Hong Kong Neo-Noir

EDINBURGH STUDIES IN EAST ASIAN FILM
Series Editor: Margaret Hillenbrand

Available and forthcoming titles

Independent Chinese Documentary
Dan Edwards

Ozu, History and the Representation of the Everyday
Woojeong Joo

Memory, Subjectivity and Independent Chinese Cinema
Qi Wang

Hong Kong Neo-Noir
Edited by Esther C. M. Yau and Tony Williams

www.edinburghuniversitypress.com/series/eseaf

Hong Kong Neo-Noir

Edited by Esther C. M. Yau and
Tony Williams

EDINBURGH
University Press

Edinburgh University Press is one of the leading university presses in the UK. We publish academic books and journals in our selected subject areas across the humanities and social sciences, combining cutting-edge scholarship with high editorial and production values to produce academic works of lasting importance. For more information visit our website: edinburghuniversitypress.com

© editorial matter and organisation Esther C. M. Yau and Tony Williams, 2017
© the chapters their several authors, 2017

Edinburgh University Press Ltd
The Tun – Holyrood Road
12 (2f) Jackson's Entry
Edinburgh EH8 8PJ

Typeset in 10/13 Chaparral Pro by
IDSUK (DataConnection) Ltd

A CIP record for this book is available from the British Library

ISBN 978 1 4744 1266 7 (hardback)
ISBN 978 1 4744 1267 4 (webready PDF)
ISBN 978 1 4744 1268 1 (epub)

The right of the contributors to be identified as authors of this work has been asserted in accordance with the Copyright, Designs and Patents Act 1988 and the Copyright and Related Rights Regulations 2003 (SI No. 2498).

Contents

List of Figures — vii
Acknowledgements — ix
Notes on the Contributors — xi

Introduction: Hong Kong Neo-Noir — 1
Esther C. M. Yau and Tony Williams

Part One Seeds of Noir in Hong Kong Cinema

1 'A Rose by Any Other Name': Wong Tin-lam's *The Wild, Wild Rose* as Melodrama Musical Noir Hybrid — 13
   Lisa Odham Stokes

2 Black and Red: Post-War Hong Kong Noir and its Interrelation with Progressive Cinema, 1947–57 — 30
   Law Kar

3 Sword, Fist or Gun? The 1970s Origins of Contemporary Hong Kong Noir — 51
   Kristof Van den Troost

Part Two Neo-Noir Films in Close-Up

4 Doubled Indemnity: Fruit Chan and the Meta-Fictions of Hong Kong Neo-Noir — 77
   Adam Bingham

5 *Running on Karma*: Hong Kong Noir and the Political Unconscious — 97
   Gina Marchetti

6	*Beyond Hypothermia*: Cool Women Killers in Hong Kong Cinema	118
	David Desser	
7	Tech-Noir: A Sub-Genre May not Exist in Hong Kong Science Fiction Films	140
	Kwai-Cheung Lo	

Part Three Cosmopolitan Cityspace and Neo-Noir

8	Location Filmmaking and the Hong Kong Crime Film: Anatomy of a Scene	159
	Julian Stringer	
9	*Running Out of Time*, *Hard-Boiled* and 24-Hour Cityspace	178
	Kenneth E. Hall	
10	Exiled in Macau: Hong Kong Neo-Noir and Paradoxical Lyricism	198
	Jinhee Choi	
11	The Tentacles of History: *Shinjuku Incident*'s Return of the Repressed	216
	Tony Williams	

Bibliography	233
Filmography	245
Index	254

Figures

1.1	Grace Chang, aka Gě Lán, actress and singer in *The Wild, Wild Rose*	26
2.1	A scene from the Shanghai noir *The Devils*	33
2.2	Bai Guang in *Destroy*	41
2.3	Cantonese noir *Mysterious Murder*	47
3.1	In *The Teahouse*, the formation of a triad-like community	56
3.2	Noir meets martial arts meets exploitation in *Kiss of Death*	64
4.1	Subverting heroic bloodshed	85
4.2	Death and escape	88
4.3	The city as illusory whole	89
4.4	Violence and magic realism in *The Longest Summer*	93
5.1	'You are the Buddha in my heart'	106
5.2	The decapitated woman	109
6.1	The beautiful, ultra-modern girl with a gun: *So Close*	134
6.2	The cool female assassin: *Beyond Hypothermia*	137
8.1	*Full Alert*: a bravura car chase that seems to encompass half of Hong Kong	165
8.2	*Full Alert* preserves disappearing Hong Kong locations on film	166
8.3	*Full Alert*'s ambitious car chase scene takes in a litany of actual Hong Kong locations	170
9.1	Jack Bauer spies on terrorists	186
9.2	Cops and robbers in split-screen display in *Breaking News*	195
10.1	*Exiled*: the four, led by Blaze, walk through the forest	205
10.2	*Exiled*: a high-angle shot of the hotel lobby	206
10.3	*Exiled*: both horizontal and vertical axes of action are established	207
10.4	*Exiled*: the camera cuts to the opposite end of the room	208
10.5	*Exiled*: a darkly lit gunfight scene that blurs the audience vision	208
10.6	Lin is locked in the room after her futile attempt to run away in *After This Our Exile*	211

10.7	Opening sequence of *After This Our Exile*	212
11.1	Chinese Invasion v. 2	222
11.2	Imperialist Echoes	224
11.3	Frankenstein Monster v. 1	225

Acknowledgements

The editors thank the contributors for their excellent work and patience. We thank Dr Margaret Hillenbrand of the University of Oxford and Editor of the Edinburgh Series on East Asian Film, for her encouragement. We wish to thank Gillian Leslie, Commissioning Editor at Edinburgh University Press, for her enthusiastic and continuous support of the project, and Rebecca Mackenzie for her assistance in production.

Esther C. M. Yau thanks her colleagues in the Department of Comparative Literature for their intellectual support of cinema studies. She thanks Winnie Fu of Hong Kong Film Archive for her expert advice and help. She thanks Jenny Kar-Kei Wong and Florence Yik-Yu Lo for their help at various stages of the production of the book.

Research assistance in preparation of the book was funded in part by the Hsu Long-Sing Research Fund of the Faculty of Arts at the University of Hong Kong. Esther Yau thanks previous Dean Kam Louie and Interim Dean Douglas Kerr for their kind support.

Notes on the Contributors

Adam Bingham has a PhD in Japanese cinema from the University of Sheffield, for which he undertook a study of Takeshi Kitano and Authorship, Genre and Stardom in Japanese cinema. He taught Film Studies at the University of Sheffield for three years before taking up his current post at Edge Hill University in Lancashire. He writes regularly for *Senses of Cinema*, *Electric Sheep*, *Asian Cinema Journal* and *Cineaste* in America and *CineAction* in Canada. In addition, he is currently working as an editor for the UK-based publishers Intellect. He is editing two volumes of their Critical Directory of World Cinema series, on East Central European and Indian cinema, the former of which was published in 2011 and the latter in 2015. He has also written *Japanese Cinema since Hana-Bi*, published by Edinburgh University Press in 2015. He has also written film reviews and essays for several other volumes in this series, including Japan, China, Korea, Sweden and Great Britain, and he has a chapter in an upcoming book on visions of 'The End' in cinema: his paper is dedicated to the myriad notions of the apocalypse in the cinema of Ingmar Bergman. His current research interests include Asian new wave cinemas and the work of Kiyoshi Kurosawa.

Jinhee Choi is Senior Lecturer of Film Studies at King's College London. She is the author of *The South Korean Film Renaissance: Local Hitmakers Global Provocateurs* (2010) and the co-editor of *Cine-Ethics: Ethical Dimensions of Film Theory, Practice and Spectatorship* (2014), *Horror to the Extreme: Changing Boundaries in Asian Cinema* (2009) and *The Philosophy of Film and Motion Pictures* (2005). She is currently working on a book girlhood in contemporary Korean cinema.

David Desser is Emeritus Professor of Cinema Studies, University of Illinois. He has authored and edited eleven books, most recently *Small Cinemas in Global Markets* (co-author, 2014). His best known works include *The Samurai Films of Akira Kurosawa* (1983), *Eros plus Massacre: An Introduction to the Japanese New Wave Cinema* (1988), *Reframing Japanese Cinema: Authorship, Genre, History* (co-editor, 1992), *American Jewish Filmmakers* (co-author, 2nd edn 2004),

The Cinema of Hong Kong: History, Arts, Identity (co-editor, 2000) and *Ozu's Tokyo Story* (editor, 2010). He is a former editor of *Cinema Journal* and founding co-editor of the *Journal of Japanese and Korean Cinema*. He provided commentary on Criterion DVD editions of *Tokyo Story* and *Seven Samurai*. He has also authored the programme notes along with audio introductions and extensive commentary on the films of Kiju Yoshida from Arrow Films in the UK.

Kenneth E. Hall is Professor of Spanish at East Tennessee State University. He has taught at the University of North Dakota and at Wake Forest University. His publications include *John Woo's The Killer* (2009), *Stonewall Jackson and Religious Faith in Military Command* (2005), *John Woo: The Films* (2000) and *Guillermo Cabrera Infante and the Cinema* (1989). He is also a regular contributor to *Studies in the Western*. He lives with his family in Johnson City, Tennessee.

Law Kar was a programmer for the Hong Kong International Film Festival and Hong Kong Film Archive. His English publications include *Hong Kong Cinema – A Cross Cultural View* (co-author, 2004) and *From Art form to Platform, Hong Kong Plays and Performances 1900–1941* (co-author, 1999). He has contributed chapters to *The Cinema of Hong Kong – History, Arts, Identity* (2000), *At Full Speed – Hong Kong Cinema in a Borderless World* (2001) and *Forever China* (2008). He is now a project researcher for Hong Kong Film Archive.

Kwai-Cheung Lo, Professor in the Department of Humanities and Creative Writing at Hong Kong Baptist University, is a specialist in trans-Chinese cinemas and cultural studies. He is the author of *Excess and Masculinity in Asian Cultural Productions* (2010) and *Chinese Face/Off: The Transnational Popular Culture of Hong Kong* (2005). His academic articles appear in *Postcolonial Studies, Camera Obscura, Cultural Studies, boundary 2, positions: east asia cultures critique, Modern Chinese Literature and Culture*, etc. Also a creative writer in Chinese language, his Chinese publications include short stories, poems, interviews, play scripts, and cultural and literary criticisms. He has been working on the issues in relation to the racial minorities in Hong Kong and China. Some of the research output has already been published, including a book entitled *Xianggang: duoyidianyanse* (Colours of Hong Kong: Racial Minorities in the Local Community). Currently he is working on a project of ethnic minority cinema in China.

Gina Marchetti teaches in the Department of Comparative Literature, School of Humanities, at the University of Hong Kong. Her books include *Romance* and the 'Yellow Peril': Race, Sex and Discursive Strategies in Hollywood Fiction (1993), *Andrew Lau and Alan Mak's INFERNAL AFFAIRS. The Trilogy* (2007) and *From Tian'anmen to Times Square: Transnational China and the Chinese Diaspora on Global Screens* (2006), as well as several co-edited volumes, including *Hong Kong Screenscapes: From the New Wave to the Digital Frontier*, co-edited with Esther M. K. Cheung and Tan See-Kam (2011), *The Chinese Diaspora on American Screens: Race, Sex, and Cinema* (2012) and, most recently, *A Companion to Hong Kong Cinema* (2015), co-edited with Esther M. K. Cheung and Esther C. M. Yau.

Lisa Odham Stokes teaches Humanities and Film at Seminole State College in Central Florida. She is co-author of *City on Fire: Hong Kong Cinema* and author of *The Historical Dictionary of Hong Kong Cinema* and *Peter Ho-Sun Chan's He's a Woman, She's a Man*. She has published numerous articles on film with a special interest in Hong Kong. She is a programmer for the Florida Film Festival.

Julian Stringer is Associate Professor in Film and Television Studies at the University of Nottingham. He has published widely on Hong Kong, Chinese and East Asian cinema, transnational filmmaking and international film festivals, and his books include *New Korean Cinema* (co-editor, Edinburgh University Press, 2005), *Japanese Cinema: Texts and Contexts* (co-editor, 2007) and *Japanese Cinema: Critical Concepts in Media and Cultural Studies* (co-editor, 2015). He is currently completing *The Korean Cinema Book* (co-edited with Nikki J. Y. Lee) and *Regarding Film Festivals*. In recent years he has organised academic conferences in Beijing, Kuala Lumpur and Shanghai.

Kristof Van den Troost is a lecturer at the Centre for China Studies at the Chinese University of Hong Kong. His essays have appeared in *Chinese and Japanese Films on the Second World War* (ed. Wilson, Tsu and King-fai, 2014), *Always in the Dark: A Study of Hong Kong Gangster Films* (ed. Po Fung, 2014) and in the journal *Asian Cinema* (2016). Currently he is working on a book on the history of the crime film in Hong Kong.

Tony Williams is Professor and Area Head of Film Studies in the Department of English at Southern Illinois University, Carbondale. He has written extensively on south-east Asian cinema for the journal *Asian Cinema*. His recent publications include *John Woo's Bullet in the Head* (2009) and *George A. Romero: Interviews* (2011). The second edition of *Vietnam War Films* co-edited with Jean-Jacques Malo is scheduled for publication in 2012. He is currently at work editing an anthology of essays on the work of independent director

Evans Chan as well as the second extended edition of *George A. Romero: Knight of the Living*.

Esther C. M. Yau teaches in the Department of Comparative Literature, School of Humanities, at the University of Hong Kong. She is the editor of *At Full Speed: Hong Kong Cinema in a Borderless World* (2001) and co-editor of *New Chinese Cinemas* (1994) and 'Asia/Pacific: a Spectral Surface', a special issue of *positions: east asia cultures critique*. Her essays have been published in a number of journals and anthologies including *Chinese Connections: Critical Perspectives on Film, Identity, and Diaspora* (2009) and *Hong Kong Screenscapes: from the New Wave to the Digital Frontier* (2011). Her most recent essay on Hong Kong cinema is published in *A Companion to Hong Kong Cinema* (2015), which she co-edited with Esther M. K. Cheung and Gina Marchetti.

Introduction: Hong Kong Neo-Noir

Esther C. M. Yau and
Tony Williams

'Film noir' is now such a common term in cinematic analysis that another book on the subject, especially in its neo-noir development, may appear superfluous. Yet discoveries are occurring all the time, necessitating the rewriting of assumptions in film history, and this is especially true of other national cinemas, especially Japan and Korea, that have their own versions of noir and neo-noir. Despite the seeming redundancy of the term 'national' in an era of globalisation and transnational changes, the 'local' always adds some distinctive nuance to a style that may be borrowed from outside. Hence the importance of critical voices to define what distinctive nuances may exist especially in a supposedly globalised era. To cite any examples of national noir remains a problem since the national variations often reworked outside influences for their own particular concerns. Concerning three aspects of different national cinemas, America, Britain and France had their distinctive nuances and styles more often than not influenced by cultural and historical changes. Classical American film noir extended from 1940 to 1958, affected by the historical turmoil of wartime and post-war development. British film noir began earlier, in 1937, with *The Green Cockatoo* directed by the American William Cameron Menzies and photographed by Mutz Greenbaum (Max Greene), a refugee from Nazi Germany, with the story written by Graham Greene. Like its American counterpart, British film noir reflected post-war concerns, especially the beginning of the end of Empire, austerity, rising crime rates, and the developing problem of juvenile delinquency infected by what was then regarded as degraded American popular culture. French film noir had a more tortuous development. Influenced especially by French poetic realism initiated by *Le Rue sans Nom* (Pierre Chenal, 1934), the style really took off as a result of the humiliation of the French Occupation and continued into the post-war period, reaching a culmination in the work of Jean-Pierre Melville, who fought in the Resistance and the Free French Army. Hong Kong film noir had its own set of historical and cultural developments that go back to post-war Shanghai cinema and developed in its own particular way during many changes in Hong Kong society, as seen in Lung Kong's *The Story of a Discharged Prisoner*

(1967), which influenced John Woo's *A Better Tomorrow* (1986) twenty years later. From those connections, Hong Kong cinema developed its own variant of neo-noir that is the subject of the essays collected in this book.

The notion of 'Hong Kong Neo-Noir' situates classic noir and neo-noir in urban modernity and cultural globalisation. Studies of noir have noted the encoding of an urban and critical sensibility towards capitalist modernity that has global and regional cinematic expressions.[1] As a phenomenon with transnational and local features, noir remains, as James Naremore has pointed out, an 'amorphous yet fascinating category in cinema'.[2] The historical and cultural characteristics that have come out of the process of adaptation, assimilation and reinvention in a particular cinema add complexity to the topic. Studies of classic film noir have alluded to changes including the adoption of colour cinematography, the end of the Hollywood studio system, the lifting of Production Code censorship, the liberalisation of values since the 1960s and self-reflexivity as what support the notion of neo-noir, a term invented to account for 'the considerable number of later pictures that have close connections or affinities with the original group'.[3] These aspects now illustrate the historical and situated nature of American films noir, from which neo-noir takes departure. Working with noir and neo-noir in the overlapping spaces of the local and the transnational, the authors of this book do not seek to come to an agreement on a definitive term of Hong Kong neo-noir, or attempt to argue for any 'national' exclusivity and coherence of an elusive style. Their essays have instead looked closely into the many shades and faces that make up the usual and unusual suspects of neo-noir, to illuminate and enrich an expanding range of global noirs.

Neo-Noir in Hong Kong Urban Modernity

The city of Hong Kong became a diaspora for the film entrepreneurs, directors, writers and artists who fled communist-occupied Shanghai after 1949. Not unlike the émigré directors who fled Nazi-occupied Europe to work in Hollywood, the south-bound directors from Shanghai also brought with them film expertise that they applied to the making of film noir, along with the genres of family melodrama and historical drama. Their work greatly enriched Hong Kong's Cantonese and Mandarin films of the 1950s. Unlike the melodramas that were hugely popular at the time and also found recognition in Hong Kong film studies, however, the small corpus of films noir in black-and-white would only receive critical attention belatedly from film historians and critics. This was also due in part to the overwhelming popularity of martial arts films in the 1970s that followed upon the meteoric rise of global *kungfu* star Bruce Lee. The untimely demise of Lee in 1973 did not stop the fever for martial arts films, but instead set Golden Harvest studio investing in action genres and martial arts stars to cultivate and expand its overseas sales. The new swordplay films, with gruelling fight scenes, excessive bloodshed and plots of betrayal were stylistically conscious, including the iconic use of colour. Individual titles also drew from Japanese samurai films and American crime films, besides from martial arts fiction. Over time, adaptation, assimilation and reinvention – the common practices in conceiving films – have cultivated a cosmopolitan cinematic interest on the part of migrant and native-born filmmakers. The film directors of the late 1970s, many of them cinephiles and some film school graduates from the UK and the US, integrated a cosmopolitan cinema orientation with critical and local sensibility. They initiated an era of location filming that put urban (dis)orientation onto the movie screen with scenes that take place in crowd-filled districts, mean streets, dimly lit public housing corridors, empty lots, new shopping malls and semi-rural borderlands.

A corpus of male-dominated 'Kowloon Noir' is said to have appeared since the 1980s. Stephen Teo has identified *The Mission* (Johnnie To, 1999), *PTU* (Johnnie To, 2003), *Election and Election II* (Johnnie To, 2005–6) as exemplars of this category.[4] Additional titles such as *City on Fire* (Ringo Lam, 1987), *The Killer* (John Woo, 1989) and *Chungking Express* (Wong Kar-wai, 1994) have also been recognised for their shades of noir. These popular features have prompted film archivists and critics to seek out precedents and contemporaries. Remaking the Euro-American conceptual frame of 'noir' by taking into consideration the noir films from the unexpected places of Hong Kong, India, Iran, Italy, Mexico and Spain, David Desser has used the innovative term 'global noir' in his analysis of the transnational circulation of noir classics and the thriving state of noir filmmaking.[5] The films that come out of these locations, according to Jennifer Fay and Justus Nieland, 'use the noir idiom to offer local reflections on the uneven development of modernity as a global force in the twentieth century.'[6]

Making crime the very spectacle of Hong Kong's capitalist modernity is an exercise in myth and anti-myth. Hong Kong's post-war rise from a British colony in Asia to a world city and financial centre entails fictions of both the lawful and the lawless. The coexistence of underworld activities with legitimate businesses makes enigmatic scenarios of intricate manoeuvres and connivances. In this respect, local neo-noir connects the narratives of disorientation, alienation and seduction to the forces of capital and empire beyond the territory's borders. The liminal status of Hong Kong between the West and China makes an interesting parallel with neo-noir, which is said to have a liminal position between commercial and art-house films. Neo-noir filmmaking in this respect can be said to have openly acknowledged the kinds of violence that shape the city's historical and contemporary powers. Conscious adaptation and assimilation of idioms common to thrillers, *policiers* and gangsters, however, have allowed for critical perspectives of the forces to appear while also restraining and eliding others.

The tales of darkness are contrary to the brightly coloured brand image of Hong Kong as 'Asia's World City' that was established in 2001 following China's takeover and the name change to Hong Kong Special Administrative Region (with the acronym HKSAR). They proffer bleak visions, wounded bodies and fatal endings tempered with fraternal bonds. Many films design intricate physical manoeuvres in a cityscape dense with traffic, pedestrians and business signs. Their personal stories are intertwined with a founding story of urban capitalism and modernity: the films stage the seduction of territory and gains (in power and money) that are the main seductions in classic noir. In place of the *femme fatale*, they are men who make merciless betrayals and who readily use violent means of all sorts (including guns, knives and animals) to take charge or get rid of rivals. Their explicitly homosocial locus has displaced the *femme fatale*, replacing her with men who are in double identity situations that enable them to carry out betrayals: the police mole in drug cartels, the gangster mole in police headquarters, and the policeman or gangster who has secretly violated the code of his group. That these men have found unexpected frankness and friendship among their enemies rather than their own kind exemplifies a sentiment different from the paranoia and anxiety directed at the increasing social visibility of astute working women in the classic noir. Considering the paradigmatic implications of displacements as this example in Hong Kong neo-noir, the examination of cultural phenomena in global noir studies will attend to resonant manifestations in American, European and world cinema contexts. Along this line of thought, the plots and figures of despair and paranoia emerging from the dissolution of utopian hope and the moral high ground that are conveyed through masculine figures of power and disillusionment, corruption, desire and anxiety are no longer limited to the study of American productions of the 1940s. Recent publications attribute a global noir phenomenon not only to the global reach of Hollywood films and American popular culture but also to places where competing capitalist economies have emerged in the world cities since the late twentieth century. In this frame of economic and cultural globalisation, a focused study of Hong Kong noir sensibility and films initiates a dialogue with the well-known as well as lesser-discussed instances of American neo-noir films, and with those of global noir.

The Hong Kong film industry has gone through many adjustments. Presently it is undergoing momentous change. Since the 1990s its products have begun to gain wider circulation and its stars have become known on world screens, in part through the interest of American critics and of Hollywood, which has assimilated many of its competitive strengths in action design and action directing. The opening up of a large Chinese market of movie-goers who grew up watching Hong Kong genre films have brought new prospects and challenges in the twenty-first century. The Chinese mainland and Hong Kong 'Closer Economic Partnership Arrangement' (CEPA, 2003 and after) that made it possible for Hong Kong films to have exhibition permits for theatrical screenings in China has greatly increased the market for these films. Scenes of crime and policing in China have appeared in Johnnie To's neo-noir films *Election II* and *Drug War* (2013). The strict censorship regime of the People's Republic of China, the cultural orientation and tastes of audiences in different provinces, and competition with China's and Hollywood's blockbuster movies are some of the pressing issues facing Hong Kong film producers and directors. The spectacle of crime continues despite these changes, while new inflections as a result of a screen presence in Mainland China with self-censorship have also emerged.

It is not too much of an exaggeration to say that nearly all male directors are directors of Hong Kong crime and crisis spectacles at one point or another. This further blurs the artificial divide between commercial genre films and art-house films. Critically acclaimed directors of art-house cinema, including Fruit Chan (*Made in Hong Kong*, 1997) and Wong Kar-wai (*As Tears Go By*, 1988; *Days of Being Wild*, 1991), made gangster movies in the 'art film' context. In the 2000s, Johnnie To (*Life without Principle*, 2011; *Vengeance*, 2009; *Sparrow*, 2006; *Election*, 2005; *Election II*, 2006; *PTU*), Andrew Lau and Alan Mak (*Infernal Affairs I, II, III*, 2002–3), Wai Ka-fai (*Mad Detective*, 2007, co-directed with Johnnie To), Yau Nai-hoi (*Eye in the Sky*, 2007), Derek Yee (*Shinjuku Incident*, 2009; *Protégé*, 2007; *One Nite in Mongkok*, 2004) and newcomer Pang Ho-cheung (*Exodus*, 2007) brought new perspectives and nuances to the stories and spectacles of crime in Hong Kong's colonial and post-colonial urban settings. An increasing consciousness of the city's unresolved contradictions and moral despair in recent films that are in part remakes of earlier Hong Kong and American classics, and an awareness of the region's political and economic crises, offer challenges regarding the frames of study of noir and neo-noir. In addition, Hong Kong cinema's own history of crime genres has brought to fame directors who established their careers in narrating a criminal modernity like John Woo (*A Better Tomorrow*, 1986), Ringo Lam (*City on Fire*, 1987) and Lawrence Lau (*Lee Rock I, II*, 1991; *Tactical Unit – No Way Out*, 2008).

Post-1997, Hong Kong crime genre films continued to be shown in the territory of the SAR. However, their seasoned directors had already been working on co-production films on the Chinese Mainland for a decade. A co-produced crime feature, Johnnie To's *Drug War* is the first staging on the Chinese Mainland of a police procedural featuring Hong Kong drug dealers engaging in gunfights with public security officers, and the film carries several putative characteristics of previous Milkyway productions, including a fatalistic ending. The film's box-office success is sure to prompt other co-productions, including between China and Hollywood. Rapid urbanisation throughout China, the building of multiplexes in second- and third-tier cities, and a large population of teenagers have provided favourable conditions for commercial cinema. Presently, romance and comedy are immensely popular and 'safe' genres. Nevertheless, stylised violence has appeared in independent Mainland productions such as *A Touch of Sin* (Jia Zhangke, 2013), *No Man's Land* (Ning Hao, 2013) and *Black Coal, Thin Ice* (Diao Yinan, 2013). A mix of alienation, rage, greed, brutality and fatalism appears in these noir features. In fact, *Black Coal, Thin Ice* is a first China-US noir co-production, which went on to win the Golden Bear Award at the 2014 Berlin International Film Festival.

Perspectives of Hong Kong Noir and Neo-Noir

This volume presents original and incisive essays on the noir films and noir idioms of Hong Kong cinema. Organised in three parts, the essays discuss the historical precedents and classics of Hong Kong noir films, the key crime films and genres related to noir, and close readings of films that reinvent noir visuality and idioms. Part One opens with a chapter by Lisa Stokes Odham on director Wong Tin-lam's noir musical *The Wild, Wild Rose* (1960), the apotheosis of Hong Kong noir origins both in its techniques and hybrid nature. The film adopts noir visual style and tweaks the characters through the incorporation of popular actress and singer Grace Chang (Ge Lan) in the role of *femme fatale* to usurp the role of the tough hard-boiled male lead. Law Kar's chapter on post-war Hong Kong noir films traces their origins to Shanghai cinema. It discusses the emergence of Bai Guang as a *femme fatale* in post-1950 Hong Kong cinema. The relocated masterful Shanghai directors Zhu Shilin, Yue Feng and Li Pingqian went on to transform noir narratives into 'Progressive films' that shaped the course of Cantonese cinema. The third chapter, by Kristof Van den Troost, gives a comprehensive overview of 1970s crime cinema as another source for Hong Kong noir films. Citing examples from the films of Chang Cheh, Van den Troost observes that martial arts films are a viable vehicle for noir stories and style. Their emphasis on action and violence, the dominance of male characters and the prominence of swords have inspired the characteristics of recent Hong Kong noirs.

Essays in Part Two make close readings of neo-noir films. Adam Bingham examines noir in Fruit Chan's *Made in Hong Kong* to demonstrate the second-hand life of the protagonist as shaped by cultural precepts outside of home. This borrowed identity has an objective correlative in Hong Kong's cinema that reworks and re-presents existing films and film paradigms. Bingham refutes Fredric Jameson's reading of nostalgia in noir films that 'evoke a lost past as a means of denying the present'[7] by stating that Fruit Chan's films, as well as the noir films of Wong Kar-wai (*Chungking Express*, 1994 and *Fallen Angels*, 1995), illustrate the difference in Hong Kong noir, with the setting and temporality that reifies the onslaught of the future in the paradigmatic image of the sleek modern cityscape. Gina Marchetti's chapter on *Running on Karma* (Johnnie To, 2003) engages with the mixed-genre film through the lens of 'ideology of form' and 'the political unconscious' elaborated by Fredric Jameson. She explores the stylistic aspects of noir, including the use of chiaroscuro shadows in the *mise-en-scène*, the dark cityscape of Hong Kong punctuated by neon lights and the glare of police-car lights, and low-key lighting suggesting the gloom of memory. After discussing the film's generic codes of detective story, crime thriller and romantic melodrama, Marchetti shows the characters as having shouldered the burden of Hong Kong's history and the themes of loss, betrayal, alienation and existential despair common to the Hollywood of the 1940s and 1950s as well as inside and outside Asia. The chapter by David Desser emphasises the transnational quality of female assassin films in the global market. After the James Bond movies featured such a figure, Luc Besson's *Nikita* (1990) 'demonstrated the global efficacy' of the motifs in the production of the female assassin. With the idea that a woman who could be a lover or a mother who is in fact a killer having struck fear in the audience, two common motifs include the (re)training of a woman to overcome her natural instincts to nurture in becoming a killer, and her redemption by bourgeois marriage. Desser discusses globalised textual operations of film examples from Hong Kong (*Naked Weapon*, Tony Ching Siu-tung, 2002), South Korea (*Shiri*, Kang Je-kyu, 1999) and a co-produced film involving China, Korea and Japan (*So Close*, Corey Yuen Kwai, 2000) to illustrate the Deleuzian notion of de-territorialisation that pertains to woman-assassin films. The discussion culminates in a close reading of *Beyond Hypothermia* (Patrick Leung Pak-kin, 1996), a Hong Kong–Korean co-production which he deems as the most genuinely noirish of the woman-assassin films. The chapter by Kwai-cheung Lo argues that 'tech-noir' is a possible sub-genre in Hong Kong sci-fi films. Lo argues that three Hong Kong 'tech-noir' films make an amorphous corpus that fits neither into noir nor sci-fi, but combines sci-fi storylines and iconography with noir sensibility and *mise-en-scène*. Completed before China's takeover of Hong Kong in 1997, they have an undertone of anxiety about the city's 'near future'. They invoke nostalgia for certain experiences of space and time that have been outmoded and rendered fragile by capitalist modernisation. Their makers exhibit an existential angst in relation to unprecedented changes in Hong Kong and reveal a sense of being in exile at home.

Part Three consists of four chapters linking the urban cityscape with noir filmmaking and films. Julian Stringer discusses the anatomy of a crime film's location filmmaking. By focusing ostensibly on the car chase scene in *Full Alert* (Ringo Lam, 1997) that covered the entirety of Hong Kong Island, Stringer explores the politics and poetics of location filmmaking in one historically specific example of the Hong Kong crime film and concludes that *Full Alert*, featuring the themes of transgression, detection and pursuit, resembles an allegory of its own production. The following chapter by Kenneth E. Hall makes a comparative study of the hard-boiled films of Hong Kong and the American television series on the concentration and limitation of time and motion. Noting the influence of Hong Kong 'action' technique on *24*, the American television series, Hall observes that the American text expresses concerns parallel to those of pre- and post-1997 Hong Kong films. In her chapter, Jinhee Choi examines the noir films set in Macao and Malaysia, which serve as a place of exile for the characters in the films. In addition to analysing the representations of transnational imagery, the essay examines the multi-faceted motivations and implications for location shooting abroad, both in terms of economic concerns and cultural connotations. Tony Williams discusses *Shinjuku Incident*, set in Japan during the 1990s, in his chapter. Starring Jackie Chan, who removed himself from his familiar star image to play a non-heroic dramatic role, Derek Yee's work is clearly influenced by Johnnie To's exploration of hidden social and political currents affecting the world of Triads and Fukasaku Kinji's epic political analysis of post-war Japanese yakuza factions, but it is also a South-east Asian global economic film noir with a revealing prologue and epilogue relevant to modern times.

This collection does not intend to define exclusively the phenomenon of Hong Kong neo-noir but rather to open the field to further debate. Many previous books, monographs and articles have referred to the term in one way or another but this collection aims to provide certain specific directions for further detailed exploration as well as to open a pathway for further discussions and redefinitions. Detailed explorations have occurred in national and transnational cinemas, rendering redundant previous definitions of noir as a peculiarly American visual style. Historical investigations have shown that the style was more universal than previously believed but that at the same time each culture borrowed from it and reworked it within its own particular concerns. This is especially true of Hong Kong neo-noir and the aim now is to show it not just as a national construction but as one influenced by the cultural and historical aspects of the past as it is now being affected by the turbulent changes of the present. Hong Kong cinema is a unique construction combining the local and the international. This is no less true of Hong Kong neo-noir.

Notes

1. Spicer, 'Introduction: The Problem of Film Noir', in Bould et al. (eds), *Neo Noir*.
2. Naremore, 'Foreword', p. xix. James Naremore is the author of a seminal study, *More Than Night: Film Noir in its Contexts*.
3. Naremore, 'Foreword', p. xx.
4. Teo, *Director in Action: Johnnie To and the Hong Kong Action Film*.
5. Desser, 'Global Noir: Genre Film in the Age of Transnationalism'.
6. Fay and Nieland, *Film noir: Hard-Boiled Modernity and the Cultures of Globalisation*, p. 70.
7. Bingham, 'Chapter 4. Doubled Indemnity: Fruit Chan and the Meta-Fictions of Hong Kong Neo-Noir' in this volume.

PART ONE
SEEDS OF NOIR IN HONG KONG CINEMA

Chapter 1
'A Rose by Any Other Name': Wong Tin-lam's *The Wild, Wild Rose* as Melodrama Musical Noir Hybrid

Lisa Odham Stokes

Wong Tin-lam's *The Wild, Wild Rose* (aka *Love of the Wild Rose*), released into Hong Kong theatres on 5 October 1960, remains critically well received and popular today. Shu Kei describes it as 'the most distinguished film among MP&GI's [Motion Pictures and General Investment Ltd] 200-odd library . . . arguably the most extraordinary Mandarin film of the 1960s'.[1] Described as a noir musical, *Rose* may not be Hong Kong's first noir,[2] but in its style and genre blending, it serves as the apotheosis of early Hong Kong noir, raising the bar for Hong Kong noirs/neo-noirs to come, anticipating standard mixed genres of future Hong Kong film, and creating urban visuals that comment on the Hong Kong of its day. While discussions continue as to whether noir is a genre or style, attuned audiences, academic and popular alike, know noir when seeing it, paradoxically and simultaneously drawn into and forbidden from its world. The widely recognised noir signatures – visual style (black-and-white photography, low-key lighting and shadow effects, low-angled, dutched and disorienting camerawork), downbeat, alienated characters, and cynical attitudes towards life – define a body of work, referenced by the historical period of distinctive output, from 1941 to 1953. With the Western and lush Hollywood musical, film noir may be a truly American nostalgic formation. Most of its screenwriters, the story material on which the movies are based, and its cinematographers are American-born, while some major directors – from Curtiz to Wilder – were émigrés to Hollywood. Hollywood noir style widely influenced cinema, from Melville's *Le Samourai* (1967) to Woo's *Hard-Boiled* (1992). Colour Hollywood productions like Polanski's *Chinatown* (1974) and Hanson's *L.A. Confidential* (1997) are set in 1940s Los Angeles and are more realistic tonally than the earlier historical period. The corruption-oozing *Chinatown*, an origin story of contemporary Los Angeles development, serves as our consummate noir. Set in Los Angeles, Ridley Scott's cyberpunk *Blade Runner* (1982) offers up tech noir, set in the near future, its technological gadgetry and plotting reflecting a gritty realism rather than nostalgia.

Rose draws upon several period American noirs and tweaks them, synthesising noir style with melodrama and musical. In searches of international cinema, I've discovered no films combining musical, noir and melodrama in such a hybrid form. The remotest similarity, combining musical numbers with noir, would be BBC mini-series Potter's *The Singing Detective* (1986), and its film version, Gordon's *The Singing Detective* (2003). The film starred Robert Downey, Jr as the delusional, hallucinating writer dreaming musicals and paranoid plots. But these dark comedies' tone bears no relationship to *Rose*'s melodramatic fateful tension and loose plotting. Being a musical, *Rose* incorporates Mandarin popular song and borrows from Western operas. Symptomatic of its time, the film provides a Hong Kong interpretation of Hollywood musicals, a half-dozen numbers performed by popular star Grace Chang, playing the protagonist/titular character, overlaid with uncertainty amid cigarette smoke and roses. *Rose* embraces nostalgia as *wenyi pian* (prominent 1950s Chinese melodrama). Both *Rose*'s mood and titular character are not unlike popular movie candy M&M, introduced in 1941 (along with film noir) – a hard shell with a soft inside. In *Rose* Chang reinvents the 'doomed songstress' for a new generation, just as director Wong creates new form – melodrama musical noir – an eponymous hybrid that creates urban visual subtext.[3]

Rose was made when *wenyi pian* and strong women dominated Hong Kong box offices. *Wenyi*, combining *wenxue* (literature) and *yishu* (art), refers to early twentieth-century literature, and *wenyi pian* (movies) dates from late 1920s Shanghai movies emphasising drama, plot, character and adaptations. Its stories emphasising women became conventional. Along this line, *Rose* offers up a strong female, a weak male protagonist (Zhang Yang plays spoiled son and ineffectual lover) and a tragic love story. *Rose* absorbs the Chinese sub-genre tradition of 'doomed songstress' (earlier established by Zhou Xuan and Bai Guang). The melodrama appealed to women while noir machismo attracted men. The popularity of female stars like Chang and others, including Pak Yin, Fong Yim-fan, Li Lihua, Lin Dai, Jeanette Lin Cui, You Min, Julie Yeh Feng and Li Mei, arose from their appearances in stories centring on extended families featuring dutiful daughters, virtuous/neglected wives, caring mothers and sexual creatures. In *Rose*, the protagonist Deng Sijia, however, usurps the tough hard-boiled male role – cynical, pursuing his own downfall – while also playing noir *femme fatale* – sexy, manipulative, desperate, lonely and vain. She dominates screen time. For *femmes fatales*, men and love are playthings, merely part of a wager. For the jaded tough, underestimating the opposite sex will bring doom.

The primary setting for *Rose* is the New Ritz nightclub. Major scenes are set in this sound stage and take place at night in a dark world, with a few jarring daytime scenes. Nightclubs figure prominently in Hollywood noir, from London-set *Night and the City* (Dassin, 1950) to Los Angeles-set *In a Lonely Place* (Ray, 1950). Such a setting is 'a fixture in noir . . . the symbolism of the potentially dangerous night spot is crucial'.[4] In *Rose*, engaged former teacher Hanhua (Zhang Yang) reluctantly accepts a job as pianist in the club, even though 'proper' people would see such as decadent and disreputable. Wong cites the nightclub setting of many earlier Shanghai films[5] and American noirs, where gangsters rub shoulders with mostly male clientele, employees are little people with few choices, and anything can happen and does. The New Ritz Club really existed. In the 1950s, Hong Kong's North Point swelled with thousands of Chinese émigrés from the Mainland, settling in this district, following China's civil war. As the community's population was primarily rich merchants and middle-class Shanghainese, who brought with them a sophisticated culture and language, the area was dubbed 'Little Shanghai'. For business, men took guests to newly opened clubs or went themselves to fool around with women.[6] These émigrés exemplify Hong Kong's newly emergent middle class. Wong relates that he 'very seldom visited nightclubs, so I had to do some field research at the company's expense. In half a month I'd visited various nightclubs and saw quite a lot.'[7]

As with much noir, *Rose*'s look and feel is prominent over plotting. Wong criticised the story as 'quite confused and incomplete', explaining: 'Plots are disconnected, some are just half done, so I've to rewrite it . . . Qin [screenwriter Qin Yifu] is well educated and a writer with insight, but she is not professional. When she is in good spirits, she writes out some parts. This way the script is not well-connected, and I have to write it all over.'[8] Gaps are filled by a prevailing style that overrides the ellipses, raising uncertainties, particularly about 1960s Hong Kong, discussed later. Writing of noir, Ray notes the gap between plots (with reconciliation and/or happy endings) and visual style that 'seemed to operate at an entirely different level of intensity, conveying anxieties not suggested by the stories themselves'.[9] He suggests German expressionism influenced Hollywood émigré directors, like Siodmak (*The Killers*, 1946), Curtiz (*Mildred Pierce*, 1945) and Wilder (*Double Indemnity*, 1944), and including first-generation American-born German Ray (*In a Lonely Place*, 1950). Noir visuals appear in Wong's film's style. Shot in black and white, with suggestive *mise-en-scène* and editing, the film moves in and out of shadows, exploiting low-key lighting with strong contrasts, creating an atmosphere in which fatalism envelopes characters and audience alike.

Superstar Grace Chang's career trajectory partly depends upon *Rose*. It can be described as the pinnacle of her career. Born in 1934 in Nanjing, Chang grew up in Shanghai, receiving Peking Opera training before moving to Hong Kong in 1949. Discovered by director Bu Wancang, she enrolled in his Taishan Acting Class, and debuted in his *Seven Sisters* (aka *Seven Maidens*, 1953), singing two songs. From romantic melodrama *Surprise* (Tao Qin, 1956), in which Chang's character murders a misperceived rival and commits suicide, to romance *Torrents of Desire* (Chiang Nan, 1958), in which childhood sweethearts fight desires but don't prevent tragedy, songs appeared. Chang's talent for singing was recognised early; she received vocal training from childhood. To enhance her natural talent, she underwent whatever additional special training was required throughout her career. Chang became the face, body and voice of Hong Kong Mandarin musicals from the late 1950s to the mid-1960s. She remains well known for her stirring performances in tragic Mandarin musicals and melodramas. In her best roles, she delivered a triple whammy, as a memorable actress, strong singer and dancer, and beautiful woman.[10] Versatile, she made comedies, such as satirical *Wine, Women and Money* (aka *Booze, Boobs, and Bucks*, Ma-Xu Weibang, 1957) and romantic comedy *Our Dream Car* (directed and written by Evan Yang, 1959). When Chang became a contract player for MP&GI, Robert Chung was general manager and Stephen Soong production manager; under their tutelage these genres thrived within a studio system drawing upon a female star stable not unlike the old Hollywood system. Evan Yang became Chang's frequent, fruitful collaborator, on films like *Mambo Girl* (1957), *My Darling Sister* (1959), *Air Hostess* (1959), *Spring Song* (1959), *Forever Yours* (1960), *Sun, Moon and Star* (1961) and *Because of Her* (1963). Chang's most artistically productive period began in 1957, ending with her 1963 retirement (after marriage, a practice still followed by females). Chang appeared in thirty films during an eleven-year cinematic run. Her popularity as a singer remains. She guested on the US Dinah Shore Show in 1959 (one of the 'favourite entertainers of the Orient'), seen by sixty million viewers. In 1961, US Capitol Records released her Chinese songs album. Signed to Pathé, Chang produced numerous recordings, re-released in the 1990s.

Before *Rose*, Chang was cast as wholesome girl-next-door types. *Mambo Girl* is exemplary. Essentially a family melodrama musical, *Girl* showcases Chang's talent, written expressly for her.[11] She plays Kailing, eldest daughter in a middle-class family, with an effervescent personality and a talent for singing and dancing. Typically, women are front and centre with jealousy between rival adolescent girls and contrasts between birth and adoptive mothers. The film (in stark black and white) opens with a lively mambo dance sequence, and the clothes and floor patterning pop during close-ups of Chang's legs dancing; the camera pulls back to reveal young people enjoying new, western dancing. Chang's characterisation of Kailing is non-sexualised and refreshing, urban and authentically Hong Kong, celebrating youth, the new and the emergent middle class. The non-threatening domestic setting serves as the family business, a toy store, and Kailing's father is representative of the burgeoning entrepreneurial immigrant middle class. Family values, modernity, thriving commerce and prosperity are part of the optimism the story expresses.

In *Rose*, the character provided a mature part for Chang,[12] especially compared to *Girl*, with an emphasis on 'girl', as contrasted with Sijia's 'woman'. Sijia offers forbidden fruit, appearing initially as the *femme fatale* out to hurt men. She's bold, sexy and on the prowl. She is, as Law Kar describes, a 'North Point Carmen'.[13] She makes a bet she can seduce Hanhua in a matter of days, insisting she can 'captivate any man'. The seduction scene, by zipper,[14] appears a case of spider to fly – Sijia turns the calendar with a satisfied smile. However, the lure backfires, as Sijia realises her love, even denying the won bet. We learn nothing of Sijia's past, but understand a hidden, bitter life story; Cyclops, her husband, a paroled underworld figure, demands her back. Superficially, as immediate foil to Sijia is Hanhau's fiancée Suxin (meaning plain, simple and pure hearted); Sijia's name ('Si' meaning thought of fondly, lovingly; 'Jia' meaning good, nice, fine) suggests Hanhua abandons Suxin for feelings he has – his thoughts are only of Sijia. (And the Chinese title, *Love of the Wild Rose*, reinforces this.) By story's end, Suxin understands Sijia's sacrifices; rather than feel the foil, she empathises. Sijia's characterisation usurps the usual noir male's jaundiced view of life. She's hurt, but we don't know how. World-weariness envelops her. She doubles as *femme fatale* who is in charge, and as doomed songstress with a heart of gold and moral centre, despite being a 'bad woman', who cannot overcome fate. As in much noir, the female is often misunderstood, her appearance deceptive. The filmmakers satisfy prevailing norms of strong female characters but play with the western noir protagonist's makeup, erasing the hard-boiled male detective, replacing him with a strong but ultimately vulnerable woman. Sijia wins a catfight with a competing singer, satisfying noir's male gaze and characterising her as a 'tigress', but lacking the physical strength to fend off Cyclops, she is ultimately dependent on a male, Hanhua, to act.

Co-star Zhang Yang typified weak males superseded by strong women in 1950s–60s Hong Kong melodramas/comedies, often paired with popular leading actresses. In *Rose* he plays a pampered son whose mother prepares him a special dish even though she's poor and hungry. He is passive, agonised and impotent, although gentle and tender-hearted. The name Hanhua (proper and traditional, serving as a reminder of Chinese roots) reinforces the social propriety he gives up for love. The movie shows and satisfies desire. Primarily female audiences could romanticise sensitive, dreamy Zhang. In *Rose*, he is caught in a tangled web. Women could sympathise because he is done in by a 'bad woman'. Circumstances get beyond his control. He goes on the lam with Sijia, having beaten and left Cyclops for dead. Hunted by police and sent to jail, he shames his family. By choosing Sijia over his fiancée, he brings further disgrace. Unemployed, jealous and alcoholic, he loses himself. Sijia's former prey becomes predator when he strangles her; during the closing moments, he is horrified by what he has done. Superficially, with Sijia's death, the *femme fatale* is punished and women get the message to be subservient to their husbands. However, because of Grace Chang's casting, women responded differently. They could vicariously experience dominating men and escape chauvinistic husbands, becoming no-nonsense, strong women and 'bad girls', albeit at a safe distance from real life. Female viewers empathised with her suffering. And yet . . . Grace Chang emerges memorably triumphant in a woman's picture, fated to suffer at the hands of the very love she belittles for most of the picture. Unforgettable images and sounds of her effervescent celebration of a woman in love in 'Jajambo' remain indelible, providing not only a self-confident woman but also an alternative memory for female audiences. Chang will forever be associated with the song. At the 2002 Hong Kong International Film Festival panel 'Stars of MP&GI', the scene played as Chang reprised the song. Attendee Roger Lee recalls the audience 'singing and screaming to the screen together with Grace . . . By the end of the song, everybody was misty-eyed.'[15]

Popular 1940s–50s Hollywood noirs and musicals contribute to *Rose*'s visual style, running the gamut from Hitchcock's noirish thriller *Suspicion* (1941) to Preminger's musical *Porgy and Bess* (1959).[16] Director Wong explains, 'I've borrowed here and there from western movies', but he never specified which films.[17] The noirs and musical I focus on below serve as films that possibly influenced Wong's approach to *Rose*; certainly they enrich our appreciation of *Rose*. Furthermore, what Wong intends and how the picture engages are two distinctive elements, each affecting the other, the unconscious level at which a filmmaker works remaining.[18] To my thinking, these Hollywood movies, popular in Hong Kong prior to *Rose*'s release, deserve discussion as influences: *Gilda* (Vidor, 1946), starring Rita Hayworth and Glen Ford; *Carmen Jones* (Preminger, 1954), staring Dorothy Dandridge and Harry Belafonte; and *Party Girl* (Ray, 1958), starring Cyd Charisse and Robert Taylor.

Gilda serves as an exemplary hybrid noir, combining noir with women's pictures; the titular character, played by 'bombshell' Hayworth, appears as *femme fatale* to former lover Johnny Farrell's (Ford) hard-boiled gambler and misogynist (marrying Gilda to punish her for her perceived abuse of his supposedly deceased friend/boss Mundson). Although *Rose* does not play *Gilda*'s love triangle straight (between husband and former lover), it shifts the triangle to bad woman-lover-and-fiancée. *Gilda*, like *Rose*, was sound stage-bound; most action occurs in Mundson's shady nightclub, as *Rose* is primarily club-set. Furthermore, *Gilda* features resonant music and dancing (Sijia dances through the club with her aroused audience) and two musical numbers by Hayworth, 'Amado Mio' ('Love Me Forever', with swaying hips) and the infamous 'Put the Blame on Mame', a titillating striptease as Hayworth removes only a long glove and her pearls, despite her shimmying, shaking, and a shot from her chest up, in which she appears to be naked. Her intent is to get under Johnny's skin, just as Sijia lures Hanhua with the 'Habanera'. There's even a 'zipper moment' between Gilda and Mundson. The movie oozes sexual heat between Hayworth and Ford, 'more a tango than a movie . . . The script is a pretext for watching overheated players enact a dance of sexual passion.'[19] Beyond the sexuality, Gilda is stronger than either man, and more honest with herself – finale revealing, she rejects the *femme fatale* role she was given to play, and like Sijia, remains faithful to her lover. The movie poster for *Gilda* read 'There never was a woman like Gilda', at least not – arguably – until Sijia, the Wild Rose.

Similar to Sijia as *Rose*, *Party Girl* Vicki Gay (Charisse) proclaims, 'I'm a party girl. I go out with men for money. The money I want. The men you can keep.' She has the cynical attitude down cold, as does her dirty mob lawyer/lover Thomas Farrell (Taylor), physically crippled as symbolic malaise. As in *Rose*, a couple is pitted against a corrupt society and mob boss, a villain not unlike Cyclops. A nightclub features as primary setting, as in *Rose* and much noir. Farrell, like Hanhua, goes to jail. The opening title reads 'Chicago in the early '30s', but unlike Ray's other realistic pictures, this one has a 'surreal, fantastical quality' throughout, due largely to musical numbers.[20] Set-bound like *Rose*, *Party* uses dancer Charisse in erotic modern dance numbers in place of *Rose*'s songs, but to similar effect – to lure men. Whereas *Gilda* and *Party* conclude with couples reunited, how happy their endings will be is unclear, as both suffer immensely, and reassembling normal lives together remains questionable. Normality doesn't exist in the noir world. *Rose*'s ending goes further.

While much is owed to Hollywood noir, as Wong borrows and reinvents, the Hollywood musical cannot be overlooked. Preminger had seen Billy Rose's Broadway production of *Carmen Jones* but was dissatisfied with its loose structure, and determined to make a 'dramatic film with music rather than a conventional film musical'.[21] Shot in CinemaScope, *Jones* features Bizet's musical score, a story loosely adapted from Prosper Mérimée's novella (the basis of Bizet's opera). Just as in *Rose*, songs comment on action and character. Preminger shifted story to World War II-era North Carolina and used an all-black cast. The titular character, highly sexualised (Dandridge), is described as a 'hip swinging floozy'; her doomed love interest, Joe (Belafonte), like Hanhua, is engaged to a simple, pure, loving young woman. As in *Rose*, songs comment on character and further action. The required catfight, nightclub setting, premonition of doom, and a finale (strangling) appear. This Carmen leaves two-timing Joe for a rich lover, whereas Sijia lies to Hanhua about an imaginary sugar daddy. Despite this difference, many elements appear that Wong possibly drew upon.

Rose's musical elements are striking from the start. Opening credits, accompanied by overture-like instrumental, project a splintering of light from stage spots establishing the rose motif and Sijia's film, from start to (her) finish. The entire scene plays in darkness, with fill light on stairs and sheet music. She appears backlit in silhouette next to a gigantic rose scaled to human size; then, with a rose between her teeth, she dances, descending a series of steps with fancy footwork focused on while the credits appear.[22] More credits appear on rose-motifed sheet music, the pages turned by Sijia's hand. Besides the 'overture', sheet music announces the importance of music to the film. The rose, traditionally symbolic of romantic love, is metonymically identified with the character, and hence the character with the film's title. Aural and visual elements are somewhat ominously toned, with numerous pauses. Already, Sijia claims space.

Following the credits are six musical numbers organic to the film, the majority adapted from western opera, with two Mandarin popular songs, exploiting Chang's strengths as singer and dancer. In order, they are: the 'Habanera' ('Love is just a plaything') from Bizet's *Carmen*; 'La donna é mobile' ('All women are capricious') from Verdi's *Rigoletto*; 'Bei jedem walzerschritt' ('The Merry Widow Waltz') from Lehár's *The Merry Widow*; the Mandarin contemporary song 'Sympathy'; the Mandarin pop song 'Jajambo'; and 'Un bel dì, vedremo' ('One beautiful day, we will see') from Puccini's *Madama Butterfly*. There is also a flamenco dance. Yao Min and Hattori Ryoichi adapted/rearranged musical numbers with modified rhythms and intact melodies; Li Jun-ching adapted lyrics, keeping them close to the originals but altered to fit the themes of passion and destruction related to the modern, urbanised songstress. Operas, using diatonic scales and chromatic tone colourisation, provide a nostalgic western element (established operas from a cultural canon used on a mid-twentieth-century stage) and quote the exoticised East (nineteenth-century western operas' depictions of/borrowings from the East) and sinocised West (Hong Kong modernisation transferred to Chinese tradition and culture). The songs are revelatory. The selection serves numerous purposes. First, the songs define Hong Kong as assimilation of East and West – a colony in transition to modernisation. Second, they set tone, and serve as a basic story arc. Third, they replace voiceover narration typical of noir, overtaking plotting – commenting on situation and action. Fourth, they enrich characterisation, specifically Sijia's, commenting on her unfolding relationship with Hanhua.

The progression of the songs is significant, providing missing plotting. With the first number, *Carmen*'s 'Habanera', Sijia throws down the gauntlet. The following two numbers are delivered tauntingly, aggressively and seductively. From *Rigoletto*, Chang dresses in a man's cape and hat, reprising the misogynistic Duke of Mantua's aria 'La donna é mobile'. (When she asks Hanhua to play the piece, he is shocked, asking, 'You want to sing this?', to which she replies, 'Why not? You don't think I can?') Their piano 'duet' follows. However, the next song, contemporary Japanese blues-inflected Mandarin 'Sympathy', is not directed at Hanhua, but at the audience, suggesting her misery, delivered sorrowfully, sadly. The flamenco number follows, and in contrast to 'Sympathy' an immediate, jarring jump cut from the couple's unseen love-making to an extreme close-up appears of Chang joyfully belting out the *shidaiqu* (Mandarin pop) modern mambo/cha-cha beat number 'Jajambo' – a woman irrevocably, undeniably, exuberantly, ecstatically in love. Her singing and acting chops carry the day. If only we ended here. But *Madama Butterfly*'s hope, faith and despair follow in the poignant 'One Beautiful Day', foreshadowing Butterfly's suicide and Sijia's betrayal. Contrasting with opener 'Habanera', Mandarin and French sung, primarily dominating the film and establishing Sijia as wild seductress and victimiser, we discover *Madama Butterfly* gets the last word, achingly heartbreaking, due to Chang's puissant performance. Suggesting her character's own demise, Sijia in close-ups is revealed no longer as the wild rose, but the tamed flower aware of the song's meaning for her after sacrificing her happiness to spare her lover's life.

Sijia literally dances her way into Hanhua's life with the opening 'Habanera' adaptation, which haunts the rest of the film. She begins seated on a stool, strumming a guitar. 'Love is just an ordinary thing that's not special at all/Men are only for fun, nothing marvellous either,' she snarls, making her way offstage into the audience, her costume slit to show her full legs, as she flirts with men, before she narrows her attack on Hanhua, giving a long exhale, drawing out her words. Numerous cuts occur between them, with his reaction shots to her performance, as she draws him in. Swinging her hips, taunting him, blowing him a kiss as he sweats and squirms, she's delighted. A close-up two shot appears as she embraces his neck; he pulls away, fearful. But she has him at hello, and warns, 'If I fall in love with you, you are going to die by my hand.' Thus, Sijia as the *femme fatale* begins and dominates the story. The song is repeated with others in the final montage, but it hovers over the film as a palimpsest, ever present, until *Madama Butterfly*. What does Rose's/Sijia's love mean? The Chinese title can be read numerous ways – the love of wildness, the kind of love the character portrays, even love for her.

Bizet's *Carmen*, as primary source material, hovers over the film, despite many other allusions. Since *Rose*, numerous other versions of *Carmen* have appeared, and *Rose*'s influence on any of these film versions is possible. A few worth mentioning include Suzuki's *Kawachi Karumen/Carmen from Kawachi* (1966), starring Nogawa Yumiko in the titular role, and Saura's *Carmen* (1983) with Laura del Sol; in the former, monochrome visuals switch with colours to emphasise various emotions; in the latter, Saura's pretext is actors/dancers/singers rehearsing a *Carmen* production, with a doubling effect whereby the rehearsal story overlaps with the developing relationship between the chief dancer and the choreographer/director – audiences often get caught out. More recently, Aranda's *Carmen* (2003) returned to Mérimée's novella author as character. Travelling to 1830s Southern Spain, he meets both Carmen and José, while the latter's woeful tale as he awaits execution (told in flashback) is told to Mérimée. Sexuality, rather than love, rules the relationship between this couple, but Carmen is defined by freedom. This is not to underestimate the significance and influence of *Madama Butterfly*. While *Carmen* dominates *Rose*'s story, *Madama Butterfly* is also important regarding its dénouement. Other film versions of *Madama Butterfly* have appeared including Cronenberg's *M. Butterfly* (1993), turning the tragedy into a gay love story. Both operas and adaptations address love and betrayal.

Rose is typical and atypical of MP&GI productions.[23] MP&GI's output was known for mixing the traditional and the new, and blending East with West. Its approach was to satisfy westernised middle-class tastes. *Rose*'s citations from Hollywood films and music are evident. The film mixes old and new, eastern and western characteristics. The western element should come as no surprise. General Manager Robert Chung and most MP&GI management were repatriates familiar with western ways. Beijing-born Chung studied in Tianjin, Shanghai and Hong Kong, later interning at Hollywood's Fox Studios. He is chiefly credited with introducing western production and management to MP&GI.²⁴ Wong somewhat modestly insisted on the collaborative aspects of making *Rose*, singling out Chung. Lee aptly refers to an 'MP&GI state of mind' to describe the late 1950s–early 1960s movies the studio produced and the movie theatre climate. '[They] portrayed a perfectly balanced dreamlike lifestyle where choices were simple, interpersonal relationships were never betrayed, and problems (no matter how complicated) were eventually resolved. This state of mind turns into an escapist's safe haven when life becomes too hard to bear.'²⁵ *Rose*'s primary characters have dreams too, but the film explodes them, exploiting melodrama. No escape is available for the couple from social stigma and a corrupt world. The protagonist sacrifices her happiness to save her lover, leading to no happy ending.

Writing of Hollywood musicals (which inspired some MP&GI productions), Ray observes that 'with so many fifties movies, the intent of these films was obviously different from their effect . . . with a loss of faith in the American dream'.²⁶ Likewise *Rose*, as a musical genre film, questions the 'dreamlike lifestyle'²⁷ exemplified by many period MP&GI films. Middle-class accumulation, prosperity and rapid development marked the then-colony's transitional period, far enough from wartime for it to be a growingly indistinct memory and distant enough from the late 1960s unrest to come. Many films feature modernisation and acquisition, a new consumerism and fascination with the new – new cars, household appliances and luxurious active nightlife. For all *Rose*'s main characters, due to its noir elements, life is Hobbesian – nasty, brutish and short. Hard times are alluded to from the beginning, with Hanhua willing to demean himself for a nightclub job. Sijia struggles, her pianist friend loses his job and breaks down when he cannot care for his ill wife, Sijia's roommate makes her living as a prostitute, and Hanhua is finally unemployed. Peter Rist notes 'the consistent use of money as a kind of sacrifice to support someone else'²⁸ and this money doesn't come cheaply or easily. The 3D (dirty, dangerous and demeaning) jobs emerging in Hong Kong as the tiger leaps are dangerous, dirty and, for Sijia, deadly. As with much noir, hard work does not pay off for everybody, and not for *Rose*'s main characters.

By 1960, Hong Kong's economic miracle as a world city was underway. Decimated by Japanese occupation during wartime, with an estimated one million people emigrating, Hong Kong faced economic collapse. Chinese immigration (largely from Guangdong, Shanghai and other commercial centres) began in 1948, as the nationalist government faced defeat by the communists. Hong Kong took advantage of a large and cheap labour pool, and by the 1950s the then colony exploited local and regional capital input and government tax incentives favourable to entrepreneurs. By the 1960s, tax policies were attracting foreign investors. In *Rose*, economic clashes of the emerging modern tiger are subjugated to the personal – catfights between women, petty jealousies, the difficulties of earning a living or caring for an ill wife, and a rogue cruel and amoral gangster husband/entrepreneur lurking. But modern Hong Kong is clearly defined by space.

Whereas in noir, location shooting and narrative city space contribute to characterisation, plot, atmosphere and theme, here few exteriors are visible. *Rose*'s urban visuals register as absence rather than presence with stage sets and interiors substituting, suggesting an insular, female space. Urban space is replaced by Sijia's close-up after close-up, singing, shrugging, laughing, pouting, smirking and crying. In contrast, Hanhua exists as adjunct, in reaction shots to her. From the opening credits, the songstress claims stage space as her own; as musical numbers are introduced, she invades the club space as she interacts with the clientele. Men, and sometimes women, become her victims, what Muller, describing noir settings, calls 'the choreography of a nightly mating dance'.[29] Sijia is inexorably linked to disreputableness and danger, setting tone and establishing pungent atmospherics where seduction, crime and love happen, all within her female space.[30] The ultimate female, Hong Kong herself, tied to a colonial culture in a love/hate relationship with its coloniser, prospering by economic expansion, is expressed by Sijia's independence but ultimate subjugation of love for a man. Similarly, weak Hanhua represents Hong Kong as a certain kind of son to the motherland. While the independence/subjugation duality indicates gender politics characterising periodic melodrama Cantonese film – female submission to one man, strong women/weak males, and the misogyny of conventional noir, it metaphorically situates Hong Kong–British relations.

Spatial dynamics threaten. Sound stage sets border on the claustrophobic, creating tension as fate closes in. Stifled as they attempt life together, the couple have transgressed social proprieties, casting their fates to the winds; inevitably, both will be punished for their passionate impropriety. As star-crossed lovers, pitted against all and finally each other, incapable of overcoming circumstances, they cannot defy fate. The city looms unseen, except for an exterior upon Hanhua's rain-drenched prison release, returning to Sijia rather than choose his fiancée and mother. In one of *Rose*'s few long shots, characters are swallowed up by a large space of street, undefined, unpopulated rectangular facades – modern Hong Kong defined abstractly, an engulfing emptiness. One would never know it is a small densely populated place from its look. Here, 'presence of absence'[31] reflects a transitional Hong

Kong, modernising but repressed, subjugated like Sijia. What registers in the film as high anxiety (the tight shots, the primary absence of urban space, and the numerous close-ups) reflects the mood of growing dissatisfaction with the inequities of British rule during simultaneous economic expansion. It makes sense that MP&GI became known for working its magic on sound stages during this transitional period. This aspect reinforces that dream factory sets substitute for real conflicts, political and economic, *in gestu*, that Hong Kongers would face in the near future. But 'all's well, ends well' as the middle class expands and prosperity (for some) grows. In this sense *Rose*'s ultimate despair and desperation remain exceptional among MP&GI product. Beyond stylised sets of nightclubs, the film includes social realist scenes, specifically the plain rooms of Hanhua's mother and those shared by the couple, and the wife's sickbed of Sijia's fired pianist friend to whom she remains loyal. The film explicitly comments on the difficulties of talented, down on their luck people in securing jobs when they are not well integrated into the 1960s Hong Kong business model.

By the 1980s, Hong Kong cinema's international heyday, when its output was secondary only to the United States and India, male action would dominate the industry, and over the next thirty years, anxiety over the 1997 return to the Mainland, the 1997–8 Asian economic crisis, SARS and globalisation would emerge as subtexts for films. While martial arts genre female warriors appeared, as well as dramedies (Chan's *He's a Woman, She's a Man*, 1994) and 'women's pictures' (Kwan's *Rouge*, 1988 and *Centre Stage*, 1992), heroic bloodshed defined the 1980s. Beginning with Woo's *A Better Tomorrow* (1986), a lone outsider hero emerged, defined by Chow Yun-fat's charm. Woo adapted the plot from Lung Kong's *Story of a Discharged Prisoner* (1967), but enhanced the film with noir elements. In *The Killer* (1989), he channelled Melville's *Le Samourai*, and by the era's end, in his Hong Kong swansong, the titular *Hard-Boiled* indicates the dominant style. Even Donnie Yen's low-budget bang for your buck *Ballistic Kiss* (1998), with its plaintive tone, indicates neo-noir. A few years later, Alan Mak/Andrew Lau's *Infernal Affairs* trilogy (2002–3) and Johnnie To's Milkyway Image productions have noir signings writ large. Hong Kong noir continues to evolve. So far, absent are women as feisty and prominent as Chang in *Rose*; instead they are ancillary to the men. (To find strong women characters one must turn to the few female filmmakers like Ann Hui, Cheung Yuen-ting and Sylvia Chang). Furthermore, contemporary Hong Kong noirs and neo-noirs are not sound stage-bound, offering up actual Hong Kong space as *femme fatale*. Hong Kong's mean streets still seduce and destroy.

Figure 1.1 Grace Chang, aka *Gě Lán*, actress and singer who plays *femme fatale* and doomed songstress with a heart of gold in *The Wild, Wild Rose*.

Notes

1. Shu Kei, 'Notes on MP & GI', p. 99.
2. Law Kar and Frank Bren argue that Bai Guang's 1940s and '50s films 'can best be described as Hong Kong noir'. See Kar and Bren, *Hong Kong Cinema*, p. 272; with collaboration by Sam Ho. In Yue Feng's *An Unfaithful Woman* (aka *A Forgotten Woman*) and *Blood-Stained Begonias* (both 1949), Bai played the *femme fatale* straight. Rather than Hong Kong noir origins, I am interested in the distinctiveness of *Rose* which combines melodrama, musical and noir styles, and eastern and western genres, establishing a hybrid nature for future Hong Kong film and its noir and neo-noir descendants, as well as the claustrophobic way it defines Hong Kong space. MP&GI aficionado Roger Lee points out that another Wong Tin-lam film, *Death Traps* (released 8 December 1960) is 'almost a film noir movie from MP&GI': Roger Lee, email to the author, 9 December 2010. I am grateful to both Law Kar and Roger Lee for their input on this project.
3. Writing about *wenyi pian*, Stephen Teo reminds us that 'the more a genre adapts to modern sensibilities, the more it retains characteristics of the well-tried genre'. I will argue that while *Rose* abounds with elements of the Chinese melodrama, it just as likely does so with elements of the musical genre and noir features, making it an unusual hybrid defining Hong Kong urban space more by its absence than presence. See Teo, 'Chinese Melodrama', p. 211.

4. Muller, *Dark City*, p. 29. Muller is the founder and president of the Film Noir Foundation in California, US.
5. As a native-born (1928) Shanghainese, Wong would have been exposed to many of these films.
6. Law Kar, email to the author, 26 July 2010.
7. Wong Tin-lam interview by Angel Shing and Ain-ling Wong in Wong and Shing (eds), *Director Wong Tin-Lam*, p. 64. I am indebted to Law Kar for providing me with the translation.
8. Ibid., p. 63.
9. Ray, *A Certain Tendency of the Hollywood Cinema*, pp. 160–1.
10. Chang was nominated for Best Actress at the Asia Film Awards for *Rose*, but Shaw Brothers' Linda Lin Dai won her fourth award for Tao Qin's *Love Parade*. Many female filmgoers (*tai-tais*) were noticeably upset, considering this unfair; articles still appear regarding this perceived injustice: Terence Chang, email to the author, 26 October 2010. I am grateful to Terence Chang for his input on this project.
11. In an interview with Sam Ho, Chang remarks she didn't have any dance training, but loved to dance, and that the key to her dancing was hard work in rehearsal. In fact, she was out dancing the mambo in a club and MP&GI bosses noticed how good she was. Hence, the origins of *Mambo Girl*. See Ho, 'Excerpts from an Interview with Ge Lan', pp. 88–9.
12. Shu Kei reports that Chang says writer Chin Yu wanted to write 'a completely different' role for her. Chang baulked at the script and suggested Julie Yeh Feng (known for playing sexy roles), but Chin insisted. Chang also revealed that she and Wong were 'overcome with anxiety during the shoot' due to her image. In Shu Kei, 'Notes on MP & GI', p. 86.

    Although Chang remarked she was proud of *Rose*, she much preferred her character and performance in Evan Yang's *Forever Yours*. The romantic melodrama was released on 7 April 1960, six months prior to *Rose*'s release date. Even though Chang worked with Wong again (and Hattori and much of the crew of *Rose*), in her final completed picture *Because of Her* (released on 31 July 1963), she said her favourite film is *Forever Yours*, in which she played a Pepsi plant clerk who falls in love with an ill man, considering the part more befitting. *Forever Yours* is a story of two simple people attempting to defy fate. The movie co-stars Kelly Lai Chen, who plays a tubercular man able to overcome his illness through love, only to be killed in an auto accident. Chang endures as a single mother vowing to keep their seaside home and raise their son, in whom her husband lives on. She explained that her mind was not on her work in her final film, as she was already a housewife, and that had she been married making *Rose*, she would have been embarrassed, especially by the sexy costumes. Roger Lee attended the Panel Discussion on 'Stars of MP&GI' in tandem with the 2002 Hong Kong International Film Festival, and recollects Chang's comments: Roger Lee, email to the author, 25 October 2010.
13. Leo Lee Ou-fan quotes Law Kar in Lee, 'The Popular and the Classical: Reminiscences on *The Wild, Wild Rose*', p. 177. Law explains that he remembered and played upon the

title of a Japanese film, *Hanoi Carmen*. He also points to Wong Kar-wai's *As Tears Go By* (1988), whose Chinese title is *Mongkok Carmen*, referring to Maggie Cheung's character: Law Kar, email to the author, 26 July 2010. Wong, of course, would also make his love song to the disappeared Shanghainese community of his youth in the 1960s, in *In the Mood for Love* (2000). See also my close read of the film in Stokes, 'Being There and Gone', pp. 127–49.

14. Wong relates, 'Grace Chang had never acted in a role like this before, playing a bad woman. I tried to persuade her to try. Robert Chung contributed some good ideas, like how she seduces Zhang Yang by first asking him to help her take off her clothes. That means she is willing and encouraging. The seduction comes from Robert's teaching, not mine. I was too young at the time and didn't know much about that kind of thing.' Wong and Shing (eds), *Director Wong Tin-Lam*, p. 64.

15. Roger Lee, email to the author, 22 October 2010.

16. Hollywood films widely screened in Hong Kong in the 1940s and '50s, preceding the making of *Rose*, include: Alfred Hitchcock's *Suspicion* (1941), Raoul Walsh's *High Sierra* (1941), Otto Preminger's *Laura* (1944), Billy Wilder's *Double Indemnity* (1944), Michael Curtiz's *Mildred Pierce* (1945), Alfred Hitchcock's *Spellbound* (1945), Billy Wilder's *Lost Weekend* (1945), Howard Hawks' *The Big Sleep* (1946), King Vidor's *Duel in the Sun* (1946), Robert Siodmark's *The Killers* (1946), Charles Vidor's *Gilda* (1946), John M. Stahl's *Leave Her to Heaven* (1947), Max Ophüls' *Letter from an Unknown Woman* (1948), John Huston's *The Treasure of the Sierra Madre* (1948), John Huston's *Key Largo* (1948), Anatole Litvak's *The Snake Pit* (1948), William Keighley's *Street Without a Name* (1948), Don Siegel's *Night Unto Night* (1949), Michael Curtiz's *Flamingo Road* (1949), Felix Jacoves' *Homicide* (1949), Billy Wilder's *Sunset Boulevard* (1950), Jules Dassin's *Night and the City* (1950), Henry Hathaway's *Niagara Falls* (1952), Alfred Hitchcock's *I Confess* (1953), Otto Preminger's *Carmen Jones* (1954), Henry King's *Love is a Many Splendored Thing* (1955), Charles Vidor's *Love Me or Leave Me* (1955), Jules Dassin's *Rififi* (1956), Gerd Oswald's *Kiss before Dying* (1956), Douglas Sirk's *Interlude* (1957), Nicholas Ray's *Party Girl* (1958), Otto Preminger's *Porgy & Bess* (1959).

17. Wong and Shing (eds), *Director Wong Tin-Lam*, p. 64.

18. Wong explains, 'The story comes from *Carmen* and *Madame Butterfly* and the ideas basically come from [writer] Qin Yu and [MP&GI General Manager] Robert Chung, with the collaboration of a few assistants in the script department. I had no part in it . . . I had not read or seen *Carmen* in a play or onstage': Wong and Shing (eds), *Director Wong Tin-Lam*, pp. 63–4. Wong claimed he was given the job because of the success of his *All in the Family* (1959), a family melodrama starring Lucilla Yu Min, Lo Wei, Kelly Lai Chin and Kitty Ting Hao. I should also note that the 83-year-old Wong passed away during my writing, on 16 November 2010. He directed more than 120 films, acted in over sixty and produced nine.

19. Muller also reminds us that when the first atomic bomb was tested at the Bikini Atoll, among the armada of ships one was renamed 'Gilda' with a portrait of Hayworth in a nightie on its side, hence the bombshell attribution. Muller, *Dark City*, pp. 97–8.

20. Ursini, 'Party Girl', pp. 222–3.
21. Preminger, *Otto Preminger*, p. 133.
22. Wong credits art director Fei Bai-yi with the idea, also noting Fei was good friends with MP&GI General Manager Robert Chung: Wong and Shing (eds), *Director Wong Tin-Lam*, p. 64.
23. An attendee at the panel discussion at the 2002 HKIFF, Lee compares the stars' reminiscences of Loke Wan Tho, founder of International Films/MP&GI/Cathay (tragically killed in an airplane crash in 1964) to the Medici in Italy, responsible for creating the 'golden age of the Hong Kong film industry': Roger Lee, email to the author, 22 October 2010.
24. Chung, 'A Southeast Asian Tycoon and His Movie Dream', pp. 43–4.
25. Lee, email to the author, 22 October 2010.
26. Ray uses Gene Kelly movies as typical: 'Kelly displayed a kind of desperation that one had never sensed in Astaire', Ray, *A Certain Tendency of the Hollywood Cinema*, pp. 167–8.
27. Lee, email to the author, 22 October 2010.
28. Rist, 'Neglected "Classical" Periods'.
29. Muller, *Dark City*, p. 29.
30. In an early scene, the double-sided club serves as the territory of two females, with Sijia dominating. The catfight that results further sets in motion the relationship between Sijia and Hanhua, as she resents his intervention but admires his physical prowess – there's a meta-filmic nod to martial arts in his fighting. MP&GI's competition, Shaw Brothers, produced numerous martial arts films (*wuxia pian*) during this era, although their productions were regarded as uncultured compared to MP&GI movies.
31. For use of this concept, see Abbas, *Hong Kong: Culture and the Politics of Disappearance*.

Chapter 2
Black and Red: Post-War Hong Kong Noir and its Interrelation with Progressive Cinema, 1947–57

Law Kar

Shanghai noir emerged in the immediate post-war years as a response to Hollywood imports. China's war against Japan (1937–45) had scarcely ended in August 1945 when its people faced another kind of 'invasion' from movies of the USA. Having been deprived of Hollywood pictures during wartime, China's filmgoers embraced American imports while local filmmakers looked on with envy and anxiety. From 1946 to 1949, hundreds of American releases flourished on Chinese screens, among them war, espionage, musicals, romantic love and crime pictures the most popular genres.[1] Chinese cinema, including that of Hong Kong, fought back by producing genre films of similar and mixed conventions. The latter combined melodramas, musicals and comedies with darker elements of murder, crime, suicide, horror and psychological dissociation. In no other comparable period were audiences of Chinese cinema so drawn to the dark side of human nature.

Some of these productions can now be identified wholly or partly under the description of film noir, or what is called '*heise dianying*' (dark film) in Chinese. As we know, the term itself is never singly or homogeneously defined, and it is not my intention to differentiate these films as a genre but rather as a 'feeling' and 'tone'. In this chapter I examine the dark elements and pessimistic tone in post-war Chinese cinema and its extension from Shanghai to Hong Kong involving key directors, actresses and films, along with specific cinema and social contexts.

Right after the war ended, the nationalist government took over the film industry in Shanghai, Peking and Manchuria, centralising film production and distribution under state control. The move was to disallow Chinese communists from using film for ideological propagation. In Nanking, the state-owned China Productions and two small studios were given support to produce nationalist propaganda and educational films; in Peking and Shanghai, China Film Studio was reorganised to become the biggest state-owned studios producing commercial films and newsreels. These studios were well equipped with facilities taken over from the Japanese occupiers and gave their employees regular salaries at a time of economic depression. Filmmakers from Chungking, Peking and Hong Kong were thus attracted to work in the state studios, under the condition of censorship that prohibited propagation of undesirable political and social messages. The civil war that broke out in 1946 and the subsequent economic turmoil nevertheless greatly weakened the execution of this film policy.

Emergent Shanghai Noir and its Critics

Two noir films, *From Night to Dawn* (1946) and *Code No. 1* (1946), were postwar blockbusters. Produced by the China Film Studio in Peking, both films were directed by Tu Guangqi and were released nationwide in mid-1947.[2]

The first feature has a love-hate drama about an engineer who falls in love with the daughter of his antagonist, a wealthy merchant who proves to have been a wartime traitor. The second, *Code No. 1*, is a more complex story of spy-versus-spy set in Japanese-occupied Peking. A nationalist (KMT) agent gains employment with a wealthy Chinese who is collaborating with the Japanese. The agent's real employer, the Chinese government, needs crucial information hidden in the traitor's house, which is well guarded by Japanese soldiers. The traitor's wife is actually a former lover of the agent, who meanwhile falls in love with her daughter. Finally, the wife kills her husband to protect both the KMT spy and her daughter before revealing that she is the KMT's 'Secret Agent Sky No.1 – Code Number One'.[3] The feature reportedly 'broke all box office records for a Chinese film', leading to a series of spy movies produced in Shanghai and Hong Kong, making Tu one of China's most popular directors and a leading expert in film noir.

The years 1947–9 witnessed a strong trend towards murder, detective, horror and thriller films made by big and small companies in Shanghai and Hong Kong. Released nationwide as well as having circulated among Chinese communities of South-east Asia, they received enthusiastic reviews along with negative criticism; the latter deplored Chinese pictures becoming increasingly sensational, and poorer in quality despite a higher quantity. One critic complained that scriptwriters and directors too often ignored reality to churn out old formulas, thus leading

Chinese cinema nowhere as spy films aped *Code No. 1* while their love stories were poorly constructed with paper-thin characterisation. Reporting on Hong Kong cinema for 1948, one writer savaged its cheap, made-in-bulk Cantonese movies that pushed sex, violence, mystery and fantasy into the realms of obscenity and absurdity.[4]

Similar criticisms appeared among critics in South-east Asia. Singapore's *Screen Voice* of 15 September 1948, for example, editorialised against post-war Chinese filmmakers who exploited sensationalism à la Hollywood for the totally inappropriate social conditions of China:

> People of the Dollar Country may crave such novelties, always needing newer sensations to stimulate and enrich their lives. They eat steak and fine bread so, naturally, look around for ice cream [eye candy] to top off the feast. But China is a poor country with serious problems everywhere. Most of our people are so poor they eat grass roots and tree skins and cannot afford this kind of enjoyment. Our urgent needs are freedom, sunshine and water. Seizing and transplanting Hollywood formulae for sex, fighting and killing is a *cul de sac* for Chinese cinema.[5]

China was indeed in turmoil during the immediate 'handover' and 'recovery' years following the Sino-Japanese War. Crime and corruption abounded, innocent people were charged with treason, while real wartime traitors retained power. Then came the civil war from mid-1946 between the nationalists and the communists. It brought great economic depression and soaring inflation, while Chinese people lost confidence in an increasingly corrupt and incompetent nationalist government. Rural people with no other hope fled to the big cities, making urban life even harder. Such pressures made Shanghai, China's greatest city and the heart of its national economy, ripe for a 'heart attack'.

Shanghai Noir vs Hollywood Noir in the Post-war Shanghai Film Industry

Among the Mainland cities, Shanghai still ran a regular film industry in the immediate post-war years. In spite of the grim conditions noted by the critic above, along with an economic depression, the film industry flourished.[6] People clearly needed escape from their daily pains and anguish, while movie-going remained the cheapest option, particularly for working-class and jobless people since there were second-, third- and even fourth-run venues with progressively cheaper tickets than first-run cinemas.[7]

Meanwhile, pro-communist or 'progressive' filmmakers infiltrated post-war nationalist film studios, whereas their own, Kun Lun film studio, was supported by 'patriotic capitalists'. These filmmakers tried to make films that reflected cruel reality but the censors strictly inspected all film productions and scripts so that social/political criticism was minimised, forcing 'progressive' filmmakers to convey messages by stealth. The most popular movie at the time, now regarded as a classic of post-war progressive cinema, was *The Spring River Flows East* (Cai Chusheng and Zheng Junli, 1947), a melodrama focusing on a family whose painful wartime experiences were in no way relieved by the 1945 victory. Logically, they wondered (aloud), would nothing ever get better (?), the film typically sugaring the message with sensual women and mildly sensational love scenes. Another progressive film, *Night Lodging* (Huang Zuolin, 1947), dissected a cross-section of tenants in a low-class hotel for their inherent goodness or evil, their individual motives driven by love or hatred and their complicated relations leading to betrayal and murder: 'Eighty per cent of the scenes in *Night Lodging* take place at night. This makes it the first Chinese film to consist mainly of night scenes.'[8] In *The Devils* (Xu Changlin, 1948), a group of Chinese bandits cooperate with the Japanese to control a small town. But conflicts of interest, lust for the same women and competition for power lead to their killing one another. The film satirised wartime human vices while associating them with contemporary social and economic corruption.

Figure 2.1 A scene from the Shanghai noir *The Devils* (1948).

In such 'progressive' (read: leftist) films, significant noir elements and visual styles expressed the sufferings of ordinary people and their resentments against those in power, lightened by some sensual onscreen excitement. Non-leftist filmmakers focused more generally on entertainments as diversions from the hardships of life, or vented personal frustrations through stories depicting human weaknesses, passions, crimes and struggles in a terrain somewhere between the extremes of good and evil. Thus emerged the murder, detective, horror, thriller and spy genre films throughout 1947–9, many packaged with noir features to make them more competitive with Hollywood imports and nationalist government-sponsored productions.

This fashionable trend in post-war Shanghai might be considered as a reaction to American noir films. Still, it grew out of society's disappointments and anger vis-à-vis the establishment's corrupt central government and unrighteous people with wealth and power in general. Nationalist government-imposed censorship that eliminated 'offensive' elements, either political or 'moral', bound filmmakers to very strict rules: forbidden were depictions of explicit sex and violence, or of social disorder and crimes portrayed in any great detail; criminals had to be punished or ultimately repentant, moral values reconfirmed and conflicts resolved. To avoid being banned or heavily cut, films turned from external social conflicts to internal emotional ones, many concerning illicit love foreshadowing crimes of passion via complicated plots and characterisations (rather than action as such) to grab attention. Sexual elements were cautiously handled – a woman in a swimsuit lying on a beach or one in pyjamas lying in bed beside a man were about as risqué as they got – and no blood could be visible in violent scenes. Even so, of 162 features submitted in 1948, forty-eight had to be cut.[9]

Perhaps Shanghai noir was influenced by Hollywood in many ways, but it is difficult even now to analyse and compare their respective styles and scenes since almost all contemporary examples from Shanghai remain locked away in Chinese archives. Nevertheless, through viewing what are available and by examining contemporary scenarios and stills, we find that Chinese filmmakers used many conventions familiar to Hollywood noir: low-key lighting; long flashback sequences; the confession of a prisoner or victim to introduce the story; a murder or gunshot in the opening scene; the disposal of dead bodies on rainy days or foggy nights; a woman smoking and holding a gun confronting an unarmed man; a soldier returning from war to discover his wife involved with a secret admirer; or a climactic chase in which the bad guy falls from on high. American film historian Jay Leyda saw *Doubt in the Boudoir* (Xu Changlin, 1948) to find that 'it was an imitation of [Alfred] Hitchcock's *Suspicion*

(1941)'.[10] In fact, the released film adopted the same Chinese title used for *Suspicion* itself and proved an instant hit. Nonetheless, Shanghai and Hong Kong noir clearly also borrowed from local cultural traditions and were thus better geared to the tastes of Chinese audiences whose social and economic conditions differed greatly from those in the United States. This point is explored in more detail below.

At the time, Shanghai cinema was hampered by the severe constraints of poor facilities, strong external competition and rigid censorship. With the economic environment worsening consistently throughout 1948–9, films had to be made cheaply and fast to recover costs in studios that were wartime leftovers with old facilities, and film stocks were difficult to obtain. From mid-1948, decreased importation of American films benefited the industry but Chinese films were still not good enough in either quality or quantity to fill the gap.[11] Even government-run studios lacked adequate resources and reined in production while renting out space to independent companies. Despite all that, numerous films with complicated plots of crime, murder and illicit love appeared because they could be cheaply made and cheap thrills sold tickets. Chinese films produced and released in Shanghai amounted to sixty-seven in 1948 and fifty-seven in 1949.[12]

Shanghai Cinema Lives On in Hong Kong

In the immediate post-war years, three major film companies made Mandarin-language films in Hong Kong for the all-China market. Financed by Mainland investors, these were: Great China Film Company (est. 1946), Yung Hwa Motion Picture Industries Ltd (est. 1948) and Great Wall Pictures Corporation (est. 1949). They attracted many Shanghai émigrés to Hong Kong and, after 1949, many more joined as escapees fearing life under communism.[13] These émigrés contributed to the advancement of Hong Kong's Mandarin cinema, whose films numbered several distinguished noirs.

The overall situation of post-war cinema was little better in Hong Kong, although the territory's general economic and social conditions bettered those in Shanghai. From late 1946, Hong Kong production resumed despite the poor facilities, low budgets and insufficiently sized companies, the main exception being Yung Hwa, well equipped to produce medium- to large-scale productions, but mainly epic, high-brow *wenyi pian* (literary art films) and melodramas in the Chinese classical style with an output of only three films per annum on average. Great China was the major Chinese company regularly providing films for the market; for example, thirty-four Mandarin- and eight Cantonese-language pictures in 1947–8.[14] Most of its Mandarin films in that period, using medium- or low-sized budgets, were made for both Mainland and local markets. Among them were three spy films, two detective stories, two black comedies and three melodramas with strong noir elements. Cantonese films, on the other hand, had by far the lowest budgets. Many smaller companies produced mainly low-cost Cantonese quickies often finished within one to two weeks but which were warmly welcomed in Hong Kong and Nanyang (Chinese communities of South-east Asia), bolstering Hong Kong's annual feature production to 141 in 1948 and 179 in 1949,[15] more than doubling that of Shanghai.

As in Shanghai during the three calendar years 1947–9, Hong Kong produced many spy movies. They reawakened the traumas of the recent anti-Japanese war, showed respect for the heroic acts of Chinese fighters, and expressed hatred towards wartime traitors. The thrillers that embraced murder, detective yarns and horror proved popular, as did melodramas, swordplay adventures and farces. My own estimate for this three-year period indicates that twenty espionage films plus more than twenty others all employed noir elements.

Cantonese Film and Urbanity

Hong Kong's first Cantonese spy film, *The Spy Lovers in the Dangerous City* (But Fu), released in April 1947, was a great box-office success. This was followed by *Female Spy 76* (Ren Pengnian) in July, a Mandarin-language production by Great China that paved the way for more. The same year also saw the rising film popularity of crimes of passion, real murder cases, underground wartime resistance, and 'good' and 'bad' thieves. However, most were poorly made with plots too loosely constructed, unimposing characters and unconvincing action, even though censorship in Hong Kong was more relaxed than Shanghai's regarding sex and violence, such that gang fights and crime scenes could be portrayed in more detail, and half-nude dancers and women in sexy postures were quite common in Cantonese films. However, in contrast to the Shanghai noirs with their strong sense of the city, one can barely feel contemporary local urban life at all in their Hong Kong counterparts, in which stories often played out in the wartime milieus of Hong Kong, Guangzhou, Shanghai and rural China where underground activities took place. Some were fanciful stories that could happen anywhere, and films featuring contemporary, urban Hong Kong were fragmentary and non-specific. Perhaps the filmmakers were so haunted by wartime memories that they felt alienated from contemporary reality or had been absent from Hong Kong too long to retain any immediate 'feel' for the city. Furthermore, there was little urban life as such to depict dramatically – immediate post-war Hong Kong was too poor and shabby.

When the Japanese occupied Hong Kong (1941–5), film production ceased. Cantonese filmmakers who fled then in time returned post-war to resume work found it hard to adjust to the new environment, whereas most Mandarin-language filmmakers had been working in urban Shanghai or Chungking during the war. Apart from the fact that post-war Cantonese films were made so cheaply and for the 'lower-end' market, they were generally inferior to the territory's Mandarin films creatively and technically during 1946–9.

Yet Cantonese cinema grew out of a local, popular culture while readily assimilating elements from abroad. Some of them adapted local pulp novels, stage operas, radio novels, martial arts novels and comics, as well as assimilating popular songs and detective stories from Shanghai, western popular dances and music, and stories from Hollywood films by localising them as part of Hong Kong culture. When Hong Kong eventually recovered economically, Cantonese cinema progressed rapidly in the 1950s to more perceptibly mirror the changing urban landscape.

Noir Classics of Hong Kong and their Masters

In 1948–9, during the last stages of China's civil war, with the national economy falling apart, numerous Shanghai filmmakers went to Hong Kong to live and work there as exiles. Their filmmaking skills and knowledge included a propensity to explore the darker side of human nature, partly because it was a fad in Shanghai and partly to express their own experiences of social injustice, bureaucratic corruption and other evils of humanity evident under the Japanese occupation and in the immediate post-war years. Among them, director Wang Yan arrived with his actress wife, Yuan Meiyun, to make *Desire* (1946) and stayed to make more. Zhang Shichuan and He Zhaozhang came to direct *An All-Consuming Love* (1947) before returning to Shanghai. Both films were melodramas with noir elements that evoked painful experiences of wartime and beyond. Other veteran directors like He Feiguang, Bu Wancang, Yang Gongliang, Dan Duyu, Ren Pengnian, Zhu Shilin, Yue Feng and Li Pingqian all came to make one-off films in the territory or remained to make more. Among the latter, Zhu, Yue and Li made the most distinguished Hong Kong films, some setting the highest standards of classic Chinese noir.

Zhu Shilin remained working in Shanghai during the Japanese Occupation, then, to avoid being tried for collaboration with the enemy, arrived in Hong Kong by 1946 to make his first post-war film, *Two Persons in Trouble Unsympathetic to Each Other* (1946). His film dramatises the mixed fortunes and cruelties of middle- to upper-class people living in a housing estate of occupied Shanghai and who, through cowardice or selfishness, remain impervious to the life and death of others during an air raid – a realistic depiction of human nature in wartime. Zhu made four films in 1947 for Great China Studio, the second and third being family melodramas while the fourth, *Where is My Darling?* (1947), was a black comedy satirising human vanity and illusion with a noir visual style rarely seen in China till then. The film develops its rather fantastical and horrific adventure around a pretty young girl pressured by her father to marry a wealthy husband. She must pretend to live in a big house by remaining in the one she has entered by chance and that's when the adventure begins. She gets locked inside, lost in darkness, half-scared to death by rats and by a drunk caretaker who tries to rape her and whom, after a fight, she thinks she has killed. At dawn, she arrives back home exhausted, only to find that her boyfriend and a policeman have come to rescue her!

Zhu's visual style is both weird and realistic, the pace slow but masterfully weighted to involve and surprise the audience. Sadly, Zhu's film disappoints with an ending where conflicts between father and daughter and between upper- and lower-class people are too easily resolved. The wealthy young master promises to marry the miserable young woman – happy ending. As in many Shanghai noir films, conflicts are too easily fixed, moral sense and family values eventually reign, all wrongs are righted and life goes back to normal.

Like Zhu Shilin, Yue Feng was a well-established director long before coming to Hong Kong. His directorial debut, *The Raging Tide* (1933), was acclaimed by leftist critics as a pioneer 'progressive' work despite being severely cut by the censor. He then turned to more straightforward entertainment, becoming a veteran in various genres. After the war, Yue went to Hong Kong to direct a Great China-produced 'progressive' melodrama, *Three Females* (1947), with a tragic story of three women in urban Shanghai.

Yue then returned to Shanghai to make several popular noirs, such as *The Incredible Rose* (aka *Roses are Prickly*, 1947), a story that foreshadowed Eileen Chang's novella *Lust, Caution*, later filmed under that title by Ang Lee in a China/US/Taiwan co-production (2007). A female undercover agent is ordered to penetrate a Japanese encampment to kill a Chinese traitor therein, only to fall in love with him. When her comrades are killed by enemy agents, she determines to kill him by sacrificing her own life. Other examples are *Murder in the Forest* (1949) and *Night of the Killing* (1949): both are detective films, with Bai Guang as the female lead in the latter. Subsequently, director Yue Feng and actress Bai Guang were recruited by Great Wall in Hong Kong to work on the studio's two inaugural features of 1949.

The first, *A Forgotten Woman* (1949), was adapted from Leo Tolstoy's last novel, *Resurrection* (1899), and tells the story of a country girl (Bai Guang) who is seduced and abandoned by the young master (Yan Jun) of the home that employs her. Now pregnant, she flees to Shanghai where, in order to raise her child, she becomes a prostitute. Years pass before Bai is eventually arrested and tried on suspicion of murdering her abusive pimp. The trial judge (Yan Jun) is actually her old lover, the former 'young master'. Found not guilty, she is released, but instead of reigniting happier days, she leaves the now-remorseful judge, putting their child in his permanent care. *A Forgotten Woman* might be called a progressive film noir. It starts with a prison scene where the judge visits Bai, who refuses to make any confession. Her tragic story unfolds in flashback beginning some ten years earlier, a convention long familiar to film noir but with an ending that is clearly non-conventional. Bai is freed not only from prison but also from the control of men, good or bad, to go her own way as a truly free woman.

The second, *Blood Will Tell* (aka *Blood-stained Begonia*, 1949), is a stylistically better thriller, or 'blood melodrama', that has many of the same cast and crew as in *A Forgotten Woman*. Yue Feng fully exercised his own cinematic style to tell a murder story (reportedly borrowed from a Hollywood film and rewritten by Tao Qin) to achieve good dramatic tension. The setting is early Republican China (1911–49), with Bai Guang cast as a typical *femme fatale* here married to a 'good thief' nicknamed 'Red Begonia' (Yan Jun) who steals from the rich to aid the poor. He decides to retire following the birth of his daughter but his unsatisfied wife (Bai) double-crosses him by stealing jewels from a famous songstress and tries to run away with her new lover. The enraged Yan kills her lover and entrusts the daughter to his old friend, a police inspector, before surrendering himself to the authorities. Years later, the daughter has grown up and is about to be happily married. Bai, meanwhile, is managing a brothel and, as she is short of cash, turns up at the home of the retired inspector to demand money, otherwise she will reveal the whole truth about the inspector's 'daughter'. Made aware of this, Yan escapes from prison to seek revenge on Bai, in the process forcing her to fall to her death – unrepentant – from a high rooftop. After watching the marriage ceremony of his daughter, Yan finally accompanies the police back to prison.

The melodrama works well under Yu's elaborate visual style that balances subtle emotions with thrilling excitement. Bai was by then already the most popular star in Shanghai, playing harsh undercover agents or wicked women, highly, sensually attractive as a *femme fatale* who manipulates men with her sex appeal and women with her wit. Long celebrated as a 'bad woman' for her carefree behaviour both on- and off-screen, she is fondly remembered as a distinguished singer, as an outstanding sexy star and as a strong woman who dared to go her own way in a male-dominated society.

Li Pingqian was also a colleague of directors Zhu and Yue (above) in the wartime Japanese-owned Huaying studios. After directing several melodramas in Shanghai, including the post-war thriller *The Murderer* (1948), he went to Hong Kong in 1948 to direct Yung Hwa studio's *Our Husband* (1949), a well-made melodrama built around the story of a *femme fatale* who uses her one-night stand with a wealthy businessman (it produces a baby) to blackmail the man's wife. It plays on the psychology of two women (Sun Jinglu and Li Lihua) who claim to love the same man, utilising plot points and scenes borrowed from unidentified Hollywood pictures.

Li Pingqian soon switched to Great Wall to make *A Strange Woman* (1950), Bai Guang's last film for that studio. *A Strange Woman* was adapted from the 'book' of Puccini's stage opera, *Tosca*, by screenwriter Yao Ke for release as a screen thriller in early 1950. Yao's script set it in the 1920s when warlords were resisting the Northern Expedition, Sun Yat-sen's military attempt (from 1924) to unify a China then fractured by local provincial strongmen in what we now call the 'warlord era' (1917–27). Once again, the film paired Bai Guang and Yan Jun – Bai as a Peking Opera singer helping her revolutionary lover obtain important information from the warlord's camp in Peking. When her lover is captured by secret police, she begs the warlord's head of secret police (Yan), who desires her, for freedom for her lover in exchange for her body. Yan assents but soon breaks his promise by executing the captive. Upon hearing this, Bai lures Yan to his bedroom and kills him there with his own gun. The technical precision made Li's film into an atmospheric, intensely emotional thriller. It was a box-office hit too, encouraging Li to stay and make *The Awful Truth* (1950), a brilliant black comedy starring Li Lihua that ridiculed the human vices and social injustices of post-war Shanghai when official corruption prevailed and the economy collapsed. Director Li would head the production team of Great Wall when it turned 'leftist' in 1950.

The above three films (*A Forgotten Woman*, *Blood Will Tell* and *A Strange Woman*), all starring Bai Guang and Yan Jun, intentionally or otherwise form a trilogy that set the mode of classic Chinese film noir. They borrowed selective noir concepts, elements and techniques from the west while effectively giving them a Chinese context, neither diluting the Chinese characteristics nor the cultural values. For instance, they depicted the vices of feudalism while reaffirming family values over individualism; they emphasised historical continuity rather than modernity; they contrasted rural and urban life rather than using cities alone as mere 'concrete jungles'. Just as interestingly, the films clearly chart changing attitudes towards women. Females were often victims but they evolved into stronger, mentally tougher creatures whether as songstress or prostitute figures, or as spies or *femme fatales*. Women carried guns or knives and were as thoughtful and ingenious as men. Chinese noirs had no equivalent to tough guy Humphrey Bogart; rather, they have quite a few tough women like Bai Guang who was the most beloved (or hated) of all. With Bai as a famous and popular singer, there was no lack of her songs as a bonus in these films featuring her.

Figure 2.2 Bai Guang, famous post-war singer and *femme fatale*, as she appeared in *Destroy* (1952).

Femmes Fatales

Bai Guang was not the only successful *femme fatale*. If she were the Rita Hayworth or Ava Gardner of Shanghai/Hong Kong noir, then Ouyang Shafei was its Barbara Stanwyck or Gloria Grahame. After her appearance in *Code Number One*, Ouyang starred in numerous Shanghai spy, detective and melodramatic films, reaching her peak in 1948. She starred opposite Bai in *Missing Document* (1948), one of the biggest hits of that year. She went on to marry Tu Guangqi, director of *Code Number One* and the master of Shanghai noir, moving with him to Hong Kong in 1950 to act in several noirs, and started a long career in acting. Apart from playing wicked women, Ouyang appeared in many Hong Kong films in various roles, from good housewife to rich man's mistress to care-free high-society lady. Ouyang herself was justly famous for her elegant charm and cool beauty.

Sun Jinglu was another versatile actress whose roles varied from innocent young girl (*Where is My Darling?*) to *femme fatale* (*Our Husband*). Her qualities of sensitive facial expression and subtle sex appeal were comparable to those of Gene Tierney or Jane Greer. And Pak Yin, who played a spy disguised as a social butterfly to seduce the enemy in *The Spy Lovers in the Dangerous City*, appeared in *The Return of the Lascivious Woman's Soul* (1948) as twin sisters, one lascivious and one virtuous, and as the 'devil woman' in *The Devil Woman in Black* (1949), a social butterfly in a Japanese occupied city who falls in love with a Chinese pilot and sacrifices herself to save him. In *Blood-Stained Azaleas* (1951) she played a typical *femme fatale*. She then played mostly good wife/mother roles in the 1950s and '60s, and became one of the prettiest and most popular stars in Cantonese cinema.

Hong Kong Cinema Left and Right

As China split into two – the Mainland (excluding Hong Kong's part of the Kowloon peninsula) and Formosa/Taiwan – Mandarin cinema was divided into 'leftist' and 'rightist' camps after 1951. The former was supported by Beijing, the latter by Taiwan with added funds from the United States. Their respective aims were not overt political propaganda but to 'educate' people through entertainment as a long-term cultural investment.

Apart from aiming at local audiences in Hong Kong, the leftist cinema there targeted the Nanyang market. The rightists, on the other hand, aimed at both Nanyang and Taiwan. Both had to face ultra-conservative audiences in Nanyang and Taiwan where strict government censorship efficiently suppressed political propaganda, scenes of sex and violence, and 'antisocial' elements. Hong Kong's colonial government actively spotted sensitive political materials in post-war films and provided internal guidelines on all undesirable elements. Later, as conflict in Hong Kong between labour and capitalist management escalated from 1948 onwards, thereby accelerating strikes and social disorder with communist support, the government re-enforced censorship by encoding do's and don'ts in its Film Censorship Standards of 1953. Hong Kong government officials, recognising that 'visual images have always had the ability to arouse a strong emotive response in an audience', strove to 'prevent the colony from becoming an arena of Communist/KMT political conflict'.[16]

Such restraints drove leftist and rightist cinemas to become *de facto* commercial middle-of-the-road entertainments providing wholesome fare for local and overseas audiences while embedding mild social messages and moral instruction. From Singapore and Malaya, the Cathay Organisation invested in Hong Kong by establishing MP&GI (Motion Pictures and General Investments Co. Ltd) in 1957, with its own studios inspiring the Shaws to do likewise by building the largest studio in South-east Asia. Thus arrived the 'big studios era' of Hong Kong, with Shaw Brothers and Cathay competing to maximise their markets in South-east Asia and Taiwan from their base in Hong Kong, both gravitating to the 'right' while the leftist Great Wall and Feng Huang studios continued to extend *their* audiences among overseas Chinese communities except in Taiwan.

Both 'left' and 'right' tried hard to negotiate with the Hong Kong establishment by filtering out sensitive or offensive elements, including social disorder, crime, explicit sex and violence, to concentrate on family or romantic melodramas, comedies, musicals and historical epics, all having less and less to do with the harsh reality of life in Hong Kong. In that sense they were ever-more distanced from the implications of 'left' and 'right' by more closely aping mainstream Hollywood entertainments that made dreams come true and celebrated sentimentality, family values, fair play and virtuous living. Eventually, throughout the 1960s, Hong Kong's studio giants – MP&GI, Shaw Brothers and Great Wall – were all producing films as dream factories.

Grey Film and Noir gets Greyer

Several 'progressive' filmmakers were part of what might be called 'Grey Cinema' in Hong Kong in 1948–50, its films responding to changing political winds when the nationalist government crumbled under the emergent New China. Some such films were released as late as 1951. They incorporated noir elements and styles into what were really social tragedies, family melodramas and romances severely criticising the 'old' society under the nationalist regime, showing the sufferings and oppression of common people who thus arose in opposition.

The better examples (Mandarin-language films) include: *Everlasting Green* (Ouyang Yuqian, 1948); *The Lexicon of Love* (Wang Yin, 1948); *A Peasant's Tragedy* (Wu Zuguang, 1949); *Way to Love* (Ouyang Yuqian, 1949); *Floating Family* (Gu Eryi, 1949); *Hearts Aflame* (Yuen Jun, 1949); *A Fisherman's Honour* (Cheng Bugao, 1949); *Quietly Flows the Jialing River* (Zhang Min, 1949); *Little Shrimp* (Wu Zuguang, 1949); *Wintry Journey* (Zhang Min, 1950); *Peasant Takes a Wife* (Gu Eryi, 1950); *The Insulted and the Injured* (Liu Qiong, 1950); *Home, Sweet Home* (Yue Feng, 1950); *The Fiery Phoenix* (Wang Weiyi, 1950); and *The Victims* (Gu Eryi, 1951). The few Cantonese films added to this list include: *Tears of the Pearl River* (Wang Weiyi, 1950); *Laughters and Tears* (Lau Fong, 1950); *Kaleidoscope* (in ten episodes by ten directors, 1950); *Tragedy in Canton* (Lo Dun, 1951); and *The Kid* (Fung Fung, 1950). As has often happened, some directors of these films returned to the Mainland in 1950–2 before the door was gradually closed to Hong Kong-made films for the Mainland Chinese market.

The 1950s did little for the development of Chinese film noir, although the genre's style and icons show up in sundry melodramas, tragedies and comedies of the day to provide dramatic tension. But, as a 'genre' (a false name for a mode of expression covering 'crime' movies, Westerns and other real genres), film noir had virtually disappeared midway through that decade. The last interesting Mandarin noirs appeared before 1952, when Shanghai's film veterans took advantage of the new creative possibilities of elements now considered to typify 'film noir', inspired also by the dawn of New China, as a way of greater self-expression. For example, Zhu Shilin's *The Flower Girl* (aka *Flora* 1951), a satire cum thriller based on Guy de Maupassant's short story, *Boule de Suif* (1880). Maupassant's story dealt with French passengers in a stagecoach from Rouen traversing a Prussian-occupied zone during the Franco-Prussian War (1870–1). Zhu's film similarly highlights human weaknesses that surface among members of a group in a somewhat similar situation – the bus passengers crossing a Japanese checkpoint in wartime China are delayed by a Japanese officer who wants the group's prettiest passenger, Flora (Li Lihua). Internal group conflicts erupt that involve three travelling couples, two nurses, a driver and Flora herself as she resists the officer while bearing the contempt of fellow passengers. Finally, as the sole passenger with real courage, Flora sacrifices herself to save the others. The sure characterisations, pacing and cinematic style deliver a powerful, sensitively played, highly emotional drama reaching deep into hearts and minds. Zhu then turned to family melodrama, satire and light comedy with Hong Kong settings for Feng Huang Film Company and seldom touched film noir again.

The previously mentioned black comedy, *The Awful Truth* (written by Tao Qin, 1950), remains one of Li Pingqian's best in the field, weaving its superb *mise-en-scène* around seven characters propelled on a self-interested wild goose chase for money and sexual satisfaction. Several narrative lines alternate one gripping scene after another, moving characters in and out of the sets beautifully with photography and art direction perfectly matched to an appealing visual style, all helping to make this film so touching.

Home, Sweet Home (Yue Feng, 1950) deals with mainland villagers who emigrate with high hopes to Hong Kong to get employment as labourers. But then they have to endure unexpected cruelties and oppression from the locals before all return, hurt and disappointed, to the Mainland. Yue Feng successfully injects a noir style into this tragedy containing a strong note of social protest and a plea for better human values.

Bu Wancang, director of the epic, internationally distributed *The Soul of China* (1948), made two noirs in 1951–2. *Destroy* (1952), being the second film, starred Bai Guang. Inspired by Alfred Hitchcock's *Spellbound* (1945), its story is likewise about a man (Wang Hao) who thinks he has killed someone while trying hard to rediscover his own lost identity. Writer Tao Qin rearranged the characters and plot to have the woman (Bai Guang), who loves and wants to redeem the man, having the identity of a sing-song girl rather than a psychoanalyst (played by Ingrid Bergman in the Hitchcock film). However, Bai fails since both the man's wife and the police who have accused him of murder cannot recognise him, the accused having so thoroughly changed his appearance. By eliminating the dream sequences and psychoanalysis from its Hitchcockian precedent, *Destroy* becomes a detective story with complicated plotlines and a tragic ending in which even true love fails to redeem the hero. Bai's role combines a *femme fatale* with an angel, first luring a man to commit a crime before trying desperately and vainly to save him. Unfortunately, the script is far superior to its near-pedestrian direction.

Tao Qin soon became a director/writer and after making a few films for Great Wall joined International Films in 1955 to make *Surprise* (1956), a thriller 'with action, climax and suspense!', one of his last noirs and an entry in the third South East Asian Film Festival (later known as the Asian Film Festival and Asia-Pacific Film Festival). He then directed mostly melodramas, comedies and musicals, seldom touching film noir again.

Tu Guangqi directed classic noirs in the 1950s and continued making noir melodramas and romances into the 1960s. As a director, he had a long and interesting career that is worth further study. His films were made in the mode of Shanghai noir, and they exuded Shanghai nostalgia and a Mainland mentality.

Cantonese Films Catching Up

Stimulated by strong competition from Mandarin cinema, Cantonese filmmakers improved their marketing strategies and filmmaking techniques in the 1950s. Director Lee Tit paired with Tong Tik-sang to make the *Mysterious Murder* (1951), proving that the Cantonese could make noir films as well as the Shanghainese given longer production times and bigger budgets. An excellent script, good casting with exquisite lighting and camerawork (Ho Luk-ying) elevated this film to an artistic high seldom achieved in China's immediate post-war years. The same year saw *Blood-Stained Azaleas* (1951) directed by Lee Sun-fung from an original story by Ng Chor-fan, who also played the central figure, a man in distress employed and exploited by an amorous woman (Pak Yin). Aided by Ho's camerawork, Lee displayed his mastery of dramatic pace and cinematic style as inspired by Hollywood noir. The film concerned the tragic fate of an innocent couple (Ng Chor-fan and Siu Yin-fei) divided by the war and again by the boss/*femme fatale* (Pak Yin) when they return to a post-war city so busy with trading and high-risk financial speculation in 1951. The boss/*femme fatale* symbolises both the city and capitalism – a lure and a threat.

Serious Cantonese filmmakers sympathetic to the deprived or lower-end people of society were sensitive to the social changes affecting their daily lives then and in the years to follow. Cantonese films increasingly came to terms with urban reality – the shortages of housing, education and medical care, the horrible working conditions for labourers and women, the great gaps between the poor and rich, and so on. Their city was mired in social injustices, exploitation, ill-aimed desires and all sorts of evils, but their critical attitudes were watered down to pass censorship through wrappings of sensational melodrama, satire and 'noir' features, and indeed any kind of entertainment. Still, one can sense in these films the changing urban life of Hong Kong along with the pains and frustration of its populace.

The Comeback of Noir in New Hong Kong Cinema

Throughout the late 1950s and early 1960s, film noir characteristics returned in force to Cantonese cinema. Kwong Ngai Film Company led the market by

Figure 2.3 Cantonese noir *Mysterious Murder* (1951): the detective happened to be her ex-boyfriend.

producing a series of detectives titled *999* plus numerous 'blood melodramas' in the mid- to late '50s, the success of which led to more of the same. The latter were churned out by the Cantonese Units of Shaw Brothers and of MP&GI. Union Film Enterprise Ltd, labelled as 'left' at the time, also produced seventeen films with strong noir elements between 1957 and 1964, among them *I Want to Live* (1960). Directed by Lee Tit, the film incorporated Italian neorealism and American noir styles to make a brilliant movie that depicted human weakness and social injustice within a robbery story. Taken from the Italian film *La città si difende* (Pietro Germi, 1951) and somewhat reminiscent of Stanley Kubrick's *The Killing* (1956), the film depicts four men deprived of job and dignity who band together to rob Hong Kong Royal Jockey Club, and one by one they are tracked down by the police. MP&GI produced *The Wild, Wild Rose* (1960) directed by Wong Tin-lam (aka Wang Tianlin) and starring Grace Chang. It fused melodrama, musical and thriller into one of the best noirs of the 1960s at a time when Hong Kong cinema had already developed a stronger urban sensibility.

Hong Kong was turning into a modern city in the 1960s. The subjects that were forbidden before, such as organised crime, bank robberies, or even specifically robbing the Royal Hong Kong Jockey Club, began to appear on screen. The government censors were still protective of the image of the Royal Hong Kong Police Force, so policemen in uniform remained off-limits for a long time, and policemen in plain clothes and police inspectors were all 'good guys'. In the late 1960s, especially after the 1967 Riot, more police inspectors appeared in leading roles, and the taboo on their relation with the criminals was lifted. With films having their own urban flavour and colour, the local film industry fully emerged from the shadow of Shanghai.

Director Lung Kong, who had acted in several Cantonese noirs, was inspired by the noir precedents to make *Story of a Discharged Prisoner* (1967). In turn this film can be taken as the classic that (might have) inspired such films as Ann Hui's *The Secret* (1979) or Alex Cheung's *Cops and Robbers* (1979) and *Man on the Brink* (1981), as well as John Woo and Tsui Hark's remake of Lung Kong's *Discharged Prisoner* as *A Better Tomorrow* (1986). Thus developed the 'neo-noir' period of Hong Kong cinema.

Author's note: This chapter is a revised and updated version of an essay previously published in the twenty-fourth Beijing College Student Film Festival 2013 catalogue, *Cross-century Frames: Hong Kong Film (1914–2014)*. I would like to thank my friend Frank Bren for polishing my English text and Professor Lisa Stokes for giving me valuable comments.

Notes

1. According to *The History of the Development of Chinese Cinema*, American features shown in Shanghai between 1946 and 1949 numbered 1083: see Cheng et al. (eds), *Zhongguo dianying fazhan shi* [*The History of the Development of Chinese Cinema*]. In 1946 alone there were 352 compared to sixteen Chinese features (see Vol. 2, p. 162). According to a government report in January 1950, of 356 features shown in China in 1948, 271 were foreign and eighty-five Chinese: see Ding, *Yingxiang Zhongguo*, p. 158.
2. China Film Studios (*Zhongyang dianying sheying cang*), reorganised as a commercial enterprise in 1947, was actually owned by the nationalist government, with one studio set up in Peking (closed in early 1949) and two in Shanghai.
3. The film was adapted from the popular stage play *Wild Rose*, which had received an award from the wartime government in Chongqing and critical success generally, though the leftist press had roundly attacked it. The play's final scene, in which Sky No.1 is killed, was less explicit onscreen, leaving the audience to guess the outcome.

4. See Zhou, 'The Chinese Film Scene Today', 1 January 1949; and Xiang, 'Exploring the Hong Kong Film Scene', 15 September 1948.
5. See the Editorial of *Screen Voice* of Singapore, 'Sex, Fighting, Killing', 15 September 1948.
6. In Peking, almost all productions were from China Film Studio, whose total production numbered seventeen features during 1946–8 before closing down in 1948; the government-run Chang Chun Film Studio produced just three features (1947–8) before folding. In Nanking, just a few features, educational shorts and documentaries were made by government-run studios, as well as educational films by Nanking University. Canton had very few productions. No productions are recorded from other cities.
7. See for instance Wang, '*Minguo nianjian meiguo dianying zaihua shichang yanjiu*', pp. 57–65. To support this finding, the author, citing producer/distributor Wu Xingzai's data, notes that 'lower class' Chinese increasingly provided cinema audiences throughout 1947–8. A front-page story in *Qing Qing Film* of 20 October 1948 reports Chinese films doing good business and that first-run theatres formerly showing American movies had switched to Chinese product, drawing consistently full houses with long queues for tickets.
8. As quoted from *Qing Qing Film*, 16 May 1948, in Hu, *Projecting a Nation*, p. 187.
9. Cheng et al. (eds), *The History of the Development of Chinese Cinema*, p. 159.
10. Leyda, *Dianying/Electric Shadows*, p. 164.
11. See the front-page article, 'Chinese Movies Fill the Void', *Qingqing dianying* [*Qing Qing Film*], 20 October 1948.
12. According to estimates listed by *Qing Qing Film* in its 1 January issues of both 1948 and 1949 – including films made in Hong Kong. The 1949 figure is a rough estimate of films already finished plus those then in progress.
13. During 1946–9 the many big names going to Hong Kong for its political and economical stability included: actresses Zhou Xuan (周璇), Li Lihua (李麗華), Butterfly Wu (胡蝶), Bai Guang (白光), Bai Yang (白楊), Ouyang Shafei (歐陽莎菲) and Sun Jinglu (孫景路); actors Liu Qiong (劉瓊), Xu Xi (舒適), Tao Jin (陶金) and Han Fei (韓非); directors Zhu Shilin (朱石麟), Bu Wancang (卜萬蒼), Li Pingqian (李萍倩), Zhang Junxiang (張駿祥), Ma-Xu Weibang (馬徐維邦) and Tu Guangqi (屠光啟); and playwrights Ouyang Yuqian (歐陽予倩), Yao Ke (姚克), Ke Ling (柯靈) and Shen Ji (沈寂). Others travelled between the two cities to work, most of them staying in Hong Kong from 1949, and included: actress Yuen Meiwan (袁美雲); actors Yan Jun (嚴俊) and Wang Yin (王引); and directors Yue Feng (岳楓) and Fang Peilin (方沛霖).
14. This data comes from Fu (ed.), *Hong Kong Filmography*, Vol. 2, 1942–9. But, according to my 13 June 1994 interview with Weng Linwen, who had worked in the promotion department of Great China, some of its films were contracted out or else acquired externally for distribution before being released as if they were produced by Great China itself.
15. Data taken from Fu, *Hong Kong Filmography*, Vol. 2, 1942–9.

16. See Kenny Ng's 'Political Film Censorship in Colonial Hong Kong', a research paper presented at the 'Conference on the Cold War Factor in Hong Kong Cinema, 1950s–1970s', October 2006, as published in Chinese in the anthology, *Cold War and Hong Kong Cinema*. See Ng, '*Lengzhan shiqi Xianggang dianying de zhenzhi shencha*', pp. 53–70.

Chapter 3
Sword, Fist or Gun? The 1970s Origins of Contemporary Hong Kong Noir[1]

Kristof Van den Troost

Introduction

The late 1960s and early 1970s were a turbulent period in Hong Kong history. Rapid social and political changes were taking place as a younger, local-born generation became more vocal in opposing British colonial policies and practices. Around the same time, a unique Hong Kong popular culture and identity began to take shape – an evolution in which television and cinema played no small part. While these developments are well known, this essay will shed light on the so far neglected role of the crime thriller in the indigenisation of Hong Kong cinema. The city's Cantonese and Mandarin film industries had been producing crime films since mid-century, but in the late 1960s a radical shift took place in the genre that still reverberates today. This break with the past was a phenomenon in the industry at large: in general, male stars replaced female ones, while action substituted for melodrama. The roots of Hong Kong's celebrated crime films of the 1980s, 1990s and 2000s are thus properly traced to this period.

The decision to deal with the history of the crime thriller in this anthology on Hong Kong film noir might need some explanation. Unlike 1940s and 1950s Hong Kong noir, which appeared mostly in the form of melodramas, more recent Hong Kong noir films are almost exclusively situated in the (action) crime genre exemplified by the output of John Woo in the 1980s and Johnnie To's Milkyway Image in the late 1990s and 2000s.[2] It thus makes sense to look at the roots of the modern crime thriller in the 1970s. This essay will argue that the modern Hong Kong crime film to some extent sprouted from the *kungfu* cinema of the early 1970s. It will also argue that current noir films from Hong Kong have their roots in the martial arts films of that decade: while a full-blown Hong Kong noir trend would only begin to materialise in the late 1980s, the seeds for this development were already present several years earlier.

The above argument follows from an understanding of film noir as an ultimately very blurry critical category – or a 'phenomenon', as Frank Krutnik calls it.[3] There are nevertheless certain characteristics of film noir that frequently recur in the literature on the topic. These characteristics include expressionist style, the presence of a hard-boiled detective and a *femme fatale*, a fascination with psychological abnormality, and a pessimistic world view (often evidenced by a fatalistic ending). None of these characteristics is essential for a film to be considered noir, although the more of them that are present, the likelier it is for the film to be perceived as such.[4]

Although this essay focuses mainly on films of the 1970s, the pioneering work of Cantonese directors such as Lung Kong and Chan Man in the second half of the 1960s deserves some mention. Chan Man is the lesser known of the two, but it was in fact his 1966 film *A Go-Go Teenager* (aka *The Dreadnaught*) that first explored some of the themes and concerns central to Lung Kong's more successful films, such as *Story of a Discharged Prisoner* (1967) – the inspiration for John Woo's seminal *A Better Tomorrow* (1986) – *The Window* (1968) and *Teddy Girls* (1969). In Chan's work, we get one of the first depictions of an honourable gangster and his relationship with a brother on the other side of the law, a central theme in many Hong Kong crime films, especially in the late 1980s. These films also feature more realistic violence compared to their predecessors, and make more use of real locations in the city.[5]

The 1970s Crime Film
Chang Cheh: Godfather of the Hong Kong Gangster Film

As mentioned above, Hong Kong cinema in the late 1960s witnessed a dramatic shift from being predominantly feminine and melodramatic to being masculine and action-oriented. Shaw Brothers director Chang Cheh was the key player in this change through his active promotion of what he called '*yanggang*' (meaning 'virile, masculine') martial arts films.[6] While the late 1960s witnessed the popularity of 'new style' swordplay (or *wuxia*) films, the next decade saw the rise of *kungfu*, which remained dominant until the late 1970s. Unlike the *wuxia* film, which was considered a northern Chinese tradition, *kungfu* was thought of as a southern Chinese style, and the shift towards it signalled a wider trend towards localisation.[7]

Again, Chang played a pivotal role in this shift from *wuxia* to *kungfu*, and shaped many of what would later become *kungfu* films' genre characteristics. One important element was the change of setting: instead of the Imperial China depicted in the *wuxia* films, *kungfu* moved closer to the present, to the Republican period (1912–49). Examples of such films by Chang are *Vengeance!* (1970),

The Duel (1971), *Boxer from Shantung* (1972) and *Man of Iron* (1972).⁸ Each of these films also illustrates a development related to the different time period: the appearance of urban gangster protagonists.

In *Vengeance!* the villains are treacherous, conniving local strongmen who do not hesitate to break the law if the situation demands it. Chang's depiction of a town controlled by corrupt forces is reminiscent of noir, and the film will be discussed at length below. *The Duel* is more clearly set in a criminal environment with feuding gangs and other thematic concerns that bring to mind Francis Ford Coppola's *The Godfather* (1972), although it in fact predates that film. *Boxer from Shantung* and *Man of Iron*, on the other hand, are reminiscent of the classical Hollywood gangster film, depicting the rise and fall of an immigrant gangster in the big city (Shanghai), and ending with the sympathetic gangster's tragic death.

The use of contemporary settings became common as well. An example is Chang's *Duel of Fists* (1971). The film was apparently made in anticipation of Bruce Lee's *The Big Boss* (1971), which came out a few weeks later, as both films are set in Thailand. *Duel of Fists*, *The Big Boss* and *The Angry Guest* (1972, *Duel of Fists*' sequel) point at another trend: the use of foreign settings in an attempt to 'go global'. Indeed, *Duel of Fists* and *The Angry Guest* at times feel like travelogues when throughout the film local celebrations, monuments and scenery are shown without any narrative function at all. In this regard it is interesting to note that, following his international success, Bruce Lee moved from Thailand in *The Big Boss* to Italy in *The Way of the Dragon* (1972), and eventually to an unspecified 'international' environment reminiscent of the James Bond films in the Hollywood-produced *Enter the Dragon* (1973).

A final point worth remarking on in view of the later development of the crime film is the working-class associations of the *kungfu* hero. This working-class or 'ghetto' identity was central to Stuart Kaminsky's pioneering article on the *kungfu* film, and remains a point of scholarly interest up to the present.⁹ Kaminsky states that 'the *Kungfu* [sic] hero . . . is invariably a lower class working figure who has no extended interest in society'.¹⁰ Moreover, the final villain is usually rich and oppresses the lower classes. Although the protagonist always destroys this final villain by the end of the film, he is subsequently often placed under arrest to face punishment for having violated the law. As Kaminsky argues, however, 'the law itself, as in American gangster films of the 1930s, is almost non-existent in *Kungfu* [sic] films. These are not films of law, but of myth.'¹¹

The shared class identity of *kungfu* and gangster heroes hinted at by Kaminsky is one of the main reasons why the two genres easily mixed in Hong Kong cinema.¹² *Kungfu* and crime films alike frequently express a deep distrust towards the rule of law, which is perceived as protecting the interests of the establishment. The triad gangster is an excellent type to channel local frustrations with a modern capitalist society: not only does he occasion the condemnation of capitalist excess (as his Hollywood cousin does), he also represents a 'traditionally Chinese', supposedly more humane, way of ordering society (vis-à-vis one based on 'western' rule of law). The ambivalent attitude towards the rule of law will be explored in more detail in the discussion of *The Teahouse* (1974) below. For now it can be concluded that triad characters fulfil a dual function in action-crime films: gangster heroes personify a traditional, more noble and idealistic world view, while gangster villains represent the corrupting influences of capitalism and materialism, having become exploiters themselves. The main conflict in action-oriented gangster films is very often between these two types of characters, and usually ends with the demise of the exploiters.[13] This working-class allegiance of Hong Kong crime films remained dominant throughout the 1970s and the 1980s (think, for example, of Woo's gun-toting heroes) but started to disappear in the late 1990s – not coincidentally, also the time when Hong Kong films became less action-oriented.[14]

Although few viewers would think of *The Big Boss* as a crime film, it certainly marked a move towards this genre. The modern Hong Kong crime film would take further shape as a result of the increasing indigenisation of Hong Kong cinema. Conversely, the genre also played a crucial role in this broader development.

Making the Gangster Local

The decision to shoot Bruce Lee's *The Way of the Dragon* in Italy might or might not have been influenced by the global success of *The Godfather*, but the latter obviously inspired Ng See-yuen to travel to Rome to shoot the *kungfu* gangster film *Little Godfather from Hong Kong* (1974). The logical next step was to look at Hong Kong's very own criminal societies, the triads. This shift was significant: instead of making films 'international' by using foreign settings, actors, languages, etc., the idea was now to become globally successful by making films more 'local'.[15]

Localisation was a logical development, as around 1974 Hong Kong's previously dominant Mandarin cinema was experiencing difficulties. The death of Bruce Lee brought an end to the *kungfu* craze in the west, while an economic crisis affected box-office earnings. On top of that, the important South-East Asian markets started to impose import quotas or taxes on Mandarin films. Hence, the Hong Kong film industry had an incentive to look inwards, and when in 1973 Chor Yuen's Cantonese-language comedy *The House of 72 Tenants* (1973) beat Bruce Lee's *Enter the Dragon* at the local box office, studio executives realised the potential profits to be reaped from the local market. The fortunes of Cantonese filmmaking turned for the better.¹⁶

The use of Cantonese was not the only reason for the success of *The House of 72 Tenants* and the many Cantonese productions that soon followed. Probably even more important was their grounding in local society and popular culture, and in this regard television played a key role. *The House of 72 Tenants*, for instance, was a highly localised version of an old Shanghai play, which had been performed by the Hong Kong Drama Troupe in 1964, and was broadcasted as a television play as well. The film featured many television actors, especially from the popular Cantonese variety show *Enjoy Yourself Tonight* (1967–94).¹⁷

The trend towards indigenisation also involved shooting on location in the city. We can look again at Chang Cheh's work as a barometer of what was happening in the industry. In 1973 Chang co-directed *The Delinquent* with a young protégé, Kuei Chih-hung. The film contains Chang's usual themes and protagonists: it focuses on a rebellious working-class youth who violently avenges the death of his father and finally dies by impalement. But it also has a grittier, more realistic feel to it that betrays the hand of the Hong Kong-raised Kuei. That the younger director was behind the urban grittiness and realism became clear with a film he made the next year, *The Teahouse*, which marked a significant breakthrough of localism in Hong Kong cinema.¹⁸

Although opened by recent immigrants from Mainland China, the teahouse of the film's title is of a distinct Hong Kong variety – it is one of the territory's famous *cha chaan teng* – and its clientele is a veritable cross-section of local society in the 1970s. The film and its sequel, *Big Brother Cheng* (1975), have loose plots consisting of short episodes that comment on the crime problem in Hong Kong – a hot social topic at the time. Stressing the community values also important in *The House of 72 Tenants* (values recalling Cantonese films of the 1950s), the two films also expressed a profound lack of confidence in the authorities and the rule of law. The owner of the teahouse, Big Brother Cheng (Chan Kuan-tai), grows increasingly disillusioned with the police and the judicial system and decides to take justice into his own hands. His protection of the weak and his punishment of the corrupt rich eventually turn him into a kind of urban Robin Hood. In fact, Cheng and his friends also increasingly resemble a triad organisation, and are mistakenly believed to be one by both real triad gangsters and the police.¹⁹

Despite the favourable depiction of a triad-like kind of justice administered by Cheng, the films also paint an ambivalent picture of the real triads: a good triad group is juxtaposed with a bad one. The films' characters repeatedly comment that righteous triad bosses are becoming a rarity – a sentiment shared

Figure 3.1 In *The Teahouse* (1974), a lack of faith in the judicial system leads to the formation of a triad-like community.

by the protagonists in Woo's 1980s films and a recurring theme in gangster films to this day. The explicit approval of the vigilante justice and triad-like behaviour of Cheng and his friends apparently was deemed too controversial at the time, and the second film ends – very unconvincingly – with the revelation that Cheng is in fact an undercover policeman.[20] Distrust of the law and the authorities, and the preference for a vigilante or traditional triad-style justice, are sentiments that would remain prominent in crime films until at least the early 1990s.[21]

Many of the first localised crime films tried to appeal to audiences by depicting real cases that drew a lot of media attention. One early example was Ching Gong's *Kidnap* (1974), based on a famous kidnapping case that took place between 1959 and 1961.[22] A year later, Chor Yuen made a rare foray into the contemporary action-drama with *The Big Holdup* (1975). The inspiration for this film probably came from the 1974 robbery of the Po Sang Bank, an event that caused a sensation when it was broadcast live on Hong Kong television. When in 1975 another spectacular robbery took place (this time of the Hang Seng Bank), Ng See-yuen was quick to cash in: his *Million Dollars Snatch* (1976) was a realistic reconstruction of the events and became a modest box-office success. The film's docudrama approach was similar to the style of Ng's earlier account of the establishment of the Independent Commission Against Corruption (ICAC) in *Anti-Corruption* (1975, discussed below) and pioneered a long strain of realistic crime films in Hong Kong. Realising the appeal of sensational crime films, Shaw Brothers soon launched a series called *The Criminals* (1976–7).[23] The five films in this series each contained two to four short episodes depicting real crimes. Kuei Chih-hung's contributions dominated, but other frequent crime film directors Hua Shan (aka Hua Yihong) and Sun Chung also participated.

The 1970s saw the downfall of several powerful drug lords, and their life stories would inspire filmmakers for decades to come. The most notorious of them, Ng Sik-ho, had many policemen on his payroll, but was nevertheless arrested and in 1975 sentenced to thirty years in jail. While a figure strongly resembling him appeared in *Anti-Corruption*, Ng also inspired a series of films dealing with international drug trafficking and crime lords. Films about the illegal drug trade included most prominently Leong Po-chih and Josephine Siao's *Jumping Ash* (1976), a film often touted as a precursor to the New Wave, as well as Stanley Siu's *The Rascal Billionaire* (1978), which was based on the story of the Ma Brothers, who in the 1970s controlled one of the major Chaozhou gangs in Hong Kong. Another film belonging to this trend was Sun Chung's *The Drug Connection* (aka *The Sexy Killer*, 1976), in which a woman single-handedly takes on a drug syndicate.[24]

The films of the late 1970s were strongly localised, not only in their settings, real-life inspiration and the use of Cantonese, but also through their depiction of triad rituals. This already occurred in *The Teahouse* in 1974, and remained a point of fascination in many pictures that followed. Of note in this regard is a series of films directed and/or produced by Chung Kwok-yan, which often used numbers in their titles – the numbers being code words used by the triads.[25] Examples of such films are *Ironside 426* (Lam Gwok-cheung, 1977) and *Gang of Four* (Hua Shan, 1978).

The Police Film

An account of the 1970s crime film would not be complete without discussing that mirror image of the gangster – the policeman. Hong Kong directors started to shoot modern police thrillers in the mid-1970s. In comparison to films focusing on gangsters, police films were less common, and it is noteworthy that very often these 'lawmen' appeared as criminals themselves – either as undercover cops, or as corrupt officers colluding with gangsters. Examples of the former are the Hong Kong-Australia co-production *The Man from Hong Kong* (Jimmy Wang Yu and Brian Trenchard-Smith, 1975) and *Ironside 426*. This last film is especially noteworthy as it deals with an undercover cop who climbs up the triad ranks and eventually has to choose between his duty as a police officer and his loyalty to his gang brothers. This plot foreshadows that of major Hong Kong films such as *City on Fire* (Ringo Lam, 1987) and the *Infernal Affairs* (Andrew Lau and Alan Mak, 2002–3) trilogy.

The primary inspiration for films dealing with corrupt policemen was the establishment of the ICAC in 1974.[26] As mentioned before, the events leading up to the creation of ICAC were fairly realistically depicted in Ng See-yuen's *Anti-Corruption*. The film focuses on an honest British policeman who comes to work in Hong Kong. Although he is initially committed to fighting crime, the attractions of wealth and power prove too much for him: when he starts to accept bribes, he climbs the career ladder smoothly and amasses an immense fortune. Eventually he is caught and brought to justice. A noteworthy sequence shows the Englishman being treated to a night out by his Chinese colleagues: in a scene that would later be adopted in *A Better Tomorrow*, one of them burns a banknote to light his cigarette.[27]

Chang Cheh again played the role of pioneer by co-directing (with Tsai Yang-ming) the first local police film, *Police Force* (1973). In this film, Chang altered his usual motifs of vengeance and gruesome heroic death, probably to placate the real-life Hong Kong police.[28] *Police Force* has its fair share of *kungfu* violence and gun battles, but its depiction of police training, practices and procedures pushes it more towards the modern police film compared to the few other contemporary films featuring cops, where *kungfu* fighting is pretty much the only concern. Three years later, in 1976, the more realistic *Jumping Ash* proved the appeal of this new kind of thriller by topping the local box office. Its impact was reflected in Shaw Brothers' *The Criminals* series: the three final instalments released in 1977 all contained episodes approaching crime from the police point-of-view. In the same year, Yeung Kuen's *Hot Blood* (1977) prefigured Danny Lee's 1980s cop thrillers with their sympathetic portrayal of the daily activities and frustrations of the average cop. At the end of the decade, *Vice Squad 633* (1979) explored new terrain by focusing on the role of police informers, while several early New Wave works (including Alex Cheung's important *Cops and Robbers* [1979]) set higher standards for the industry as a whole. A local tradition of police films had taken root.[29]

The Seeds of Hong Kong Noir

In a postscript to *A Study of Hong Kong Cinema in the 1970s*, Li Cheuk-to puts forward cynicism as *the* attitude typical of 1970s Hong Kong filmmaking and television. According to Li, films of this decade became increasingly fatalistic, morally ambiguous, materialistic and anti-traditional.[30] With neo-noir films achieving success in Hollywood, it seemed like the right time for a Hong Kong noir trend to blossom. That this did not fully materialise can be attributed to the dominance of period martial arts and comedy during most of the decade (although, as will be shown below, period martial arts could function as a vehicle for noir style and themes). The seeds for modern Hong Kong noir were planted in Chang Cheh's late 1960s and early 1970s films, and can also be found in a number of other works throughout the decade.

Traces of Noir in Martial Arts Films

> I was often asked about the characters in my films, that the knights-errant are not as 'upright' as traditional ones. Indeed they are, and I don't like two-dimensional characters. Modern audience [sic] also has learned to accept non-traditional, multi-dimensional characters . . . Sometimes, the 'bandit' gets more sympathy than the 'soldier.' Earlier films about the knight-errant punishing the wicked or lawman getting the bandits are now considered outmoded and old-fashioned. I have contributed to this development.[31]

This quote from Chang Cheh's autobiography touches upon some of the characteristics of his works that can be considered noirish. Firstly, there is his assertion that he created 'non-traditional, multi-dimensional characters': the boundary between good and evil in his films is less clear-cut, and sometimes the conventionally 'bad' protagonist is given a more positive, sympathetic treatment. Secondly, Chang explicitly mentions a 'modern' audience that can appreciate moral complexity: this resonates with Naremore's argument for an understanding of film noir as situated between modernist art and traditional sensationalist melodrama.[32] Chang correctly assumed that a better educated and generally more prosperous audience familiar with the complexities of modern urban life would be able to appreciate the more ambiguous characters in his films and their tortuous struggles with a corrupt environment.

Another important Chang theme, fatalism, is also present in many films noirs. As Jerry Liu writes about Chang's heroes: 'The heroic individual blindly submits to the fatal cycle of cause and effect while exercising little control over his own actions, except to conform to certain "moral" obligations arising from loyalty, friendship, and love.'[33] This type of heroism survives in Hong Kong cinema to this day, to a large extent via John Woo's similarly fatalistic but 'moral' heroes. While more pessimistic than the many Hollywood films where the hero survives, the affirmation of positive moral values ultimately steers Woo's and Chang's films away from the darkest visions of some films noirs: even if their moral hero dies in the end, at least he has usually first removed the 'evil' in the diegetic world of the film.[34]

As mentioned before, Chang is most recognised for his role in shifting Hong Kong cinema from a female-centred industry to a male-centred one. As in recent Hong Kong noir, his films nonetheless often give small but crucial parts to women. These parts generally fit into the 'mother' vs 'whore' dichotomy.[35] In a wide array of genres in Hong Kong and elsewhere, women of the latter type habitually contribute to or even directly cause the demise of the male hero. The martial arts film is no different: the male hero is often threatened by aggressively sexual *femmes fatales* and generally has to avoid them to preserve his integrity and physical strength.[36]

Of all Chang Cheh films, *Vengeance!* is probably the one that comes closest to film noir. In this film the wife of opera actor Guan Yulou (Ti Lung) is having an affair with a local aristocrat. With the help of other powerful members of the local elite, this aristocrat sets up a trap for Yulou and has him killed. The rest of the plot concerns Yulou's brother Xiaolou (David Chiang) arriving in town and setting out to take revenge. Xiaolou succeeds, but at the cost of his own life. Thematically, the film thus contains the typical noirish elements of many Chang films: the unfaithful *femme fatale* wife, and the presence of a fatalistic but moral hero. We are also introduced to the archetypical noir city: the men responsible for Yulou's death are the ones who are running the city – as Xiaolou is told shortly after his arrival, 'the whole town is involved'. Xiaolou's presence disturbs the balance of power and a cycle of violence erupts, in which the former partners-in-crime turn on each other. While John Boorman's neo-noir *Point Blank* (1967) is an obvious influence,[37] one can also find similarities with other hallmarks of the literary and cinematic noir canon, such as Dashiell Hammett's 1929 novel *Red Harvest* and the *Sin City* comic book series (1991–2), recently adapted into film (Frank Miller and Robert Rodriguez, 2005 and 2014).

The discussion of the visual style of *Vengeance!* and other noirish Hong Kong films of the 1970s requires a consideration of visual style and colour in classical Hollywood film noir and neo-noir. Referring to an influential article by Janey Place and Lowell Peterson, Steve Neale lists some of the visual elements often associated with noir: 'such visual motifs as portraits and mirror reflection, choker close-ups, the use of wide-angle lenses and visual distortion, cutting from extreme close-up to high-angle long shot . . . and the extreme high-angle long shot'.[38] According to many commentators, the most important visual marker of noir is low-key lighting: its strong contrasts between light and darkness, its famous chiaroscuro obscuring parts of faces, rooms and urban settings. After positing this conventional account of noir's visual style, however, Neale goes on to deconstruct its claims, questioning both the prevalence of these elements in film noir, and the extent to which this visual style is exclusive to it. Neale's numerous examples illustrate that films classified as film noir not always contain low-key lighting and other 'noir' visuals, and that high-contrast lighting was prevalent in much filmmaking preceding the appearance of noir in 1940s Hollywood.[39] This once more confirms the famous incoherence of film noir as a category. The use of colours in a type of film that lends itself extremely well to black-and-white filmmaking further problematises conceptions of what is considered a film noir and what is not.

As Kathrina Glitre points out, chiaroscuro lighting is particularly suited to black-and-white film, and transposing it to colour filmmaking involves a number of complications. Most crucially, while black-and-white film is limited to various degrees of light and dark (tonal contrast), colour film also brings into play hue (the actual colours) and saturation (the strength of the colours). So, although some films noirs use conventional black-and-white lighting set-ups to create chiaroscuro (for example, *Slightly Scarlet* [Alan Dwan, 1956], shot by famous noir cinematographer John Alton), colour noirs often complement tonal contrast with colour contrast (*Leave Her to Heaven* [John M. Stahl, 1945] is a good example of this tendency).[40] In her article, Glitre contrasts the use of colour in classical noirs with that in 'modernist neo-noirs' that started to appear in the 1960s.[41] Due to the technical limitations of colour film stock in the 1960s and 1970s, achieving chiaroscuro was quite difficult, and the low-key look is consequently not that common in this period.[42] This seems to have been true for Hong Kong films as well: while chiaroscuro was not uncommon in the local films of the late 1940s and the 1950s, high-contrast lighting is rare in the 1970s. Indeed, Shaw Brothers colour films from the early 1960s onwards are characterised by their bright look and their use of vibrant, saturated primary colours, similar to the Technicolor look of 1950s Hollywood films. While creating an overview of the colour strategies employed in 1970s Hong Kong noir precursors (as Glitre does for Hollywood noir) is beyond the scope of this paper, the discussion of *Vengeance!* (and some of the other films below) can indicate how the stylistic elements of colour noir were sometimes coupled to noirish themes and plots.

In *Vengeance!*, Chang employs low-key lighting in a surprising way: chiaroscuro predominates in romantic scenes between Xiaolou and his lover, rather than the scenes where he encounters and fights his enemies. In one remarkable scene, an almost entirely dark room is shot at some length: a barely visible Xiaolou is sitting still at a table until seconds later his lover switches on the light. Possibly, Chang opted for high visibility during scenes of conflict simply to showcase the film's excellent production design and stylish martial arts sequences. There is, however, one major exception to this strategy: the first fight between Xiaolou and some thugs in the theatre. During this protracted scene, Xiaolou and his adversaries move the fight above-stage: shadows obscure faces, while (extreme) low- and high-angle shots occur frequently.[43] The colour design of the film is executed carefully and sometimes works in tandem with the chiaroscuro: one lovemaking scene concludes with a high-angle shot showing the couple lying on the bed, with an out-of-focus red paper butterfly in the foreground adding nice contrast to a *mise-en-scène* overwhelmed by areas of black and white.[44]

Most of Chang's films in the 1970s belong in the first place to the *kungfu* genre. In that other branch of martial arts cinema, the swordplay movie, a stylish noir aesthetic and atmosphere also surfaced occasionally. One particular sub-genre – the detective martial arts film – lent itself remarkably well to a film noir atmosphere. Good examples of noir-like detective swordplay films are *Black Tavern* (Yip Wing-cho, 1972), where in the typical *wuxia* setting of the inn various wandering swordsmen engage in murderous intrigue to obtain a mysterious treasure, and *Ambush* (Ho Meng-hua, 1973), in which a young official is wrongly suspected of being an accomplice in a robbery and tries to clear his name by finding the true culprit and recovering the loot. The most outstanding 1970s director in this particular sub-genre was Chor Yuen. One of his best works is 1972's *Intimate Confessions of a Chinese Courtesan*.[45]

Chor's film offers an innovative mix of martial arts and erotic thriller. A young girl, Ai Nu (Lily Ho), is kidnapped by a gang and sold to a brothel run by Chun Yi (Betty Pei), an icy lesbian madam. Ai Nu at first refuses to cooperate, but a series of cruel punishments (including rape by several local dignitaries) seemingly force her into submission. After becoming the brothel's most desired courtesan and learning deadly martial arts skills from Chun Yi, Ai Nu starts to assassinate the men who raped her years earlier. A young official (Yueh Hua) investigates and quickly realises Ai Nu is behind the murders, but is unable to stop her since she receives protection from Chun Yi, who has fallen in love with her. With all the rapists killed, Ai Nu murders the men who kidnapped her as a child and finally turns against Chun Yi. When the madam is dying after fighting side by side with her, Ai Nu reveals she never loved her but grants her a last kiss. This kiss turns out to be poisonous: the two women die together.

Featuring not one but two *femmes fatales* in major roles, *Intimate Confessions* offers no happy ending, leaving only one character alive: the detective-like upright official who was unable to prevent the catastrophe. Visually, the film avoids chiaroscuro lighting, although it stages most of its action at night. In fact, *Intimate Confessions* can, despite its gory storyline, be considered a visual masterpiece of the studio era: the nightly swordfights in the snow are beautifully shot, and the attention to detail and setting is probably the most careful among Chor's numerous 1970s swordplay films. The fights in the snow also seem to betray some Japanese influence, possibly from Toshiro Mifune's famous fight in *The Sword of Doom* (Okamoto Kihachi, 1966).

It could be argued that much of the film noir characteristics of 1970s Hong Kong martial arts cinema are the result of the influence from Japanese *chanbara* films and revisionist Westerns (including Italian 'spaghetti Westerns'). A complex network of linkages is at work here: the first film of Sergio Leone's 'The Man With No Name' trilogy, *A Fistful of Dollars* (1964), was an unofficial remake of Kurosawa Akira's *Yojimbo* (1961). *Yojimbo*, in turn, is often said to have been inspired by Dashiell Hammett's noir novel *Red Harvest*. Whether Hammett's novel was a direct inspiration or not, it is clear that both in Japanese *chanbara* and in the Western a revisionist trend developed in the 1960s, involving a cynical and darker approach to the subject matter and its heroes, who often became more morally ambivalent.[46] To find noirish overtones in contemporary Hong Kong martial arts films is thus not that surprising. After all, as the exciting cinematography of Japanese *chanbara* was copied and improved upon by Hong Kong filmmakers, and Ennio Morricone's film scores were shamelessly employed in countless *kungfu* flicks, it seems quite logical that the morally grey characters and cynical storylines of these foreign films would appeal to directors as well.[47]

Noir Elements in Contemporary Crime Films

Although rare, a few 1970s contemporary crime films also had shades of noir. The above-mentioned *The Delinquent*, for instance, prefigures the dark and gritty look of later Hong Kong noir films, with recurring shots of dark, neon-lit streets, desolate urban settings (public housing estates, a warehouse, a lumber factory, a scrapyard and so on), and even a hallucination sequence. Some of the most remarkable visuals of the film occur at the beginning and the end: the opening credits show the male protagonist bursting in slow-motion through several large drawings of Hong Kong urban settings. Green, red and pink light is used in this scene, causing all other colours to disappear. The credits then come up in screaming colours, while the protagonist attacks us (the camera) in various brightly coloured negative shots ending in freeze-frames. The soundtrack with loud, often dissonant rock music punctuated by screams contributes to the powerful anger expressed through these images. As the film makes clear, the anger here is that of a working-class youth in an utterly corrupt and materialistic city. The final shots conclude the film on a similar note: as the protagonist lies dying and we hear his fading heartbeat, a fish-eye lens is employed to show passers-by looking at him. While the images are in black and white at first, colour soon floods in and the final image is of another, similarly angry youngster fighting a gang somewhere in the city. The final freeze-frame is of this youngster raising his hand and screaming, as if in defiance of an unfair society. As with the film's realist touches and frequent use of location shooting, the visual noir elements are most likely the work of Kuei Chih-hung, who co-directed the film with Chang Cheh. Other Kuei films, such as *The Lady Professional* (1971), *The Teahouse*, *Big Brother Cheng* and *Killer Constable* (1980, discussed below), seem to confirm this assessment.

One remarkably grim film worth highlighting is *Kiss of Death* (Ho Meng-hua, 1973), which contained a 1970s version of the *femme fatale*.[48] *Kiss of Death* has a slightly more complex plot than the average action flick and combines cynicism and despair with the sexploitation trend of the 1970s. At the start of the film, the 'heroine', Chu Ling (Chen Ping), is brutally raped by a gang. Not only is Chu psychologically traumatised, she soon discovers that she has caught a deadly venereal disease as well. Unable to resume her life, she quits her job at the factory, leaves the home of her uncaring parents and goes to work as a hostess in a nightclub. She soon falls in love with the crippled nightclub owner Wang (Lo Lieh), who is a *kungfu* expert and who teaches her some fighting skills so that she can take revenge on her rapists. When Chu begins to eliminate the gang members one by one, she uses in true *femme fatale* fashion her feminine charm to get close to them. In a final showdown with the remaining gang members, Chu is victorious but afterwards dies from her wounds.

Quite similar in plot to *Intimate Confessions of a Chinese Courtesan*, *Kiss of Death* in fact had the same scriptwriter, Qiu Gangjian.[49] *Kiss of Death* is more obviously set in a film noir milieu: the action takes place in dark alleys, abandoned apartment buildings and the seedy nightclub where Chu works – at one point she even kills one of the rapists in a gothic cemetery. Typical for noir are also the many shadows, the sometimes barely visible faces and the glaring neon lights of the nightclub district. In a striking final image, nightclub owner Wang picks up Chu's lifeless body and stands in silent despair while the police arrive and surround him. This scene is overwhelmingly dark, with some red and blue neon reflecting on the wet asphalt, and only Wang and Chu brightly lit.

Figure 3.2 Noir meets martial arts meets exploitation in the rape-revenge film *Kiss of Death* (1973).

Kiss of Death (and, to a lesser extent, *Intimate Confessions of a Chinese Courtesan*) can also be regarded as a Hong Kong contribution to the international 1970s cycle of rape-revenge films. While the exploitation element is obvious in *Kiss of Death*, however, it should be stressed that, unlike many films in the genre, the rape scene is short and shocking mostly through montage and *mise-en-scène* rather than through explicit detail. Much more attention is paid to the aftermath: Chu's dealing with her trauma, the discovery of her disease, her relationship with Wang and friendship with one of the other bargirls, and finally the series of murders she commits to get her revenge. The affinities between classical Hollywood film noir and the rape-revenge film are rather obvious: rape-revenge films take film noir's *femme fatale* and put her at the centre of a more violent and sexually explicit tale that is, however, equally – if not more – despairing and fatalistic.[50]

Conclusion

Not only does *Kiss of Death* reveal the affinities between film noir and the rape-revenge film, it is also proof of the interconnectedness of noir, martial arts and crime cinema. This interconnectedness is most strikingly illustrated by the parallels between three films made over two decades of Hong Kong cinema: Chang Cheh's *The Invincible Fist* (1969), Kuei Chih-hung's *Killer Constable* and John Woo's *The Killer* (1989). *The Killer*, now often considered Woo's most noir-like film, contains a famous scene in which Chow Yun-fat's assassin and Danny Lee's cop face off in the apartment of Chow's blind girlfriend (Sally Yeh).[51] To not upset the innocent girl, the two opponents pretend to be old friends and engage in silly banter – all the while pointing guns at one another. An almost identical scene takes place in Kuei's noirish swordplay film between the 'killer constable' and a robber he is trying to catch. Here, of course, the men are holding swords instead of guns.

Made at the beginning of a new decade, *Killer Constable* can be said to fully realise the noir potential already present in Chang Cheh's martial arts films. Chang and especially Kuei's sympathy for the common man and his fight against a corrupt and criminal elite is here recast as the domination of Han Chinese by corrupt and greedy Manchu rulers during the late Qing dynasty. A constable known for killing the criminals he catches is ordered to investigate a theft from the imperial treasury. He duly finds and kills the culprits, but loses all of his trusted lieutenants in the process. Finally, he finds himself betrayed by his own boss, a court official who uses him to get rid of accomplices in a heist he has masterminded himself. Hence, the protagonist's character flaws lead, in true noir fashion, to his own demise. Also cinematically, Kuei turns the film into a true *wuxia* noir. Beautifully realised chiaroscuro dominates many of the scenes taking place at night, and Kuei goes as far as staging several fights in (simulated) moonlight. In other night scenes, colour strengthens the overall chiaroscuro effect, with Kuei using blue and amber source lighting to create colour contrast in a way that recalls *Leave Her to Heaven*. One could add to this list other noir flourishes such as several extreme low-angle shots of the constable with the sun right behind his head (creating another type of high-contrast look), and recurring shots of the protagonist partly obscured by bars or the shadows they cast, indicating from the very beginning that he is trapped by fate.

As in *The Killer*, the lawman and one of the criminals eventually grow to respect one another through their adherence to a shared code of loyalty and righteousness in a corrupt world. Both Woo and Kuei probably took inspiration from their mentor Chang Cheh's *The Invincible Fist*, who in turn might have taken the scene with the blind girl from Lung Kong's *The Window*. The films thus exemplify an important part of the lineage of film noir and crime films in Hong Kong: from late 1960s social problem films, through Chang's and Kuei's work, to the work of Woo in the 1980s. Hong Kong noir would eventually be at its most despairing in the late 1990s and 2000s, when directors such as Johnnie To began to deconstruct the heroism of the earlier films.[52]

This chapter has shown how in the 1970s important transformations took place in Hong Kong filmmaking that would determine the appearance of Hong Kong noir and crime films in subsequent decades. It has traced some of the roots of modern action-crime films back to early 1970s *kungfu* films (especially the work of Chang Cheh), and has argued that (period) martial arts films are a viable vehicle for noir stories and style, as well as an important influence on the particular characteristics of more recent Hong Kong noirs (through the centrality of action and violence, and the dominance of male characters, among others).[53] While the noirish elements in 1970s martial arts films are suggested to be, to some extent, the result of the influence of foreign genres such as Japanese *chanbara* and revisionist Westerns, it is also argued that the crime film went through a crucial process of indigenisation, and that it, in turn, played an important role in the indigenisation of Hong Kong cinema as a whole.

At the end of the 1970s, a new group of filmmakers appeared on the scene, giving rise to the phenomenon that is often described as the Hong Kong New Wave, or New Hong Kong Cinema. Interestingly, many of the young directors chose to make their debuts in the crime genre and opted for bleak stories with a 'fatalistic noirish look'.[54] While the contributions of this new generation can hardly be underestimated, it is clear that they built on the work of previous directors. At the start of a new golden age in the film industry, the noir-like (action) crime film was ready to become the genre with which Hong Kong is today most associated.

Notes

1. This article is based on a chapter in my PhD dissertation on the history of the Hong Kong crime film. I would like to thank my dissertation supervisor, Ann Huss, for her valuable support and advice, and the editors of this anthology for their constructive comments on an earlier draft.
2. As will become clearer below, film noir is not treated as a distinct genre here. Thomas Schatz sees film noir as 'a system of visual and thematic conventions which were not associated with any specific genre or story formula': see Schatz, *Hollywood Genres*, p. 112. Genres marked by the film noir 'style' include melodramas, Westerns, gangster films, and Hitchcock's psychological thrillers (ibid.). When looked at from this angle, the association of film noir with melodrama in one period and crime films in another is not that unusual.
3. Krutnik, *In a Lonely Street*, p. 24.
4. The sources used to define these characteristics and come to this understanding of film noir are Collier, 'The Noir East', pp. 137–58; Kaplan (ed.), *Women in Film noir*; Krutnik, *In a Lonely Street*; Naremore, *More than Night*; Neale, *Genre and Hollywood*; and Spicer (ed.), *European Film noir*.
5. Several of these works are often associated with the 'youth problem' films of the late 1960s, indicating a certain overlap between the two genres. As Fu Po-shek has pointed out, these films were an attempt to lure back younger audiences with displays of youth culture, although the filmmakers could not resist a degree of didacticism: see Fu, 'The 1960s', p. 82. This last element marks an important difference with most of the films appearing in the 1970s.
6. Chang, *Chang Cheh*, p. 150.
7. This is of course a generalisation: many *kungfu* films were made by émigré directors from the north and set in cities like Shanghai. Also, quite a few swordplay films were made in Cantonese and/or choreographed by 'Southerners' like Lau Kar-leung (aka Liu Chia-liang). See Bordwell, *Planet Hong Kong*, 1st edn, p. 206.
8. In his memoir, Chang Cheh admitted to having got the inspiration to make films set in the early Republican era from Japanese cinema, in particular from a sub-genre of Japanese films set during the Meiji Restoration period (c. 1868–1912): see Chang, *Chang Cheh*, pp. 88–9.
9. For a recent example of this argument, see Morris, 'Transnational Imagination in Action Cinema', pp. 181–99.
10. Kaminsky, 'Kung Fu Film as Ghetto Myth', p. 132.
11. Ibid. p. 137. Many of Kaminsky's remarks resonate with Ariel Dorfman's insightful analyses of superheroes in American culture: see Dorfman, *Empire's Old Clothes*, pp. 67–131.
12. The working-class hero is in fact predominant in low-budget action films globally, as Meaghan Morris has pointed out. In parallel with the gangster hero, the working-class hard-boiled cop also started to appear in Hong Kong action crime films of this period.

13. There exist influential cultural precedents for the depiction of heroic criminality in the face of a corrupt regime. A figure such as Robin Hood is the western equivalent of the 'outlaws of the marsh' depicted in the Yuan Dynasty *Shuihu zhuan* (Water Margin), one of the four great classical novels of Chinese literature. Tellingly, Chang Cheh directed three martial arts films based on sections of the novel: *The Water Margin* (1972), *The Delightful Forest* (1972) and *All Men Are Brothers* (1975).
14. An excellent example is the influential *Infernal Affairs* trilogy (2002–3), which almost entirely eschews action sequences and is clearly set in an upper middle-class milieu.
15. This 'globalisation-through-localisation' strategy has remained important to Hong Kong film production to the present, and reflects a stronger self-confidence: filmmakers believe that movies with a strong Hong Kong flavour will find acceptance elsewhere as well. The attempts to make films more 'global' have not been given up either: this topic has been widely discussed in recent scholarship on 'transnational' Chinese cinema. To give just a few examples: Chris Berry and Mary Farquhar mention several Hong Kong films in their discussions of 'transnational' Chinese cinema in *China on Screen*: see Berry and Farquhar, *China on Screen*, pp. 1–16, 66–74, 195–222; as does Gina Marchetti in *From Tian'anmen to Times Square*: see Marchetti, *From Tian'anmen to Times Square*, pp. 1–68, 157–218. Focusing on Hong Kong cinema with a similar interest in the effects of globalisation are works edited by Esther C. M. Yau: see Yau (ed.), *At Full Speed*; Esther Cheung and Chu Yiu-wai: see Cheung and Chu (eds), *Between Home and World*; Gina Marchetti and Tan See-kam: see Marchetti and Tan (eds), *Hong Kong Film, Hollywood and the New Global Cinema*; and many more. One could argue that starting from the late 1990s, when Hong Kong cinema entered its continuing downward spiral, this self-confidence was shaken, and that as a result more efforts were made to appeal to other markets.
16. Writing in 1974, on the cusp of the Cantonese revival, I. C. Jarvie describes the change in the studios' attitude towards the local market. While in the mid-1960s, people working for the Cathay and Shaw Brothers studios told him that the Hong Kong market was so small that its audiences barely mattered in the preparatory calculations for making Mandarin films, this attitude had completely changed by the early 1970s: a film could recoup several million in Hong Kong alone, and even the international co-productions initiated at the height of the *kungfu* craze were only trial balloons – the producers still had their eyes fixed on the local audience: see Jarvie, *Window on Hong Kong*, pp. 56–64. Jarvie did not foresee the spectacular return of Cantonese cinema, and at the time he suggested that Mandarin and western films were more successful than Cantonese features because they better reflected the modern lifestyle of the colony, in contrast to the 'backward' world of Cantonese films. With the advantage of hindsight, it seems obvious that when Cantonese cinema modernised under the influence of television, local dialect features would naturally displace Mandarin filmmaking.

17. Teo, 'The 1970s', pp. 95, 109.
18. *The Teahouse* and *Big Brother Cheng* were based on a popular Hong Kong comic book series called *Xiao Liumang* (Little Rascals), later renamed *Long Hu Men* (Dragon and Tiger): see Lui and Yiu, 'Intrigue is Hard to Defend', p. 172.
19. This impression was possibly strengthened at the time by the star image of Chan Kuan-tai, who had in 1972 portrayed righteous and charismatic gangsters in *Boxer from Shantung* and *Man of Iron*.
20. An interesting spin-off from the Brother Cheng films is *Big Bad Sis* (1976), which can be regarded as a feminist version of the earlier films. The film adds a gender angle to the crime-ridden milieu of Hong Kong: the 'Big Bad Sis' is a female factory worker (Chen Ping) who teaches her colleagues to defend themselves against male sexual predators and who organises them into a sort of sisterhood. While this film might sound like a feminist manifesto of sorts, it should be pointed out that it simultaneously contains elements of sexploitation that would seem to contradict any progressive reading of it.
21. Criminals were often portrayed with sympathy, and many films featured likeable gangster figures endowed with loyalty and righteousness. Pretty soon, however, there also appeared films that brought the glamorisation of gangsters to a new height, thereby continuing a tendency visible in several post-war films, especially in the Cantonese 'Jane Bond films' of the late 1960s (for an account of this peculiar genre, see Sam Ho's article, 'Licensed to Kick Men'). This was already visible in the 1976 film *Brotherhood*, but reached a high point in films starring Alan Tang. *The Rascal Billionaire* (1978) was one of those films, but more successful was *Law Don* (1979), which obviously took its inspiration from the *Godfather* series. Throughout, *Law Don* stresses the leader's strict application of the triad laws (the *jiafa*), and Tang's character has nothing of the ambiguity of a Michael Corleone: he does not kill his transgressing brothers, for instance – instead they commit ritual suicide once they realise their mistakes.
22. The same case also inspired the 1989 film *Sentenced to Hang* (1989), directed by Taylor Wong and produced by Johnny Mak. It was the last case in which the death penalty was carried out in Hong Kong.
23. *Kidnap* and *Anti-Corruption* were very successful at the box office, while Johnny Mak's Rediffusion Television crime drama series *Ten Sensational Cases* (1975–6) was very popular as well.
24. *The Drug Connection* can also be considered part of a series of films dealing with powerful female crime bosses or crime fighters. *Brotherhood* (Hua Shan, 1976), for instance, features an evil female triad boss, while an episode of the second *The Criminals* film, 'Mama-san', focuses on a tough Madam running a brothel and getting involved in a murder. *The Drug Connection* was not the only film to combine the two motifs of the narcotics trade and powerful female gangsters/crime fighters. Another example was *The Drug Queen* (Richard Yeung Kuen, 1976), which offers a sympathetic portrait of a female drug trafficker upholding underworld values.
25. Fang, *John Woo's A Better Tomorrow*, p. 33.

26. Armed with the draconian Prevention of Bribery Ordinance of December 1970, the police had started an investigation into one of its senior officers, Chief Superintendent Peter Godber. When sufficient evidence was gathered two years later and action was taken against Godber, the officer used his privileged access at the airport to slip past border control and escape to England. This case ignited a public campaign against corruption to which the new Governor MacLehose reacted by creating the ICAC. Soon after, Godber was extradited back to Hong Kong and tried with wide media coverage. These events were instrumental in changing popular opinion regarding the government and police corruption, and the ICAC would in time become an important source of pride for Hong Kong people: see Tsang, *A Modern History of Hong Kong*, pp. 203–4.

27. Another film dealing with a corrupt cop is *Payoff* (Wa Yan, aka Chung Kwok-yan, 1979). In this film a police inspector attempts to lord it over Hong Kong's underworld.

28. Judging from the abundant documentary-like footage illustrating the professionalism and training of the law enforcers, this was necessary because the film was made with police support. Compared with other 1970s films, *Police Force* is amazingly positive about the police, especially when one considers that it was shot a year before the ICAC was established and widespread police corruption began to be tackled. The hero in *Police Force* is a youth (Wong Chung) whose close friend is murdered; he pledges vengeance and joins the police to achieve it. When years later he finally catches the culprit, he has to make a choice: avenge his friend, or serve the public and safeguard the reputation of the force. He chooses the latter, and as a result is able to bring down a powerful crime syndicate.

29. The influence of Hollywood should not be neglected, of course. Just like *The Godfather* had a strong impact on the Hong Kong gangster film, so did Hollywood's surge of big-budget police thrillers like *The French Connection* (William Friedkin, 1971), *Dirty Harry* (Don Siegel, 1971) and *Serpico* (Sidney Lumet, 1973) influence the appearance of the police film. Both Bordwell and Teo have remarked on the similarities between *Jumping Ash* and *The French Connection* (Teo, *Hong Kong Cinema*, p. 145; Bordwell, *Planet Hong Kong*, p. 150), and the latter's popularity most likely led to the English titles of films dealing with the drug trade (although not from a police point-of-view), such as *The Drug Connection* and *Amsterdam Connection* (Fan Meisheng and Law Kei, 1978). Similarly, *Serpico*'s story of an honest cop in a corrupt police force resonates with the theme of *Anti-Corruption*. A final resemblance between Hollywood and Hong Kong police films of the 1970s is that they are very often based on real cases. In this regard, the cop thriller also participated in the indigenisation drive of Hong Kong cinema, going for more realistic depictions of local crime and law enforcement, and extensive location shooting.

30. Li, 'Postscript', pp. 128–30.
31. Chang, *Chang Cheh*, p. 143.
32. Naremore, *More than Night*, pp. 40–95.
33. Liu, 'Chang Cheh', p. 161.

The 1970s Origins of Contemporary Hong Kong Noir 71

34. Since the mid-1990s, this type of hero is frequently deconstructed and discarded, resulting in a more cynical and despairing version of Hong Kong noir.
35. In an interview with the author, Johnnie To pointed towards Westerns and 1970s films with Steve McQueen as an influence on the limited, more or less stereotypical roles women play in his own films.
36. Another type common to martial arts films is the 'good prostitute' who helps the hero, but is usually tragically killed as a result.
37. Not only do both films feature a somewhat enigmatic and stoic hero determined to kill his way towards the achievement of his goal, but Chang also incorporates some striking stylistic and plot elements from the Boorman film (for instance, the famous sound effect of Walker's reverberating steps as he walks in a long corridor reappear in *Vengeance!* to add atmosphere to Xiaolou's ominous arrival in the town; a villain is outwitted by the hero and is as a result killed by his own sniper; etc.).
38. Neale, *Genre and Hollywood*, p. 170.
39. Neale, *Genre and Hollywood*, pp. 170–3.
40. Glitre, 'Under the Neon Rainbow', pp. 11–15.
41. The 'classical' period of film noir is usually considered to have ended in the late 1950s.
42. Glitre names *Klute* (1971), *The Parallax View* (1974) and *Taxi Driver* (1976) as examples of neo-noir films that did achieve a darker style: see Glitre, 'Under the Neon Rainbow', p. 16.
43. Cross-cutting in this scene highlights the similarities between the fight on-stage and the one taking place above it – a strategy employed at various times throughout the film, most memorably in the final battle of Yulou.
44. The contrast between neutral colours and saturated primary colours is one of the major strategies/conventions Glitre attributes to neo-noir: see Glitre, 'Under the Neon Rainbow', p. 16. Another striking element of the colour design of the film is the use of clothing: most major male characters wear black or white clothes, while their henchmen are usually in grey-blue outfits. Women, however, add colours by being dressed in warm colours such as red and pink. Most striking is Xiaolou's dress code: when he is with his lover, he usually wears a white shirt, but when he meets his enemies he is dressed entirely in black. A crucial exception is the final battle, for which Xiaolou is dressed entirely in white. Before this battle starts, one of the characters even suggests he change his clothes. This is not motivated by anything in the plot and thus serves to highlight his appearance: Xiaolou refuses to change into another outfit, making his bright red blood stand out clearly as he gradually sustains more wounds in the course of the fight.
45. Starting from 1976, Chor directed a series of adaptations of Gu Long's martial arts novels. Illustrating the link between martial arts and crime films, the first of these adaptations, *Killer Clans* (1976), was in fact inspired by Coppola's *The Godfather*. According to Sek Kei, some details in *Killer Clans* were carbon copies of the American film: see Sek, 'Cross-over Romanticism', p. 80. Detective and mystery elements recurred frequently in other Gu Long adaptations by Chor Yuen, including

successful films such as *The Magic Blade* (1976), *Clans of Intrigue* (1977), *The Sentimental Swordsman* (1977), etc.

46. Discussing Sam Peckinpah's Westerns, for instance, Stephen Prince notes how in these films 'the signs of historical eclipse are manifest', how historical forces are undermining the lives of the heroes, and how Peckinpah set the primitive codes of honour of his outlaw protagonists against 'the barbarism of Vietnam-era America': see Prince, 'Genre and Violence in the Work of Kurosawa and Peckinpah', p. 336. This of course brings to mind John Woo's films, but also the work of Chang Cheh, who spoke of Peckinpah's as well as Leone's influence on his films: see Chang, *Chang Cheh*, pp. 89–90. Kurosawa is likewise often regarded as an important influence on different generations of Hong Kong directors, including Chang, Woo and Johnnie To.
47. Kinnia Yau offers a detailed account of Japanese–Hong Kong interactions in action cinema: see Yau, 'Interactions between Japanese and Hong Kong Action Cinemas', pp. 35–48.
48. The film's director Ho Meng-hua was also responsible for the above-mentioned *wuxia* thriller *Ambush* and the despairing indictment of authoritarian state power in the minor cult classic, *The Flying Guillotine* (1975).
49. Early in his career, Qiu Gangjian wrote several scripts for Chang Cheh. In the 1980s and 1990s he was involved in many Hong Kong New Wave films, such as Ann Hui's *The Story of Woo Viet* (1981) and *Boat People* (1983), and Stanley Kwan's *Rouge* (1988), *Centre Stage* (1991) and *Full Moon in New York* (1990). As can be seen from the above examples, his scripts often feature strong female characters.
50. In her *The New Avengers*, Jacinda Read also points out the similarities of (neo-)noir with rape-revenge films and erotic thrillers: see Read, *The New Avengers*. For a classic analysis of the rape-revenge genre, see Carol Clover's *Men, Women and Chainsaws*, especially Chapter 3, 'Getting Even': Clover, *Men, Women, and Chain Saws*, pp. 114–65. Rape-revenge films did not become a very popular genre in 1970s and 1980s Hong Kong, but a few were made over the years, including Dennis Yu's *The Beasts* (1980), Lee Chi-ngai's *Vengeance is Mine* (1988) and Lam Nai-choi's *Her Vengeance* (1988). This last film is interesting as it is a remake of *Kiss of Death* but questions the original's (and with it much of Hong Kong cinema's) endorsement of bloody vengeance and heroic death. In the 1990s, more films of the type were made, especially during the Category III boom at the beginning of the decade.
51. *The Killer*'s similarities to film noir receive attention throughout Kenneth Hall's book on the film.
52. This linear history of Hong Kong noir is meant to reflect the main trend over the decades. In reality, the development of noir in Hong Kong is of course not that straightforward. As this essay has shown, noir-like films already existed in the 1970s, and several 1980s and 1990s works of Ringo Lam, for instance, could be considered as precursors to the very despairing and cynical noirs of the late 1990s. The Lam film best exemplifying the director's pioneering role is *City on Fire* (1987). Usually considered as part of the spate of hero films that followed Woo's *A Better*

Tomorrow (1986), Lam takes the genre into darker regions. His heroes are much more human, complex and vulnerable than Woo's, and his villains are not all purged from the world by the end of the film. *City on Fire* also has a moody, jazzy soundtrack, and was, according to cinematographer Andrew Lau, the first Hong Kong film to use blue toning, giving it a new kind of noir look.

53. That this is just one possible manifestation of Hong Kong noir is indicated by the female-dominated noir melodramas of the 1940s and 1950s.
54. Teo, 'Hong Kong's New Wave in Retrospect', p. 17.

PART TWO
NEO-NOIR FILMS IN CLOSE-UP

Chapter 4
Doubled Indemnity: Fruit Chan and the Meta-Fictions of Hong Kong Neo-Noir

Adam Bingham

If it is true to say that the film noir remains one of the most unstable, amorphous and contested of film genres – with even its status as such, as a distinct generic entity, being called into question by a number of scholars and critics who would rather categorise it as a style, a historical moment, a cycle, a series, a mood – then it follows that it should find a responsive home in the quixotic universe of Hong Kong filmmaking. In a quasi-national cinema more than commensurate to a disparate confluence of genres, the fluid boundaries of even the canonical wave of Hollywood noir films that predominated between 1944 and 1958 would appear to offer a model that could be readily assimilated into its paradigmatic stylistic and narrative norms. Indeed, quite apart from the oft-quoted designation of Hong Kong as a 'Hollywood of the East'[1] (which signifies more than just the local and international commercial dominance of their respective industries), one may point to the fact that a certain self-reflexive potentiality can be located within the noir canon. It may even be argued that film noir represents the first real site of cinematic experimentation within classical Hollywood, with works such as *Lady in the Lake* (Robert Montgomery, 1947), *Sorry, Wrong Number* (Anatole Litvak, 1948) and *Sunset Boulevard* (Billy Wilder, 1950) employing complex, convoluted narrational strategies that frustrate the narrative and stylistic transparency inherent in studio-era US filmmaking, while conversely many of the most esoteric and ambitious Hollywood films in recent memory – such as the works of Quentin Tarantino, David Fincher (especially *Fight Club* [1999]), Christopher Nolan (*Memento* [2000]) and Steven Soderbergh (*The Underneath* [1995]) – adapt and appropriate the tenets of noir as an organising principle, a register within which to frame their variously circumscribed and fatalistic stories.

Moreover, like the melodrama (in many respects its generic mirror image), film noir operated within a heightened register of visual expressivity, becoming a loaded adjective (noir-esque) that could then be applied to other, ostensibly diverse, genres. There have been noir Westerns like *High Sierra* (Raoul Walsh, 1941), *Blood on the Moon* (Robert Wise, 1948) and *The Furies* (Anthony Mann, 1950); noir road movies like *Detour* (Edgar G. Ulmer, 1945) and *Thieves' Highway* (Jules Dassin, 1949); noir science-fiction films such as *Kiss Me Deadly* (Robert Aldrich, 1955) and *Blade Runner* (Ridley Scott, 1982); gothic noir like *The House on Telegraph Hill* (Robert Wise, 1951); and noir-esque domestic melodrama like *Mildred Pierce* (Michael Curtiz, 1945), *Daisy Kenyon* (Otto Preminger, 1947) and *The Reckless Moment* (Max Ophüls, 1949). There have also been horror films with a noir style – *Cat People* (Jacques Tourneur, 1942), *The Seventh Victim* (Mark Robson, 1943) – social-problem pictures like *Border Incident* (Anthony Mann, 1949), even documentary noir in a late 1940s series of works ignited by *The House on 92nd Street* (Henry Hathaway, 1945) and comprising detailed procedural and investigative works such as *T-Men* (Anthony Mann, 1947), *13 Rue Madeleine* (Henry Hathaway, 1947) and *Call Northside 777* (Henry Hathaway, 1947).

Given this stylisation of *mise-en-scène* and complex, ambiguous generic identity built upon numerous interconnecting sub-sets that potentially frustrate or compromise narrative transparency, American film noir can be read as a markedly intertextual cinematic entity, something further underlined in the lineage that has been seen to feed into its specificity in Hollywood filmmaking. It has been variously constructed as the offspring of German expressionism, French impressionism and poetic realism, the 1930s Universal horror cycle, the 1930s Warner Bros gangster cycle, literary detective fiction and existentialism, even wartime documentary filmmaking that began to employ new lightweight cameras and faster film stock that facilitated the location shooting that became a defining feature of many noir narratives. As such, a majority of these films may be understood as foregrounding or problematising the act and process of storytelling and narration. They contain an implicitly meta-fictive import that, in line with Linda Hutcheon's definition of the term as 'a fiction that includes within itself a commentary on its own narrative',[2] allows one to conceive of them as calling attention to their constructed-ness; not, perhaps, in the typically modernist sense of Brechtian distanciation, but certainly with regard to laying bare some of the ideological processes that underpin Hollywood narratives, especially with regard to the positioning of women as objects of the male gaze (something that the *femme fatale* often explicitly usurps and/or rebukes).

It is precisely through this route that Hong Kong cinema begins to enter the discourse. As Theresa L. Gellar has argued, 'film noir's stylistic elements . . . highlight the irreducible tensions and conflicts that are the stuff of contemporary transnationalism',[3] and within neo-noir this tension and anxiety has been felt particularly strongly. The fact that Tarantino's feature debut *Reservoir Dogs* (1992) famously reworked the scenario of Ringo Lam's cult Hong Kong thriller *City on Fire* (1987) is only one example of a reciprocated transnational intertextuality that has long been perceived as central to Hong Kong cinema and the socio-cultural specificity of its post-modernity – what Stephen Teo (invoking Fredric Jameson) has characterised as a freeform site of 'cannibalisation ... a tangible symptom of an omnipresent, omnivorous and well-nigh libidinal historicism'.[4] Taking this characterisation as a locus of noir cinema, it is possible to begin to construct an alternative corpus, or at least a markedly different pathway, into the already canonised body of work, the key to which (as the title of Lam's film suggests) can be located in visions of the city, the modern urban sprawl. Even more than the earlier cycle of American gangster films popularised at Warner Bros in the 1930s, visions of the noxious urban environment predominated in, and in fact came to define, noir cinema. As Edward Dimendberg[5] in particular has noted, given the continued ambiguity of a term whose parameters and salient features few can agree on, might we not conceive of the commonality of the cityscape as a decisive determinant on the noir-esque? Is not the perceived archetypicality of the noir image – of a rain-drenched city street, shimmering in low-key, high-contrast black-and-white *mise-en-scène* and refracted through a canted camera and destabilised compositional architecture – indicative of a world thrown entirely out of kilter, a 'noir urbanism'?[6]

The Hong Kong crime film, especially those of the heroic bloodshed sub-genre that came to make up such a vital part of the New Wave in the 1980s under the heightened directorial auspices of John Woo, Ringo Lam, Kirk Wong and others, has drawn on the specific space of urban modernity associated with film noir, on the milieu of the venal cityscape as a repository of criminality and corruption. Such an image has remained endemic in any number of Hong Kong films; indeed, it has arguably offered as paradigmatic an image as the aforementioned noir archetype. However, independent Cantonese cinema has offered a contrastive model of neo-noir that seeks to subvert the typically contextual (post-World War II) meta-narratives of their US studio counterparts and to make visible a socio-cultural paradigm shift wherein the flux of colonial national identity was of particular import. But to what extent does this particular approach carry any weight or meaning with regard to Hong Kong cinema? And how can perceptions of Hollywood paradigms inform and infuse our understanding of Hong Kong, especially during the upheavals of its immediate pre- and post-1997 filmic exegeses? Going further, can the example of film noir offer any meaningful framework within which to elucidate the thematics of independent Hong Kong cinema? The transnational dialogue between Hollywood and Hong Kong suggests that the answer may lie in the affirmative, and this paper will look at the work of one Hong Kong director in particular – namely Fruit Chan, a figure who remains of almost singular importance within Cantonese independent filmmaking and who has arguably done more than any of his contemporaries to adapt and appropriate the tenets of perceived canonical film noir. For this I will principally be concerned with his trilogy of films comprising *Made in Hong Kong* (1997), *The Longest Summer* (1998) and *Little Cheung* (1999) – what has been termed the 'handover trilogy' for its insistent focus on the problems surrounding the 1997 cessation of Hong Kong to Chinese sovereignty. The post-modern vision of Hong Kong in this director's films stresses the city's status as an imaginary, received and narrativised space, one depicted and focalised through the filter of both character consciousness and ambiguous nationality. It is also concerned with crime and urban space, and makes specific play with post-colonial Hong Kong in flux, presenting a cityscape comparable to the post-war environment in which noir initially thrived in the US: that is, one in which a marked process of reconceptualisation was underway (the latter of actual spatial environs in the major cities, the former to do with population, wherein among other things a Chinese state-enforced migration policy continues to bring new immigrants into its Special Administrative Region). I will thus use the concept of film noir in order to elucidate points of contrast and commonality, to probe the fractures and fissures that open up between disparate or competing narrative, generic, methodological, even industrial norms (in the sense of the fault line between studio and independent production). Chan is a director whose films occupy a veritable panoply of liminal spaces, the productive tension or interplay between which makes his work especially receptive both to studies of coloniality and post- or neo-coloniality (the socio-historical space in-between which two states both *Made in Hong Kong* and *The Longest Summer* were produced) and also to film noir and its particular intertextuality, and this will form the central focus of the paper.

A further, contrastive aspect to the analysis of Fruit Chan's work will take the form of a study of the noir paradigm in other Asian national cinemas, chiefly Japan and, briefly, Taiwan. In the noir films of these countries a noir framework was adopted as an index of a new cinema in a transformed society (in Japan in the post-war, post-occupation period; in Taiwan as one of the salient generic determinants of the new Taiwanese cinema of Hou Hsiao-hsien, Edward Yang and Tsai Ming-liang). This particular approach will also allow a concomitant analysis of the use value of noir as a critical term with regard to

Hong Kong filmmaking, something that has been almost wholly absent from critical discourse on this national cinema. In addition, Wong Kar-wai further offers an important juxtaposition in presenting a colonial, pre-1997 vision of Hong Kong to compare with the post-1997 work of Chan, and this will help to shape the view of the specificity of the latter's noir films as contrasted with those that came to fruition prior to the handover to China.

Eastern Noir

In a paper about film noir and its dystopic images of the American city, Mark Shiel[7] has usefully summarised the ways in which the post-war predominance of this cinematic mode has been cited by commentators as a response to numerous cinematic and socio-historical crises. These relate particularly to Hollywood itself (a crisis in 'the classical codes and conventions of representation favoured by the . . . studio system')[8] and to patriarchal society and masculinity: that is, to men returning from the war to find newly independent women who had been mobilised as a workforce during the conflict and thus whose hitherto prevalent role as housewives and homemakers had been challenged and destabilised.

The notion of film noir as a crisis cinema – as a reaction to social malaise – is a pertinent concept with regard to Asian filmmaking. Although the parameters of noir and neo-noir that can be found in Japan and China consist of markedly different paradigmatic structures and, in some cases, of highly contrastive characterisations, one can nonetheless point to a fundamental similarity between Hollywood, Hong Kong and Japan with regard to the social dimension and impetus that their respective noir films contain, the fears and pressures they articulate. Japanese cinema in particular offered a series of films made at the country's oldest studio Nikkatsu in the late 1950s that traded very heavily on the iconography and circumscribed structures of US noir. Titles such as *I Am Waiting* (*Ore wa matteru ze*, Kurahara Koreyoshi, 1957), *Rusty Knife* (*Sabita naifu*, Masuda Toshio, 1958), Suzuki Seijun's *Take Aim at the Police Van* (*Sono gososha o nerae*, 1960) and *Cruel Story of a Gun* (*Kenju zankoku monogatari*, Furukawa Takumi, 1964) offer a stepping stone between their trans-Pacific forebears and the strains exemplified both in Hong Kong and in other Asian cinemas, including Taiwan and Mainland China. They combine the iconography, fatalistic mood, intertextuality and many of the typical *dramatis personae* of American noir with a concern for youth that would subsequently find its complement in the new Taiwanese cinema of the 1980s and the following decade's sixth generation of Chinese filmmakers in works such as Jia Zhangke's *Pickpocket* (aka

Xiaowu, 1998), Zhang Yuan's seminal *Beijing Bastards* (1993) and Wang Xiaoshuai's minimalist, affectless *Drifters* (2003). This latter aspect serves as a marker of a country that was itself at this time experiencing a state of figurative postwar infancy and adolescence, with an attendant identity crisis. Indeed, the title of Furukawa Takumi's *Cruel Story of a Gun* is a spin on Oshima Nagisa's Japanese New Wave polemic and pivotal youth film *Cruel Story of Youth* (*Seishun zankoku monogatari*, 1960), from a director who had already made the first real *taiyozoku* film, *Season of the Sun* (*Taiyo no kisetsu*, 1956).

Appearing at a crucial socio-political fault line between the end of the American occupation of Japan (officially 1952 but only widely accepted within Japan in 1955)[9] and the subsequent growth of the country's miracle bubble economy that gained momentum in the early 1960s, these films are less overtly concerned with the urban sprawl and stylised *mise-en-scène* of canonical noir than with its engagement with modern society, its direct intervention in the seismic changes affecting the post-war landscape of America. In this they implicitly allegorise the contemporary state of Japan, featuring as several of them do characters trying to escape and break free from their immediate past. The very title of the first key film in this series, *I Am Waiting*, connotes something of the limbo experienced by the protagonist, who is an ex-boxer cum bar-owner waiting for word from his brother to escape Japan and join him in Brazil. The comparable *Rusty Knife*, starring the same actor (Ishihara Yujiro), goes a step further by directly equating its central character with the national body itself. Like Japan, he is haunted by his recent past, a past associated with crime and personal corruption, and like his country he is currently struggling against the lure and glamour of capital, represented in the narrative by the money he is offered to avoid testifying against a criminal boss.

Intriguingly, in Japan these works are known collectively as *mukokuseki akushun*, or 'borderless action' films. Such a designation connotes something of the transnational cachet of these works, the fact that, following the aforementioned *taiyozoku* films, Nikkatsu attempted to meld the youth film dynamics of what had rapidly become their niche genre and its attendant demographic with the then-popular forms of US noir and even French poetic realism. *I Am Waiting* contains overt parallels with Marcel Carné. The fact that its protagonist is running from a troubled past and awaiting an uncertain future recalls *Daybreak* (*Le jour se lève*, 1939), in which Jean Gabin remains holed-up in an apartment waiting for the dawn and his irreversible appointment with fate, while the moody, run-down port setting where the action transpires strongly resembles that of *Port of Shadows* (*Le quai des brumes*, 1938). Subsequent works in the cycle took this aesthetic to extremes. *A Colt is my Passport* (*Koruto wa ore no passport*, Nomura Takashi, 1967) takes a number of the accoutrements of the spaghetti Western – such as an Ennio Morricone-esque guitar-led score and a climax in which the protagonist faces off against a gang across a vast, empty wasteland – and mixes them with a prototypical *yakuza* film plot structure and characters to make a truly international noir. It is as though the film's myriad constituent stylistic and narrative paradigms are flaunted in order to highlight the futility of seeking homogeneity: both in world cinema (particularly post-*nouvelle vague*) and in a country like Japan, whose (post)-modernity in the twentieth century, especially following its post-war occupation, was largely comprised of a matrix of appropriations of foreign influences.

Made In, and About, Hong Kong

A direct dialogue can be traced here with Hong Kong neo-noir cinema. The concept of Hong Kong filmmaking as a 'borderless cinema' – the fact that it has been perceived to occupy a focal point of transnational cinematic capital whose films operate 'across the boundaries of time, culture and conventions . . . [offering] a wide range of sensations and an escapism that both stimulate and saturate the imagination by blasting apart a banal contemporary world'[10] – is a prevalent one. Many have noted that, at least from the time of its New Wave onwards (the late 1970s), Hong Kong cinema has often sought to appropriate, to take, rework and re-present diverse aspects of other films, genres and cinematic/artistic paradigms (something that was stressed recently in an epic, seven-part documentary on the history of Hong Kong filmmaking that outlined the diverse determinants on 'local' culture). *Made in Hong Kong* exemplifies this trend of amalgamation. The film follows a troubled protagonist named Autumn Moon, a teenage boy from a broken home who, along with his retarded friend and a terminally ill girl named Ping, eschews school and works on the periphery of organised crime as a debt collector. As Esther M. K. Cheung has noted, Chan's film may be seen as a reaction to the popular *Young and Dangerous* (Andrew Lau, 1996–2000) films, a series of comic book adaptations that ran to seven chapters and which celebrated a modernised form of the traditional concept of heroism known as *jianghu* through its focus on a group of youths within the triads.[11] More pertinent, however, is the fact that the three protagonists and their relationships in this film carry distinct echoes of Wong Kar-wai's feature debut *As Tears Go By* (1988), a film that itself reworked the scenario and central characters from Martin Scorsese's *Mean Streets* (1973). The protagonist of Wong's film also exists in a violent criminal milieu, and his life is similarly defined on the one hand by the friend for whom he is responsible and whose altercations with rivals continue to impinge upon his life, and on the other by his burgeoning relationship with his cousin, who lives on an outlying island and who originally comes to stay with him while being treated for a potentially serious illness. This not only foregrounds intertextuality as an extra-diegetic norm but acts as an objective correlative to the protagonist, whose life and identity is to an extent second-hand, shaped by external, particularly cultural, precepts in lieu of any viable positive influence closer to home. He, like Ping, has been left without a father (an apt nod to a city state caught between, as it were, competing father figures), and through the prominent American movie posters that adorn the bedroom walls of both characters it becomes apparent that their lives exist as much in an interior, imaginary realm as any tenable phenomenological 'reality' (Moon also refers to Sylvester Stallone when talking about his retarded friend, who is named Sylvester, as well as to Julia Roberts when he teases Ping about being a prostitute during one of their first meetings).

The voiceover by Moon, who narrates the film at a point following his death (though importantly, unlike *Sunset Boulevard*, this is not made clear until the end of the narrative), reinscribes this thematic of a dual identity by making of the whole narrative a past present, a present that is already in the past. In a cinema that has been much preoccupied with memory and nostalgia, and with the politics of what Ackbar Abbas has famously termed 'dis-appearance'[12] (the pre-1997 sense that the cultural specificity of Hong Kong was being overlooked because new means of commensurate representation had not been employed), such a dual temporality explicitly problematises the notion of looking back to the past as a means of negating the future (a concept with some debt to the nostalgic imperatives of post-modernity as defined by Fredric Jameson). The film's schema of time is almost Heideggerian in being located in an unstable present that contains and indeed remains in its own past while continually hurtling forward towards the future, towards death. The protagonist's name connotes such a facet, to the extent that it offers a potent and double-barrelled allusion to ageing – each word connoting a temporal death (of summer and of daytime respectively) – while in an even more explicit nod to noir, both women in the film directly signify death, though not the overtly castrating demise associated with the *femme fatale*. Rather they connote an actual bodily torpor visited upon their own person. Their deaths draw Moon to them as a locus of his desire. He has recurring wet dreams about Susan following her suicide, and only begins to openly fantasise about Ping after learning of her terminal illness, precisely as though the void of their dying draws him in, becomes bound up in his life (and, indeed, vice versa, as it is when Moon lays dying in hospital following a stabbing that both Ping and Sylvester die).

This then helps to frame the narrative as an implicitly meta-fictional construct, something that becomes especially apparent in those scenes that overtly present a fantasy on Moon's part. For instance, when he is sent to kill someone by his boss, we see a number of versions of this assassination: or, more properly, of Moon's anxious actions before the event. Again, here we find Chan subverting several of the tenets of a dominant practice of filmmaking, this time the typical *découpage* associated with the stylised Hong Kong heroic bloodshed narrative. Here slow-motion is typically employed to enhance movement and action, to stretch and elasticate time the better to accentuate balletic motion and invigorate and heighten dramatic momentum. Chan, in contradistinction, retards the time before action through a repetition of slow-motion shots that merely follow Moon in the build-up to his attempt on a man's life. Given there is an explicit fantasy in this scene, in which Moon kills the man and runs away (something subsequently revealed not to have taken place, as he in fact is unable to pull the trigger at the crucial time), his actions are thus complicated rather than celebrated, with the slow-motion serving to subvert the sense of heroic motion specifically by psychologising it, making of it yet another infertile interior space rather than an exterior action.

Figure 4.1 Subverting heroic bloodshed.

Moon's reflections and remembrances shape and define the narrative. But beyond several overt lamentations for disaffected youth (again, like Japan, we can read a figurative infancy into Hong Kong's handover from one parent to another) his narration also stresses the impossibility of cogent storytelling or indeed of a satisfying meta-narrative of the city that can encompass the experiential subjectivity of these characters. Early in the film, during a conversation between Moon and a friend, the latter mentions his social worker fiancée, which then necessitates an abrupt change of scene to follow up on who she is and what her relationship is to Moon, a change that explicitly negates Moon's control of the narrative. An even more marked example occurs later when Moon stops at a public toilet (which carnivalesque site of embedded stories would go on to occupy the focus of a more recent Chan film, entitled *Public Toilet* [2002]). He is about to leave when another youth enters and chops off the arm of a man who is urinating in a cubicle, berating him as he does so for raping his younger sister. This incident leads Moon to ruminate on the fact that 'everyone has their story to tell'. Each personal micro-narrative comprises a tiny fragment of a whole, much as the roles and performances that male noir protagonists tend to feature in (often 'cast' by the *femme fatale*) demonstrate the extent to which personal identity is bound up in victimhood,[13] a capitulation to a narrative designed and executed by another, an actor in the creation of a figurative director. By the end of the film, a multitude of voiceovers take over the storytelling from Moon, offering a proliferation of points of view that Christine Gledhill[14] has noted as one of the prevalent features of noir filmmaking. Moon's voice and control of the narrative segues into those of Susan, Ping and, finally, of a radio address playing a speech by Chairman Mao about China's glorious youth. This ironic, official and officious narration further sets a grand narrative against a contrastive personal story that comments upon its intractability and perhaps suggests the inexorable and fatalistic undertow of Chinese nationality (the image under this scene tellingly features a kite lodged in a tree – a potent symbol already employed in a comparable context of discursive nationhood by Tian Zhuangzhuang in *The Blue Kite* [1993]).

There is, then, little if any of the nostalgic thematic of many other Hong Kong films made in the late 1980s and early 1990s in *Made in Hong Kong*. The concept of nostalgia is, however, hardly anathema to studies of neo-noir cinema. Fredric Jameson[15] and others have talked about how modern noir films evoke a lost past as a means of denying the present. They over-invest in antiquated cinematic visions of yesteryear, whereas *Made in Hong Kong*'s setting and temporality stress an inexorable spiral into the future. The past, for Chan, only reifies the onslaught of the future, which in discourse on Hong Kong finds its paradigmatic image in the sleek modern cityscape. At the same time as these notions connect *Made in Hong Kong* to US film noir, they also serve to connect Chan's film to the work of Wong Kar-wai, whose noir-esque diptych of *Chungking Express* (1994) and *Fallen Angels* (1995) uses a range of different voiceovers to express the thoughts and feelings of each film's competing, similarly lost protagonists. The effect is very much one of stasis and control, of finding a moment of respite and reflection within a cityscape that, as Wong's dizzying style connotes, is perennially on the move. Both films open with frenetic scenes following characters moving determinedly, rapidly, through the crowded environs of Hong Kong, and are captured in a stop-motion technique that heightens a sense of extreme motion while simultaneously de-familiarising the environment, abstracting the characters from any concrete sense of space. Wong stresses this still further by conflating personal and public space; *Chungking Express* and *Fallen Angels* both feature characters whose apartments are continuously broken into, while in the former the central arena for the working through of feelings and emotions, not to mention the site of private reverie, even of epiphany, is the very public and quotidian space of a fast-food stall. He collapses and conflates the two realms as though to stress a subjective response to the city that implicitly challenges hitherto demarcated boundaries and offers a correlative to the above in terms of the self and Other, the problem of constructing a stable sense of selfhood and personal identity in a world that is perennially in flux. As Moon notes in *Made in Hong Kong*, it 'is moving too fast. So fast that just when you adjust yourself to it . . . it's another brand new world',[16] and the ghost of post-coloniality from this point of view becomes a means of problematising and questioning self as much as Other.

If this intertextual melange offers one prominent instance of constructedness, then it is also by this circuitous route that the city itself becomes most keenly felt in *Made in Hong Kong*. Esther M. K. Cheung has written in detail about what she terms the 'ghostly' or 'spectral' city[17] – an urban site characterised by a figurative sense of homelessness in a drab lower-class environment and by a loss of the real at a moment of great social change. Chan locates a crucial slippage between the entity of the city in its hypothetical, contradictory totality and those perceptions of it that accrue within and between the cracks, the figurative fragmented spaces that challenge its spatial coherence and what we might term its 'known-ness'. In other words, micro-narratives of urban modernity predominate amid a general post-modern affectivity, and it is the tension between these two modes that narrates into being the idea, or concept, of the city as a macrocosmic space as well as reclassifying the aforementioned anxiety between the weight of a problematic past and the spectre of an uncertain future. David Harvey has discussed destruction as a specifically modern narrative, of tearing down the old to make way for the new.[18] For Chan this pertains to the handover, and is literally reflected in the urban spaces of *Made in Hong Kong* to the extent that one sees numerous construction sites throughout the film, sites in the process of transformation, of becoming, while a key scene in a graveyard (an ironic moment of escape for the young protagonists) further cements the past as a key aspect of the present. These moments offer a modern paradigm, a literal modernist landscape that is tempered by the post-modern landscape of the film's intertextuality, its generic pastiche (noir and otherwise), in order to suggest an indeterminacy over temporal order, and by extension Chan's Hong Kong is similarly caught or suspended between Britain and China, coloniality and post-coloniality. Its status as a colony appears to be coming to an end – the title of the film appears to posit a specifically Cantonese identity – but does Chinese sovereignty offer an end to this colonisation? Does it present any tenable change, especially for Hong Kong's lower-class citizens?

Figure 4.2   Death and escape.

Moreover, to what extent do the city spaces that we see act as a viable microcosm of Hong Kong? There are only a handful of moments when the city is seen in any complete way, typically through Moon's apartment window as he surveys its skyline before him, a sight that he contemplates through the figurative bars of the blinds that further connote a sense of imprisonment. In addition, the steely blue palette of Chan's *mise-en-scène* in these scenes recalls

Figure 4.3 The city as illusory whole.

the similarly expressionistic presentation of the recurring images of Susan as she prepares and undertakes her suicide, thereby further stressing the deathly pallor of the alienating, metaphysical city. These shots are like urban appropriations of Caspar David Friedrich paintings, with a solitary human figure in diminished perspective contemplating the impenetrable vastness beyond, a whole that remains illusory, as fragile and tenuous as his perception of it and his or her place within it.

In this it is instructive to contrast *Made in Hong Kong* with regard to Taiwanese New Wave directors, particularly Edward Yang and Tsai Ming-liang in *A Brighter Summer Day* (1991) and *Rebels of the Neon God* (1992) respectively. The chief arena of convergence here underlines the central difference attendant upon eastern noir cinema, but which comes to the fore in works by Yang, Tsai and indeed Hou Hsaio-hsien: namely, a youthful cast, subject matter and perspective, which typically takes the form of a narrative built around a protracted and complex coming of age. Hou's *The Boys from Fengkuei* (1983) is most pertinent, contrasting as it does the city and its rural environs. The story concerns a group of three variously delinquent youths who, after having dropped out of school in their titular home town (a coastal village), decide to move away to the city to try to make their way. The idea of the city as a perceived, meta-fictive space – that is, a location whose specificity resides in a multitude of competing, overlapping microcosmic stories that imbricate the illusory concept of a whole and coherent site – comes increasingly to the fore in this film. Cinema-going figures prominently in the narrative. A con played on Ah-ching and his friends in the city sees the gang tricked into going to the top floor of a derelict building where, they are told, they will find a cinema that is playing films in widescreen and in colour. This is then revealed to be the space for a yet-to-be-fitted large window, with the panoramic view of the city beyond figuring literally as the scope screen and metaphorically as a narrative in *medias res*, an endless story playing on a loop that is both witnessed and narrated into existence by the hapless protagonists and their experiential encounter with this urban milieu. It also underlines the scopic imperative attendant upon the protagonists' alienation from the city, the fact that they stand outside and look at it as an (illusory) whole, much as Moon does through his window, his own movie screen.

Made in Hong Kong similarly depicts an unstable, uncertain and heterogeneous space in which boundaries become confused, bleed into one another. Indeed, implicit in the film's temporal schema is the notion that the only personal space is within oneself, the space of interiority. The death of one of Moon's friends occurs when he has retreated into himself while listening to music and fantasising with a gun and thus cannot hear the desperate knocking on his door (something further emphasised in Chan's close-ups of the gun being completely abstracted from the diegesis, appearing only as a silhouetted object against a plain white background), and this factors into a dialogue between this film and Hollywood films noir. Often in the former the city is presented not only as a centre 'of vice and corruption'[19] but also in a documentary fashion that records its modern reality. *Call Northside 777*, for instance, begins with a historical exposition of Chicago, from the great fire of 1871 to its construction as a modern metropolis, while works such as *The Naked City* (Jules Dassin, 1948), *Criss Cross* (Robert Siodmak, 1949) and *The Big Combo* (Joseph H. Lewis, 1955) among numerous others all open with images of the city that are held beyond any immediate narrative import, existing as it were outside and beyond the realms of the narrative and framing their subsequent implicit meta-fictions. Conversely, the aforementioned Japanese noir *Rusty Knife* also begins with a comparably discursive prologue detailing the criminal malaise afflicting the typical new Japanese town of Udaka where the action transpires, a contextual record of a reality that frames the story as a modern fable of old world criminality in a new and different Japan.

Chan, however, does not follow this example. Indeed, he goes further by working explicitly in contravention of the grammar and syntax of commercial filmmaking. The opening shot of the film is a lateral track along a fence bordering a basketball court in which the protagonist is playing this game. There is no establishing shot, and the camera is already in motion when the scene begins, and such elements of conventional analytical editing are withheld throughout to construct a vision of the city not as a tangible, complete entity but an elusive, centrifugal space that perennially seems to be emanating outwards from some indefinable centre. It is a city of the mind and the psyche as much as a physical milieu, with the sub-textual point being that a symbiotic relationship may be uncovered between individual and state, at least to the extent that precepts of British-ness or Chinese-ness do not fully elucidate the subjectivity of at least a section of Hong Kong citizens. Physical space remains indeterminate in an appropriation of this precept, its sense that British or Chinese nationhood ultimately means little as far as subjects like Moon are concerned, subjects who fall between the cracks of society and to whom national identity is not necessarily a pressing concern.

Fireworks

Chan capitalised on the immediate, indeed almost overnight, success of *Made in Hong Kong* with a film that has tended to be forgotten, or at best marginalised, in critical discourse on his work. *The Longest Summer*, made in 1998, is the film that contributed to what would subsequently become the 'handover trilogy', and is the closest appropriation of an action thriller in the director's filmography. It details the attempt to rob a bank carried out by a group of ex-soldiers from the Hong Kong Military Service Corps (the 31 March 1997 disbandment of which is depicted in the film's opening scene) who have fallen on hard times due to the impending handover. The protagonist, Ga-yin, is already on the margins of crime, as his younger brother (played by Sam Lee, the lead in *Made in Hong Kong*) works for a triad boss and procures work for his older sibling, and against the backdrop of the three months leading up to both the handover and the robbery his life and sense of selfhood are thrown into turmoil and disorder.

There is in this scenario a potentially allegorical import, something dramatised most overtly in a scene relatively late in the film when Ga-yin begins to violently berate himself, screaming in his apartment that he does not know who he is while smashing a mirror in an explicit rendering of a confused identity. Like *Made in Hong Kong*, however, *The Longest Summer* frustrates such a reading; it reworks its overtly noir narrative (with echoes of the heist thriller found in such canonical works as *The Asphalt Jungle* [John Huston, 1950] and *The Killing* [Stanley Kubrick, 1956] or *Odds Against Tomorrow* [Robert Wise, 1959]) and protagonist (who takes his place beside such American figures as 'Rip' Murdock in *Dead Reckoning* [John Cromwell, 1947], Joe Parkson in *Act of Violence* [Fred Zinnemann, 1948] and, of course, Travis Bickle in *Taxi Driver* [Martin Scorsese, 1976], in that he is an ex-soldier tainted by violence and warfare and struggling with civilian life) in order to reposition the concept of genre, or at least a rigidly stratified narrative framework, as a figurative entity. That is, Ga-yin's trajectory over the course of the narrative is located within the personal struggles attendant upon leaving behind a highly structured and regimented way of life in law and order and of moving on to an aimless life of crime. Noir, indeed the concept of genre cinema (so prized by Ackbar Abbas as one of the keys to understanding 1980s Hong Kong cinema),[20] becomes in *The Longest Summer* a metaphorical construct redolent of such an ordered, predictable existence, with Chan's directorial departure in this neo-noir serving to underline the protagonist's transmigration, the disorder following his heretofore relatively stable life.

The film is thus explicitly located in a context of noir cinema, which Chan then employs as a point of departure in order to emphasise both sameness and difference in what appears as a pertinent commentary on the state of post-coloniality. Chan's employment of a broadly discursive backdrop to the action of the film, the fact that certain scenes take place alongside (and were in fact filmed concurrently with) the ceremonial celebrations of the handover, is a crucial aspect of the film and a further link to the aforementioned documentary-esque procedural noirs. However, Chan does not present his actual footage with an eye to offering a real sense of the city, or to validating his characters through a verisimilitudinous context; rather the point of such a strategy in *The Longest Summer* is precisely to undermine and frustrate such a textual taxonomy, to destabilise any clear distinction between the 'real' and the 'fictional', between what is 'true' and what is not, so as to problematise readings of the 'post' in post-colonial. The fact that many characters in the film stay at home and simply watch the handover festivities on television further underlines the distance from 'reality' for many of the populous, and stresses an imaginary space of disconnection rather than an actual union. Once again, it is the imaginary, illusory space that predominates, the meta-fictions of lives lived in the amorphous spaces that defy and deny the master narrative of the city-as-metropolis through the mediating agent of the post-modern practices of televisual consumption as theorised by Jean Baudrillard in particular.

Notions of trust and betrayal, to say nothing of violence (emotional as well as physical), arise as by-products of life in this noir-esque city. In *Made in Hong Kong*, the fact that both Sylvester and Ping die when Moon becomes absent in their lives figures as a symbolic index of the extent to which lives become intertwined and interconnected within the environs of this teeming urban milieu. Indeed, like the classical noir protagonist whose own actions imperil only himself, Moon here cannot even trust or depend upon his own person to act: that is, he is not only unable to rescue his friends but he also fails to kill when called upon. He cannot save or indeed take lives, something that complicates his fateful self-immolation by undermining any element of choice or decision on his part. It is, as the structure of the narrative underlines, a story already told, played out and exhausted. The implicitly suicidal trajectory of the canonical noir hero is frequently cast as the inexorable dance of Eros and Thanatos. Here, by contrast, the in-built obsolescence of especially the female characters of Ping and Susan (both killed by an absent male) overturns the concept of the *femme fatale*. They signify the solemn procession of their own deaths rather than the castration-fuelled demise of the smitten male protagonist, and the question subtly arises as to the social subjectivity of the city as a stage for this interior drama. The amorphous spaces that accrue around the protagonists become external manifestations of interior malaise. In other words, Hong Kong circa 1997 is allegorised within these fateful stories as an explicitly constructed location with no a priori phenomenological veracity: a city, in effect, breathed into life by the characters whose experiences of its environs echo the urban space as Lacanian mirror (that is, an autonomous, complete Other that confers fragmentation on the desiring proto-subject) as theorised in particular by Rob Lapsley.[21] And it is this immediate, experiential drive that structures the film beyond any overt socio-political exegesis in Chan's work. Ultimately, in *Made in Hong Kong*, if the (British) King is dead, then long live the (Chinese) King.

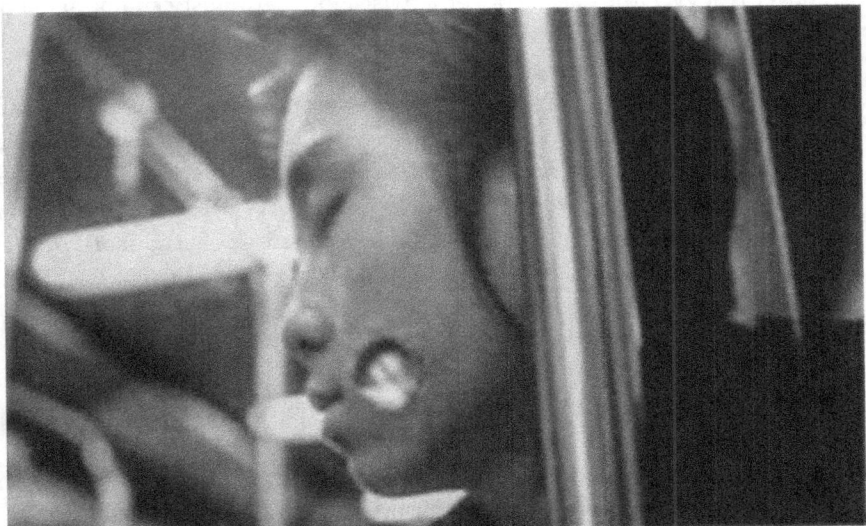

Figure 4.4 Violence and magic realism in *The Longest Summer*.

The Longest Summer takes these inter-personal dynamics a stage further in depicting the national betrayal of former soldiers in the military service corps, whose disenfranchisement surrounding the handover feeds the criminal plot that drives the narrative. Heightened, almost magic-realist, moments such as the encounter on a train with a soldier whose face carries a hole sizeable enough to look through amply demonstrate the ways in which violence marks Cantonese citizens who, unlike their forebears in *Made in Hong Kong*, here seem fated not to die. In its final scene, a brief epilogue set in summer 1998, Chan makes perhaps his most damning statement on the vagaries of memory and remembrance as they pertain to the violence of the teeming sub-strata of Hong Kong. Ga-yin, who was last seen being shot in the head, is recognised by a woman he had become close to, the daughter of his crime syndicate boss. However, he appears not to reciprocate the recognition, and begins to berate the woman for bothering him, while simultaneously (and captured in the same long mobile take that makes a sequence shot of the whole scene) a taxi driver who had earlier been affected by a used tampon left in his car by a group of school girls takes revenge on the young ladies by smearing faeces on them. It is a comic moment, and taken alongside Ga-yin's memory figures in a juxtaposition of forgetting (something important) and remembering (something trivial) that contrasts with *Made in Hong Kong* by stressing a future based on a denial of the past. Conversely, the final moments of the final work in the handover trilogy, *Little Cheung* (an otherwise more naturalistic drama about a young boy and his family in working-class Mong Kok), offer an adumbration not of personal but perhaps of spatial memory. The titular young protagonist, in a moment of dejection and in a further appropriation on Chan's part of magical realism, sees before him on the street the central characters of both *Made in Hong Kong* and *The Longest Summer*. They appear as residual images of those who have slipped through the cracks and transgressed the city's physical limits and boundaries to appear as the horror genre's central motif of the return of the repressed: the reappearance of what has been suppressed and oppressed by the rapid economic expansion of Hong Kong, and a damning vision of what lies in wait for the young adolescent of *Little Cheung*, and maybe the figurative adolescent that was Hong Kong as it moved from one parent to another. Magic realism is often perceived to be a specifically post-colonial register, a means of countering a reality thought to be in service of white first-world hegemony; it is also often described as an entirely objective artistic mode, and its spectre here as part of an interior landscape subverts such an imperative as a way to invoke, only to then counterpoint and frustrate, post-coloniality as a clear socio-political context.

The myriad forms and features associated with canonical Hollywood film noir have found little direct currency in discourse on Hong Kong cinema, perhaps because of a relative paucity of any overt engagement with or appropriation of its perceived salient iconography. The dialectical relationship opened up in the work of Fruit Chan between past and present, life and death, subject and object, facilitates a fractious textual as well as narrative and thematic space that has significant ramifications for the representation of the singularity of Hong Kong. In particular, given the explicit treatment of 1997 and the handover of Hong Kong to China, Chan's early films allow for a discourse on the dialectics of colonial and post-colonial, and the viability of such an approach, as facilitated by a study of neo-noir cinema, lays precisely in this form's insistent, experiential mapping of urban space and the deep anxiety over its development and change, its competing modernity and post-modernity. With regard to Hong Kong, the import of noir cinema arises less in any meta-narrative of the city's socio-historicity (although this is certainly discernible in some films that do carry a more overt narrativisation of seismic social change, such as the *Infernal Affairs* trilogy [Andrew Lau and Alan Mak, 2002–3]) but rather in the independent cinematic arena of emphasising the untenability of grand narratives with regard to what may be termed the social subjectivity of the city – the fact that it can be broken down into a multitude of overlapping, competing micro-narratives that trace an imaginary, illusory space rather than a comprehensible locale. It is here that Fruit Chan's work is most valuable; it stresses the lack of validity surrounding a majority of discourse about Hong Kong's supposed post-coloniality by problematising any clear notion of national identity, any stable self against which to mark on Other.

Chan's protagonists also follow a noir template in that they underline a sense of problematic masculine selfhood predicated upon encounters with women. The fact that Chan also stresses a perception of the city, a subjective response, rather than any viable objective reality, makes it plain that no grand narrative of nationality can completely elucidate the story of citizenship, especially of those alienated lives lived and lost on and around its periphery. Ultimately, if it is true, as Susan Hayward argues, that 'film noir articulated the repressed needs of American culture',[22] then it is particularly instructive with regard to Hong Kong for the extent to which it maps out a veritable matrix of perspectives on and responses to cultural and cinematic (post)modernity, typically with the city at its core. And in a cinema so accustomed to appropriation and assimilation this markedly transnational mode may well be argued to offer the most pointed and potent framework for understanding the almost singular nature of this stasis-in-change that has defined Hong Kong's recent history.

Notes

1. Ciecko, 'Hong Kong: Cinematic Cycles of Grief and Glory', p. 171.
2. Hutcheon, *Narcissistic Narrative*, p. 2.
3. Gellar, 'Transnational Noir', p. 173.
4. Teo, *Hong Kong Cinema*, p. 243.
5. Dimendberg, *Film noir and the Spaces of Modernity*.
6. Prakash (ed.), *Noir Urbanisms*.
7. Shiel, 'A Regional Geography of Film Noir', pp. 77–8.
8. Ibid., p. 77.
9. An economic white paper was published in Japan in 1956. It began with the proclamation (soon to be a proud slogan) that 'the post-war is over', and is generally regarded as the impetus behind governmental reform and the foundational moment of the subsequent growth of the Japanese economy.
10. Yau, 'Introduction', p. 1.
11. Cheung, *Fruit Chan's* Made in Hong Kong, pp. 60–78.
12. Abbas, 'The New Hong Kong Cinema and the *Déjà Disparu*', pp. 80–1.
13. This is a key point, as film noir thrives on and breeds masochistic masculinity that proffers a death drive as part of a vicious circle wherein this Thanatos arises as the spectre of the Eros facilitated by the *femme fatale*.
14. Gledhill, 'Klute 1', p. 14.
15. See Jameson, *Postmodernism*, pp. 1–66.
16. If it seems a little too presumptuous and over-simplified to read the impending spectre of the post-colonial into Wong's images then it is worth stressing the presence of an Indian community in the central setting of the Chungking Mansion, not simply a diasporic minority in Hong Kong but, by extension, another once-colonised country that has recently embarked upon its own post-war post-coloniality.
17. Cheung, *Fruit Chan's* Made in Hong Kong, pp. 79–124.
18. Harvey, *The Condition of Postmodernity*, pp. 17–22.
19. Straw, 'Urban Confidential', p. 87.
20. Abbas, 'The New Hong Kong Cinema and the *Déjà Disparu*', pp. 72–99.
21. Lapsley, 'Mainly in Cities and at Night', pp. 186–208.
22. Hayward, *Cinema Studies*, p. 132.

Chapter 5
Running on Karma: Hong Kong Noir and the Political Unconscious

Gina Marchetti

Film scholars routinely approach Johnny To's films in relation to film noir conventions.[1] *Running on Karma* (2003, co-directed with Wai Ka-fai), however, at first glance, may not appear to fit the noir portion of the director's oeuvre. The film is a generic hybrid that moves from dark comedy to horror and from the supernatural thriller to the improbable romance. However, when viewed in the context of the rest of To's work, as well as within the framework of his production company Milkyway Image and his other collaborations with Wai Ka-fai, a certain insistent stylistic consistency emerges that resonates with noir. Chiaroscuro shadows faces within the *mise-en-scène*; the cityscape of Hong Kong appears in murky darkness punctuated by the neon of nightclub signs and the glare of police-car lights; exteriors outside the city take on the quality of dreamscapes displaced from the daylight by the low-key gloom of memory. Images materialise, as the theme of karmic return implies, 'out of the past', and, as in film noir generally, the characters shoulder this burden of history (social, cultural, political and personal). The bare outline of the film's plot, however, does not immediately connect it to the hard-boiled detectives, alluring *femmes fatales*, persistent pessimism and sinister ambience usually associated with noir. A former Buddhist monk from Mainland China turned bodybuilder/male stripper (played by Andy Lau in a muscle suit), who can 'see' the past lives of people he encounters, comes to the aid of a Hong Kong policewoman, Lee Fung-yee (Cecilia Cheung), who suffers from very 'bad karma'. Although the film does deal with crime investigations, the noir connection to this story seems strained, at best. Its supernatural elements and bloody murders draw it closer, in fact, to the horror film, and its carefully choreographed martial arts sequences, including a balletic demonstration of martial artistry using a Kleenex, links it to the *wuxia pian*. Moreover, *Running on Karma* also falls into the romantic comedy mould of an earlier teaming of Johnnie To–Wai Ka-fai and Andy Lau, *Love on a Diet* (2001), in which Lau performs in a fat suit rather than a muscle suit opposite Sammi Cheng instead of Cecilia Cheung.

From the first glimpse of Lau in the outrageous, oversized suit that must convincingly serve as his 'birthday suit' in 'the naked city' as well, romance, action, horror, fantasy and perhaps satire seem to figure more prominently in the generic mix than film noir. However, Hong Kong's post-modern cinema does not offer clear generic distinctions, and film noir has been described as a 'style' rather than a 'genre' by scholars,[2] so finding noir in *Running on Karma* may not be so astonishing after all. Although Andy Lau's muscle suit and strip-club routine may situate him within the realm of the comic or grotesque, his divided character, desperate search for justice and his own conflicted engagement with good and evil place him in the company of film noir's hard-boiled anti-heroes. The film also draws liberally on noir conventions, including chiaroscuro lighting, claustrophobic urban spaces, flashbacks, and a sense of the dark side of human nature and the inextricable machinations of fate.

Given the enormous differences between America's post-World War II malaise and Hong Kong's post-handover disquiet, the fact that noir as a style and constellation of narrative conventions still has creative currency across cultures, continents and decades may not be readily apparent. However, *Running on Karma*'s engagement with noir goes beyond the surface to encompass themes of loss, betrayal, predestination, alienation and existential despair common to both Hollywood in the 1940s and '50s and Hong Kong after 1997 (known as the Hong Kong Special Administrative Region, or HKSAR). Nonetheless, as Joelle Collier points out, it must be kept in mind that Hong Kong noir has to do with the 'anxieties of post-modern Asia, not postwar America . . .'[3]

Noir visualises a nightmarish world linked to historical trauma. Fredric Jameson's notion of the 'political unconscious', therefore, may be useful as a way of connecting Hong Kong noir to Hollywood/European/global film culture. As Jameson notes, the concept provides a way to 'restore' a buried history to the interpretation of a text:

> It is in detecting the traces of that uninterrupted narrative, in restoring to the surface of the text the repressed and buried reality of this fundamental history, that the doctrine of a political unconscious finds its function and necessity.[4]

> History is what hurts, it is what refuses desire and sets inexorable limits to individual as well as collective praxis, which its 'ruses' turn into grisly and ironic reversals of their overt intention.[5]

History 'hurts' in *Running on Karma*, and this chapter probes how the film engages with the political moment through its citation of noir elements.

Hong Kong Noir

In their compendium on Hong Kong popular cinema, *Sex and Zen & a Bullet in the Head*, Stefan Hammond and Mike Wilkins define 'Hong Kong noir' as follows:

> With 1997 – and the return of Hong Kong to the People's Republic of China – looming large on the horizon, the development of Hong Kong's own brand of film noir was a natural. Not surprisingly, HK noir hit its stride right after the Tiananmen Square massacre in 1989, reflecting the panicky fear of life with a brutal new landlord... Like the Hollywood offerings, Hong Kong noir is gloomy and cynical. But as with everything Hong Kong borrows from Hollywood, HK filmmakers have taken noir and made it uniquely their own. Hong Kong noir is both darker and more colourful, bleaker and more humorous.[6]

While Hammond and Wilkins link the genesis of Hong Kong noir to the period between 1989 and 1997, noir elements exist in Hong Kong productions, influenced by global aesthetic trends, made during the Cold War era as well.[7] The resurgence of noir after 1989, however, is striking. James Naremore characterises Wong Kar-wai's *Chungking Express* (1994), for example, as 'inflected by the French New Wave's fascination with noir'.[8] As neo-noir became a fixture in post-modern cinema globally, Hong Kong continued to develop its own aesthetic and philosophical conversation with film noir's dark imagery. With the uncertainty following the handover and the economic slump in the wake of the Asian financial crisis the same year, films turned, as Esther Yau has noted, to 'bleak emotions'[9] explored through noir conventions.

The year 2003 prompted filmmakers, in addition to To and Wai, to respond to a series of crises within and outside the film industry with films featuring dark themes. Accompanying a slump in production, Hong Kong faced added challenges with the SARS epidemic, an economic downturn, and the controversy surrounding Article 23 that year. A broadly drafted anti-sedition document, Article 23 would amend Hong Kong's Basic Law to enable the government to take action against groups and individuals seen as 'state security threats' to the Chinese nation; however, mass demonstrations on 1 July 2003,[10] the anniversary of the territory's change in sovereignty, put the legislation on hold indefinitely. If Article 23 had been enacted, several religious groups, including the Buddhist sect the Falun Gong (aka Falun Dafa) and the Roman Catholic Church, would have come under scrutiny because of their status in the People's Republic of China (PRC). The SARS epidemic earlier in the year created a different set of border tensions, when it became clear to the world media that the PRC had not communicated the gravity of the crisis in a timely manner, which may have exacerbated its severity in the HKSAR. Noir pessimism also flies in the face of the cultivated optimism associated with China's burgeoning capitalism. Noir elements in several films appeared to speak, then, to the suspicion of the state, anxieties surrounding public security, and a general malaise associated with 2003.

Scholarly debate still dogs the concept of 'film noir', and few agree on whether the phenomenon can best be described as a 'genre', a 'movement', a 'sensibility', a 'style' or, as Slavoj Žižek calls it, 'an anamorphotic distortion'.[11] Historically, it may best be seen as an aesthetic encounter with the pessimism, cynicism and anxiety associated with key events. Scholars trace its origins to the hard-boiled anti-heroes popular during the Great Depression and the nightmarish crime stories associated with German expressionism. Noir appeared to reach its Hollywood zenith in the post-World War II economic slump, and darkened during the beginning of the Cold War and the growth of the nuclear threat. Valorised by French critics and capturing the imagination of world filmmakers, film noir became part of a global cinematic idiom. Revivified during the closing days of the Vietnam War, when Watergate and Nixon's resignation marked a new political nadir for America, 'neo-noir' surfaced at a time when Hollywood experienced its own drop in box-office revenues.

Roman Polanski's *Chinatown* (1974) exemplifies this iteration of noir, which adds colour cinematography, a post-Watergate political climate and the moral exhaustion of the era to the mix. The immigrant director, Depression-era urban setting, chiaroscuro lighting, divided anti-hero, mysterious *femme fatale*, sinister supporting cast, Orientalist flourishes and themes of fatalism, despair and corruption remain, but with a post-modern attention to the surface – the self-consciousness of the auteur's signature, the Hollywood glamour of the stars, and the care given to period details and the feeling of stylistic exhaustion. Polanski's film deals with a fatalistic assessment of personal and political corruption using visual and narrative conventions associated with noir classics such as *The Big Sleep* (Howard Hawks, 1946) or *The Lady from Shanghai* (Orson Welles, 1948);[12] however, *Chinatown* also functions as a film about those earlier motion pictures, as a 'nostalgia film' in Fredric Jameson's use of the term.

As a pastiche of several ostensibly incompatible genres, *Running on Karma* takes up neo-noir at an even greater distance. Horror, action, martial arts, comedy, romance and melodrama all contribute generic elements to the mix, but noir, as a style, a constellation of themes or a sensibility, seems to hold the film together. In fact, its noir elements resonate with the mood of the times – depressed, diseased, panicked, anxious, paranoid, hysterical, under threat and subject to fate, bad luck or 'bad karma'. As a story that deals with characters that move between Hong Kong and the PRC, noir conventions also help to navigate these geographic and psychological boundaries. Noir has its obsession with borders – the line between 'Chinatown' and the rest of the city (usually LA, sometimes San Francisco or New York), the border with Mexico in films such as *Touch of Evil* (Orson Welles, 1958), and, of course, the line between 'good' and 'evil' complicated by the convoluted plots that characterise these films. For *Running on Karma*, the border between Hong Kong and Shenzhen becomes an exemplar of the tensions between the HKSAR and the PRC, exacerbated by Article 23 and the apparent bungling of information that allowed the SARS epidemic to escalate out of control in Hong Kong. Twin cities, magnifying the vices of each other, Hong Kong and Shenzhen stand as noir cities of the night – doused in rain, neon flickering off slick surfaces, harsh shadows hiding nightmarish dangers, theatres of violence and bloodshed.

Just as the *Infernal Affairs* (Andrew Lau and Alan Mak, 2002–3) trilogy (particularly in Part II and Part III) took up these issues and wedded them to Buddhist religious themes,[13] *Running on Karma* appears to be attempting, on one level, to address tensions between Hong Kong and the PRC with an allegory based on a Buddhist conception of fate. Andy Lau, in fact, stars in *Running on Karma* as well as *Infernal Affairs I* and *III*.[14] The marriage of noir with Buddhist conceptions of karma lies at the heart of *Running on Karma*. Johnnie To makes this quite explicit in an interview:

> . . . it was a way to really get the audience more interested in this Buddhist philosophy of Karma, this feeling of cause and effect, meaning that what you do today will have a result, some sort of consequence, in the future. These are the kinds of philosophy we wanted to do, and having Andy Lau in special makeup made the film more acceptable for audiences in HK.[15]

In this respect, the film appears to be in conversation with other films and celebrities from around the world that have taken up Buddhist themes to criticise the 'consequences' of the PRC's policies directly or indirectly. In an article published by *Time* titled 'Can Hollywood Afford to Make Films China Doesn't Like?', Erica Ho cites films such as *Kundun* (Martin Scorsese, 1997) and *Seven Years in Tibet* (Jean-Jacques Annaud, 1997), as well as Sharon Stone's misstep on calling the Sichuan earthquake the result of 'karma' because of Beijing's suppression of Tibetan protests in 2008.[16] Richard Gere, a devotee of the Dalai Lama, of course, is *persona non grata* in China, and Bernardo Bertolucci's *Little Buddha* (1994), in many ways, acts in dialectical opposition to his pre-Tiananmen crackdown *Last Emperor* (1987) by using Tibetan Buddhism as a political device.

Films from the PRC also contain Buddhist elements. However, the Buddhist motifs generally downplay any religious or philosophical significance and remain tied to martial arts history (for example, *Shaolin Temple* [Cheung Yam-yim, 1982]) or classic fairy tales (for example, *Journey to the West* [Stephen Chow and Derek Kwok Chi-kin, 2013]). *Running on Karma*'s invocation of 'karma' serves a very different purpose. It acts as a means to separate the filmmakers' vision from Chinese governmental policy and to carve out a separate ideological space for local Hong Kong concerns. The references to Buddhism also link up with American and European cinematic discourses critical of the PRC, and they resonate with a sense of transcendental justice and spirituality at a time of tremendous public tragedy and civic upheaval in Hong Kong. Karma also speaks to noir fatalism, cyclical repetitions, funereal concerns and the complexity of the human psyche – including its submerged dark side.

While the flashbacks motivated by Big's ability to see the past place the film within the orbit of noir's obsession with fate, psychological trauma and horrors coming from 'out of the past'[17] to haunt the film's protagonists, it also allows for the contemplation of another 'sensitive' topic in the PRC. In this case, Big sees the past life of policewoman Lee Fung-yee as a World War II-era Japanese soldier who beheads Chinese prisoners of war.[18] Periodic flare-ups of anti-Japanese sentiment in China point to a rather complicated cross-border provenance for the image. Cold War realignment of political and economic interests forced Hong Kong to work through the Japanese Occupation and Taiwan to deal with the Japanese colonial period differently than the PRC, where ongoing political, economic and territorial disputes exacerbate the trauma of the Pacific War.

The decision to make an apparently upright exemplar of the law a reincarnation of a Japanese war criminal, therefore, gives pause. While ostensibly calling for the transcendence of past trauma through forgiveness and reconciliation by merging the war criminal with an 'innocent' woman, it also seems to resonate with the negative reactions to the increased paramilitary powers Article

23 would have given the police. Even the benevolent Lee harbours the 'sins' of the past, and the government, embodied here by the police force, may not be in the best position to uphold 'justice'. Instead, the mystic working out of karma becomes the province of the Buddhist monk/illegal sex worker – the most maligned and marginalised element in cross-border culture. It seems as if To and Wai had a checklist of material that would irritate the Chinese censors – Buddhist mystics, ghosts and other supernatural apparitions, and Japanese war criminals (potentially seen as 'not so bad' because of their karmic connection to starlet Cecilia Cheung).

The Noir Anti-Hero[19]

Film noir specialises in existential crises of identity visualised through shadowy *mise-en-scène* and extreme, canted angles representing the murkiness of perception and the nightmare of morally divided souls. The noir anti-hero embodies this – hopelessly flawed, violent, morally ambivalent, a seeker of truth who encounters only lies. As improbable as the device of the muscle suit might make this, Big, in point of fact, displays many of the characteristics associated with this classic noir protagonist. Although he has turned his back on temple life, Big continues to search for the 'truth', albeit in the urban gutters of Hong Kong and Shenzhen. He has an intimacy with the nocturnal, seedier side of life (for example, strip clubs, prostitutes), harbours a moral ambivalence (for example, engages in sex work, smokes, drinks), attracts violence, has nihilistic tendencies, and lives as a social outsider disturbed by a past that he cannot seem to transcend. He lives on the wrong side of the law and throws the establishment's darker excesses into sharp relief as a prisoner beaten by the police. Because the legal system proves ineffectual, he takes justice into his own hands and operates outside the law in order to fight crime and attempt to re-establish a modicum of justice in a corrupt society. In this respect, he stands on the cusp between the superhero and the anti-hero. His extraordinary *kungfu* allows him to scale walls, leap from rooftops and apparently defy gravity. He sometimes appears to function more like Superman or Batman, outside the law but within its moral parameters, rather than as the noir anti-hero who remains mired in a world of corruption with little hope of salvation.

Part of what makes *Running on Karma* compelling, in fact, involves the way in which Big's moral ambivalence stays in play throughout the film. Although the narrative establishes the character's apparent 'goodness' at the outset, it depicts Big's moral standing as complicated by more than his immigration status, sex work, taste for cigarettes and liquor, and brushes with the law. As Stephen Teo points out, Big's body concretises this divided nature via the latex suit:

> The body suit thus gives the impression of a denaturalised body which To turned into a narrative advantage. The swollen, denaturalised body removes Big from his inner natural body such that we see the body suit as a transcendental cover enclosing the proverbial garden of the soul, thus emphasizing a discrepancy between body and soul.[20]

Even though Big has turned his back on his Buddhist past, his compassionate core revives when he sees Lee's karma as a threat to an otherwise upright person. He helps her police investigations, saves her from violent death on more than one occasion and, overall, shores up the side of virtue. However, the body suit and what Chris Holmlund might call an 'impossible body'[21] keep the artifice of the film at the forefront and the embrace of Big as heroic in check. Something excessive and exposed in Big inextricably links him to film noir. Joan Copjec observes: 'The noir hero is embarrassed by a visibility that he carries around like an excess body for which he can find no proper place.'[22]

The noir elements of the film, moreover, complicate this picture of Big's virtue. Particularly in neo-noir films that bridge the horror and detective genres,[23] the protagonist can emerge as the villain of the piece (for example, *Angel Heart*, Alan Parker, 1987). Leading a shadowy existence at the edges of society, only Big's unflappable good humour appears to keep the suspicion at bay that he may be on the lam because he, in fact, murdered Jade, a young woman near his monastery. He remains, throughout the film, an inconsistent, divided, often incoherent and somewhat inscrutable character.

As Jameson points out, schizophrenia characterises the post-modern condition as 'an experience of isolated, disconnected, discontinuous material signifiers which fail to link up into a coherent sentence'.[24] Hong Kong's 'one country, two systems' status as well contributes to a general feeling of discontinuity and division in a way that localises the global malaise Jameson describes. *Running on Karma* provides ample evidence that vertiginous alterations in narrative time, space, genre and characterisation mark Hong Kong noir as aesthetically post-modern. Big's character mirrors the shifts from comedy to melodrama, from superhero action to supernatural horror, as well as from *wuxia* chivalry to noir bleakness. Indeed, the darkness at the depths of his character revolves around the fact he is a murderer. Although the plot confirms that he killed a bird rather than a woman, he does confront himself as a killer – on a par with Lee's Japanese war criminal and Sun Ko as his friend Jade's murderer.

Film noir enshrined the doppelgänger as a fixture rooted in the German expressionist sensibilities the European immigrant directors brought with them to Hollywood. The doppelgänger figures in many post-1997 Hong Kong films, including the Milkyway productions *Running Out of Time* (Johnnie To, 1999) and *The Longest Nite* (Patrick Yau Tat-chi, 1998), as well as the *Infernal Affairs* trilogy. In *Running on Karma*, Big strongly resembles the killer Sun Ko. Both find Jade and Lee attractive (presumably sexually). While Big may be inclined to protect his platonic female friends, Sun Ko's desire turns to violence in each case. Given that Sun Ko remains an out-of-focus entity until the very end of the film, *Running on Karma* keeps the imaginative possibility open that Sun Ko may be Big. Although the film limits speculation by including Big's fellow monks' testimony to support their comrade's innocence, Big's intimacy with vice, his violent power, his suspect psychological state and inconsistent behaviour point to a darker possibility.

This haunts Big throughout most of the film and keeps a noir sense of gloom and doubt in play. As Big sees Lee as both the righteous Hong Kong cop and Japanese war criminal, he also sees himself as both the spiritually superior monk and a vengeful, base, sexually depraved killer. A flashback shows Big, maddened by the murder of Jade, striking out at a tree with his staff. A bird falls from the tree, dead, and Big sits in front of its corpse for seven days and nights. The film visualises this with a process shot showing both the sun and the moon in an azure-tinted sky. Even nature appears to contain impossible, schizophrenic contradictions. Big gets up, strips off his monk's robes, and walks away from the tree naked (putting the manufactured muscle suit on display). This epiphany under a tree, of course, alludes to Buddha's enlightenment while meditating under the Bodhi tree; however, in this case, the authenticity of the monk's spiritual malaise vies with the artifice of the filmmaker's kitschy exhibition of ersatz flesh. Noir darkness may be constrained by the uneasy balance of comic excess and a close encounter with the cosmic consciousness of karma, but Big remains a 'killer' nonetheless.

Later, after Lee's murder, Big literally fights a version of himself – a future self who has presumably killed Sun Ko and is spattered with blood. Big confronts his doppelgänger in a cave – psychologically, the dark recesses of the unconscious, spiritually, the depths of the soul – overseen by statues of Buddha. The cave serves as a womb for a psychic rebirth out of the black shadows of noir film conventions. Blooded by a blow from the staff, the two versions

Figure 5.1 'You are the Buddha in my heart.'

of Big tumble out of the cave, throw away the staff, face each other and assume meditative postures. Big articulates this enlightenment as: 'You are the Buddha in my heart' (Figure 5.1).

Big goes back to the tree where he had stripped off his robe after Jade's murder, puts on the tattered garment and walks away again – echoing the earlier scene. Five years later, he finally meets up with Sun Ko and, not surprisingly, they look like twins – with soiled, threadbare robes, scraggy beards and long, matted hair. Big embraces his adversary, leads him back to civilisation and, presumably, incarceration at the village police station. Big, who has reduced in size during his years in the wilderness, so that Andy Lau no longer needs to wear his muscle suit, shaves his beard and his head, accepts a clean monk's robe from the police, takes a cigarette from one cop's pocket, lights it, and walks off towards the camera, a faint smile on his face.

Both noir and the spiritual left behind, the film concludes with the contradictory image of a clean-shaven monk enjoying the inappropriate vice of smoking a cigarette. Big is no longer plagued by vengeful rage or his own darkly violent urges, and the ostensible villain has been peacefully captured; however, the film allows a cynical hint of noir to remain behind in a puff of smoke. Unlike classic noir in which the anti-hero, if not dead, generally carries on as a broken wreck in even worse shape than at the outset, Big has the last laugh – whether this is evidence of the character's 'good' karma or a symbol of Hong Kong cinema's ability to survive various crises remains moot.

The *Femme Fatale*

As many film scholars have noted,[25] women in noir tend to fall into two distinct types – the inaccessible virgin or the *femme fatale*. Frequently, these two types merge into one character, who may appear innocent at the outset and turn villainous at the end, or vice versa. As a product of a generic mix with noir overtones, Lee appears to hover above this dichotomy. Like the classic *femme fatale*, contact with her must be associated with death, and every time Big looks at her he sees her past as a Japanese war criminal. Like all noir characters, Lee carries her past with her as a terrifying burden that impinges on her present life.

Like most noir women, Lee has a knack for luring the protagonist into danger – often against his better judgement. From the opening at the strip club, she serves as Big's most ardent fan as well as a source of trouble. Undercover, Lee cheers on the gyrating Big until he drops his jockstrap and the rest of the squad raid the joint. She proudly stays in place, as the other female spectators scatter, and holds up her police ID. Although on the 'right' side of the law, Lee is duplicitous, and Big runs to escape a woman whose approving glance had encouraged his performance a moment earlier. In this case, Lee's 'bad karma' drew her into a profession that would put her in the line of fire until she could 'atone' for her World War II crimes. As Big soon sees, Lee's past haunts her – literally shown in superimposed images of beheadings – and he reluctantly attempts to save her from her destiny, a clearly futile task.

Unlike the classic noir *femme fatale*, Lee has no conscious access to the past that plagues her. She suffers from war trauma and related guilt at a remove. Only Big, a Mainlander, and her trip to the PRC to sacrifice herself for his sake, connect her to this past and a 'sin' that must be expiated on Mainland Chinese soil. Through Lee, then, the connection between China's historical past and Hong Kong's present becomes part of an allegory of sin, sacrifice and redemption. She functions as a *femme fatale*, but with a difference.

In most classic noir, the *femme fatale* represents the independent woman out of control – manipulative, covetous, aggressive, treacherous and ruthless – the cinematic incarnation of the woman on the home front during World War II working outside the home and far from male supervision. The noir heroine, however, also has a vulnerable side, subject to victimisation again because of the breakdown of male authority. Neo-noir continues to work through the complications of the dramatic changes in women's status in what some call a 'post-feminist' society. Lee embodies some of the ambivalence associated with contemporary career women inside and outside of Asia. She is an independent, single woman who proudly tells Big of her career choice and desire to help her family through her job, and has no problem enjoying her work by encouraging a male stripper to bare it all.

However, after introducing Lee as a legal force antagonistic to Big, the film quickly switches gears. Big sees Lee as 'good', and this becomes an important premise for the narrative, taking Lee away from the duplicitous *femme fatale* of noir and placing her in the other category of the 'good' woman. However, Lee still poses a moral dilemma for Big. As a Buddhist who accepts karma, he should do nothing to save Lee. However, as a compassionate man enamoured of a pretty woman, he has difficulty not intervening to help her. Lee's vulnerability must stay in play to keep the plot in motion. Her strength must be spiritual rather than physical or mental. Lee, in fact, is not a very effective cop, and she displays little talent as a policewoman in the film. Rather, she relies on Big to solve her cases as well as to save her life. In fact, although she has a career, she leaves little behind when she decides to sacrifice herself and accept a violent death as 'punishment' for her former life.

As in most noir films, the heart of the mystery involves a woman and, whether 'good' or 'bad', she draws the protagonist into danger. As the host for the soul of a Japanese war criminal, Lee holds tremendous power that represents unquestionable evil. However, she is also a fragile, young woman, ready to sacrifice herself for a man. Her ostensible independence and the male protagonist's inability to save her may speak to a crisis in traditional gender roles or in patriarchal authority. However, her typically 'feminine' attributes, displayed when she tenderly bandages Big's wrist, patiently waits for him on the sidewalk curb and warmly holds his hand as they walk, uphold a conservative desire to return to more clearly defined and demarcated gender roles. Noir nostalgia extends beyond style to include a yearning for more traditional sex-gender norms coupled to a comforting spirituality associated with established religions.

Lee's severed head swinging in a tree in the wilderness, therefore, speaks to more than the wrapping up of a plot line that demands karmic punishment for past crimes. Noir men may be castrated and unable to exercise masculine authority in a world that has ostensibly stripped them of their former power; that is, prior to the horrors of the atom bomb, the Holocaust, the battlefields of World War II and the emancipation of women. However, noir women suffer a parallel fate. If the men lack balls, the women lose their heads (for example, independent thought, reason, intelligence and individual ambition). It seems important, then, for Big to cradle Jade's bloody head in flashback and caress Lee's headless corpse before he confronts his own violent desires in the narrative (Figure 5.2).

Figure 5.2 The decapitated woman.

The decapitated woman appears to allow the divided man to achieve some illusion of wholeness. Lee's journey leads her to accept her fate as a victim of male violence. The film reiterates her willing acceptance of the necessity of her violent death at several points, so that there can be no doubt about it. Lee tells Big about her plan at a *dai pai dong* (an informal outdoor restaurant), records it on her camcorder and addresses the camera directly to articulate her intentions. Some critics have compared the use of the video diary coupled to the horror of a maniacal killer to *The Blair Witch Project* (Daniel Myrick and Eduardo Sánchez, 1999).[26] However, the inclusion of a motion picture featuring a female author's subjective appraisal of a situation running parallel to the film proper points to an important aspect of *Running on Karma*'s noir self-reflexivity. Noir very often relies on first-person narration, on a limited perspective and on questionable perceptions. Not only are memory, illusion and various psychological states highlighted in noir, but the act of storytelling itself – the reliability of the narrator and, by extension, the filmmaker – comes into question as a fundamental attribute of the form.

Running on Karma includes Big's visions, flashbacks narrated by his spiritual master from the temple and Lee's stories about her life before becoming a cop; however, the video diary and the juxtaposition of past and present that characterises the narrative at its climax offer a particularly telling insight into its gender politics. Lee records her own death as well as the events leading up to her murder, which show the gradual erasure of her identity. As Tong Ching-siu points out: 'The film is clearly a more literal interpretation of the concept of redemption through "self-erasure".'[27] All the points on her journey up the mountain allow her to envision the perspectives of Sun Ko, Jade and Big, while her own identity seems to vanish. She visits the cave where Sun Ko likely lived for a time, pronounces it hell-like and remarks, 'I feel sorry for Sun Ko.' She goes to the edge of the cliff where Big gave up his pursuit of Sun Ko and, surrounded by drifting pollen, catches one piece in her palm. Later, close to the end of the film, this moment appears again and a close-up of her hand releases the pollen into the air.

The image conjures up many possible associations. Given Lee's karmic connection to the Japanese military, it may resonate with the wartime association of soldiers with falling cherry blossoms – beautiful, but dead and doomed to decay, a necessary loss marking the seasons and the promise of the continuation of the cycles of nature from death to rebirth. Her enlightened sacrifice parallels Big's turn away from revenge. The two, of course, operate in tandem with one or the other, leading the spiritual way at various points in the narrative.

This becomes particularly clear when Lee jumps out of a van, blasting techno music, to greet Big when he unexpectedly turns up in Hong Kong to participate in a body-building competition. Out of contact since Big informed Lee of her karmic circumstances, Big does not know what to make of Lee's bright red wig, trendy green clothing and neon fingernail polish. She appears to have taken a page from Big's book and decided to immerse herself in a hedonistic lifestyle. Later, at the competition, Lee reveals that she has been undercover and continues to follow the straight and narrow despite the troubling news of her bad karma. At this point, she tells Big she has decided to sacrifice her life to help him with his quest. Thus, this resignation to a violent fate becomes part of Lee's destiny as a woman. As such, the noir link to the punishment of the *femme fatale* continues to operate.

Wearing the mask of a profligate hussy, Lee plays with the various aspects of her identity as Japanese soldier, Chinese cop, youthful hedonist and sacrificial offering. However, she still sacrifices herself for men – to expiate the 'sins' of the war criminal and to reconcile Big to the loss of Jade, allowing him to step away from revenge. Whether taken as an image of Buddhist compassion or as the embodiment of noir's 'dangerous' female, Lee's severed head may transcend its narrative significance as furthering Big's transformation and moving the plot along. Big's 'castration' (or submission to fate/compassion for life) is shown through the removal of Andy Lau's muscle suit; time passes, his body shrinks, and he can embrace his enemy. However, Lee pays a different price for her acquiescence to the moral order. She loses her head. The visual power of Lee's severed head, in fact, seems to bring noir's violent exoticism and its legacy of Orientalism together in the figure of the alluring, decapitated woman.

Noir Orientalism

As Gordon Slethaug[28] and Joelle Collier[29] have pointed out, one of the abiding characteristics of film noir is its investment in Orientalism. In addition to featuring orientalia in the *mise-en-scène* in the form of Buddhist statues, incense burners, bamboo fixtures and dragon motifs, many noir classics offer excursions to Chinatown or references to characters' past Asian travels as key ingredients of their plots. Most of these references point towards Asia as 'decadent', 'inscrutable', 'occult', 'dangerous', 'inconstant' and 'feminine'. The classic *femme fatale* in films such as *The Lady from Shanghai* generally link the 'evil' part of the Orient's alterity to predatory sexuality. Noir also misreads eastern mysticism as nihilism, fatalism, passivity, diametrically opposed to western humanism, and the realisation of what Freud called 'masochism' or the 'death drive'. Forged during America's Pacific wars with Japan, Korea and, later, Vietnam, classic noir and neo-noir operate alongside discourses featuring the 'Oriental' as victimised, emasculated allies in need of support, and as sub-human vermin in need of extermination.

Drawing liberally on noir elements, *Running on Karma* does not neglect these Orientalist tropes. However, it may not be as easy to see them as such because the film moves these Orientalist fixtures to a Hong Kong/Chinese setting. As Gary Xu observes:

> To scholars of cinema and to Asian audiences, Hong Kong cinema might appear to be transnational, hybrid, and multifaceted, but to Western audiences Hong Kong cinema is singularly Chinese and Oriental.[30]

For the Hong Kong audience, 'Hong Kong' may be secular, modern and rational, while 'China' represents spirituality, irrationality and physical impoverishment. Thus, the world of temple grottoes and ancient stone Buddhas highlights the exotic qualities of 'China' for a domestic Hong Kong as well as a western audience.

Sun Ko and the monks residing at the Grotto Temple represent the extremes of Orientalist configurations of the Mainland. They provide a glimpse of traditional

China that appears to represent Hong Kong's 'surrogate or underground self,'[31] to use a phrase from Edward Said. Sun Ko stands as the embodiment of a China that seems primitive, violent, uncivilised, anti-social and inarticulate. Big's brother monks serve as Sun Ko's antithesis. They represent the transcendental peace and spiritual order of Buddhist asceticism. However, at both extremes, these Mainland representatives remain irrational and beyond the reach of the modern world, and, as such, stand in marked contrast to the materialism of urban Hong Kong. Sun Ko stays mute, while one of the Buddhist masters is blind, and both gesture towards China as limited – subaltern, unable to speak, and blind to the contemporary world. The Mainland may hold the key to spiritual transcendence, but when Big puts a cigarette in his mouth and turns his back on the Chinese police at the end of the film, Andy Lau, a quintessentially Hong Kong star, walks away from the 'Orient', with the cigarette in his lips pointing in a different direction.

This dark Orientalism is not limited to the depiction of Mainland China, however, and Japan and India provide other instances of Hong Kong's 'others' operating as 'underground' versions of an implicitly HKSAR 'self'. They are Mainland China's principal Asian 'others' – China having fought wars with both in the twentieth century – as well as Hong Kong cinema's 'others', boasting two of the region's oldest and largest film industries. The Japanese and South Asian references mark moments of historical trauma – occupation and imperial conquest – that may resonate with the current status of the territory. The reincarnation of a Japanese war criminal in the body of a Hong Kong policewoman re-enacts the 1941 occupation of the colony (echoing, perhaps, the 1997 handover). The criminal investigation of a murder in Hong Kong's Indian community also has historical resonances. The South Asian community has been a fixture in Hong Kong since the colonial period, often associated with the British imperial administration and, particularly, the police and military. As a visibly non-Chinese ethnic minority, they also often suffer from prejudice in Hong Kong.

Big and Lee come together because of an investigation of a murderous feud between two yogi adepts. Big's ability to read karma allows him to connect the yogis to their earlier incarnations as Chinese martial artists, easing the slippage between *kungfu* action and the contortions of the yoga master who hides within tin cans and shopping bags. The Hong Kong woman in the mix had been a beetle who lost a limb during an ancient battle between the two men. The past lives of the two Hong Kong women, then, as an insect and a Japanese war criminal, put them at an added disadvantage. Within the karmic system, they seem – as non-human and inhuman – far from Nirvana. There also seems to be a further connection here between film noir and Asian spirituality. As both noir and Buddhist teachings suggest, appearances are illusory, deceptive and fleeting; the façade of the beautiful woman (the *femme fatale*) contains the soul of an insect or killer.

Much has been made of the 'self-Orientalisation' of China's Fifth Generation filmmakers, and debates on these films continue to rage.[32] However, the same phenomenon may contribute to the perceptual disconnect that Gary Xu notes between Asian and western viewers of Hong Kong films. *Running on Karma*, for example, appears to be 'transnational, hybrid, and multifaceted' as a postmodern mix of genres, narrative complications and character inconsistencies, but also 'singularly Chinese and Oriental' as a Buddhist fable of karma and spiritual redemption, traditional Chinese religious practices and mysticism. The tropes linked to film noir – transcending global film genres but concretising particular character types such as the anti-hero and the *femme fatale*, a dark visual style, and a world view associated with moral ambivalence, cynicism, pessimism – provide another dimension to the film's Orientalism. Film noir brings the contradictory, transnational hybridity of global cinema and the 'singularly Chinese and Oriental' together in film noir in a way that highlights the alterity of Hong Kong's 'others' in the form of Mainland monks and serial killers as well as South Asian yogis.

The Noir Wake-Up Call

Buddhist cosmic consciousness vies with film noir alienation throughout *Running on Karma*. The repeated use of high-angle crane shots to dwarf the characters in the shadowy corridors of Hong Kong streets, for example, could be seen as a cosmic vision of the insignificance of humanity or as a noir distanced perspective that belittles its doomed characters. The camera, in a scene featuring a grotto with stone icons, literally takes the perspective of a Buddhist statue looking down on the characters below it, and this could be interpreted as Buddhist transcendence or noir alienation.

Empty shots punctuate the film. Notably, the depiction of Lee's murder ends with a striking shot of stillness. Sun Ko grabs Lee from behind, while she films the site of Big's epiphany under the tree. Her camcorder flies from her hand, and an image in its viewfinder shows Sun Ko taking up a boulder to strike her at a distance. A cut indicates the continuation of the action without the mediation of the video camera. The final shot in the sequence displays Lee's severed head hanging in the tree out of focus with the video camera on the ground and only a green shoot in focus – small and thin – in the foreground. Nature – green and promising rebirth – provides a visibly sharp reminder of the impermanence of human life – even when 'mummified', as André Bazin might say, through motion picture technology. The human head hangs out of focus in the depths of the shot. This image, empty of living human beings, resonates with film noir's anti-humanist, nihilistic undercurrents, but it also visually and viscerally reiterates a tenet of Buddhist philosophy regarding the impermanence of human life and the individual's relative insignificance within the cosmos.

Big locates Lee's body by following the sound of her watch, and the chronometer's alarm also signals the filmmakers' awareness of popular crime clichés. Justin Lin's *Better Luck Tomorrow* (2002) opens with the sound of a beeper going off in the backyard of a suburban home where a corpse has been buried hastily. In an episode of the television show *Columbo* (1971–2003), entitled 'Columbo Cries Wolf' (1990), the detective finds the corpse by following the sound of a beeper-watch. In other words, the alarm watch has cinematic antecedents that prevent it from being taken as 'new'. The intra-textual association of the watch with Lee's longing for Big and her tragic fate vies with the hackneyed intertextual connection that reduces it to a used and recycled bit of cinematic business.

In *Running on Karma*, the alarm sounds as 'dead time', announcing the location of her corpse, showing where the body is buried. Karmic cycles move into generic cycles, and the watch, too, figures as a significant element in many of Johnnie To and Wai Ka-fai's films as well as in the work of Hong Kong auteurs such as Wong Kar-wai and Tsui Hark. The marking of Hong Kong's time as a colony before the 1997 change in sovereignty explains the obsessive interest in timepieces at one level; however, the concern with marking time characterises post-modern concerns with history, memory, nostalgia and amnesia more generally. Accelerated and obsessive, disorienting and forgotten, new technologies and current labour practices mark time differently than in the pre-digital, Fordist, industrialised economy of the past. Esther Yau notes that this 'anachronistic temporality' disrupts the 'empty time of a world city': 'anachronistic time provokes a sense of accountability for the injustices and unfulfilled expectations of the past, and a respect for justice toward humans already dead or not yet alive'.[33] The 'dead time' associated with the buried watch, then, links it to Jameson's 'political unconscious'. History has been buried, but corpses have a way of being resurrected and bringing with them the traumas that refuse to remain underground. The alarm watch links *Running on Karma* to contemporary global culture as well as situating it within Hong Kong cinema and, specifically, within the To–Wai oeuvre.

In the classic noir *Sunset Boulevard* (Billy Wilder, 1950), Joe Gillis (played by William Holden, star of Hollywood–Hong Kong fantasies *The World of Suzie Wong* [Richard Quine, 1960] and *Love is a Many-Splendored Thing* [Henry King,

1955]) gets trapped on his way out of the decaying Hollywood mansion owned by Norma Desmond (Gloria Swanson) by the chain of his pocket watch. Time never seems to be on the side of the noir anti-hero. In *Running on Karma*, 'bad timing' and 'bad karma' mark a cultural and aesthetic common ground between film noir and Asian culture. Noir tropes link the film to the cinematic past, allow it to speak to the present, and travel beyond the borders of Hong Kong or the Asia market. Film noir as a dark indictment of post-war society or a cynical vision of human depravity speaks to world cinema. As an element in the multicultural mix that characterises the oeuvre of Hong Kong filmmakers such as Johnnie To and Wai Ka-fai, it allows *Running on Karma* to differentiate itself from Mainland Chinese films and speak across the European/Hollywood art film/commercial entertainment divide.

However, given that film noir only figures as an element of a much more elaborate pastiche of world cinema in *Running on Karma*, the use of noir conventions appears to be quite self-conscious and strategic. Noir allows for the expression of a mood related to global/local affairs, from economic downturns to crises in gender identities, and operates as a cinematic shorthand that speaks to the HKSAR–PRC border. Misogyny, Orientalism, cynicism and paranoia get thrown into the mix as well, complicating the ideological picture and allowing darker images to rub against the film's comic encounters, martial arts action and superhero fantasies. If noir has always been associated with crises inside and outside of film culture, then *Running on Karma* complicates the 'political unconscious' of noir even further by refusing any sense of aesthetic 'purity' of form. Given the uncertainties of the marketplace for Hong Kong film, as well as the various crises connected to Hong Kong as a place, the dramatic variations in tone, generic plurality and inconsistencies in form speak to the historical moment as well as imaginatively move beyond it with a wink, a nod, and a puff on Andy Lau's cigarette.

Notes

1. See, for example, Rist, 'Scenes of "in-Action" and Noir Characteristics in the Films of Johnnie To (Kei-Fung)', pp. 159–63. To's affinity for French-inflected noir (for example, Jean-Pierre Melville) is also noted in Ingham, *Johnnie To Kei-Fung's* PTU. Ingham also notes To's affinity for the noir works of Japanese director Kurosawa Akira. For an appraisal of the western critical reception of Johnnie To, see Jost, 'The Rise of Johnnie To': http://www.hkcinemagic.com/fr/pdf/The-Rise-of-Johnnie-To-Marie-Jost-HKCinemagic-PDF-version.pdf (last accessed 15 January 2015).
2. For definitions of noir, see Silver and Ursini (eds), *Film Noir Reader*. Silver and Ursini have also collaborated on other collections of key critical essays on film noir.
3. Collier, 'The Noir East', p. 138. For another consideration of Hong Kong cinema in relation to Asian Noir, see Lee, 'The Shadow of Outlaws in Asian Noir', pp. 118–35.

4. Jameson, *The Political Unconscious*, p. 20.
5. Ibid., p. 102.
6. Hammond and Wilkins, *Sex and Zen and a Bullet in the Head*, pp. 127–8.
7. See Van den Troost, 'The Hong Kong Crime Film'. For more on the global dimensions of film noir (including its impact on Hong Kong film), see Fay and Nieland, *Film noir*.
8. Naremore, *More than Night*, p. 228.
9. Yau, 'The Spirits of Capital and Haunting Sounds', pp. 249–62.
10. For more on the demonstrations against Article 23, see the website created by the *Hong Kong Human Rights Monitor* dedicated to the controversy surrounding the proposed amendment: http://www.article23.org.hk/english/main.htm (last accessed 14 January 2015).
11. Žižek, '"The Thing That Thinks"', p. 199.
12. For a discussion of the reworking of *The Lady from Shanghai* in *The Longest Nite*, see Collier, 'The Noir East'.
13. See my reading of the trilogy in Marchetti, *Andrew Lau and Alan Mak's* Infernal Affairs – The Trilogy.
14. For more on the similarities between *Running on Karma* and *Infernal Affairs*, see Leary, 'What Goes around, Comes around': http://www.sensesofcinema.com/2004/feature-articles/infernal_affairs_ii/ (last accessed 15 January 2015). For more on the depiction of 'karma' in films made after 1997, see Lee, *Hong Kong Cinema Since 1997*. For a consideration of 'karma' as part of Wai Ka-fai's oeuvre, see Longtin, 'The Buddha's Gaze', pp. 88–9.
15. Austen, 'CSB Interviews Johnnie To': http://www.cinemastrikesback.com/?p=1470 (last accessed 15 January 2015).
16. Ho, 'Can Hollywood Afford to Make Films China Doesn't Like?': http://content.time.com/time/world/article/0,8599,2072194,00.html (last accessed 15 January 2015).
17. One of the classics of noir cinema is entitled *Out of the Past* (Jacques Tourneur, 1947).
18. Hong Kong is also haunted by the ghosts of the Japanese Occupation in Ann Hui's *Spooky Bunch* (1980).
19. For more on noir masculinity, see Krutnik, *In a Lonely Street*.
20. Teo, *Director in Action*, p. 165.
21. Holmlund, *Impossible Bodies*.
22. Copjec, 'Introduction', p. ix.
23. For more on the 'gothic' noir, see Morgan, 'Reconfiguring Gothic Mythology', pp. 74–86.
24. Jameson, 'Postmodernism and the Consumer Society', p. 119.
25. See the essays collected in Kaplan (ed.), *Women in Film noir*.
26. *The Blair Witch* connection is mentioned in Nix, '*Running on Karma* (2003) Movie Review': http://www.beyondhollywood.com/running-on-karma-2003-movie-review (last accessed 20 January 2015).
27. Tong, 'Notes on Wai Ka-Fai's Narratives of Redemption', pp. 94–6.

28. Slethaug, 'The Exotic and Oriental as Decoy', pp. 161–84. For more on Orientalism and film noir, see Loza, 'Orientalism and Film Noir: (Un)Mapping Textual Territories and (En)Countering the Narratives', pp. 161–74.
29. Collier, 'The Noir East'.
30. Xu, *Sinascape: Contemporary Chinese Cinema*, p. 135.
31. Said, *Orientalism*, p. 3.
32. See Chow, *Primitive Passions*. See also Chu, 'The Importance of Being Chinese', pp. 183–206.
33. Yau, 'The Spirits of Capital and Haunting Sounds', p. 255.

Chapter 6
Beyond Hypothermia: Cool Women Killers in Hong Kong Cinema

David Desser

We should not be overly surprised that, given the long tradition of female warriors in Hong Kong martial arts cinema, we find modern-day women among the ranks of killers. Yet, given this very tradition, it is perhaps a bit surprising that we do not find more of them. In a global context we note that on a typical web-based fan site of the 'The Top 100 Hitman/Assassin Films of All Time', only thirteen movies feature women assassins and in a couple of them they are part of an ensemble.[1] However, we find enough of them spread throughout the modern-day filmic *jianghu* to make it worth our while to examine this image.

What we will also see is the inherently transnational character of the female assassin films. This is not just to chalk this up to distribution demands – the need for Hong Kong cinema to have overseas markets. While that is certainly the case for many films produced with the obvious intention of garnering overseas appeal, other films manage to do this by trading on Hong Kong itself – its own image, its own cinema – as a globalised site. To say that there is a clearly staked-out Hong Kong 'brand' is to state what is by now well known. To state also that this brand has become somewhat diluted by influence and imitation, not to mention the exchange of personnel between Hong Kong and overseas cinemas, is also to note that Hong Kong cinema has long participated in a chain of transnational borrowings and has always had the need to reinvent itself to account for its own success. The female assassin, then, should be seen in the context of such films made within other globalised cinematic sites: Hollywood, Japan, France. And thus we have the need to trace this fascinating figure through its many incarnations, keeping a watchful eye on Hong Kong in the process.

It is likely that the figure of the woman assassin first appears in the James Bond films. She is, of course, merely a supporting player, a temporary obstacle in Bond's quest to eradicate the latest global threat. Many Bond villainesses attempt to seduce Bond into a trap; they are not, however, the actual assassins (for example, Bonita in *Goldfinger* [Guy Hamilton, 1964], Fiona Volpe in *Thunderball* [Terence Young, 1965]). Helga Brandt in *You Only Live Twice* (Lewis Gilbert, 1967) is closer to the archetypal female assassin, pretending to fall in love with Bond only to try to kill him. However, she also tends to be more laughable than lethal. Let us take the figure of Grace Jones' May Day in *A View to a Kill* (John Glen, 1985). Her efforts to crush Bond between her powerful thighs may be an obvious symbol of the fear of women's sexuality, but it nevertheless speaks to some of the deep-seated ambivalence felt towards this figure. Jones' androgyny and stature similarly speak to the ambiguities of a woman taking on a role more usually, if we may not say, traditionally, reserved for the male. By 1995, with Famke Janssen in the role of Xenia Onatopp in *GoldenEye* (Martin Campbell), the figure of the beautiful but deadly *femme fatale* was well-established in world cinema.

It is fairly well known that the James Bond films had a significant impact on the Hong Kong Mandarin cinema. The inherently transnational character of the Bond films was reproduced in *Asia-Pol* (1967), directed by Matsuo Akinori under the Chinese pseudonym Mak Chi-woh. A co-production between Shaw Brothers and Japan's Nikkatsu Studios, the film boasted Japanese locales and a number of Nikkatsu's major stars, including Shishido Jo as the villain and Asaoka Ruriko as the Miss Moneypenny equivalent. Jimmy Wang Yu, soon to be catapulted into the rank of superstar with the release of *One-Armed Swordsman* (Chang Cheh, 1967) a month after this film, plays the James Bond equivalent and Shaws' attractive Fang Ying plays a sister he never knew he had. *Inter-Pol*, released just one month later, also had a pseudonymous Japanese director at its helm in the form of Nakahira Ko, credited as Yeung Shu-hei. Tang Ching, a handsome and versatile star, plays Agent 009 (the Chinese title translates as 'Special Agent 009'); Shaws' glamorous star Margaret Tu Chuan plays the villainous leader of a counterfeiting ring; and the stunning Tina Chin Fei lends sex appeal to this glossy reworking of the James Bond myth.

However, there was already a screen Agent 009 in Hong Kong released at the very beginning of 1967, one perhaps unjustly forgotten in the rush-to-judgement that claims Shaws was male-dominated at this time, in the form of the *yanggang* films of Chang Cheh. In this distaff version of James Bond, Agent 009 was portrayed in the comely form of Lily Ho Li-li, who must infiltrate a gang of master criminals. Tang Ching presages his role as 009 by playing Dark Angel C7, sexpot Fanny Fan Lai is Dark Angel B1 and the always-welcome Tina Chin Fei is the villainess in tight dresses. *Angel with the Iron Fists*

(1967), directed by Lo Wei, was successful enough to warrant a sequel, *The Angel Strikes Again* (1968), with Lo Wei again directing Lily Ho.

Without doubt the most outrageous of all Mandarin films in the James Bond mode was *Temptress of a Thousand Faces* (Jeng Cheong-woh, aka Cheng Chang-ho, 1969). The Korean Jeng brings a sense of sheer pleasure to this film that is closer perhaps to the 1960s television classic *Mission: Impossible* (1966–73) than to the Bond films, with its villainous temptress a master of masks. Things get positively giddy when protagonist Ji Ying poses as the temptress, who then decides to pose as her, leading at one point to a fight between identical Ji Yings in the form of a partially undressed Tina Chin. Jeong's more familiar *Five Fingers of Death* (aka *King Boxer*, 1972) is presaged here in the use of a musical motif that accompanies the action scenes.

The most interesting of the Mandarin movies is *The Lady Professional* (1971). Lily Ho again stars under the direction of Matsuo Akinori in this, the second and final film he directed at Shaws. First off, it borrows the title of a Cantonese series of action-women films, and second, it takes pains to demonstrate why the female assassin (the translation of the Chinese title *Nushashou*) undertakes her assignments to kill. This is the closest a Hong Kong film will come for three decades to having an actual 'woman killer' as the sympathetic protagonist.

Temptress of a Thousand Faces and *The Lady Professional* are well known to fans of Hong Kong cinema. Not so a number of Cantonese-dialect films made just prior to and at the same time as the Mandarin-language movies. Given the nature of the Cantonese industry at the time, the films were highly responsive to their female-dominated audience, made with very low budgets on very short shooting schedules. These films quickly came to be dubbed 'Jane Bond' movies and they far exceed in number what was produced in the bigger-budget, colour films of the Shaw Brothers Studio. The action-woman within a kind of Bond-like universe of gadgets, gizmos and good-heartedness was presaged by *The Story of Wong Ang the Heroine* (Yam Pang-nin, 1960).

> The pulp fiction series 'Oriole, The Flying Heroine', which originated in Shanghai in the 1940s and remained popular in Hong Kong in the 1960s, was a major influence on the Jane Bond films, its titled heroine a precursor of the quick-witted, fast-fisted, and good-hearted Jane. *The Story of Wong Ang the Heroine*, adapted from the series before Hollywood's James Bond tidal wave, provides an interesting study on the impact of the 007 craze on Hong Kong popular culture.[2]

The beloved, oft-cited and remade *The Black Rose* (1965), directed by the talented Chor Yuen and starring three of Cantonese cinema's greatest stars, Patrick Tse Yin, Nam Hung and Connie Chan Po-chu, is often credited as initiating the Jane Bond cycle, though it is the story of two sisters and their Robin Hood-like penchant for thievery of the rich and giving to the poor. Esther Yau notes the similarities not to James Bond, but to Batman. A masked and caped-figure, the Black Rose is a kind of urban vigilante; a person from the wealthy class, she possesses the 'forms of mobility and the plentitude of resources'[3] that characterise Bruce Wayne as Batman. Though Yau sees the film as essentially conservative, compared to film noir's radical underpinnings, it does rely on a certain cynicism and questioning of society.[4] With its night-time action, the film obviously recalls the essence of film noir, though given the rapidity with which Cantonese films were produced and the very low budgets with which they had to operate, the expressionistic, Rembrandt-like lighting of noir is absent. *Spy With My Face* (1966), a sequel to *The Black Rose*, further set the Jane Bond genre on its course.

> Director Chor Yuen, emboldened by the success of the original, takes the Bond influence up a notch. The arch villain is not just a crooked businessman, but the head of a powerful crime syndicate, lording over an army of thugs while headquartering in a secret hideout equipped with an endless array of high/low-tech devices. Connie Chan Po-chu, with her embodiment of both the fairy Jade Girl and the fierce fighting woman, eclipses Nam Hung as the film's true star, establishing herself as the Jane Bond prototype.[5]

Though the film is more comic and outrageous than *Black Rose*, more Bond-like in its use of gimmicks and gadgets, it also, unusually, features a moment in which the heroine kills the bad guy.[6] In fact, all of the films in this cycle were less Jane Bond and more film noir – it's just that Bond had more cachet at that historical juncture.

The year 1966 also saw *The Dark Heroine Muk Lan-fa* (aka *The Black Musketeer 'F'*, Law Chi; her name is a variation of the Chinese characters used for Hua Mulan as in films like *The Story of Hua Mulan* [Chan Pei and Gu Wenzong, 1951] and *Lady General Hua Mulan* [Yue Feng, 1964], just scrambling them up in a different order). The title character is based on a popular series of pulp fiction written by martial arts novelist and scriptwriter I Kuang, who wrote many of Chang Cheh and Chor Yuen's martial arts films. The action direction of this film boasts the most significant team of martial arts directors of the era, Lau Kar-leung (aka Liu Chia-liang) and Tong Gai. The unjustly forgotten Suet Nei portrays the title character, supported by Kenneth Tsang Kong, Roy Chiao Hung and the redoubtable Sek Kin in a typically villainous role. Although Lan-fa begins as a Black Rose-style cat-burglar, when she is recruited by a secret police organisation she leaves her Robin Hood activities behind to fight major, world-class criminals. Two more films would follow, first in 1966 and then a year later.

But it was Connie Chan Po-Chu, perhaps the most important of the 'Seven Princesses of the Cantonese Cinema' (certainly along with Josephine Siao Fong-fong), who would most particularly embody the Jane Bond figure. In 1966 she would make four more such films, the first of which, *Lady Bond* (aka *Chivalrous Girl*, Mok Hong-see), possesses the Chinese title of *Nushashou* (female assassin), the film from which *The Lady Professional* took its title. Connie is most assuredly not a female assassin; 'Chivalrous Girl' is a far better title. Still a teenager, Connie is more pop-star cute than James Bond deadly. Nevertheless, this veteran of martial arts films was a convincing action star and the *nushashou* would become something of a signature role for her with films like *Return of Lady Bond* (Mok Hong-see, 1966); *Lady in Distress: The Invincible Fighter* (aka *Dragnet of the Law*, Mok Hong-see, 1967), which featured in a bit part David Chiang Da-wei, soon to be a superstar in the Mandarin martial arts cinema under director Chang Cheh; and *The Flying Killer* (aka *The Perilous Rescue*, *Chivalrous Girl in the Air*, Mok Hong-see, 1967). All these films had fight choreography by Lau Kar-leung and Tong Gai, and they all use the *nushashou* Chinese characters in their titles. Chan would also in 1966 make *Lady Black Cat* (Chiang Wai-kwong, 1966) for the Daai Chi Company, which had a nice run of films in the mid-1960s specialising (though not exclusively) in female actioners, including *Lady Black Cat Strikes Again* (aka *The Wild Black Cat, Part Two*, Chiang Wai-kwong, 1967). Yet another Jane Bond-style film in 1966 was *Girl Detective 001* (Lung To).

One thing about Connie Chan and the Cantonese cinema itself was that it was prone to making films fast and cheap; perennially under-funded and almost totally dependent on the Hong Kong market, filmmakers had little choice. Thus Connie would make thirty-two films in 1967 (not an unprecedented number for an actor in a single year; for example, see Kwan Tak-hing in 1956). Many of these films continued the Jane Bond image and action: *The Black Killer* (aka *Dangerous Appointment*, Chiang Wai-kwong, 1967) from the Daai Chi Company is one of the most important of these films, presaging the Japanese films of a few years later. Here, Sek Kin portrays a gang boss who has kidnapped Connie's uncle. She goes undercover as a young tough and successfully gains his trust until the inevitable moment of revelation and betrayal.[7] Once again the action choreography was handled by Lau Kar-leung and Tong Gai. Other action-women movies of 1967 for Connie include *She's So Brave!* (aka *The Heroine*, Ling Yun); *The Black Swan* (Ling Yun); *A Death Pass*, directed by Chor Yuen; *The Golden Swallow* (Chiang Wai-kwong) for the Daai Chi Company (not to be confused with the 1968 film of the same English title by Chang Cheh); and *Lady with a Cat's Eyes* (aka *Cat-Eyed Beauty*, Law Chi), in which Chan is actually a secret agent who works with Kenneth Tsang Kong. She would portray a secret agent again at the end of the Jane Bond cycle (and the temporary end of the Cantonese cinema) in 1970 with *Secret Agent No. 1* (Tso Tat-wah). The film boasts an all-star cast in support of Connie Chan in the famous forms of Walter Tso Tat-wah (who also directed), Wong Fei-hung himself, Kwan Tak-hing, Nancy Sit Ka-yin, Lui Kei, Suet Nei and Lydia Shum Tin-ha.

Josephine Siao would also get in on the action with her Jane Bond-type films in 1967, including *The Lady Killer* (aka *Bat Girl*, Wong Fung) with Sek Kin and Lydia Shum; *Lightning Killer* (Chiang Wai-kwong); *The Professionals* (aka *Golden Gull*, Chan Man) with action direction by Lau Kar-leung and Tong Gai, and co-starring Patrick Tse-yin, Lau Kar-Leug, Tong Gai, Lau Kar-wing (aka Liu Chia-yung) and Yuen Woo-ping, made by the very important Kong Ngee company; and *The Golden Cat* (Chiang Wai-kwong) for the Daai Chi Company. Though some of the films of Suet Nei, Connie Chan and Josephine Siao have been resurrected for showings in Hong Kong, they remain little known and, more to the point, had little direct influence. A film like *The Black Killer* might presage the Japanese films to come, but whether it made an impact outside Hong Kong is unlikely. More likely might be the Mandarin-language *The Lady Professional*, considering that Shaw Brothers had a relationship with some of the major Japanese studios and that the film's director was Japanese. However, by this point, East, South and South-east Asia had become enamoured of martial arts movies and the slick modern films were quickly becoming strictly local commodities.

Global Assassins

The hitwoman, the female assassin as the central protagonist, is introduced into world cinema by Luc Besson in 1990 with his protean French film, *Nikita*. Remade as a Hong Kong film, an American film and two North American television series, Besson's film demonstrated the global efficacy of the various motifs that go into the production of the female assassin. This is not to say that the female assassin as the central protagonist had no precursors. Any Asian cultist knows the infamous *Zero Woman: Red Handcuffs* (Noda Yukio, 1974). Starring Sugimoto Miki, a fashion model whose film career lasted barely more than half a decade in the 1970s, *Zero Woman: Red Handcuffs* belongs to a specifically Japanese genre known as 'pinky violence'. These Toei-produced films give their women much more agency than typical exploitation films, and the sex and violence is just as likely to be initiated by the women as by any would-be gangster or male rival.[8] Unlike so many of the pinky violence films which feature a violent *sukeban* (girl gang boss), *Zero Woman* focuses on a cop. Imprisoned for the revenge killing of a diplomat, she is freed by a secret governmental agency in order to track down the kidnapped daughter of a powerful political figure. She is given explicit orders to rescue the girl and kill the kidnappers. It is this disjunction between her earlier revenge killing which netted her a prison term and the official sanction to track down and kill the gang members that is part of the noir world of hypocrisy, corruption and easy violence. The noir setting is quite apparent as 'Rei pursues her prey into a neon-lit nocturnal Tokyo underworld of night clubs and noodle joints . . .'[9] Due to its extreme content the film had little overseas distribution, awaiting the era of home video for its subsequent cult fandom.

For the knowledgeable Tom Mes, *Zero Woman* provides the foundation for Besson's *La Femme Nikita*: '[she] is saved from the gallows and forced to become an agent for the top secret Division Zero of the Tokyo police department'.[10] What is new in the original *Zero Woman* film, and which Besson's film and its remakes take up, is that the killer woman is the central protagonist. In the Besson film she undergoes a transformative process, becoming a *femme fatale*, a deadly woman, for a shadowy governmental agency, and in that sense she loses her own agency, that is, her identity, however repulsive or marginal it might once have been. It is this transformation of identity, the moulding of a young woman into something different, that is most striking in this and subsequent hitwoman films. It is a motif not present in classic hitman films like *Le Samourai* (Jean-Pierre Melville, 1967), *The Mechanic* (Michael Winner, 1972), *The Killer* (John Woo, 1989) or Besson's own *Leon* (aka, *Leon: The Professional*, 1994). These hitmen come to us fully formed. But the women must be transformed.

We see this transformation, this moulding, of the girl or young woman into a killer not just in the direct remakes of *Nikita*, but in film after film featuring the female assassin. This motif is ubiquitous to the point where it reveals the heart of the issue with the figure of the hitwoman. The fully formed hitman is no surprise; he may not require any backstory at all, let alone the kind of extensive training sequences found in the female variation. It is as if the male propensity for violence and killing is a given, an innate characteristic. But a woman needs some kind of (re)training. There is something far more duplicitous in the image of the classic *femme fatale* than in something like a traitor among men, precisely because we imagine a woman to be more honest, more natural, than a man. The idea that a person who could be a lover or a mother is in fact a killer strikes an elemental chord of fear, especially in men (and perhaps a delightful *frisson* in women). And that is why so many female assassin films, especially those from Asia, also include elements of nudity, sex and lesbianism – common exploitation elements to be sure, but in this case those that strike deeply into the ambiguous heart of the genre.

No less important to the genre, and another motif that speaks to and redresses the gender confusion and imbalance of the hitwoman, is her rejection of her assassin's life once she falls in love. Out in the world, she keeps her life a secret, especially when she falls in love with an ordinary man. But once she does, she comes to desire the prosaic life: marriage, children and the mundane. Even in films like *Nikita* and *Point of No Return* (the 1993 American remake by John Badham), where the violent *femmes* had no middle-class life previous to their transformation, bourgeois values and lifestyle become their fondest desires. This, too, works to contain their killer selves, as if all women must desire nothing so much as romantic love followed by the joys of homemaking. The transformation of the young woman into a trained killer and her redemption by bourgeois marriage become the twin pillars of the genre.

In the wake of *Nikita* and *Point of No Return* we find the concept of the 'Zero Woman' (Rei is her name, but 'rei' also means zero in Japanese) revived in the 1990s, first as a theatrical film in 1995, then as low-budget straight-to-video entries thereafter, with five in all in the '90s. Tom Mes notes:

> In an example of cinema's inherently transnational nature (not to mention a great deal of irony) the idea to dust off the concept of [the original *Zero Woman*] was most likely influenced by the international success of . . . *La Femme Nikita*, a film that made female assassins a temporary hot topic . . . *Zero Woman* was Japan's attempt to jump onto the bandwagon, adding more than a touch of S&M (in what could be read as a nod to the delightfully insane ero-guro works of Teruo Ishii, the first straight-to-video *Zero Woman* pits its heroine against a bondage-fetishist dwarf in a torture dungeon) but little in the way of inspiration.[11]

It might or might not be 'inspiration', but in each entry the Zero Woman assassin working for a secret group within the Tokyo Police Department is played by a different actress. The important motif of lesbianism is apparent in *Zero Woman: Dangerous Game* (Takahara Hidekazu, 1998), where Rei falls in love with a gangster's mistress whom she is assigned to protect. The lesbianism is rather overt with a love scene between the two women – handled quite delicately, especially for a 'B' movie whose intended audience would be happy to see a longer, more explicit scene.

Contemporaneous with the revival of the 'Zero Woman' was another exploitation video, produced by Toei Video Company, but one rather nicely done with an interesting regional flavour to it. *Beautiful Beast* (Ikeda Toshiharu, 1995) focuses on a half-Japanese, half-Chinese woman from the Mainland who goes to Japan seeking revenge on the yakuza boss who had her sister killed. In addition to the yakuza boss, Ran, known as the Black Orchid, also discovers that a Taiwanese triad leader is implicated in her sister's murder. She is provided with a backstory, if an unlikely one. Nevertheless, we come to know how she came to be so deadly: she served as a Red Army commando, fought as a guerrilla in Afghanistan, and now works for the 'Untouchables', a triad group in Hong Kong.

Shooting on video with low budgets and only marginally skilled, if beautiful, actresses enabled Toei to release a spate of films in a kind of 'Beautiful' (*utsukushiki*) cycle. Replete with plenty of nudity, violence and action sequences, the films gave the 'girls with guns' cycle some of its proudest moments. Among them surely is *Beautiful Killing Machine* (Hara Takahito, 1996). Its female protagonist has the unlikely name of Cheryl, a former assassin-turned-bodyguard whose latest protectee is a jewel thief from Hong Kong, the target of killers who want the cache of diamonds she stole. When Cheryl kills them all, the gang sends the invincible Owl after her. As in so many of these killer-women films, Cheryl's past is revealed to us in order that we may understand how things came to pass. In this case, there is a plot twist that is unique in the genre, and if it helps us understand how she can be so tough in her numerous fight sequences, it also (literally) blurs the gender distinctions that are central to the killer-women genre. For Cheryl, it turns out, used to be a kick-boxer – a male kick-boxer. She fell in love with another male kick-boxer and underwent gender reassignment in order to make love to him. The film does not use a transgender actress, but still this plot point throws into relief the issues of gender, femininity and masculinity that the female-assassin film relies on.

Hong Kong got in on the female-killer film almost immediately following the international success of *Nikita*. *Black Cat* (Stephen Shin Gei-yin, 1991) is a direct remake, and although one could spend some time on the differences – Catherine, who starts the film living in upstate New York, is more mature than Nikita; the film spends more time on her problems and degradation before becoming an assassin (the first twenty minutes of a ninety-minute film); she has a microchip implanted in her brain in order to improve her skills and to better control her – the similarities are striking. The most important of these is what Besson also brought to the fore: the inherently bourgeois values of the female assassin. We see that as soon as she falls in love she wants to abandon her life of killing. This may speak to the ambiguity at the heart of the genre, too. Heterosexual normativity acts as some kind of 'cure' for the non-feminine side of the woman; marriage will tame her wild side. *Nikita*, *Black Cat* and Hollywood's *Point of No Return* all insist on this motif and it will obtain throughout the genre as it does in a major Hollywood film like *Long Kiss Goodnight* (Renny Harlin, 1996). In *Black Cat*, Catherine does not abandon her assassin ways. Knowing that the CIA will kill her lover, she does it herself – or so her superiors think. We see that he has survived, although she goes away with Brian, her handler.

Black Cat has no Hong Kong locales: shot primarily in Canada, with one sequence in New York City and one in Japan, it also relies strongly on English. (As often happens in Asian films, the English speakers are drawn from the US, the UK and Australia without regard for logic and they are generally poor actors.) On the one hand, the use of English and non-Hong Kong spaces may be justified by the fact that Erica, née Catherine, is employed by the CIA. On the other hand, this removal of the film and its characters from Hong Kong suggests Deleuze and Guattari's concept of 'deterritorialisation'.[12] In the transformation from Catherine to Erica we see something of the fluid and weakened nature of human subjectivity in advanced capitalist cultures, a motif taken up even more strongly in *Black Cat 2* (Stephen Shin Gei-yin, 1992). Here Erica has a new microchip implanted in her brain intended to wipe clean her previous memories; and with its Russia-set story, the process of deterritorialisation is complete. The issue of memory and identity is a cognisant of this in the uncoupling of culture from its originary point. Here we might also invoke Anthony Giddens and the concept of 'disembedding'. Giddens writes: 'By disembedding I mean the "lifting out" of social relations from local contexts of interaction and their restructuring across indefinite spans of time-space.'[13]

Deterritorialisation in terms of geography and identity is very much apparent in the nearly hysterical *Naked Killer* (Clarence Fok Yiu-leung, 1992), the first effort from Wong Jing's Workshop Ltd. Wong Jing is both notorious among Hong Kong film fans and something of a cult figure. He went all out for this effort, both following and extending the female-killer film form. As a result, the film is a cult favourite. Like many cult films, one wouldn't say it was particularly good, and some might say it's so bad that it's good, but for our purposes it reveals the dark heart of the formula.

One could rattle off the motifs that producer-writer Wong Jing includes. The heroine, Kitty (an obvious derivation of 'Cat'), is a wild child of the streets who demonstrates a talent for killing men who have tried to molest her; she is taken under the wing of Sister Cindy, an older trained killer who shows Kitty some of the tricks of the trade while trying to seduce her; when Kitty is ready she gets a new identity, though here the use of a relationship with Tinam, who meets her after her transformation, prevents her from slipping into a new mental space. In opposition to Kitty and Cindy there is Princess, a lesbian trained by Cindy, and her Japanese lover, Baby, also an assassin. Kitty's relationship with Tinam gives her pause regarding her newly acquired skills.

This structural breakdown gives no indication of the over-the-top action sequences – which are typical Hong Kong-style constructivism but whose average shot length is under three seconds – and the rather explicit sex scenes, both hetero and lesbian. Indeed, in one sequence the film cuts between the love-making of Tinam and Kitty and Princess and Baby. The film certainly justified its Category III rating (it is rated 'R' in the US and '18' in the UK), and it is a bit surprising to see such relatively graphic sex and nudity in a Hong Kong film. Such a surprise also apparently was the case with co-star Carrie Ng Ka-lai. In every scene she is wearing long gloves, which may make the lesbian sex a bit kinkier, but was supposedly due to her discomfort simulating the sex.[14] A needlessly apocalyptic ending does nothing so much as seem to preclude the possibility of a sequel. This being Hong Kong and its commercially driven cinema, however, Wong Jing found a way: he simply co-starred Simon Yam Tat-wah and Chingmy Yau Suk-ching in a film called *Naked Killer 2: Raped by an Angel* (Andrew Lau Wai-keung, 1993) and a series was off and running. Further entries dispensed with the 'Naked Killer' sobriquet and stuck with 'Raped by an Angel'. All made in the late 1990s, none features a female assassin.

A Taste of Killing and Romance (Veronica Chan Jing-yee, 1994), which features superstars Andy Lau and Anita Yuen, deserves more space than can be devoted to it here. Suffice to say that its dual protagonists are both hired assassins who fall in love, but whose professions are unbeknown to the other. (In its basic plot it might look forward to the later Hollywood blockbuster

Mr and Mrs Smith [Doug Liman, 2005], but this later film is played for laughs, a kind of explosive screwball Comedy of Remarriage.) This gives the film a chance to explore not only the bourgeois desires of the hitwoman, but also the man. Their desire to leave their old life behind comes up against hired killers who have no such ideals. This is the only female-killer film directed by a woman and is, in fact, the only film Veronica Chan directed. Stylish and stylised in a way that looks forward to the best of Johnnie To and Alan Mak Siu-fai (whose *A War Named Desire* [2000] features an unusual turn for Gigi Leung in a major supporting role as a cool and collected killer who falls, gently, for Francis Ng's ex-triad member now living in Thailand), one wonders what is responsible for the truncated career of a talented woman.

Her Name is Cat, directed by the inimitable Clarence Fok in 1998, from a script by producer Wong Jing, stars Almen Wong Pui-ha in the title role of a female assassin who was recruited and trained in her youth in the PRC amid starvation and hardship. Sent to Hong Kong to assassinate triad leaders, she becomes enamoured of sex with cop John and consumerism in the form of TV and instant food. As in *A Taste of Killing and Romance*, the attraction between cop and killer is made manifest by their opposite gender. What John Woo understood so well in *The Killer* – the essential similarity between the law and the outlaw and the homoerotic attraction between them – is more able to be literalised when the genders are opposite. Only later will we see an instance of same-sex attraction between women on opposite sides of the law. As typically happens, the desire to leave the life behind is impeded by assassins and gangsters who will not easily let the romantic couple off the hook.

In *Shiri* (Kang Je-kyu, 1999), South Korea's blockbuster entry into global cinema, we are presented with a mature vision of the silent assassin, a woman who kills both from afar and close up. She is perfidious, a *femme fatale* to the extent that she tricks her fiancé, an agent with the South Korean equivalent of the FBI, into planting bugs in the agency's office, allowing her always to be one step ahead of her antagonists. Yet she also reveals a more 'feminine' side when she actually falls in love with her boyfriend. The question of identity is at the forefront of her characterisation. A rigorous and quite shocking training sequence opens the film, wherein all the recruits are first honed to physical perfection and taught to kill without mercy until the climactic moment when they kill each other, last man standing, so to speak, winning the right to infiltrate South Korea as an assassin. This training sequence is meant to brutalise and thus dehumanise her so that when she assumes the identity of Lee Myung-hyun there will be no danger of her expressing any real sympathy or humanity towards her duped fiancé. One of the earliest films of the *hallyu*, the Korean Wave, *Shiri* is in every way a globalised work, a Hollywood-style blockbuster utilising the specifically Korean content of the North–South divide handled at both the macro-level – North Korean agents infiltrate the South to wreak havoc – and the micro-level – Lee Myung-hyun's torn loyalty to both the North and South – along with a style that in every way recalls the action spectaculars of both Hollywood and Hong Kong. A huge hit in South Korea as well as a film that received substantial release and critical and commercial respect in both regional and international markets, including America, *Shiri* proved the utility of an action film with a female killer containing both local and global characteristics.

The most commercially successful of any of the women-killers films has surely been Quentin Tarantino's *Kill Bill I* and *II* (2003–4), a wide-ranging pastiche, indeed a mash-up, of genres like the spaghetti Western, the Japanese samurai film and the Hong Kong martial arts movie. The film demonstrates, as if any proof were needed, that Tarantino knows his movies; and among the things he knows is that women killers are made, not born. What he also knows is that Asia has been the birthing ground of so many female killers. The general idea and some specific cinematic quotations in *Kill Bill* derive from the Japanese *Lady Snowblood* (Fujita Toshiya, 1973). Starring Kaji Meiko, the film tells the blood-filled tale of a woman literally born to seek vengeance. Yuki (snow) is born in prison to a mother whose husband and son were murdered and she was tortured and raped. Sent to jail for killing one of the men who raped her, she conceives and gives birth to her daughter while in prison; her dying request is that her daughter be taught to kill and seek vengeance. Trained by a priest in the way of the sword, Yuki undertakes her bloody quest when she has fully mastered the martial arts.

It was only appropriate that Kaji Meiko would net the starring role in this first female-killer film from Japan. She was already one of the Queens of the Bs with the influential and popular five-film 'Stray Cat' series, Nikkatsu Studios' answer to Toei's pinky violence. *Stray Cat Rock: Female Juvenile Delinquent Leader* (Hasebe Yasuharu, 1970), the first entry, introduces most of the series' primary elements – ultra-modern Tokyo (the film is set in Shinjuku), rock 'n' roll, night clubs, street fighting and clear feminist undertones. The most famous film in the series is *Stray Cat Rock: Sex Hunter* (Hasebe Yasuharu, 1970). Despite its lurid title, the film is an interesting look at the issue of mixed-race people in Japan, especially half-Black/half-Japanese teenagers. Set near the US Naval Base at Yokosuka, instead of the youth-culture centre that is Shinjuku, this entry obviously wants to say something about foreign influence in Japan, but also to decry the treatment of mixed-race off-spring of US servicemen. The film continues the use of rock music, this time featuring the all-female group the Golden Half, all of whose members are mixed race. And, of course, the centrality of the all-girl gang drives the plot.

As the 'Stray Cat' series came to an end, Kaji Meiko moved right into an even more violent series. Here, revenge elements combine with fantasy aspects in the cult favourite *Female Convict: Scorpion* series (1972–3). These women-in-prison films are part of the same exploitation cycle as the 'Zero Woman' films, but Sasori, the Scorpion, is not a trained killer, just a woman possessed by a strong sense of outrage and a desire for vengeance. The fourth, and final, entry in the series, *Female Convict Scorpion: Grudge Song* (Hasebe Yasuharu, 1973), was released four weeks after the first of the two *Lady Snowblood* films. The move from a modern setting of her previous series to the period setting of the *Lady Snowblood* duology was an interesting move at a time when the samurai or *chanbara* film was pretty well on its way out. Perhaps that is why Lady Snowblood made only two movie appearances.

Female Convict #701: Scorpion (Ito Shunya,1972), the first in the series, was remade in Hong Kong by Joe Ma Wai-ho in 2008, starring Japanese actress Mizuno Miki in the title role of *Sasori*. It is an odd film, with Hong Kong stars like Simon Yam, Sam Lee and Lam Suet featured alongside a Japanese superstar like Ishibashi Ryo. Like the original it concerns a woman who is not a trained killer to begin with, sent to prison for a murder she was forced to commit. With a typical, yet revealing Hong Kong-style twist, when she escapes from prison she determines to seek revenge, but in order to do so must learn *kungfu*. Thus we get the rebirth of the woman from a mild-mannered housewife to a trained killer and we get a lengthy training segment. Its hybridised status as a Japan/Hong Kong co-production, with a Hong Kong filmmaker directing a cast of Hong Kong and Japanese stars in a remake of a Japanese film, made this a festival favourite. *Sasori* premiered at the New York Asian Film Festival and played at the prestigious Fantasia Film Festival in Montreal. It seems to have had no release in Hong Kong, however.

Lady Snowblood, too, was remade in Hong Kong as *Broken Oath* (1977) by *kungfu* master director Jeng Cheong-woh (who had earlier made the internationally successful *Five Fingers of Death*, 1972). Produced by Golden Harvest, the film stars Angela Mao Ying in the role originated by Kaji. As in the earlier Japanese film, the female killer is not really an assassin for hire, but a woman on the trail of vengeance. As in the original, she is birthed in prison by a mother who dies in childbirth, then given over to a Buddhist temple where she learns martial arts. With an enviable supporting cast, including Sammo Hung Kam-bo, Han Ying-chieh and Bruce Leung Siu-lung, the film also features future director Corey Yuen Kwai in a small role as a bodyguard.

The globalised mash-up that is *Kill Bill* was presaged by two Hong Kong films produced immediately prior to Tarantino's effort. *Naked Weapon* (Tony Ching Siu-tung, 2002) is in every way a globalised work, with producer-writer Wong Jing perhaps imagining the riches that fell upon *Crouching Tiger, Hidden Dragon* (Ang Lee, 2000) two years earlier. That it was an abysmal failure at the Hong Kong box office and received no US theatrical release might serve to underscore the need for films perhaps to include more of the local in order to succeed within the global. Nevertheless, the film picks up on the manner in which killer women remain suitable subjects for examining the effects of deterritorialisation upon former colonised spaces. The film's globalised content may be seen throughout its textual operations, ranging from its production in English featuring a multi-ethnic cast; its various locations, climaxing in Hong Kong; Hong Kong-style action and martial arts sequences; and a sexual content in excess of the typical Hong Kong action movie. If we sift out all of these elements we may see more clearly what this film means by globalisation and we will also see how this very globalisation leads to the deterritorialised identities of the women.

The film features Maggie Q in her first starring role and co-stars Chinese-American actress Anya Wu, billed solely as 'Anya', a compression of her Chinese given name, An Ya. (Interestingly, Maggie Q would go on to star in a successful American television adaptation of *Nikita* from 2010 to 2013.) The film also features Daniel Wu and Cheng Pei-pei, and Almen Wong as Madam M, the cruel but effective trainer of the women assassins. As with so many female-killer films the origins of her skills in severe and secret training are revealed at length, in this case in a locale far removed from Hong Kong. We see the kidnapping of a multi-national group of teenage female athletes, gymnasts and martial artists. We see them go through years of vigorous and rigorous training, their original identities gradually stripped away, until such time as, *Shiri*-like, they are ordered to kill each other, last one standing getting the job of global assassin. Katherine (Anya) and Charlene (Maggie Q) refuse to kill each other, though Li Fei has no such qualms, killing her boon companion right off the bat. Madam M decides to let the three of them live and, after being drugged and repeatedly raped to get rid of their last remaining vestiges of modesty and bourgeois womanhood, off they go on their multiple killing assignments.

Complicating Charlene's life is her meeting with Jack (Daniel Wu), a capable, sympathetic CIA operative trying to stop 'the China Doll Killers'. Jack captures Charlene after a hit she makes in Hong Kong and although she soon escapes, they have pretty well fallen in love. Jack wants to find a way not to send her to prison; Charlene wants to find a way to leave her assassin's life behind – especially after, with Jack's help, she recovers her memories of her happy childhood and wishes to see her mother (Cheng Pei-pei), which she does. Thus both a middle-class life and romantic love conspire to convince the killer to grasp onto those bourgeois values that no woman assassin can resist.

Though we can easily ascribe the few sex scenes and the hints of lesbianism to the film's exploitation agenda, in fact they are also part of the globalising agenda. Since there are far more scenes of graphic sexuality and nudity to be found in the action-women mode than is apparent here (for example, *Naked Killer*), the point of the sex scenes is to bring the film more in line with contemporary standards of world cinema, rather than the more tame Hong Kong category II films that make up the bulk of their output. Though not handled especially graphically, the rape scene is perhaps the only one of questionable taste in terms of its (relative) explicitness and longevity. Otherwise, one should expect a film about women who are trained to use everything they possess as part of their arsenal of death, including sex, to feature a little sex. The hints of lesbian love between Katherine and Charlene can just as easily be interpreted as close female bonding amid horrible circumstances as of genuine expressions of female friendship. In any case, seen today, most of the sex sequences might not even be out of place in Hindi movies, the most restrictive and 'puritanical' of the world's global cinemas. (And one reason, though not the only one, that keeps Bollywood off mainstream or Art screens in the US.)

Another thoroughly globalised film of 2002 was *So Close* (Corey Yuen Kwai). Made by Columbia Pictures Film Production Asia, which had struck pay dirt with *Crouching Tiger, Hidden Dragon*, following upon the critical success of *The Road Home* (Zhang Yimou, 1999), which it had distributed, *So Close* was obviously pitched towards the regional and global markets. Director Cory [sic] Yuen had previously directed multi-national casts in films such as *No Retreat, No Surrender* (1986) and *No Retreat, No Surrender 2* (1987); had helped push New Style martial arts films to greater heights with the serio-comic *Fong Sai Yuk* (1993) and its sequel; and had also worked with Shannon Lee, daughter of Bruce Lee, on *Enter the Eagles* (1998), among other films. He had proven both a master of Hollywood-style storytelling and had worked with a CGI-heavy Hong Kong production in *The Avenging Fist* (2001). Given the all-star cast, the big budget and the effects-heavy stunts to be utilised, Cory Yuen seemed like the perfect choice for this transnationally geared film.

The first index of the film's cross-border production may be seen not just in its all-star cast, but in the fact that the three Chinas, South Korea and Japan are all represented. The multi-lingual, multi-racial Karen Mok is an actress associated with Hong Kong; Shu Qi, another Hong Kong star, was born and raised in Taiwan, acting in light sex films before transitioning to mainstream success; Zhao Wei was a rising star on the Mainland in film and television before crossing over to Hong Kong-American audiences who likely first saw her in Stephen Chow's *Shaolin Soccer* in 2001; male co-star Song Seung-heon is Korean; and long-time actor in Hong Kong films Kurata Yasuaki is Japanese.

Figure 6.1 The beautiful, ultra-modern girl with a gun: *So Close* (Corey Yuen, 2002, Columbia Pictures Film Production Asia).

So Close possesses an ultra-modern sheen, a function of the extensive use of glass surfaces, screens and white costumes. Heavy use of CGI not only creates the skyscraper that houses the villain's corporation, a glass-encased cube built around a central shaft, but is itself indicative of the modern – expensive computer graphics often separating the 'first-world blockbuster' from its would-be competitors. *So Close* even seems to be vaguely science-fictional with its use not only of GPS but also Google Earth (two years before Google acquired the application from the company that developed the technology for the CIA) and a new generation of smart phones capable of running the kind of software, or apps, only developed in the last few years. These glass buildings and high-tech screens are accompanied by the high-fashion dress of the three stars, all tall and slender (they are all actually almost the same height, slightly taller than 5'6"). In particular, white pant suits emphasise their long legs and athletic builds. Their model-like physiques are themselves indices of the global, women's bodies being a central part of the modernising project undertaken by Asian nations since the third decade of the last century.

The GPS/Google Earth eye-in-the-sky motif is matched by the ubiquity of a video camera constantly wielded by Sue. She is forever filming her sister, especially as the latter's birthday approaches. The video camera also functions as memory, as we see snippets of flashbacks to the girls' pre-adolescence, when their parents were alive. The video footage is slightly altered as a sign of its past-ness. Sue has also set up an elaborate network of cameras that operate as security, linked to a complex bank of video monitors. The combination of the Google Earth, GPS and video surveillance functions further to promote the post-modern – we are faced with nothing so much as a Foucauldian panopticon. The video has captured the girls' loss of their parents and in a flashback we see the very moment when Lynn first tentatively fired a gun – the moment, that is, of her transformation from a happy schoolgirl into a female killer. (We actually don't see any more of her training, just this one moment to suggest that it occurred.) The panopticon that has continually captured Lynn even manages to capture her death. From the entry of the hitmen out to kill her to the final moment when they succeed, all is consigned to the digital. In fact, though we see much of this sequence 'live', so to speak, we never see her final moments except through the surveillance footage – used to prove Hung's innocence of Lynn's murder, but more to the point to demonstrate that in essence her life has been lived on camera, surveilled, from her (re)birth to her final moment.

The women's skill in computer programming and operations is matched by their expertise in the martial arts. Here, too, this is a sign of the global. First, Chinese martial arts was not simply a 'brand' for Hong Kong to marshal against Hollywood's encroachment (though that would take on a more important character at this time), but also a sign of its power and reach. One could hardly stage a fight or action scene not in imitation of Hong Kong, whether close combat or wild shoot-outs. It would therefore be rather strange not to see the new-style *wushu* and 'gun-fu' at work here. The John Woo-style standoff between antagonists, use of automatic pistols in each hand and shooting while slipping, sliding and flying, and pumping multiple bullets into enemies are all in abundance. So, too, the slightly speeded-up action pioneered by Tony Ching Siu-tung and used in *Naked Weapon*.

Though there is no nudity in the film, no sex scenes as in *Naked Weapon*, there is a hint of lesbianism, a slight frisson when Zhao Wei's Sue expresses her attraction for Karen Mok's Hung and plants a gentle kiss on her lips by way of goodbye. This lesbian attraction is either rather late in developing in the film or very subtle earlier on. But in any case it functions not as exploitation – it is far too chaste for that – but both in terms of the John Woo-like relationship between cop and killer (in Woo's cinema homosocial/homosexual) and as a sign of the global – a kind of lesbian chic. Presented very sympathetically, unlike in the films of Clarence Fok, say, one feels a wistful sense of sadness at the impossibility of Sue and Hung living happily ever after.

The global in Hong Kong culture itself is also expressed in music, with Canto-pop, Mando-pop, K- and J-pop competing in a sonic marketplace. In one sequence – which might be one of those subtle hints of erotic attraction – Sue toys with Hung in a CD shop, staying just out of her sight until she gives her a CD to listen to. Hung has heard the song 'Close to You' on a surveillance video of the crime committed by Lynn and Sue; what Sue gives her is that very song, what appears to be Mai Kuraki doing a cover of the Carpenters hit on her album *Perfect Crime*. Except this song is not, in fact, on Kuraki's album, so the disc was chosen only for its apt title vis-à-vis this film. In fact, the cover of the Burt Bacharach classic is performed by Singaporean pop star Corinne May. Though it seems like a long way around just to get a disc with the title *Perfect Crime*, there is also something appropriately deterritorialised about using the disc cover of a Japanese pop star and a performance by one from Singapore – though, in fact, that would be exactly the kind of thing you could find in an HMV store in Hong Kong in 2002, which is where this sequence was obviously shot.

The most interesting of the cool female-killer films is *Beyond Hypothermia* (Patrick Leung Pak-kin, 1996). One reason is certainly that it is the most genuinely noirish of the woman-assassin films. The female assassin here is often bathed in a blue or green light; a number of scenes take place at night, some with an air of mystery and implied violence, others with a more romantic tone. The film also benefits from the skills and input of Johnnie To. This was the first production of To's newly formed Milkyway Image, and though director Patrick Leung was a protégé of John Woo – and it certainly shows – To's deeper insights and preferred kind of characters predominate. The film's odd Chinese title, *Sheshi 32 du*, refers to the fact that the heroine's body temperature is 32 degrees Celsius, which is 5 degrees below normal, or 8 degrees below normal in Fahrenheit. *Beyond Hypothermia* is the English title that tries to capture this idea.

Lau Ching-wan plays an ex-triad member, now gentle and kind, who operates a noodle shop on the streets of Hong Kong; Wu Chien-lien (Ng Sin-lin) plays a hitwoman. There is something counter-intuitive in the casting, not simply the gender reversal, but in the very idea of Wu Chien-lien as a hitwoman. There is something very ethereal about her; she is best-suited for melodramas and period films, such as *The Phantom Lover* (Ronny Yu, 1995), a remake of the Chinese classic *Song at Midnight* (Ma-Xu Weibang, 1937), itself a reworking of the old warhorse horror story, *Phantom of the Opera*, or as middle sister Jia-Chien in Ang Lee's *Eat Drink Man Woman* (1994). Another of her best roles came courtesy of Eileen Chang's story, *Eighteen Springs*, a lush historical drama directed by Ann Hui On-wah in 1997, made the year after Hui had worked as an actress for Patrick Leung on his debut feature, *Somebody Up There Likes Me* (1996).

A Hong Kong–Korean co-production, *Beyond Hypothermia* thus features a large Korean cast, especially young star Sang Woo-han as a Chow-Yun-fat-like bodyguard who vows vengeance against the mysterious hitwoman who killed his boss in Seoul. A twelve-minute sequence set in Korea details the assassination and its aftermath, shifting the film at this point to a dual-focus narrative, cutting between the female assassin (whose real name even she doesn't know, but comes to believe for a while it is Shu Lihan) and bodyguard Yichin (Yat-jing in Cantonese) and his search for the mysterious killer. The dual-focus narrative in such a short film (82 minutes) certainly detracts from the female lead. Perhaps it was part of the co-production deal to split the time between them for the film's major segments. Indeed, the English-language trailer for the film makes no mention of Lau Ching-wan or the film's romantic elements, stressing only the revenge motif on the part of the Korean killer.[15]

Figure 6.2 The cool female assassin: *Beyond Hypothermia* (Patrick Leung, 1996, Milkyway Image Company).

The sense of deterritorialisation is strongly implicated in this film in a number of ways. The use of Korean actors and locales is one such way; another is the way in which, following the opening assassination sequence, Lihan burns her passport, moves out of her flat and takes up residence in a new apartment in Hong Kong. We know this is a routine that has been done time and time before.

Her low body temperature, while not perhaps a major motif, also contributes to her sense of deterritorialisation and cultural schizophrenia. Of course, it does stand her in good stead in her first hit in an ice-house where she waits for her target for many hours, with only a light plastic coat and a hoodie to shield her from the cold. Her imperviousness to the cold rain that frequently pelts her is another sign of her cold blood. This is to say that her low body temperature is used to more effect than simply to make her a 'cold-blooded killer'. In fact, one might argue that she is thus different from most people and her body temperature is only one sign of this. In a clear resemblance to *Blade Runner* (1982), she's obsessed with photographs; having no past she longs for pictures of her family or herself. She even makes up memories that she tells to Long: of loving to sit on a swing or eat cotton candy, things she saw recently, passing a playground or making a hit on a triad member who has just bought his daughter the sugary treat. She is told of a traumatic childhood in Cambodia, where she lost her family 'in the war'. Though it is possible that this refers to US bombings and incursions into Cambodia around 1969–70, it is more likely a reference to the auto-genocide that began in 1975. In any case, this Cambodian past, her obsession with photographs and a desire to know her real name speak clearly to the issue of identity that deterritorialisation leads to and that is a commonality among the women-killers we have seen. *Beyond Hypothermia* makes this most explicit: 'Can't have photos, can't have a name, can't have a past, can't have an identity . . . you can only kill.' This is a litany that she knows only too well.

'Only women would sacrifice for love' is another homily her handler-aunt has drummed into her. But here Aunty is wrong. While Lihan is willing to sacrifice her life as an assassin, Long proves willing to sacrifice his life. Thus Lihan, the woman-killer, becomes a classic *femme fatale* for Long. The impossibility of the identity-less woman living happily ever after is denied her once again, while any man caught in her sphere is similarly denied not just a happy life, but any life at all. *Beyond Hypothermia* is the bleakest of the three post-millennium Hong Kong killer-women films, but they all manage to show that there is a point of no return for the women; having crossed the line of gender expectations, there is no going back.

Notes

1. None of the female-centred films from Hong Kong discussed in this essay is in the Flick Chart Top #100. See 'The Top 100 Hitman/Assassin Films of All Time': http://www.flickchart.com/Charts.aspx?genre=Hitman+/+Assassin+Film&perpage=100 (last accessed 28 April 2014). Such lists are, of course, debatable, but the point here is that knowledgeable film fans cannot so easily call to mind female assassin films in any great number.
2. Australian Cinematheque, 'Bond, JANE BOND': http://www.qagoma.qld.gov.au/cinematheque/past_programs/2010/bond,_jane_bond_hong_kong_action_women (last accessed 1 July 2014).
3. Yau, 'Ecology and Late Colonial Hong Kong Cinema', p. 107.
4. Ibid., p. 108.
5. Australian Cinematheque, 'Bond, JANE Bond'.
6. Yau, 'Ecology and Late Colonial Hong Kong Cinema', p. 110.
7. duriandave, '*The Black Killer* (1967)': http://hkmdb.com/db/reviews/show_review.mhtml?id=11578 (last accessed 30 June 2014).
8. One should mention a very early American hitwoman film, *Too Hot to Handle* (1977). Directed by Don Schain with an eye on the 1970s exploitation market, the film stars the very shapely Cheri Caffaro. The film combines the sexualised image of the James Bond villainess with the heroic image of the chivalrous girl, one willing, however, to reveal what is underneath the cool costumes. A cult item today, *Too Hot to Handle* is #100 on the Flick Chart Top 100 Hitman movies.
9. Saint-Cyr, 'REVIEW: Zero Woman: Red Handcuffs': http://jfilmpowwow.blogspot.hk/2010/05/review-zero-woman-red-handcuffs.html (last accessed 29 April 2014).
10. Mes, 'Zero Woman: Red Handcuffs': http://www.midnighteye.com/reviews/zero-woman-red-handcuffs/ (last accessed 29 April 2014).
11. Ibid.
12. See Deleuze and Guattari, *Anti-Oedipus*.
13. Giddens, *The Consequences of Modernity*, p. 21.
14. '*Naked Killer*': http://en.wikipedia.org/wiki/Naked_Killer (last accessed 27 April 2014).
15. asianwack, 'Beyond Hypothermia': https://youtu.be/Mm0F3oOddlA (last accessed 18 February 2015).

Chapter 7
Tech-Noir: A Sub-Genre May not Exist in Hong Kong Science Fiction Films

Kwai-Cheung Lo

Although critics nowadays talk about global noir or neo-noir (that means the revived genre does not even carry any technical cinematic features as the classic noir possesses) from various localised contexts in the age of transnationalism, the concept of film noir in cinema, at a first glance, is typically a very Euro(America)-centric way of classifying, perceiving and organising cinematic productions, which is, of course, an integral part of the hegemonic western conceptualisation or mapping of the world, subjugating widely different peoples and their cultures to parallel – if not 'universal' – historical paths of modernity.[1] However, noir as a guiding concept to generalise, group and identify the multitude of diverse different films is itself a false recognition of post-war French viewers on Hollywood cinema. It is actually not a conscious category developed from Hollywood industry but a critical object invented by French criticism in order to allow Europeans 'to love the United States while criticizing it'.[2] While noir may designate the tensions (within the west) and the paradoxical relationships between Europe and the United States, thus debunking the myth of a homogeneous west, can it then be justifiably appropriated to look at the cultures of the non-west?

If the notion of noir as an 'external misperception' may create an entirely new perspective 'invisible to those who are directly engaged in it' and exert some 'productive influence on the misperceived "original" itself',[3] what is the 'positive' effect noir can bring to our understanding of Hong Kong cinematic productions? What is the so-called hidden truth – which is supposed not to be seen without such notion – of Hong Kong cinema unfolded through the introduction of noir as a critical concept? But, once again, will such an argument using a 'distorting outside gaze' to reveal one's 'repressed inner truth' simply reinforce the legitimacy of western hegemony and violence in the transnational and transcultural milieu? Isn't it true that the western conceptual framework has already dominated today's film study? Perhaps what is at stake is not whether noir is an 'external' concept or not, but rather the instability and fluidity of the concept itself that generates a dynamic relationship with the object to be looked at, that is Hong Kong cinema, and allows the object to have a more proactive role to respond to the conceptual gaze. The interaction between noir and Hong Kong cinema, that is a fiction and its object, is no longer about how an absolutised or closed western concept is applied to categorise Chinese-language films produced by the (post)-colonial city. Rather, it is a self-doubting, self-negating notion bewaring of its own fictionality that can only realise itself and find its life through encountering undefined, multiple and volatile objects and realities.[4]

Although there might supposedly be a Sinocentric way of categorising things (yet such particular culture would be quickly defined as the other vis-à-vis the western self by the Eurocentric paradigm),[5] rejecting noir is actually not a very sensible option for analysing Hong Kong cinema, not only because its modernity – like many others – probably cannot be comprehended without reference to the west. While the themes, styles and characterisations of noir can be spotted in a large number of Hong Kong (crime) films without much difficulty, the recognition of noir as a common film genre is by no means established in the city's local industry. Seemingly, there is no consensus upon the genre among producers, directors, critics and ordinary viewers in Hong Kong, whose development for decades has been governed by excessive urban modernisation. As a result, there has been very little secondary literature in the Chinese language, in comparison to the English counterparts, using the noir notion to categorise or discuss Hong Kong productions.[6] Yet such general negligence is not identical to any form of resistance to the western concept. It may mean the filmmakers and audiences are simply under its spell and influence without knowing it – probably a perfect case of ideological operation (you don't know it but you are doing it). But to call noir an ideology is highly problematic, since noir is not even consistent in itself.

Given the fact that noir may not even enter the consciousness of the industry or even of the community, why discuss a sub-genre of 'tech-noir' or future noir in Hong Kong cinema? If noir is something operating in Hong Kong cinema without much awareness, then science fiction film, that is the 'tech', is a genre that usually embodies a self-conscious endeavour of the industry to edge Hollywood mega-production, especially in the post-1997 period when the market's focus is shifted to the Mainland where the nationalist discourse is increasingly dominant. However, sci-fi film has generally been considered a particular genre that Hong Kong or the transnational Chinese cinema is not good at. Chinese-language criticisms often lament that there has been no successful Chinese sci-fi film ever made, yet Chinese filmmakers should not give up on this genre but be committed to it relentlessly since sci-fi movies symbolise the way the future can be conquered and imagined, and how advanced technology is mastered (as proved in the ability to produce such a genre), that would be easily translated into an index of national strength and cultural (soft) power.[7] In other words, the Chinese sci-fi genre nowadays is invested with the nationalist dream for a fast rise of an upstart power with earnest longings, which are somewhat incompatible with the dark atmosphere perpetuated by noir.

So what does it mean when noir encounters sci-fi in a Hong Kong context? To look back, a younger generation of Hong Kong filmmakers who were educated in academic film knowledge might get their ideas from critics to produce their noir-style films in concrete terms, or made direct use of the Hollywood models to create their own noirs with local expressions and concerns. 'Crime as a social problem was a major theme of the new wave directors in the late '70s... The underworld was, needless to say, a murky, dark underworld in line with the film noir aspirations of the new wave film-makers.'[8] While the underworld is an attractive theme for filmmakers to articulate their views on social problems, the future world setting in the sci-fi genre also serves as an imaginative screen for them to project the city's fate. Perhaps sci-fi films made in Hong Kong convey a sense of strangeness and non-conformity in the tradition of Chinese cinema,[9] offering a different channel to challenge dominant values and to subvert conventional filmmaking, thus providing the opportunity for some provisional or partial turning or derailment of persistent institutional practices and structure. This may explain why tech-noir films first appeared on the production line of the New Wave filmmakers in 1980s Hong Kong. However, it is not merely a practice to espouse an 'external genre', that is sci-fi, for internal self-critique or self-regeneration.

Sci-Fi Noirised

In the following Hong Kong films I discuss, the use of a sci-fi setting is often combined with the noir style. Yet the noir-ness in these sci-fi movies means not only a style but an outlook towards oneself and the world. That is to say, while these Hong Kong filmmakers adopt the sci-fi genre with clear purposes, they also express certain doubts or distrust of what sci-fi represents in their understanding. If Hollywood sci-fi always portrays a crisis on a global scale that threatens the entire human species, Hong Kong sci-fi tends to take up a 'noir position' by dismissing that universality claim and preoccupying itself with some 'minor', localised and particular concerns. In short, the general obsession with global magnitude or universal extent in Hollywood sci-fi has been undermined in its Hong Kong counterpart. For the motif of human–robot dialectic and competition for the domination and control of the earth always seen in the genre, Hong Kong sci-fi is almost unconditionally on the side of human in its natural and 'uncontaminated' form against any scientific transformation of human into a partial machine or a quasi-immortal superhuman bio-system. In some conspicuous way, Hong Kong sci-fi passes on a stock image of science and technology which is simplified as some tremendous power and uncontrollable impulse, manifesting a populist anxiety about the implications of the increasingly predominant machines and mechanisation process that general Hong Kong citizens have benefited from but also found inevitable. Such a view is not necessarily an insight generated from serious reflections over scientism. Rather, it may be rooted in some conservative values and pragmatic-utilitarian world views that not only dichotomise science as something imported and imposed from the western powers but also reveal contempt towards abstract and incomprehensible scientific ideas. In this light, the human in Hong Kong sci-fi is usually invested with the pragmatic values of the local community (it does not mean that the conviction in human[ity] is absolute and neither is human seen as something eternal or timeless in these films) whereas the alien machines and the extrapolative science are reduced to be the high-sounding and intangible things from the outside world. But it is not very feasible to see the threats of science and technology as something non-structural. As a result, Hong Kong-made sci-fi film always oscillates between a fascination with and an appalling feeling towards the 'tech', revealing its ambivalent dark side and questioning its own raison d'être. In short, it is noir-ised sci-fi, or tech-noir in a broader sense.

The narrower sense of 'tech-noir', in Paul Meehan's book with the same title, refers to some 'science fiction works that exist in a more recognisably noir milieu of crime, murder, mystery, suspense, obsession, perversity, predestination, femmes (and hommes) fatales and identity transference'.[10] Ridley Scott's *Blade Runner* (1982) is named as the one that has evoked the look and formula of noir from the 1940s in a new and fantastic science fiction context, while James Cameron's *The Terminator* (1984), in which there is a dance club called 'Tech Noir' that originates the term, is considered another seminal work that further cross-pollinates the two genres. The term, however, is still rather inconsistent in grouping a cluster of sci-fi movies produced in the western world, and the category line tracing back to the German expressionist cinema of the 1920s is quite suspicious and not very convincing, demonstrating the eternal non-coincidence of the notion of genre and the real films themselves. The ambiguous identity of tech-noir in Hong Kong cinema is that, while noir hardly has any artificial purity and distinctiveness since it is never a distinctively defined genre but could be loosely understood as a way of looking at the world, the number of science fiction films produced by the Hong Kong film industry in the past couple of decades is far from adequate to be recognised as an important genre. When there are no recognisable genres to be mixed in the first place, can the derivative 'tech-noir' stand on its own in Hong Kong cinema? Film scholars will easily point out where the problem lies: '[a] significant number of films embodying analogous characteristics are thus a necessary precondition for the establishment, recognition, and consciousness of a genre, even though the number required cannot be precisely quantified'.[11]

The transnational nature of Hong Kong film, perhaps, may refute such logic of deduction, that is you must have some well-recognised 'pure genres' in large quantity at first before you can get mixed or sub-genres. Right from the beginning, Hong Kong films have never been pure in the sense that they are difficult to generically categorise. Abrupt changes of mood, style and generic reference are not uncommon in many Hong Kong films. Different generic elements could be inserted and juxtaposed in odd and illogical ways, not necessarily intending to subvert a genre or break through conventional generic discourse for new life. Though having some subversive implications for cinematic conventions and connoting the inherent contradictions of modern life, many Hong Kong films choose hybridity over purity, heterogeneity over homogeneity, probably because of a hasty production process, limited resources, disorganised systems, reliance on taken-for-granted devices, and a fatigue of creative ideas. In order to satisfy the audiences, Hong Kong movies put great emphasis on 'striking moments' snatched from other films, even though these adapted images or motifs may not always fit in the new contexts. Such an impulse leads to a 'scavenger aesthetic'[12] or 'hybrid cinema'.[13,14] The prevalent market orientation also pushes the industry to shrewdly capitalise on any popular trend by rapidly copying or remodelling a hit either imported or locally produced. Any film released could be simply a direct response to the transnational market rather than a 'naturally evolved' product from the organic development of the industry. Thus, tech-noir as a somewhat ill-defined hybrid of several ill-defined genres can be possibly used to understand a cluster of films made in Hong Kong that may not exactly fit either noir or sci-fi but combine sci-fi story lines and iconography with a certain noir sensibility and *mise-en-scène*.

New Wave Mixtures

The pioneering Hong Kong tech-noir works can be attributed to some New Wave filmmakers, like Alex Cheung, Kirk Wong and Tsui Hark, demonstrating their boldness of styles, experimental spirits and visions. Indeed, these directors had already made some noir-look crime films before attempting the sci-fi genre. It was therefore not surprising that the noir style or theme was carried forward to their other works. One of the earliest examples is *Twinkle Twinkle Little Star* (literally Interstellar Stooge, 1983) by Alex Cheung Kwokming. After making his two critically acclaimed crime features *Cops and Robbers* (1979) and *Man on the Brink* (1981) that introduced the New Wave movement in Hong Kong cinema, Cheung joined Shaw Brothers to launch the sci-fi comedy *Twinkle Twinkle Little Star* with a budget over HK$10 million, a huge investment by 1980s standards. Joining the big production company does not look, in retrospect, like a wise choice for Cheung's career. Such co-opting of New Wave directors by the mainstream was seen as a betrayal of their ideals. But since there was hardly any space for alternative filmmaking, many New Wave directors like Cheung made the decision to go into the mainstream in order to gain a foothold in the industry for their future development. Unfortunately, Cheung's works after joining Shaw Brothers no longer attracted critical acclaim or box-office success.

Twinkle Twinkle Little Star is more a parody than a science fiction in any proper sense, though Shaws had previously produced two more conventional sci-fi adventure movies, namely *The Super Inframan* (Hua Shan, 1975) and *The Mighty Peking Man* (Ho Meng-Hua, 1976), both of which were copycats: one of Japan's special-effects TV programme *Ultraman* (*Urutoraman*, 1966–7; *Ultra* series, 1966–present) and *Masked Rider* (*Kamen Raidā*, 1971–3; *Masked Rider* series, 1971–present), and the other of Hollywood's *King Kong* remake. Continuing this 'reworking' or rip-off mode of fast-lane production in Hong Kong cinema in the 1980s, Cheung's debut work for Shaws is a collage (or straightforward quotation) of many films from Hollywood and the local film industry (including, to name a few, *The Seven Year Itch* [Billy Wilder, 1955], *Star Wars* [George Lucas, 1977], *Close Encounters of the Third Kind* [Steven Spielberg, 1977], *Taxi Driver* [Martin Scorsese, 1976], *The Warlord* [Li Hanhsiang, 1972] and even his own *Cops and Robbers*), hybridising various genres (melodrama, comedy, satire, slapstick, farce, fantasy, musical, dance, horror, noir and science fiction) and mingling familiar scenes, dialogue and icons to such an extent that it looks more like a disjointed variety show than a consistent narrative. With its relatively high budget and prolonged shooting period, the hybrid dimensions of *Twinkle Twinkle Little Star* may mean more than a bricolage for production convenience. In other Hong Kong tech-noirs that came after this Cheung film, the unresolved mix of styles and genres continues, constituting a kind of 'convention' that cannot be always fully explicated and easily extrapolated. An off-hand answer could be that the noir-ness of these hybrid sci-fi films makes them more sensitive to the changing and fluid realities of the capitalist world. Their heterogeneous generic discourses and disparate styles are probably the reflections of the unsettling circumstances created by changing political situations and the increasingly intense capitalisation process.

For its noirish qualities, *Twinkle Twinkle Little Star*'s expressionistic dim lighting for alien abduction and spaceship interior scenes may be modelled on *Close Encounters of the Third Kind* and *Star Wars*, but it is its self-negation mode that displays its noir sensibility. While the vulgar jokes about rape fantasy and the over-dramatisation of the female lead Cherie Chung Chor-hung's sex appeal may repel today's audience with its feminist consciousness, its sarcastic assertion of the rudeness and extensive power of the patriarchal-capitalist gender economy provokes some further reflection. All the father figures (the rich father, the poor father, and the scientist who is the godfather of the female character), though satirised or noir-ised, have the ability to turn around the fate of the protagonists, implicitly affirming the old patriarchal power structure. What is most revealing from a supposedly funny episode is that while the male protagonist (played by James Yi Lui) tries desperately to run away from the Darth Vader villain and look for an exit from the spaceship, trying many buttons on the door, yelling 'open sesame' and other passwords to no avail, he calls his real father's name for help, being well known as the son of a popular comedian, Yee Chau-sui, in traditional Cantonese cinema.

Another cynical depiction is the press conference scene in which a number of New Wave directors, including Tsui Hark, Alan Fong, Alfred Cheung Kin-ting and Alex Cheung himself, have non-credited cameo appearances as members of the press. The conference quickly turns into a food- and cake-throwing slapstick sequence which lasts approximately four minutes, during which creamy cakes and greasy food such as spaghetti and pizza are repeatedly tossed in the faces of anyone in range, including the filmmakers. It appears less a funny scene aimed at provoking audience laughter than as one humiliating someone in this way, and this someone seems to be the filmmakers who intend to make a fool of themselves. Does Alex Cheung tell us that, with such a scene, the new energy and new realist aesthetics brought by the New Wave simply dissolve into a mess of senseless food-fighting and being wasted under the rule of corporate production? The food-throwing fight ends with the appearance of the father-figure scientist who announces that the UFO story told by the female protagonist is true and thus creates the opportunity for her as a victim of 'the close encounter of the fourth kind' – that is being raped by the aliens on the UFO – to immediately become a media darling. Once again, does the film reveal that the noises, doubts and disturbances made by the newcomers can easily be suppressed and subdued by the old authority and power structure? Though money was largely spent in making the huge spaceship and other special effects, the film appears to mock all these high-tech gadgets while placing its focus on the 'low-tech' human slapstick (in a scene where an ATM machine is blown away by a strong gust of wind, a man is revealed hiding in the machine to provide cash to customers, apparently laughing at the uselessness of mechanical technology).[15] The self-negating manner of Cheung's tech-noir exemplifies the paradox of both embracing and critiquing capitalist modernity at the same time. While the corporate capital of Hong Kong in the 1980s had already begun to dominate most features of daily life, including one's very being, *Twinkle Twinkle Little Star* reveals that any unity (identity or genre) is only constructed contrivedly since the truth is impure, incongruous, disjointed and messy.

Released in the same year was Kirk Wong's *Health Warning* (aka *Flash Future Kungfu*, 1983), a low-budget sci-fi cyberpunk thriller that apparently tries to capture *Blade Runner*'s look. A talented stylist, as shown in his previous gangster film *The Club* (1981), Wong sets the story of *Health Warning* in a twenty-first-century dystopian world where advanced technology has destroyed human spirit and young people expend all their energies in violence like underground boxing. A martial arts house tries to steer its students to the right path through disciplined training, but is assaulted by a mysterious neo-Nazi organisation that controls its members using drugs and has the ambition to rule the world by converting humans into new species. With very limited resources, the film can only describe the ruined world by means of intertitles. The tech-noir milieu is constructed by means of desolate and crumbling interiors, dim and hazy lighting, lights filtered through smoke and fans, the fuzzy cathode-ray blue of TV monitors, and electronic synthesiser music with transvestite characters, sadomasochistic scenes, homoerotic imagery, and a weird mix of punk fashions and decorative gas masks and radiation suits. Putting the old *kungfu* movie plot (martial arts disciples taking revenge on an evil force for destroying their school) into the alien world of sci-fi, Wong seems to be more conscious and enthusiastic with style and form, although the bleak world dominated by Nazi-like dictatorship could easily be over-interpreted as an allegory of Hong Kong under communist China.[16]

Style and form already carry their message. The deviant visuality of Wong's tech-noir not only aims to unsettle local viewers but also indicates his desire to reach the level set by Hollywood, even though the production conditions in Hong Kong could not make it objectively possible. *Health Warning*, however, is not exactly an imitation of Hollywood sci-fi, while noir in Hong Kong cinema is admittedly a sophisticated means to attain the spirit of Euro-American-led modernity precisely because it also comprises its self-criticising aspect. Some critics may find it ridiculous and incredible that the skin-headed neo-Nazi gang in Wong's film only use their bare hands rather than any hi-tech weapons to fight in a sci-fi setting.[17] But emphasis on *kungfu* and the human body rather than on advanced technology can be understood as a self-realising mode of responding to modernity and a rejection of the blind replication of imported sci-fi films. The *kungfu* fight scenes, on the other hand, do not necessarily stand for a nationalistic resistance towards western technology. The finale where the male protagonist has a boxing match (rather than a traditional *kungfu* duel) with the neo-Nazi leader is a long take with little choreographed action, subverting the audience's expectation for *kungfu* beauty and exposing the dullness and brutality of human violence. In short, what *kungfu* usually symbolises in Hong Kong cinema is also noir-ised and challenged in Wong's film.

Tsui Hark, a Noir Filmmaker?

If noir can be grasped as some subversive and transgressive force, Tsui Hark, whose works began with the New Wave movement, can be named as a 'noir filmmaker' since the movies he directed, produced and scripted always take advantage of new skills, violate generic boundaries or challenge conventional styles. It is always said that Tsui has much control over the creativity of his works: even when playing the role of producer, he is able to maintain creative authority over the projects. As a result, he tends to intimidate the credited directors working under him. Only a few directors with some status or whom Tsui trusts, for example, John Woo, Tony Ching Siu-tung and Ringo Lam, can stand up to him and have real collaboration on equal terms.[18] However, the problem, within a system almost entirely determined by commercialisation, is how can film which is made for a mass audience be really subversive and transgressive? How can a single person, even the so-called auteur filmmaker, bring any significant transformations to the industry and the larger system? Like other New Wave directors, Tsui's early works such as *The Butterfly Murders* (1979) and *Dangerous Encounter – 1st Kind* (1980) put across a dark vision of the world, provocatively defying certain mainstream values and assaulting conventional film styles and techniques. But all these transgressions fell into place as new conventions when Tsui was quickly co-opted into the mainstream film industry. Undoubtedly, Tsui's complete surrender to the mechanism of the mainstream industry has earned him a leading role in the Hong Kong film industry – as long as his projects work commercially, the rest will follow.

Being a master of genre films and heavily relying on the star system, Tsui still preserves his instinct to confront and violate in his commercial generic productions. The tech-noirs associated with him to be discussed here are *I Love Maria* (dir. David Chung Chi-man, prod. Tsui Hark and John Sham, act. Tsui Hark, 1988), *The Wicked City* (dir. Peter Mak Tai-kit, prod. Tsui Hark, co-scripted Tsui Hark, 1992), *Black Mask* (dir. Daniel Lee Yan-gong, prod. Tsui Hark, co-scripted Tsui Hark, 1996) and *Black Mask II* (dir. Tsui Hark, 2002). These films are generally seen by critics as works full of Tsui's traits, stamp and style. The irony, however, is that *Black Mask II*, though under Tsui's directorship, is considered entirely lacking in any of his idiosyncrasies – a weak and unlively work, like his other English-language film, *Knock Off* (1998), a failed product that is presumably made for Hollywood's taste and interest.

Though incomparable to Hollywood's standard of special-effects design, the terrorising robot carrying out a bank robbery in the central commercial district in the sci-fi comedy *I Love Maria* is still a brand-new thing in Hong Kong cinema. Tsui himself plays a main character in the film, a former member of the robot gang, and is suspected by his fellow members of having betrayed the organisation. The gang leader sends a female android modelled on his lover Maria (played by Sally Yeh Sin-man), who also happens to be Tsui's romantic interest, to kill Tsui. But Tsui and his friends (John Sham and Tony Leung Chiu-wai) accidentally get control of the droid and reprogramme her to fight for the right cause, leading to a final showdown with the evil robot gang. Having the same name as the woman robot from *Metropolis* (Fritz Lang, 1927), the female android Maria in *I Love Maria* is her copy as well as a hybrid of *Robocop* (Paul Verhoeven, 1987) and C-3PO from the *Star Wars* series. However, the Maria robot in Hong Kong tech-noir does not have any strong erotic implications as in *Metropolis*, and neither does she have any mesmerising power over the lustful men around to make them lose their self-control. Instead, Maria in Tsui's project is easily tamed and domesticated by the people who are able to programme her, very different from the wild and rebellious female characters often seen in other Tsui films. The noirish femininity is not exactly about the female protagonist being a man-hating duplicitous temptress, but in the split identity of Maria: while the human Maria is a *femme fatale* that has been finally killed by men, the droid Maria survives and becomes a good woman for the male protagonists.

I Love Maria apparently was made for laughs, and Tsui seemed to enjoy his role as an actor rather than an ambitious producer who tried to impose moral sermonising in the film. But Tsui's vision of the modern city as a dark hellish place to be destroyed in a violent way is already there. Most fight scenes (the battles between robots and humans) take place in dim-lit spaces of urban architecture. The human–machine binarism is reinforced in the way that the boss of the evil gang attempts to turn himself into a robot by transplanting a pair of mechanical arms to his body. Confronting such mechanisation of the villain and other hostile forces, the heroes emphasise their friendship, trust, brotherhood, familial-like relationship, and even humanist love for other living things (the protagonists refuse to kill a dog for its meat even when they run out of food). The reiteration of the traditional values may sound clichéd. But such a 'retreat' to old values in the sci-fi film is driven by the increasingly dehumanising institutions (the gang, the police department and the news corporation) to which the protagonists originally belong. Not necessarily revalidating the traditional collective-oriented values, the underdog characters have to strategically rely on a certain moral high ground in order to win the brutal struggle with their corrupted and heartless superiors. In these Hong Kong tech-noirs, discontent with the despotic capitalist class and the social inequalities brought by the mechanical system does not automatically lead to an unconditional embrace of the traditional morality, even though some old values have been strategically appropriated.

That machine or technology has been broadly understood as the metaphor for the totalising process of mechanisation, modernisation or administrative rationalisation can also be seen in *The Wicked City* and *Black Mask*. Although *The Wicked City*, freely adapted from a Japanese manga-anime, is set in a future where human society is invaded and infiltrated by demons called 'Rapters' that can assume human form and other shapes, it consistently alludes to the apocalyptic return of Hong Kong to China that triggers anxieties, fears and chaos. The demons, like machines, also need fuel to empower themselves. And they are also like their antagonist humans, ruled by lust and greed, designating the troublesome situation of a doomed materialist world. The human counterparts are not able to offer any alternative since the official demon-hunter organisation is also overwhelmed with bureaucracy, self-interest, betrayal and mutual distrust. But Tsui is observably more fascinated by the intractable and mutable demons than by the drab and boring humans. It is the old demon leader (played by Nakadai Tatsuya) who has an aspiration to live with humans in harmony, and it is also the half-man half-demon character (Jacky Cheung Hok-yau) who sacrifices his life to ensure the success of the rescue mission. The visual eroticisation of a female demon (played by Michelle Reis) may inspire some scenes depicting the naked female cyborg Kusanagi Motoko from the Japanese animation *Ghost in the Shell* (Oshii Mamoru, 1995), though the special effects of *The Wicked City* are obviously not as subtle as those in the latter film. Allegorising Hong Kong's political transition on the surface, the film has highly valued mutability, hybridity or cross-breeding, which is the quality of the demons as well as the essence of Hong Kong tech-noir itself. But a subject with such fluidity and flexibility can only be a collaborator of the dispersed, decentralised or networked capitalism that strives to blur many more boundaries for the imperative to the more aggressive and unlimited accumulation of capital.

The Alluding Meanings of (Post-)1997 Tech-Noirs

The cross-bred characters continue in *Black Mask*, which is about a group of super-warriors who have been genetically altered to make their bodies no longer feel pain and emotion (but having a relatively short life expectancy like the humanoid replicants in *Blade Runner*) so as to become fatally destructive weapons. But the experiment is aborted and all warriors who are now failed experiments have to be destroyed. One member (Jet Li) succeeds in escaping to Hong Kong and covers himself as a librarian in order to relearn human feelings through reading. He blends quite well with a colleague Tracy (Karen Mok) who falls for him, and best buddy Detective Rock (Lau Ching-wan) who never doubts his identity. Soon the other escapees who have been his comrades catch up with him but they become villains who try to extort money from the human world in order to cure their diseases. Now the protagonist, dressed up as Kato from *The Green Hornet* TV series (1966–7), has to stand up against his ex-comrades in defence of humanity. The action flick touches on what it means to be human and problematises the protagonist's identity and conscience (even though he no longer feels human, he seems to have an inbuilt morality of right and wrong). This search for oneself could be socially relevant in the context of Hong Kong's imminent return to China, but the essence of humanity may not generate any productive meaning if unattached to any socio-political position.

When Tsui took up the *Black Mask* project by himself six years later, he seemed to explore the identity issue in a rather unexpected way though the story is still about the genetically modified superhuman. Made originally in English with a predominantly foreign cast, *Black Mask II* was dubbed in Cantonese when released in Hong Kong. The voice cast includes Andy Lau, Louis Koo, Lau Ching-wan, Cecilia Cheung, Jordan Chan, Chapman To and other leading actors in the industry. Tsui probably got very upset by the consecutive failures of *Knock Off* and this film in the US market, and went so far as to make fun of *Black Mask II* through the Cantonese dubbing or 'voice-over', as if it were a sarcastic parody of all the stupid English-language Hong Kong films he made for Hollywood (Columbia Tristar in this case). The Cantonese soundtrack relentlessly ridicules the characters in *Black Mask II* through the voice actors, constituting a typical split between the subject of enunciation and the subject of the enunciated. Does Tsui want to alienate himself from his own work by demonstrating that the enunciated content in the film he as an auteur says 'that's him' is actually not 'him'? But the Cantonese soundtrack cannot function as an active engagement to change the film, and Tsui, like the hero in the noir narrative, is reduced to a passive noir subject that helplessly gazes at the events within which he remains caught up and for which he cannot deny responsibility.

That the noir subject is being vulnerably trapped in the strange succession of events no matter how hard s/he fights can be found in Johnnie To's two comic book-like, action heroine films, *The Heroic Trio* (1993) and *Executioners* (co-dir. Tony Ching Siu-tung, 1993), and also in Wong Kar-wai's *2046* (2004). Well received as cult films outside Hong Kong, the two tech-noirs by To cast Anita Mui, Maggie Cheung and Michelle Yeoh as a trio of superheroes in a chaotic, crime-ridden, dystopic world that may allude to *fin de siècle* Hong Kong. Not intending to promote any explicit feminist messages,[19] To uses the heroine as a vehicle of differentiation from the mainstream swordsman actions dominated by male stars in the market. The portrayal of the female protagonist Wonder Woman (Anita Mui) as a domesticated housewife under her police chief husband may play out a masculine fantasy of sexual difference as well as a certain masculine anxiety. But the action heroines may refer less to the conventional politics of gender (how women can kiss ass and topple the patriarchal authority all in an instant) than to the feelings of powerlessness in an inevitable situation. The impossible mission for the heroines to rescue all kidnapped children from insane abuse by the evil villains and the violence inflicted upon women not only serves as an exploitative means or emotional bullying of the audience. They are also the evidence of loss of control, power, certainty and self-confidence. To fabricate women as superheroes who triumphantly fight the dark forces cannot really redeem one from being an inactive and horrified witness of seeing the established system and value crumbling and being annihilated.

Apparently teasing the year set by the Chinese government for the termination of Hong Kong's so-called autonomy and its different system from the Mainland, Wong in *2046* designates '2046' as a remote future to where a time-travelling express train is bound in order for the passengers to reclaim all the lost memories in a science fiction with the same name written by the male protagonist Chow Mo-wan (Tony Leung Chiu-wai) as well as a hotel room lived in by a number of women with whom Chow passionately tangles. The visual presentations of Chow's relationships with various female characters are artistically composed shots that seem to be parts of Chow's memories of them rather than the real encounters. If *2046* can be read as a parable of Hong Kong's future, its straightforward political reference is somewhat like the 1967 riot glimpsed in fragmented newsreel footage and mentioned in Chow's casual voiceover narration, which is trivial and fleeting. But the dim, tight and claustrophobic interiors within which the characters move around and inhabit attune to their trapped inner emotional states, conveying a sense of regressive immobilisation and compelling an endless return to a 'future' that has been shelved and delayed. That the characters are transfixed by a 'future' that resists any ultimate signification may induce more interesting political readings.

The sci-fi works under the collaborative mode of production between Hong Kong and China in the twenty-first century, such as *Kungfu Cyborg: Metallic Attraction* (Jeff Lau Chun-wai, 2009), *Future X-Cops* (Wong Jing, 2010) and *City Under Siege* (Benny Chan, 2010), have carried a certain noir-ness, although the Chinese sci-fi genre has already been assigned a nationalist mission to manifest the Chinese people's desire to play a major role in shaping the world's future in the new century.[20] Although some of these tech-noirs by Hong Kong directors were set in China or demonstrated a strong presence of the Mainland, there existed certain non-synchronous elements that may relate to a past among the faster-moving rhythms and speeds of the rising nation. While anxiously imagining a techno-future for Chinese audiences, these noirish films also invoke a past, in terms of their mood or storylines, that conveys a profound nostalgia for some experiences of space and time that have been rendered outmoded and fragile by the rapid transformations of capitalist modernisation. If the Chinese sci-fi genre is supposedly marked with the allegedly optimistic face of the forthcoming Chinese century, these Chinese-language flicks directed and scripted by Hong Kong crews express an existential angst as a common reaction to the unprecedented changes in

Chinese society, the revelation of a sense of being in exile at home, as well as a lingering sentiment for the ageing of an older form (probably Hong Kong colonial) of modernity. It may be too early to judge if Hong Kong future noir confirms or problematises the noir notion and its implied hegemony, but this ambiguous, hybrid sub-genre may provide a temporary 'home' for Hong Kong cinema to find comfort with itself, and to have the flexibility either to distance itself from or draw itself closer to China.

Notes

1. As Harootunian has said, 'capitalism [through the agency of the west] was "born of colonisation and the world market" and has subsequently "universalised" history, inasmuch as it has established systematic relations of social interdependence on a global scale that have eventually encompassed noncapitalist societies. In this regard, capitalism has managed to fix a standard of measurement – world time – produced by a "single global space of co-existence," within which action and events are subject to a single, quantifiable chronology': Harootunian, *History's Disquiet*, p. 49.
2. Vernet, 'Film Noir on the Edge of Doom', p. 6.
3. Žižek, 'Da Capo Senza Fine', pp. 248–9.
4. It may tell us how a concept can never exist on its own, but has to open to be completed by realities external to itself.
5. The typical and most reputed example probably is the one from the Argentine writer Jorge Luis Borges and quoted in Foucault's *The Order of Things*: 'a "certain Chinese encyclopaedia" in which it is written that "animals are divided into: (a) belonging to the Emperor, (b) embalmed, (c) tame, (d) sucking pigs, (e) sirens, (f) fabulous, (g) stray dogs, (h) included in the present classification, . . . (n) that from a long way off look like flies"'. Foucault then comments, in a dichotomised manner, '[i]n the wonderment of this taxonomy, the thing we [Europeans] apprehend in one great leap, the thing that, by means of the fable, is demonstrated as the exotic charm of another system of thought, is the limitation of our own, the stark impossibility of thinking *that*': Foucault, *The Order of Things*, p. xv (emphasis in the original). Of course, western culture and its way of categorisation could be equally strange, fragmented and illogical if examined from a Sino-centric perspective, which, however, does not necessarily naturalise and reconfirm the east–west dichotomy thinking.
6. Those who did use the noir notion to analyse Hong Kong films are mostly published in English and written by non-local critics. See, for instance, Fay and Nieland, *Film* noir, pp. 108–15; Lee, 'The Shadow of Outlaws in Asian Noir', pp. 127–9; Collier, 'The Noir East', pp. 137–58; Rist, 'Scenes of "in-Action" and Noir Characteristics in the Films of Johnnie To (Kei-Fung)', pp. 159–63; Desser, 'Global Noir', pp. 516–36; Naremore, *More than Night*, pp. 228–9.
7. Xu, 'Xianggang kehuan dianying qianlun', pp. 51–6.
8. Teo, *Hong Kong Cinema*, p. 236.

9. One can probably argue that the so-called 'tradition' of Chinese cinema cannot be fully understood without the western mediation in the west-dominated world, no matter how hard Chinese filmmakers and scholars have endeavoured to link the filmmaking of their times to the classical traditions of Chinese opera and other forms of national arts.
10. Meehan, *Tech-Noir*, p. 1.
11. Moine, *Cinema Genre*, p. 3.
12. Bordwell, *Planet Hong Kong*, p. 11.
13. Jaffe, *Hollywood Hybrids*.
14. Neither Bordwell nor Jaffe, however, has ever attempted to historically contextualise the hybrid or scavenging characters of Hong Kong cinema in their books.
15. Its male lead, James Yi, because of his personal debt problem, disappeared for months during the shooting, thus creating big delays to the production schedule. The computer-generated images were not able to produce a substitute for the male lead.
16. For instance, Teo argues that the film is 'a rare hybrid of *kungfu* and science fiction containing a bizarre, not wholly satisfactory, allegory about Hong Kong future': Teo, *Hong Kong Cinema*, p. 158.
17. Cheuk, *Hong Kong New Wave Cinema (1978–2000)*, pp. 191–2.
18. Ho and Ho (eds), *The Swordsman and His Jiang Hu*.
19. Johnnie To explains why he has cast three women in his films: 'we thought of making a movie about female heroes, because female stars were not so expensive and we couldn't at any rate get male stars since they were all contracted to other companies. We brought together three female stars, the most popular at the time: Anita Mui, Maggie Cheung and Michelle Yeoh – a very good combination. We wanted to make it different, so we didn't want to make it in period costume . . . So the idea was to make it different, post-modern, very comic book': Teo, *Hong Kong Cinema*, p. 222.
20. Song, 'Lun Zhongguo kehuan dianying de queshi', pp. 23–4.

PART THREE
COSMOPOLITAN CITYSPACE
AND NEO-NOIR

Chapter 8
Location Filmmaking and the Hong Kong Crime Film: Anatomy of a Scene

Julian Stringer

In his important book *Film Noir and the Spaces of Modernity*, Edward Dimendberg provides a cultural geographical analysis of the 'regulation of spatial territories' in 1940s and 1950s Hollywood film noir.[1] Drawing distinctions between 'two discrete but interrelated modes' – 'centripetal space' (that is concentrated urban space, often comprised of 'immediately recognizable and recognized spaces') and 'centrifugal space' (that is non-centred or dispersed spatial tendencies) – he outlines compelling new methods for analysing this culturally and historically specific production cycle.[2] A vital component of Dimendberg's argument concerns location filmmaking. For a variety of complex reasons, post-war US film noir was a 'beneficiary of innovations that permitted greater location cinematography'.[3]

Unfortunately, however, Dimendberg overlooks the significance of a topic that would benefit from more perspicuous scholarly attention – namely, the question of how filmmakers secure permission to shoot in spaces other than a sound stage to begin with. Because Dimendberg does not approach this matter directly, he inadvertently treats the phenomenon of location filmmaking as if it happens merely by accident, chance or else an act of will. In other words, the stories that lie behind the capacity to secure and utilise real-world locations remain untold and hence hidden. Across the pages of his otherwise commendably thorough book, the processes through which post-war US films noirs arranged the capture of non-studio images appear largely inexplicable.

An example of Dimendberg's limiting conceptualisation of this key aspect of location cinematography may be found in his discussion of *Johnny One-Eye* (Robert Florey, 1950). Considering decisions made with respect to location choices, he reports that, in a departure from its prior literary source, the film transposes its New York settings from 'the abandoned brownstones in which [protagonist] Martin hides from "East Fifty-third Street over near Third Avenue" to MacDougal Street in Greenwich Village' and claims that '[A]lthough the reasons for this switch must remain a topic of speculation, one might surmise that the selection of Greenwich Village . . . provided a greater opposition to the area around Times Square.'[4] A series of unanswered questions stubbornly lurk behind such pronouncements though. Why 'must' the reasons for such a 'switch' exist merely as 'a topic of speculation'? (Surely these matters can be researched empirically?) How are such 'selections' made and implemented in the first place? What are cinema historians to do with the ideology of free choice underpinning the notion that filmmakers are able simply to pick and choose from among a host of available locations?[5] Dimendberg perceptively asks: 'How could film noir illuminate the late-modern spaces of the 1940s and 1950s to which it provided unique access?'[6] Ironically, though, he himself shies away from providing detailed explication of the specific conditions that help facilitate the 'latent transformability of a street corner into a site of observation, the city (and the cinema) as a machine for making space visible'.[7]

This chapter engages with Dimendberg's discussion of location cinematography and the crime film by posing the key research question that *Film Noir and the Spaces of Modernity* seemingly declines to pursue: How do filmmakers gain access to the spaces within which they shoot? As the analysis below hopefully demonstrates, raising such a fundamental question of location filmmaking necessarily entails consideration of some of the core working practices associated with commercial feature film production.[8]

As well as exploring how and why genre filmmakers shoot their movies in certain real-world spaces, I am also interested in the unique aesthetic possibilities facilitated by the material conditions of location filmmaking.[9] Certainly, there is much that students of film noir and neo-noir have yet to learn about what it is that filmmakers actually do once they have gained access to particular sites. The case study that follows therefore focuses on culturally and historically specific aspects of the contemporary Hong Kong crime film as a distinct production cycle.[10] In order to ensure that the analysis is as detailed and rigorous as possible, my argument is presented in light of consideration of just one scene from one individual movie.

Out in the Streets

Although questions of location filmmaking are relevant to all commercial production cycles in all periods of cinema history, they penetrate and shape Hong Kong neo-noir in highly suggestive ways. The process by which filmmakers gain access to locations, and the creative uses they make of them once there, find unique aesthetic expression in films made in the city since the early 1980s. There are a number of reasons for this.

First, filming in Hong Kong poses a series of unique logistical challenges arguably not found in quite the same combination in other major urban centres. These factors include the severe constraints of time and budget that have historically characterised the local cinema industry, a high population density carrying with it the potential for unwanted interference from bystanders, urban sound pollution, and the substantial financial premium placed on accessing some of the world's most costly real estate. As the numerous testimonies included in the valuable Hong Kong Film Archive publication *Movement, Emotion and Real Sites @ Location* demonstrate, these circumstances have structured story and style in the local cinema for decades, including the abundance of neo-noir titles produced over recent years.[11]

Second, the crime film's narrative preoccupation with themes of transgression, law-breaking, detection and pursuit means that it presents investigations of spatial restriction and access as a matter of course. Once again, while other genres and cycles, like the action movie and the heist film, also explore such tropes, the contemporary Hong Kong neo-noir does so in particular ways. Films produced elsewhere, for example Los Angeles, New York, Seoul and Tokyo, thus do not draw on themes found in the Hong Kong crime film – such as triad culture – in quite the same way or to quite the same extent.

Third, the emergence of a plethora of commercially and critically successful contemporary Hong Kong crime movies has pushed the city's filmmakers to become more competitive by seeking up-to-date ways of exploring city spaces previously unseen by cinema audiences. This phenomenon is borne out, for instance, by the increased use of roof terraces as locations since the late 1990s, as in the case of *Purple Storm* (Teddy Chen Tak-sum, 1999), *Hit Team* (Dante Lam Chiu-yin, 2001) and *Infernal Affairs* (Andrew Lau and Alan Mak, 2002).[12] In such examples, the key impulse is to capitalise upon singular locations so as to attract and hold the viewer's attention.

Fourth, in recent years the Hong Kong Film Services Office (FSO) has striven to enable filmmakers to gain access to a range of both familiar and under-represented city spaces. The FSO was established in April 1998 under the Television and Entertainment Licensing Authority after the city's Chief Executive, Tung Chee-hwa, committed the government, in his 1997 Policy Address, to a number of new initiatives designed to revive the local movie industry:

> [A]part from facilitating film production and location shooting in Hong Kong, the FSO is also tasked with maintaining a resource centre which provides information and reference materials on film production services in

Hong Kong; promoting Hong Kong films by helping organise film festivals and exhibitions in Hong Kong and abroad; helping the industry to publish trade promotion materials and promoting the long-term development of the film industry.[13]

The FSO has proudly trumpeted its successes in all of these regards, often through the use of statistics. For example, in May 1999 it stated that it had already

> liaised with more than 140 government departments and public bodies in the last year to simplify procedures and to obtain the necessary approvals for location shooting at various sites ... the FSO plays a part in winning approval for movie-makers when filming involves complicated location shooting, such as in crowded places or the use of explosives and fake weapons.[14]

It further claimed to have 'provided assistance to 142 complicated cases of location shooting in 2000';[15] and to have issued guidelines in March 2001 'on outdoor shoots which involve street closure in a bid to ease the paper work involved in gaining permission to do so'.[16] By the end of 2006, the FSO had reportedly received 614 requests from local and overseas film production companies for assistance with filming projects in Hong Kong.[17]

It is important to note that the establishment of the FSO as the government body officially charged with facilitating location shooting in Hong Kong occurred in the period following the city's return to Chinese sovereignty on 1 July 1997. Alongside the other complex changes wrought by this moment of major historical transition, then, fresh attention to the economic and cultural attractions of location shooting provided Hong Kong with opportunities to rebrand the city's image for the twenty-first century. From this point on, particular aspects of both geographical change and continuity could be designed by filmmakers in league with this local agency.[18]

Lack of space unfortunately precludes further analysis here of the FSO's role in stimulating the nature, purpose and practice of location filmmaking in Hong Kong since 1998.[19] Instead, let us consider the no less significant question of how production circumstances linked to the use and extent of real-world shooting practices shaped story and style in the local cinema in the period immediately prior to the 1997 handover. Clearly, this is a time when location services were not as available to film crews as they were to be just a few months later; the establishment of the FSO marks a watershed moment when rules and regulations concerning filming activity in the city were formalised for all to see. However, in the days before the setting up of an official organisation ostensibly charged with facilitating access to shooting permits, how were non-studio images captured? What was the old way of doing things?

Because Hong Kong's filmmakers were obliged to seek less formal methods of scouting and utilising location settings, movies made at this time are among the last to be made 'on the lam', or without the benefit of the local government's support services. The period around 1997 and 1998 therefore represents a historical movement away from the practice of shooting below the radar via use of 'stolen' locations. Significantly, this earlier style is a mode of production that has often been identified by filmmakers and critics as embodying a distinctly Hong Kong cinematic aesthetic.

A further characteristic of this particular historical moment is that some local filmmakers active at this time appear to have sought deliberately to make movies that would archive the city's visual culture by chronicling what might be on the verge of disappearing. It is therefore constructive to consider in this respect how Ackbar Abbas' well-known words on Hong Kong cinema and the *déjà disparu*' (or the notion of cultural and aesthetic disappearance linked to 1997) finds historical parallels in the context of Dimendberg's observations regarding US films of the 1940s and 1950s.[20] For example, Dimendberg notes the American film noir cycle of this period's engagement with 'urban topoi on the verge of destruction'.[21] Similar to Abbas, he talks of film noir's '[n]ostalgia for public urban space' and of how the cycle 'needs to be grasped as a means of rendering visible the often-overlooked features of the city . . . many of which soon would disappear'.[22] In short, the US crime film of the 1940s and 1950s, according to Dimendberg, provided 'an opportunity for recording architectural and urban fragments of earlier historical moments before their imminent disappearance'.[23] Something similar was to happen again in Hong Kong around 1997. To repeat, the period immediately before political transition represents a time when these shifts in consciousness and production processes were occurring. At this point, local filmmakers worked without the safety net soon to be provided by the FSO.

The crime film case study chosen for investigation hereafter explores the working practices evident at this small window of historical opportunity. As outlined below, these historical circumstances injected a sense of urgent sensitivity into everything that was done at this particular moment in time. The remainder of this chapter thus grounds its analysis in the material realities underpinning just one example of Hong Kong crime filmmaking from this period.

Full Alert

Full Alert (Ringo Lam, 1997) is neither the most famous nor most celebrated example of the contemporary Hong Kong crime film. However, it is an excellent example of the kind of quality commercial neo-noir routinely produced in the city in recent years. It has therefore been chosen for analysis as much for its typicality and modesty of production as for its excellence and flamboyance. That said, *Full Alert* certainly does have its champions. It received five nominations at the seventeenth Hong Kong Film Awards, held in April 1998, for Best Film, Best Director, Best Actor (Lau Ching-wan), Best Editing (Marco Mak and Lam Nyn Ngai) and Best Sound (Brilliant Idea Group Ltd). In addition, critic John Charles calls it a 'grim, highly engrossing crime thriller which is highlighted by deeper characterisation than HK genre films are generally known for'.[24] Stephen Teo also wrote sympathetically about it at the time of its original release, extolling a number of key virtues:

> The Hong Kong film industry remains the foremost film-making centre in the Chinese-speaking world. Taiwan and Mainland China would be hard put to come up with films as imaginative and inventive as *Too Many Ways to be No. 1*, *Task Force*, *Made in Hong Kong*, *Full Alert*, *Island of Greed*, the Tsui Hark animation *A Chinese Ghost Story* [. . .] 1997 was also the year when one of the darkest of films ever made in Hong Kong was released: Ringo Lam's *Full Alert* [. . .] There are holes in the plot that make *Full Alert* a lesser picture than the great one it could have been. But its narrative thrust effectively covers up the holes; the picture is so dramatically taut that it appears too pat. Yet, apart from coming up with a good action picture in his best form, Lam has succeeded in delineating a mood that comes as close to the inner despair of the darkest allegories of good versus evil in literature – and in half the time than [Michael] Mann's overblown *Heat*.[25]

A reworking of Lam's well-known *City on Fire* (1987), *Full Alert* marked the director's return to Hong Kong after his work in North America on the Jean-Claude Van Damme star vehicle *Maximum Risk* (Ringo Lam, 1996). Co-scripted by Lam and Lau Wing-kin, the film is set in the city in 1997 and centres on the relationship between Inspector Pao (Lau Ching-wan) and former construction demolitionist turned thief Mak Kwan (Francis Ng Chun-yu). When the former arrests the latter following the discovery of blueprints and bomb-making equipment at an apartment building murder scene, Kwan admits to accidentally killing the victim but refuses to say anything further. As Kwan is being transported to court by police, his Taiwanese crime partners then attempt to rescue him, leading to a lengthy and lethal car chase. Kwan later escapes and so the police turn their attention instead to his girlfriend, Chung Lai-hung (Amanda Lee), in the hope that she might lead them to the gang. Pao eventually determines that the criminals plan to plunder the multi-million dollar bounty held in the safe of the Hong Kong Jockey Club. After increasingly tense and bloody encounters between the cop and his adversary, Pao catches up with the gang but kills Chung during the final showdown. Unable to handle the death of his beloved, Kwan shoots himself.

Figure 8.1 *Full Alert*: a bravura car chase that seems to encompass half of Hong Kong.

In terms of choice and use of locations, one scene from *Full Alert*, occurring approximately one-third of the way through the narrative, stands out as particularly significant – namely, a 'bravura car chase that seems to encompass half of HK'.[26] This scene, planned by Lam in collaboration with car stunt coordinator Fock Wing Foo, is striking because of its ambition. Lam has claimed in interview that he made the movie precisely in order to film this particular moment, 'because I wanted to complete a film before the 1997 change of sovereignty to preserve what was still there'.[27] More than this, his desire to film the entirety of Hong Kong Island raises questions of how it is possible for a filmmaker to materially access such a geographically large and congested physical space. As Lam states:

> Since Hong Kong Island is most representative of Hong Kong, I shot it from the Island Eastern Corridor to Central in order to record the entire Hong Kong Island on film. In 10 or 20 years, the streets and signs of Central documented may not look the same again. The places are witnesses to the passage of time. It'll be interesting to watch this film again in 20 years' time. Because it's a car chase and by freezing each frame, we can see each building clearly along the way. Since I rushed to finish the film before the handover in 1997, the car chase scene took on additional meaning.[28]

Surely this is filmmaking of high ambition – an attempt to map all of Hong Kong Island as a spatial exercise in preservation. Moreover, this particular scene is injected with a frantic sense of urgency and drama, the filmmakers giving every impression of having bolted through the window of opportunity opened up via a period of political transition from one administrative system to another.

Given that *Full Alert* was made before the establishment of the FSO, its extended car chase scene raises two fundamental questions. First, how exactly

Figure 8.2 *Full Alert* preserves disappearing Hong Kong locations on film.

were the filmmakers able to capture images, apparently at will, in such congested daylight locations? Second, what aesthetic choices did they make in designing the use of these locations for maximum resonance and impact? In considering such issues it is instructive to propose at this point a twin set of conceptual terms to structure the analysis that follows: namely, between authorised and unauthorised location filmmaking practices and between controlled and uncontrolled filmmaking situations. It is also important to observe that in any given example, the relationship between these four terms is likely to be fluid and variable.

Let us therefore begin our analysis of this extraordinary moment of Hong Kong neo-noir cinema by observing that car chase scenes in action narratives pose particular challenges to filmmakers linked both to questions of authorisation as well as matters of control. After all, as Tico Romao argues in the context of a discussion of US films such as *Bullitt* (Peter Yates, 1968) and *The French Connection* (William Friedkin, 1971), pursuit sequences have their 'most proximate origins in a realist aesthetic', and 'the emotional power of these sequences derives as much from their narrative aspects, as from their spectacular character'.[29] Romao outlines how the realist nature of such scenes – that is to say, their staging on streets and roads and in actual moving vehicles instead of through use of techniques of studio trickery like rear projection – developed as a significant formal dimension of this 1960s/1970s US production cycle (to which one might add the observation that such dimensions also characterise other formally advanced commercial movie industries such as Hong Kong's).[30] Such techniques fostered a sense of 'the authenticity of the chase', further heightened by 'a range of different camera setups' that allow the viewer to observe the action as well as character reaction through multiple vantage points.[31] Significantly, Romao reports that the stunt coordinator on *The French Connection* 'sped through uncontrolled city traffic as a means to obtain realistic footage'.[32]

Such words resonate in the context of the abundance of car chase scenes found in contemporary films noirs from Hong Kong. Indeed, it is possible to argue that a key defining feature of the city's engagement with neo-noir is its realistic use of authentic urban locations. Yet while the notion of 'realism' has been central to the development of Film Studies, the concept of cinema's fidelity to actual physical spaces has seldom been considered by scholars and historians. When shooting in the streets of a city like Hong Kong, filmmakers often strive to preserve a sense of geographic actuality while embedding familiar sights and sounds in compelling narrative situations. Yet this may or may not be done through authorisation and in situations that require greater or lesser degrees of control.

According to the available evidence – which includes the film's credits as well as interviews with Lam himself – permission was granted to film at some of the locations used in *Full Alert* (for example, Victory Centre) after negotiations with the relevant authorities.[33] Other locations, such as the vault and the sewerage system, were built in the studio.[34] Still others, including the car chase scene, were filmed without recourse to the gaining of official shooting permits.[35] In the case of Lam's ambition for the car chase scene, then, location challenges were evidently solved in a straightforward manner: permission for shooting was neither sought nor granted.

In extending cinema's tradition of unauthorised and clandestine high-end car chases, *Full Alert* had to negotiate with the specific nature of Hong Kong's unique cityscape. On the one hand, this arrangement threw up numerous obstacles, such as the proximity of the abundant passersby who can clearly be seen straining to observe the action as the cars speed by in front of their eyes.[36] On the other hand, it also generated unique possibilities.

Aesthetic Dimensions

In his discussion of story and style in the 1970s US car chase film, Romao draws attention to the 'inherent narrative dimension of the pursuit structure' that characterises such scenes – in other words, their wider narrative significance.[37] This observation is of clear relevance to issues of authorised/unauthorised and controlled/uncontrolled location choice and use in *Full Alert*.

When considering the intersection of film locations and wider narrative issues in Lam's film, it is once again helpful to keep in mind *Full Alert*'s status as a historically specific crime narrative. What questions of transgression and unlawful entry drive the aesthetic dimensions of this particular Hong Kong movie? Consider in this respect the fact that *Full Alert* is not just a crime film, it is also a heist narrative.[38] It is preoccupied with the ways and means by which its various characters gain access to a series of previously restricted spaces, and with the legality or illegality of this process. The screenplay works on the principle that the film is therefore concerned with the breaching of public and private spaces by criminal and cop alike. For example, its opening scene is set in an architect's stunning apartment – a very well-chosen location – that the police's special crime bureau is preparing to raid.[39] In line with Hong Kong cinema's increasing penchant for the use of rooftop locations at this time, it takes the viewer to the top of the building where a corpse has been concealed in a water tank.

The film then starts to present key narrative information by showing images of various maps. These shots function both as a prelude to the later presentation of scenes shot on actual city streets, and as a foreshadowing of the blueprints depicting the layout of the Jockey Club vault the criminals will ultimately attempt to break into. Detailed analysis of *Full Alert* as an example of what Tom Conley terms 'cartographic cinema' lies beyond the scope of the present chapter. (As he puts it, 'films *are* maps insofar as each medium can be defined as a form of what cartographers call "locational imaging"'.[40]) Instead, it is enough to draw attention at this juncture to Conley's observation that, in *The Crazy Ray* (*Paris qui dort*, René Clair, 1924), 'the edges of sidewalks, bulkheads, and river barriers become critical zones in a field of muted social conflict'.[41]

The introduction of the first of the film's many maps at this early part of the proceedings points to how the Hong Kong crime film – and the caper movie in general – engages as a matter of course with the narrative possibilities opened by physical locations that embody social conflict by existing at the intersection between entry and refusal. This is to say that crime stories tell tales of gaining unauthorised and uncontrolled access to previously barred or controlled borders. As they cross the legal and symbolic thresholds separating the law from lawlessness, criminals (and on occasion cops) step into spaces that they have hitherto not been authorised to enter.

At this point, the narrative aspects of *Full Alert* begin to offer a commentary upon themselves. Authorised location filmmaking is legal and permitted whereas unauthorised filming is not permitted and hence potentially illegal. In Lam's film, the criminals proceed in a manner similar to how they might if they were intending to 'steal' locations for an unauthorised movie shoot.[42] First, they make choices about which locations they aim to operate within (for example, 'scouting' the Jockey Club vaults). Next they confront the task of planning where and how to access – or rather break into – these particular spaces (for example, through detailed consideration of the blueprints.) Finally, they attempt to execute the job itself with stealth and aplomb, aiming to get in and out as quickly as possible. The parallels are irresistible. Those committing major robbery and those stealing film locations face common logistical difficulties, chief among which is the question of whether the cops will intervene before there is a chance to make a safe getaway.[43]

The narrative of *Full Alert* then moves on to the question of how to bust out of jail an accomplice who may aid in the execution of the proposed criminal scheme. Once again, this is an operation that requires knowledge of the targeted location and careful planning as well as the violation of a legal threshold which people are not usually permitted to cross. Appropriately enough, scenes depicting the careful planning of this task are presented through (seemingly unauthorised) location shooting, culminating in the extended car chase when an attempt is made miraculously to spring the individual from an impossibly tight police convoy.

Another form of visual mapping of location spaces is now introduced via the first of the film's many depictions of computer surveillance monitoring on the part of the police.[44] Images of such monitors will subsequently recur throughout the narrative; for example, when the cops all look at closed-circuit pictures taken inside the prison, and when they check to see whether Kwan has an account at the Jockey Club. Here, however, they plot out the entirety of the motorcade's planned route, taking in a litany of actual physical spaces: Shek Kong, Yau Ma Tei, Nathan Road, Po Ning House, and so on.

Figure 8.3 Wan Chai: *Full Alert*'s ambitious car chase scene takes in a litany of actual Hong Kong locations.

Brief mention may also be made at this point of two other aesthetic choices which enhance the narrative elements outlined above while designing the locations for maximum resonance and impact. First, the car chase scene is punctuated, or bookended, by dual images of bars or iron railings. Its opening shot is a cryptic image, seemingly taken from inside a police van, of thick iron bars obstructing both the camera's path and access to the street in front of it.[45] Nine minutes later, the scene ends with a shot of three police officers leaning in silhouette against an iron grating while in distress over the death of a colleague. Use of such finely nuanced mirror images metaphorically suggests the way in which this entire sequence has been 'locked down' by the crew as it goes about its task of shooting under the radar while on location.[46]

Finally, what about the use of sound in this scene? The film's audio design is once again something of an accomplishment – as demonstrated by the fact that the team concerned was honoured with a Best Sound accolade at the Hong Kong Film Awards – and the car chase scene provides excellent examples of this level of professional achievement.

The scene opens on the sound of a car alarm (accompanying the mysterious image taken from beyond an iron grid), thus illustrating in auditory terms some of the film's key themes such as transgression, law-breaking, detection and pursuit. After some very brief dialogue in the gang's getaway car, the soundtrack then unravels virtually wordlessly, with the sound effects taking on the burden of delivering much of the action in auditory terms. (The entire sequence includes a relatively sparse, if highly effective, use of music.) Individual shots of cars and other forms of traffic are then presented accompanied by sounds of differing scale, volume, pitch and timbre as the vehicles accelerate, screech, brake, skid and navigate around the murderous terrain while sirens wail and gun shots ring out.

It is highly likely that the audio design for this particular scene was constructed using a combination of sounds captured on location and in the studio. Location sounds of cars speeding in tunnels and down motorways could have been (and probably were) recorded on a different day than the filming of the images. Certainly, it would have been significantly easier all round for the sound crew to record such noises at another time and another place and then to match them to the visuals captured by Lam during the intense and hectic filming operation on Hong Kong Island. In this manner, the artful construction of a complex soundscape allows the filmmakers to deliver a multi-textured audio accompaniment to the thrilling images while navigating (through an artificial assemblage of effects) Hong Kong's notorious urban sound pollution.

In sum, in terms of choice and use of all these storytelling and aesthetic mechanisms, it is possible to speak of principles of geographic accessibility in *Full Alert* functioning as a double tier of meaning. At the textual level, the film's narrative sets up a series of questions concerning whether or not a group of criminals will gain unlawful access to hitherto restricted spaces. At the extra-textual level, the film's production poses a series of material questions concerning the extent to which filmmakers have or have not sought or gained permission to shoot on location. Issues of location filmmaking in *Full Alert* are mirrored on both textual and contextual levels, and in each case the narrative enigmas are very similar. Can the crew gain access to its desired locations? Will they have to bypass officialdom? How can these unauthorised spaces be controlled for the duration of the operation? In circumventing its own procedures in a manner akin to criminals planning their next intricate heist, *Full Alert* resembles an allegory of its own production.

Finally, it is also worth pondering the significance of the film's title. During a meeting held at police headquarters the night before the motorcade is due to set off, Inspector Pao outlines the plan of action for the benefit of his team. 'Tomorrow we escort Mak Kwan along this route,' he explains while pointing at a map of Hong Kong Island. 'I want you all on full alert! We could run into these guys [that is the Taiwanese gang] at any moment!' How very tempting it is to consider this to be precisely the kind of rallying cry that Lam himself may have given his crew as he charged them with the slightly insane task of pulling off their own ambitious heist – the filming of an intricate unauthorised car chase down the full length of the island.[47] In Hong Kong thrillers produced around 1997, the lines separating police from villain are very often blurred. More than that, the process of making such movies is at times difficult to distinguish from the act of committing a crime.

Conclusion

The contemporary Hong Kong neo-noir production cycle straddles the historical line dividing the period before and after the establishment of the official body charged with facilitating access for filmmakers to the city's various locations. Since the mapping out of new spatial regulatory procedures through the formation of the Hong Kong Film Services Office in 1998, it has become easier for directors and other movie personnel to navigate the material politics of the process by which the latent transformability of real-world locations is forged into sites of cinematic observation.

However, as this chapter has sought to demonstrate through its anatomy of just one scene from *Full Alert*, the period immediately before the transition of Hong Kong's political sovereignty in 1997 – a time when filmmakers relied more upon methods of unauthorised location shooting – is on these terms of no less historical interest and importance than the period which followed it.[48] After all, pre-FSO filmmaking in Hong Kong is often celebrated precisely for its penchant for shooting 'on the lam'. *Full Alert* thus functions as a kind of historically specific psycho-geography of the city. This chapter has sought to explore both the aesthetic dimensions of this achievement as well as its grounding in pragmatic filmmaking practices.

Given *Full Alert*'s status as a well-made and compelling but largely unexceptional Hong Kong neo-noir – albeit one that deserves to be better known than it currently is – who can say how many other instructive location situations linked to this particular production cycle might profitably be explored through scholarly investigation? Issues of location filmmaking animate Hong Kong crime films in highly specific ways and lend them a sense of drama as well as authenticity. They also raise other intriguing lines of inquiry which will hopefully be followed up in future research. For example, the question of the availability (or otherwise) of insurance cover connected to filmmaking in the city, especially around stunt work and other kinds of action-oriented activities.[49]

This chapter has explored the politics and poetics of location filmmaking in just one historically specific example of the Hong Kong crime film. Analysis could of course be extended further to consider location choice and use in other Ringo Lam neo-noirs, especially those that draw upon the talents of his more regular collaborators. This challenge, as well as the task of analysing the cultural politics of location filmmaking in the post-1997 period, will have to wait for another day. In the meantime, there is no doubt that more recent Hong Kong neo-noirs have proven to be equally preoccupied with the prospect of shooting on location, especially given the benefits of opportunities secured through gaining the FSO stamp of approval. There is thus a clear need for future scholarship to pay detailed attention to the geographic analysis of important titles as varied as *The Mission* (Johnnie To, 1999), *Infernal Affairs* (Andrew Lau and Alan Mak, 2002), *Protégé* (Derek Yee, 2007) and *Vengeance* (Johnnie To, 2009).[50]

Notes

1. Dimendberg, *Film Noir and the Spaces of Modernity*, p. 47.
2. Ibid., pp. 18, 255.
3. Ibid., p. 12.
4. Ibid., p. 97. The quoted reference is from the Damon Runyon story upon which the film *Johnny One-Eye* is based.
5. Similarly, when discussing *The Street with No Name* (William Keighley, US, 1948), Dimendberg, ibid., p. 28, describes how the film 'commences with a shot of the seal of the FBI followed by a series of long shots of the exterior of its headquarters in Washington, D.C., succeeded by a statement that "wherever possible" it was photographed in the original locale'. It is the meaning and implications of that 'wherever possible' that require further consideration.
6. Ibid., p. 3.
7. Ibid., p. 33.

8. It is also worth pointing out that these working practices cut across – and hence throw into relief – Dimendberg's theoretical distinction between centripetal and centrifugal spatial tendencies.
9. For further consideration of such issues in the context of the production of a different contemporary genre – namely, US television drama – see Stringer, 'The Gathering Place: *Lost* in Oahu', pp. 73–93.
10. On the situating of film noir in Asia through empirical investigation of the historical formation of crime thrillers in one particular time and place, see Lee and Stringer, 'Film Noir in Asia', pp. 479–95.
11. Fu (ed.), *Movement, Emotion and Real Sites @ Location*.
12. Ibid., pp. 168–73.
13. Government Information Centre, 'FSO Places HK on Map of Celluloid World'. This reference, together with the primary materials cited in notes 14–17 (below), were sourced at the Hong Kong Film Archive; page references are provided where available. For a succinct overview of the work of contemporary 'film commissions', see Swann, 'From Workshop to Backlot', pp. 88–98.
14. Eddy Chan Yuk-tak, Commissioner for Television and Entertainment Licensing, quoted in Wong, 'Cameras Roll on Location as Office Chalks up Its 50th Successful Take'.
15. Government Information Centre, 'Hong Kong Remains a Safe and Attractive Place for Filming'. This particular source also reports on a 'recent incident involving a film company being asked to provide protection money by an alleged triad member for location shooting'. Insisting that this 'was an isolated case', it goes on to state that the 'incident would not affect the international reputation of Hong Kong . . . Blackmailing would not be tolerated. For the majority of cases, location shooting should remain incident free.'
16. Lau, 'Painting over the Cracks'.
17. Tsui, 'Site Seeing'. Discussing ways of branding Hong Kong for overseas markets as a modern cosmopolitan city, this article also makes the point that crime films depicting the city as a 'warren of labyrinthine streets bubbling with intrigue and menace' can be just as alluring and effective as representations of the 'usual hackneyed landmarks such as the harbourfront or bustling Central or Tsim Sha Tsui . . . Authorities are very aware of how cities should demolish stereotypes and market them beyond the conventional landmarks that draw so many visitors from overseas.'
18. The establishment of the FSO was particularly good news for filmmakers working in certain genres – for example, action films and comedies – which rely upon street and location shooting as part of their appeal.
19. Phillip Lee, the celebrated Executive Producer and owner of Hong Kong- and Beijing-based Javelin Pictures, stated in 2010 that

> [I]t's very easy to arrange shooting in Hong Kong, but for some 'big asks' like blocking entire streets, you have to be well-connected with various Government departments through the Film Service Office. For instance, with their help we could block the city's airspace for our shooting! Our planes and helicopters were able to fly above Hong Kong for the whole of these shoots.

(It is likely that Lee is referring here to the Hong Kong scenes in the 2008 noir-inflected Batman movie, *The Dark Knight* [Christopher Nolan, 2008]). Quoted in Peak, 'Hong Kong Producers Discuss Filming the City'.
20. Abbas, *Hong Kong: Culture and the Politics of Disappearance*.
21. Dimendberg, *Film Noir and the Spaces of Modernity*, p. 64.
22. Ibid., pp. 109, 121.
23. Ibid., p. 221.
24. Charles, *Hong Kong Filmography 1977–1997*, p. 118.
25. Teo, 'Sinking into Creative Depths', pp. 11, 12–13.
26. Charles, *Hong Kong Filmography, 1977–1997*, p. 118.
27. Ringo Lam, quoted in Fu, *Movement, Emotion and Real Sites @ Location*, p. 163. Clearly, his comment in this same source that 'I rushed to shoot "Bird Street" which was later demolished' resonates in the context both of Abbas' work and Dimendberg's observation that post-World War II US film noir exhibits a penchant for locations on the verge of disappearance as well as a fascination with capitalist redevelopment and transformation.
28. Lam, quoted in ibid., p. 163.
29. Romao, 'Guns and Gas', pp. 131, 132. See also Romao, 'Engines of Transformation', pp. 31–54.
30. For further consideration of this topic in the US context, see Ramaeker, 'Realism, Revisionism and Visual Style', pp. 144–63.
31. Romao, 'Guns and Gas', pp. 132, 133.
32. Ibid., p. 137.
33. Lam stated at the time of the release of *Full Alert* that

> [S]hooting films in Hong Kong has great limitations since the government will not formally cooperate with us. I am not sure whether Tung Chee-hwa will fulfill his promise of promoting the film industry. The government knows nothing about movies. Since officials do not want to shoulder their responsibility, we are happy to lie to them to make them happy. For example, when we apply for permits, we usually inform them that we are just shooting non-action scenes in public areas. Even if you tell them the truth, they won't respond in a constructive way. So it's better not telling them and they will gladly entertain your sweet talks. If we pull out a toy gun on the streets and the police spotted us, they will hold up work for an hour or two and then we can go on. This way, in case anything happens the police can tell the public that the shooting was never authorized.

Quoted in Lai and Ho, 'The Lucky One Becomes the Cop: Ringo Lam on *Full Alert*', p. 40.
34. Ibid., p. 40.
35. Lam claims that the car chase scene was shot in secret in five working days. In answer to the question of why, in later scenes, the Jockey Club was used, he answers

> No special reason. I think it is partly because there have been too many bank robbery films. But we had to shoot the scenes in secret, knowing damn sure that the Jockey Club would say no . . . even the scenes in the stands . . . The crew

just carried the equipment inside the track. They kicked us out the first day. We sneaked in again. We spent three days shooting just a few minutes of the actual film. (Ibid., p. 40.)

No need to guess whether this Hong Kong filmmaker asked for or was granted authorisation to film the aerial views of the Jockey Club in *Full Alert*.
36. To quote Lam's own words once again, his crew did not block the roads when shooting the car chase scene: 'We timed everything. We chose Sunday to reduce the risk and we informed the tram station right before shooting. I could have rented a tram to minimize the risk but that was not possible either.' Ibid., p. 40.
37. Romao, 'Guns and Gas', p. 143.
38. As Charles puts it, 'While [the break-in at the Jockey Club] seems an impossible task, Mak [Kwan] is an architectural design expert and has determined the one weak spot that will allow access', *Hong Kong Filmography, 1977–1997*, p. 118.
39. Since this is a private residential space, the obvious likelihood is that use of this particular location was secured through negotiation with its owner. Although further details are impossible to ascertain at the present time, it is possible, for example, that the deal involved a cash payment or some other form of compensation. Alternatively, the apartment could belong to an individual known to someone on the filmmaking team, in which case the process of securing usage of the site might have been significantly smoothed.
40. Conley, *Cartographic Cinema*, p. 2. Italics in original.
41. Ibid., p. 33.
42. Indeed, when describing the shenanigans his crew went through to capture the Jockey Club shots referred to in note 35 (above), Lam reports, 'To shoot a movie is to record what one feels during the shooting itself . . . I feel like a thief myself.' Quoted in Lai and Ho, 'The Lucky One Becomes the Cop', pp. 39, 40.
43. In another arguably self-reflexive moment, Inspector Pao loses his cool at the Jockey Club after low-ranking officials tell him that he needs to obtain the consent of its Board of Directors to access the vault and hence stop a major robbery from taking place. 'Permission?' rails Pao while energetically gesturing at the blueprints. 'Damn them!'
44. Such shots also serve as another form of precursor of the car chase scene, where such monitors will be deployed extensively to provide the viewer with a handy visual map of the convoy's entire route through Hong Kong Island. They thus provide a foreshadowing of action to come as well as a grounding of that action in the physical reality of authentic Hong Kong roads and streets.
45. This shot is followed by images of the Taiwanese gang hot-wiring a stolen car – another example of the criminals opening up a previously closed space by removing obstacles to access.
46. In addition, the opening shot of the following scene (which parallels the opening and closing shots of the car chase sequence) is of Kwan in prison, thus suggesting shared links between the emotional experiences of criminal and cop.
47. Another example of meta-commentary operating in the car chase scene: 'They're all crazy' observes a driver in one of the police cars with a worried look on his face

as the vehicles begin to weave at high speed in and out of trams while careering towards Wan Chai.

48.
> I still miss the days when we used to shoot on the sly. The action scenes in some Hong Kong films are exciting precisely because they were shot on the sly. The unstable camera reflects the nervousness of the cameraman [sic]. Since he [sic] was getting ready to run, the shots are quick and a bit chaotic. As the real shooting is bound to be different from the rehearsal, the shots feel extremely tense with a strong sense of reality. Even though we can apply for permission now, sometimes I would rather shoot it the old way. Instead of doing it shot by shot, we would rehearse the whole scene to capture the live tension.

Director Gordon Chan quoted in Fu, *Movement, Emotion and Real Sites @ Location*, p. 145.

49. In their insightful interview with Lam about the production of *Full Alert*, Lai and Ho ask directly whether the car chase scene is insured. 'Yes,' replies Lam, 'but only for our crew.' 'What about the pedestrians and the vehicles?' asks Ho. 'That is simply impossible because we are not authorized,' states Lam. 'Statistically, there have not been too many accidents in the past. Even the one explosion accident this year which killed a crew member happened near army headquarters. If I remember right, no civilian has ever been hurt so far; the most you can say is that our filming disturbed them.' Quoted in Lai and Ho, 'The Lucky One Becomes the Cop', p. 40.

50. See also Ingham, *Johnnie To Kei-Fung's PTU*.

Chapter 9
Running Out of Time, Hard-Boiled and 24-Hour Cityspace

Kenneth E. Hall

The *Running Out of Time* (Johnnie To, 1999, 2001) films, as well as other Hong Kong dystopic films such as *Hard-Boiled* (John Woo, 1992), share with the now-iconic American television series *24* (2001–10, summer 2014) a preoccupation with the concentration and limitation of time and motion. The Hong Kong films to be considered here express the well-known anxiety about the 1997 handover through strategies of suspense relying on limitation of time, a familiar technique transferred into an innovative setting as the lead character in each *Running Out of Time* film engages in a parodic mirroring of the 'get rich' activity so basic to the experience of Hong Kong. The parody is not only societal but cinematic, as the noir icon *D.O.A.* (Rudolph Maté, 1950), among other noir films such as *White Heat* (Raoul Walsh, 1949), *The Big Clock* (John Farrow, 1948) and *Where the Sidewalk Ends* (Otto Preminger, 1950), serves as subtext for a 'running out of time' anti-hero.[1]

While the pre-1997 apocalyptic film *Hard-Boiled* differs from *Running Out of Time* in its presentation, it nevertheless posits a familiar but hypertensive cliff-hanger scenario (a hospital held hostage, with patients and staff, by a ruthless, even deranged, gang) as a metaphor for a society losing its underpinnings. Here these texts and others intersect with the phenomenally successful American TV series *24*, which has employed a highly innovative and demanding 'real-time' strategy to play out (some would say to engender) Americans' fears of terrorist activity following 11 September 2001. The mechanics of the series rely on repeated 'cliff-hanger' situations which are significantly intensified by the 24-hour structure of the show (one hour-long episode = one hour of 'real time'), which does not permit time lapses not covered in the narrative, or other ellipses, and are complicated further by the introduction of parallel and intersecting subplots and incidents. Notably influenced by Hong Kong 'action' technique and by melodramatic practice, the series nonetheless evolves an original narrative, within an American context (often mirroring current topics in American political discourse in its plots), which expresses concerns parallel to those of certain Hong Kong films since the 1980s.

The post-1997 Hong Kong action film, specifically the gangster and cop films familiar to viewers of pre-1997 Hong Kong work like that of John Woo, Ringo Lam and Kirk Wong, features an increased emphasis on limitation of time and space and on the disappearance of the clear line between Hong Kong and Mainland China. While Mainland characters had certainly been present in earlier releases, notably the *Long Arm of the Law* (Johnny Mak Tong-hung and Michael Mak Tong-kit, 1984–90) films, their presence in Hong Kong as active participants in crime was perhaps not taken for granted as easily as in a recent film like *Flash Point* (Wilson Yip, 2008). In this Donnie Yen vehicle, the brotherhood between the Hong Kong cops is threatened and nearly destroyed by the activities of a trio of blood brothers on the run from the Chinese Mainland; in fact, the relationship between the Mainland brothers is more central to the narrative than the expected brotherhood of cops motif.

Furthermore, films like *Flash Point* and its prequel *Kill Zone* (aka *SPL*, 2005) are specifically set in pre-1997 Hong Kong, permitting a putatively nostalgic treatment of the personnel and environment of the Hong Kong police department under the colony before its linking to the enforcement organisations of the Mainland. Despite their pre-handover setting, these and other such films made after 1997 (like *Dragon Heat* [aka *Dragon Squad*, Daniel Lee, 2005] and *Invisible Target* [Benny Chan, 2007]) display a particularly unsettling ruthlessness and expenditure of destructive energy with regard to combatants as well as civilians. Especially notable in this regard is the recent film *Dragon Heat*, in which the body count among civilians caught between rival criminal organisations, mercenaries and competing groups of law enforcers is quite high, and the lives of police officers seem to be treated as just so much collateral damage. The handover also plays directly into the plot of some films, for example *Exiled* (Johnnie To, 2006), set in Macau just before the reversion to Mainland control. *Exiled* displays a somewhat befuddled policeman (Hui Siu-hung in essentially the same role as in the *Running Out of Time* films) avoiding intervention in the triad fight between Boss Fay (Simon Yam) and Curtis (Anthony Wong) because his retirement, due to the handover, is only hours away.

The triad protagonists of many of these films are motivated by the need for financial security. Even many policemen are preoccupied with the money chase (in contrast to cop heroes of pre-1997 films like *A Better Tomorrow* [John Woo, 1986], *Hard-Boiled*, and *City on Fire* [Ringo Lam, 1987], who are motivated more strongly by honour and by *esprit de corps*). Money – the getting and losing of money – is a central motif in post-1997 films from *Full Alert* (Ringo Lam, 1997) to *Exiled*. In a process akin to the 'hyphenation' discussed by Abbas with respect to the Hong Kong cityscape and its cinema, the romantic presentation of traditional values begins to be levelled into a concern with the instability of the global capital system.[2]

Exiled presents a particularly appropriate picture of the unsettled situation in Macau (and by extension, in Hong Kong) on the eve of 1 July 1997. The setting in Macau in fact adds to the sense of 'borrowed place, borrowed time'[3] because of the historically undefined nature of Macau, expressed, as Jonathan Porter observes, in its ephemeral architecture.[4] Suspense in this film revolves around several axes, the primary of which is the fate of Wo (Nick Cheung), a hitman who has left the employ of Boss Fay after nearly killing him. Fay has sent a set of hitmen led by Curtis to kill Wo, but the killers decide to postpone their action until at least the next day – significantly, the day of the handover. The impending collapse of the agreed-upon protocols in the territories soon to become PRC property extends to the performance even of contracts for assassination.

The hitmen and Wo soon become allies against Fay and local boss Keung (Lam Ka-tung), although Wo soon dies in a gunfight. Even the gunfights are presented as aleatory, with many shots missing their mark and with camera eye-lines not uniformly resolved. The hitmen escape and, chance again intervening, happen upon the route of a shipment of a ton of gold for corrupt officials. They begin to toss a coin to decide on their course of action – that is, coin toss becomes their preferred choice for decision-making. They obtain the gold, acquiring an ally in a courageous and skilled policeman who had been guarding it; and, in a nod to *The Wild Bunch* (Sam Peckinpah, 1969), they decide (minus the policeman, who stays with the bulk of the gold) to face overwhelming odds and near-certain death in a bid to rescue Wo's widow and baby from Fay and his men. The ineffectual Macau cop again declines to intervene in the fight, allowing Fay and the hitmen to kill each other (and all Fay's gunmen), and the widow and the baby to escape to the boat where the allied policeman is waiting. In a final twist, a prostitute who seems to inhabit the hotel drags the hitmen's share of the gold away.

The two *Running Out of Time* films approach the Hong Kong of the handover period from a game-playing perspective. In the first film, Cheung (Andy Lau), apparently suffering from terminal cancer (thus the title of the film, which also refers to the handover), leads sympathetic cop Inspector Ho (Lau Ching-wan) on a game of cat-and-mouse through locations in the city. The MacGuffin here is a cache of jewels apparently to be transferred to a bald crook (Waise Lee), with a stunning diamond as the central prize. Although many of the games seem harmless enough, a scene in the car driven by the cop, with Cheung as passenger, illustrates the deadliness beneath the surface, as Cheung begins to shoot randomly near pedestrians: a clear analogue to the perilous disruptions within Hong Kong society, viewed from the vantage point of a speeding cab. Society and its underpinnings are changing too fast to be managed or even predicted. At the end of the film, Cheung is shown driving away, and a woman he had met during one of his escapes is wearing the diamond. Certainly intimated is the possibility that he may reappear, throwing into question even the validity or seriousness of his illness.

While Cheung does not appear in the sequel, his gamester successor (Ekin Cheng) is a kind of leprechaun or trickster figure whose stunts lead at film's end to a whimsical outcome. Along the way the trickster plays seemingly endless games of coin toss with a heavily indebted cop (Lam Suet) who continues each time to call a losing 'Tails', finally to learn that playing has no value. The policeman becomes a Santa Claus figure, trying to give to others. Again the bases of the get-ahead capitalist system in Hong Kong are questioned, this time not only with the handover as backdrop but also appropriately during Christmas season.

Games and gambling are central as well to the sequel to this film as well as to a quite different film, *Full Alert* (Ringo Lam, 1997). In this film with echoes of *The Killing* (Stanley Kubrick, 1956), resentful engineer Mak Kwan (Francis Ng) aids a group of Taiwanese criminals in robbing a racetrack. The object of the theft is itself based in chance, as gambling winnings become a source of international contention and revenge against a system perceived as unjust. An additional element of importance in the transitional process to unification is the guilt experienced both by Inspector Pao (Lau Ching-wan) and the engineer over having killed a person; for these inhabitants of a city in flux, the past is unresolved and surfaces as nightmare. Neatly encapsulating the threat is a sequence in which a young cop and a group of schoolchildren are held hostage on a bus with a time-bomb on board: the future of the governing apparatus as well as the future of the society at large are both threatened inside a bus, an instrument of collective urban mobility. A similar if much larger threat is actually put into effect in Woo's *Hard-Boiled*, in which the ruthless Wong (Anthony Wong) attempts to kill all the patients and staff, as well as police and rescue workers, in the hospital which had served him as arsenal for his criminal enterprise. In this 1992 film, which looked ahead to post-1997 apocalyptic motifs, the urban landscape of Hong Kong became a killing ground, with SWAT teams and gangsters shooting it out from street to hospital windows.

The urban environment of Hong Kong is visualised strikingly in films such as To's gangster and cop dramas, several of which have been termed 'Kowloon Noir' by Stephen Teo.[5] One of these films in particular shows intriguing parallels to *24*: *PTU* (2003), which, as Teo notes, 'unfolds over one night', much as each season of *24* unfolds over one day. *PTU* also parallels *24* in its visualisation of urban space as 'the aftermath of a metaphysical apocalypse';[6] in *24*, this vision can be seen in scenes such as those in Season 1 when Kim Bauer and her doomed friend Janet (Jacqui Maxwell) flee from their kidnappers into a seedy area of Los Angeles inhabited by criminal and socially maladjusted denizens.

The fears surrounding the handover and its effects on Hong Kong, which was to become the Special Administrative Region (SAR), are neatly expressed in metonymic fashion in the relationship between Jimmy (Louis Koo) and Boss Lok (Simon Yam), from whom Jimmy wrests power, in *Election 2* (Johnnie To, 2006). Jimmy had made a bargain with a representative of the Chinese intelligence community that he would be able to do business on the Mainland without interference provided he became triad leader. He discovers, however, that his enterprises are to be controlled by the state, as he is expected to follow the lead of his 'mentor' in the government. Jimmy claims only to be a businessman and that he never wanted to be a gangster. He expected his version of free enterprise to proceed apace, reflecting the hopes of many Hong Kong business people that China would not interfere with the special nature of Hong Kong economic structure after the handover. Of course, the ironic fact here is that Jimmy is not a legitimate businessman, or perhaps it might be concluded ideologically that his activities merely present the underside of normal big business transactions.

Like 1 July 1997 for Hong Kong, 11 September 2001 was a watershed in United States consciousness. Perhaps even more than 1997 for Hong Kong, where the handover had been a long-anticipated event, 11 September represented for the United States a shocking point of recognition that protected insularity was no longer possible, that in a real sense the relationship of the United States to international entities had undergone a collapse, as if the national space had opened up (or had been forced open) to the degree that the former sense of isolated security was no longer operative. Predictably, the threat of penetration from outside led to a constriction of space, notably in official security terms, and time was felt to be at a premium as far as forestalling further attacks was concerned.

This framework was mirrored with especial accuracy in the television series *24*, which premiered in Fall 2001 and ran until Spring 2010. The most notable feature of the series was its 'real-time' narrative in which one hour of running time was equated to one hour of story time, and the 24 episodes per series season were equated with one day in the lives of the characters. Besides this structurally restrictive mode of presentation, the series also featured extensive use of current technology – cell phones, computers – and in fact the ubiquity of cell phone conversations in the series led directly to another distinctive technical display, the use of boxes (split-screen), at first primarily to display the participants in conversations, and increasingly as well to present or to recap the several sub-plots embedded in the narrative. The locus of the action is largely urban, set in Los Angeles during the first six seasons, and then in Washington, DC (Season 7) and in New York City (Season 8, the final year). The narrative for most seasons repeatedly shifted to the White House or to the president's retreat or command centre. One season (3) was shifted between Los Angeles and a drug cartel's headquarters in a small town in northern Mexico. Jack Bauer (Kiefer Sutherland) is the complexly heroic[7] counter-terrorism agent whose personal life intersects, chiefly tragically, with his dangerous work for CTU (the Counter Terrorist Unit), based in Los Angeles.[8] It should be noted at this point that unlike the Hong Kong films under consideration, the acquisition of money is not generally a motivation in *24*; in fact, those characters associated with desire for money are seen negatively (CTU officer George Mason [Xander Berkeley], suspected of embezzling confiscated funds; the Salazar drug family and turncoat CTU agent Nina Myers [Sarah Clarke]). Although Jack's motives may be mixed at times, no one places into doubt his heroism and his loyalty to country.[9]

The series was set in crucial power centres for global capitalism, a move certainly understandable purely in narrative terms: important US cities are magnets for terror attacks, and Washington, DC is of course the political centre. For most of the series, though, presidential politics was carried out in 'retreats' or refuges not located on the East Coast: Logan's retreat near Los Angeles, a military establishment in Oregon for Palmer, an LA facility for Palmer in Day 3 during his re-election campaign.

The Los Angeles locus is significant, as LA represents the newer, faster-moving, less staid face of modern United States – and by extension global – capitalism, as opposed to the 'older' tradition of New York, with its nineteenth-century associations. Like Hong Kong, whose ephemeral architecture reflects its disjointed historical and cultural memory,[10] Los Angeles has been the subject of purposeful 'forgetting'. Norman M. Klein says of the destruction of downtown 'ethnic communit[ies]' in Los Angeles that '[m]ost Angelinos I interview, even those who live immediately in the areas affected, have barely a dim memory that these neighbourhoods stood at all' and notes that '[t]he overall effect resembles what psychologists call "distraction," where one false memory allows another memory to be removed in plain view, without complaint – forgotten'.[11] The brief change of setting for Seasons 7 and 8 to Washington and New York, with their many sites of remembrance, respectively serves only to underline the special nature of the Los Angeles setting.

24 is a complicated hybrid of serial melodrama, with its cliff-hanger endings, highlighting of action over meditative character development, and intricate sub-plotting;[12] and neo-noir storytelling – dark cinematography, characters with conflicting motives and psychic imbalance, innocents trapped in nets of deceit and violence, societal disintegration in urban settings, and treacherous *femmes fatales*. Jack Bauer is a noir anti-hero who overlays his essential integrity and dedication to his work with acts of torture, violence and deception, admittedly carried out in the line of duty but in numerous cases shaded with a combination of personal motivation and even gratification.[13] His character becomes, by at least season 6, a psychologically damaged entity which fits well into the noir catalogue of conflicted and injured protagonists.[14] (This emotional damage is actually displayed expressionistically in his scarred body revealed during Season 6 and in the potentially terminal disease contracted by Bauer in Season 7, whose symptoms include seizures and lack of mental focus.)[15]

His terrorist adversaries are aided by a series of treacherous female characters, whose *femme fatale* status is certainly not absent from the typical melodrama but whose entrapment and frustration of Bauer and other male heroic characters (especially President David Palmer [Dennis Haysbert]) places them more firmly into the noir framework. Chief among these are Nina Myers, CTU agent turned mole (apparently planted or suborned by an undetermined agency or group before the time of the series), whose love affairs with Jack and then with CTU agent Tony Almeida (Carlos Bernard) become part of her undermining tactics; and Sherry Palmer (Penny Jerald Johnson), the manipulative and highly duplicitous wife of Senator (later President) David Palmer, whose machinations continue even after he divorces her early in the series.[16] Similar also to noir is the destructive effect of Bauer's and Palmer's careers on the unity (and in fact the very existence) of their families.

Central to the noir (or neo-noir) experience of the series is its treatment of urban, and non-urban, space. Most of the violent confrontations and threats, and even the hairbreadth rescues and escapes, are played out either on urban streets or within urban environments such as garages, apartments, office spaces – especially within the severely delimited 'secure' space of CTU – hospitals or even school buildings. The limited occasions for Bauer to egress from the city and its suburbs, such as his rescue of his family in Season 1, or his pursuit of a terrorist in Season 4 prior to his rescue of kidnapped Secretary of Defense James Heller (William Devane) and his daughter Audrey Raines (Kim Raver), only serve to underline the restrictively urban space of the narrative. As noted, much of the urban space is further compressed to the confines of the CTU building.[17]

Limitation of space is a motif of the series to such an extent that it rivals the emphasis on limitation of time. The CTU structure is filled with hallways, holding rooms and cul-de-sacs, and even when characters interact outside its confines, they tend to be placed in similarly constricting spaces: police stations with holding rooms, offices and security doors; ruined buildings with maze-like configurations (a doomed police officer in Season 1 calls the building through which she and Jack pursue a suspect 'a maze'); multi-level buildings in which the elevators and long hallways are emphasised; and underground spaces like subway stations, and, in Season 1, a 'Class 3 detention centre' (7–8 pm) hidden under a seemingly pristine wilderness area.

Open-air settings are not presented here as much less threatening than indoor, circumscribed ones. The base camp where Jack's family (wife Teri [Leslie Hope] and teenage daughter Kim [Elisha Cuthbert] are held in Season 1 by kidnappers trying to orchestrate the assassination of Senator Palmer, a physically lush area of eucalyptus groves north of Los Angeles, is nevertheless bounded by fencing topped with piano wire and guarded by heavily armed men, and within its confines the buildings comprising the camp are coldly functional and compact. Although a considerable section of Season 3 takes place in rural Mexico, the outdoors provides chiefly opportunities for violence unobserved by city authority, and the inviting confines of the ranch of drug dealer family Salazar hide burials of those dead from their ruthlessness. In *24: Redemption*, the two-hour prequel to Season 7, shot on location in South Africa, the veldt is likewise a place of threat, with child soldiers, impressed into the army by rebel leaders, engaging in wanton murder.

The composite impression is one of pervasive threat and limitation of freedom for Americans. Even the sanctum of CTU provides little protection against outside invasion: it is bombed in Season 2 by white supremacists being duped by a foreign terrorist organisation, itself manipulated by US oil interests; gassed in Season 5 by Russian separatists; and actually invaded and commandeered by a team working for an alliance between Jack's father[18] and the Chinese in Season 6. The White House is itself invaded by rebel African nationalists led by General Zuma (Tony Todd) and aided by Jonas Hodges (Jon Voight), the ruthless and self-righteous leader of a Blackwater-like organisation, in Season 7.[19]

The resultant visual style, in which the constriction of space is figured in sequences featuring closed rooms, dark hallways, basements, with a bravura use of handheld camera especially by operator Guy Skinner,[20] and abetted by the stunningly effective ostinato work of scorer Sean Callery,[21] objectifies the threatened, bunkered mindset which necessitates the activity of Jack Bauer and his colleagues.[22] In fact, the much-touted use of boxes (split-screen) at various points of each episode is mirrored in the insistent herding of agents and their targets into hallways with right angles, box-like rooms, and even into spaces above the ceiling (Bauer in the airport hostage scenes in Season 5) and airducts (Bauer again during the poison gas attack on CTU in Season 5), so that the visual surface of the narrative acquires angularity and isolation.[23]

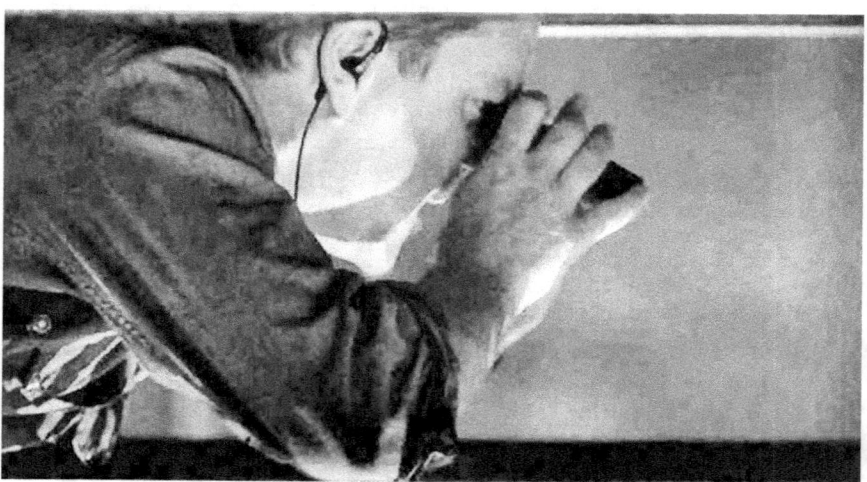

Figure 9.1 Jack Bauer spies on terrorists at the Ontario, CA airport, from his hiding place above the ceiling (24, Season 5, 9–10 am).

Similar effects are achieved in *Running Out of Time* and *Hard-Boiled*, as well as in the recent *Vengeance* (Johnnie To, 2009). *Vengeance* is quite interesting in this context as it combines threatening, violent scenarios in more accustomed closed spaces – city streets in Macau and Hong Kong, houses – with scenes in presumably idyllic settings – a park while a family picnic is taking place, a small village by the shore. Also, like Bauer but in even more extreme fashion, the protagonist Francis Costello (played by Johnny Hallyday) displays physical and mental degeneration. He is losing his memory to an extent that nearly incapacitates him, although he cannot forget the reason for the vengeance he seeks from those who killed some of his family. His degenerative mental state does not however interfere with his innate skills as a former hitman, though it does stem from exactly that past: he carries a bullet in his head which is slowly destroying his memory.

Much of the considerable mayhem in *Hard-Boiled* takes place in enclosed, constricted spaces, reflecting the cramped urban space of Hong Kong. The opening teahouse gunfight is masterfully staged around corners, down staircases, and amid tables, chairs and dishes. The fight is actually started metonymically, with a teapot (that is, a container with enclosed contents, a microcosm of the cramped space) swung violently by Tequila (Chow Yun-fat) at one of the gunrunners. Later enclosed spaces in the film include Alan's boat, where a small-scale but vicious gunfight erupts; the garage where Tequila mounts an attack on Wong's men; and, most spectacularly and extensively, the hospital where several contained spaces are explosive battlegrounds. One of these is the morgue, where Tequila and Alan are temporarily trapped by Wong's henchman Mad Dog (Phillip Kwok); the two burst from the morgue on body pallets and proceed through darkened and labyrinthine corridors as they battle adversaries who appear suddenly from outside and inside the frame – rather like negotiating a dangerous traffic pattern. Significantly, a film with much frenzied gunplay chooses to stage the fights in buildings, in corridors and on boats, in contained environments. Missing from the film are extended car chases, open-country gunfights and other features of many action movies. Woo's last Hong Kong film before his time in Hollywood clearly expressed the implosive nature of the Hong Kong urban environment with its pressurised political and social tensions.[24]

The first *Running Out of Time* film reflects, as does *24* in its own setting, the constricting yet anonymous space of urban Hong Kong. The opening shot shows actor Andy Lau ascending an enclosed staircase. As yet unidentified, his character seems to emerge from nowhere and to be sheltered, or perhaps entrapped, by the massive urban structure. This presentation strategy is not unfamiliar to *24*. Its opening shots repeatedly feature unidentified characters engaging in mysterious activities: in Day 1, a man walks hurriedly down a crowded street in Kuala Lumpur; in Day 3, a panel van drives up to a clinic and deposits a body; in Day 4, a train with a passenger carrying a chained briefcase is bombed and then attacked by an unidentified motorcyclist who retrieves the briefcase. Similar openings can be found in other seasons of the show. Only subsequent to the opening shots are the identities of the participants revealed, as is the case with To's film, with Lau's character gradually revealed to be Peter Cheung, the prankster who will engage in a contest of wits with policeman Ho (Lau Ching-wan). Aside from its roots in melodramatic narrative practice, the device has the merit of highlighting the ease with which characters in these urban dramas melt into and out of the cityscape. This is particularly true of Cheung, who seems to vanish almost at will, as he does on the street after one of his pranks (Bauer is also adept at vanishing), and whose trickster qualities are enhanced by his facility with disguises.

Until the final two seasons, as noted above, 24 was set and shot in Los Angeles.[25] Unlike the notoriously verticalised and compressed profile of Hong Kong, Los Angeles still presents a generally horizontal and extensive profile, as travellers on its complex freeways are well aware.[26] The expansive array of space in the metropolitan area and in the surrounding suburbs and towns does not thereby lend a sense of freedom to the characters in the series, but the horizontal expansion and great length of the freeway system – frequently traversed by Bauer, as especially in Seasons 4 and 5 – do contrast sharply with the intestinal twistiness and rectangular sharpness of the many interiors in the narrative. Most of the shots of characters in the narrative are either straight-on or medium-low angle, adding to the participatory position of the viewer. Rarely seen in 24, at least until the final season (8), when the locus shifted to New York, are the high-angle shots used in the recent Hong Kong action film *Invisible Target*. In this gangster film, the high-angle perspective underlines the lack of importance of the personal within the extremely compressed, verticalised space of Hong Kong. When high-angle perspective is used in 24, generally the locus is the office of the director at CTU, which overlooks the floor where much of the work takes place;[27] the kind of extreme high-altitude shots seen in *Running Out of Time II* are rare in the series. For instance, although rooftop scenes do occur in 24 on several occasions, the perspective is generally levelled to the rooftop itself (as in Day 2 and Day 5); but in *Running Out of Time II*, the opening rooftop scene with its threat of suicide is filmed with emphasis on its height over the city, so that the cityscape becomes itself part of the threatening (or, as it turns out, the game-playing) screen space. The two men on the roof edge (the prankster and the police negotiator – the cop with gambling debts [Lam Suet]) are in fact framed by two skyscrapers in the near distance which neatly encapsulate the reach and influence of global capital in Hong Kong. One building carries the logo

Philips, the other Samsung. The association of the prankster with an American bald eagle is an additional hint at the unpredictable influence of capital on an unstable society.[28]

Political instability is also a central element in the construction of 24. The fact of the location of 24, for the greater part of its run, in Los Angeles is itself significant regarding the creation of suspense within the context of 11 September as well as within a generic noir frame. The selection of the western metropolis implies a counterpoint to the New York locale of the terrorist attacks and frames the reach of terrorist threat as transcontinental. In Season 4, John Woo alumnus Arnold Vosloo's chilling Marwan[29] has his crew intercept a shipment of nuclear weapons in the Midwest (Iowa), displaying not only a close familiarity with American geography but also an apparent blanketing of the physical and political map of the country, not just the coasts or the major cities, with threats of disaster. When the crew launches a nuclear missile from the Midwest, its target is at first undetermined as its trajectory traverses the country, until it is found at almost the last moment to be Los Angeles, thus extending imminent disaster from east to west coast. Although the detonation is averted, its threat is not the first nor the last in the series to the Los Angeles area – in fact, in the season opener for Day 6, a nuclear device explodes in Valencia (a part of the town of Santa Clarita, near Los Angeles), causing thousands of deaths. The repeated micro-threats to Jack's family and colleagues are reductions of the larger threats to security and safety posed by unseen forces.

As with the anti-heroic protagonists of noir films such as *Raw Deal* (Anthony Mann, 1948) and *D.O.A.*,[30] the continued effort to survive within such a precarious environment appears expressionistically on Bauer's body. The normal ageing of actor Kiefer Sutherland during the long run of the show is augmented in Jack's physique by the murder of his wife Teri in Season 1, by severe torture in Season 2, a heroin addiction displayed in Season 3, and most especially by a long stint in a Chinese prison from which Jack returns heavily scarred and emotionally damaged in Season 6. During the course of Season 7, Bauer is infected with a lethal bioweapon which swiftly begins to destroy his mental and physical capabilities. Strikingly, Jack Bauer displays on his own person the corrosive energy of the putative terrorist threat posited at the beginning of the series.

The noir qualities of Bauer's personality begin to surface early in the series, escalating as it progresses. A notable example from the first season (the 8–9 am episode) is a clear if early instance of Bauer's increasingly divided character. Holding prisoner for the moment an innocent driver whose car he has commandeered in his escape from a Secret Service lockup, he tries to reassure her that he has no intention of harming her. Taking him at face value, she tries to leave the office where they are hiding. Jacking back the slide on his SIG, he tells her, 'Lauren, I have killed two people since midnight. I have not slept for over twenty-four hours. So maybe – maybe you should be a little more afraid of me than you are right now' (Season 1, 8–9 am). His twitching face as he points his weapon is eerily reminiscent of the basilisk stare, only interrupted by some facial movement, of William Talman in *The Hitch-Hiker* (Ida Lupino, 1953) or Kitano Takeshi in his crime films *Sonatine* (1993) and *Fireworks* (*Hana-bi*, 1997). As the season, and then the series, proceed, Bauer becomes more and more conflicted and even twisted at times, until he becomes in Season 4 a snarling avenger character (viciously breaking the finger of a former Marine who had aided Marwan). By the end of Season 7 his personality has disintegrated to the extent that he openly questions his own prior actions and sometimes seems incapable of acting as decisively as he had earlier in his career.

In an intriguing narrative turn in Season 7, initially law-observing FBI agent Renee Walker (Annie Wersching) gradually becomes a Bauer epigone or transgendered double, torturing suspects even after Bauer warns her about the consequences for her own conscience and character. When she reappears in Season 8, after her dismissal from the FBI, she is an emotionally damaged person who is subject to fits of rage and other mood swings. Her highly expressionistic demeanour acts out, as it were, Bauer's more obscured internal conflicts. Rather like Yan in the *Infernal Affairs* (Andrew Lau and Alan Mak, 2002–3) films, she goes undercover with the Russian Mafia in New York to assist in learning the location of stolen nuclear rods. Unlike Yan, however, who maintains his cover until his death, she loses control of her emotions when confronted with a mobster who had abused her on a prior undercover assignment. She had disregarded Jack's warning about going undercover given her instability (he tells her, 'Renee, I know where you are. And it's a dark place' [7–8 pm]), and she soon kills the mobster in a berserker fit of rage.[31]

Consciousness divided between two characters is common to *24* and to the presentation of Hong Kong's conflicted space and time in *Running Out of Time*. A good example of this from *24* is the doubling, not immediately apparent, between Bauer and the conflicted President Logan (Greg Itzin).[32] Both men destroy their families because of their careers; both are motivated by patriotism; both employ dubious methods to gain their ends. Certainly they are not comparable in terms of physical prowess or basic decency; Logan does many craven things to which Bauer would not stoop. Still, they do make an illuminating pair of mirror-images.[33]

In *Running Out of Time*, Cheung and Ho the cop are set up as double or mirror characters. Both are presented as loners, Cheung more so than Ho, although Ho is a typical 'workaholic' professional who does not form friendships easily and who has little patience with his inept, hesitant chief. Cheung and Ho are both highly skilled at evading and setting traps, or in another sense at playing robber and cop. Filming strategy links the two, as To employs a fast-forward or time-compression technique applied to both characters to show their spatial transitioning within scenes. They also reverse roles on occasion, as in the attempts by Ho to drive Cheung to the police station, with the characters taking alternate roles of authority (possession of a weapon) in the scenes. Another, less splashy role-reversal parallels Day 1 of *24*. Ho is tricked by Cheung into entering a protected interior space of a financial institution. Finding himself unable to escape the space as he is pursued by security personnel, he is contacted by Cheung, who has set up total surveillance on Ho through the building security system. In a much more sinister, extended and suspenseful fashion, Bauer is surveilled by the chilling Ira Gaines (Michael Massie), the kidnapper of his wife and daughter, in a bid to force him into seemingly assassinating Senator David Palmer. The surveillance follows Bauer from a hospital to the CTU headquarters and includes even the interior of the car he drives. In both instances, the criminal, whether the frightening Gaines or the mocking Cheung, turns the law-enforcement capability of surveillance on its head, entrapping the legal authority in its own web and demonstrating the vulnerability of all citizens to the abuse of surveillance technology.

In Season 7, Bauer acquires a sinister doppelgänger in Tony Almeida, his long-time colleague, thought to have died in Season 5, who returns with a mysterious agenda which turns out to be personal revenge on Wilson (Will Patton), the man behind the conspiracy which led to the death of Tony's wife Michelle Dessler (Reiko Aylesworth) and their unborn son. (Wilson is tortured and nearly killed by Agent Walker at the end of Season 7, an act which leads to Walker's dismissal from the FBI.) Like Jack, Tony displays externally the internal effects of his compromises with conscience; unlike Jack, at least until the end of Season 8, Tony allows his hatred to overcome his better nature. The governmental system in *24* destroys even its best agents; likewise, the police organisation in films like *Infernal Affairs III*, in which the triads operate with full knowledge of policemen, contributes to the destruction of men like Yan (Tony Leung Chiu-wai) and Ming (Andy Lau), who both protest their good intentions despite operating as moles on opposite sides of the law. The collapse of clear delineations in societal organisation results in both the United States and in Hong Kong in the collapse of moral clarity and certitude.[34]

Notes

1. In all the noir films mentioned, the protagonist faces a 'ticking clock' scenario. In *D.O.A.*, Frank Bigelow (Edmond O'Brien) is poisoned because he overheard a detail about a criminal enterprise, and he spends his remaining brief time (a day or two) in discovering who poisoned him. *White Heat* features a psychotic gangster, Cody Jarrett (James Cagney), whose unbalanced actions will clearly lead to his demise in short order. *The Big Clock* (remade as *No Way Out* [Roger Donaldson, 1987]), whose title refers to a huge timepiece on the building which houses the news empire of Earl Janoth (Charles Laughton), details the suspenseful hunt for a murder suspect which must be carried out by the suspect himself (George Stroud, played by Ray Milland), with all the implications of time and space limitation inherent in such a predicament. *Where the Sidewalk Ends* is the story of a brutal cop (Dana Andrews) whose search for a killer will implicate him as the actual killer, and though the killing was self-defence, the cop's own record of brutality will lead him to a possible conviction.
2. Abbas, 'Hyphenation', pp. 214–31.
3. Abbas, *Hong Kong: Culture and the Politics of Disappearance*.
4. Porter, '"The Past is Present"', pp. 63–100.
5. Teo, *Director in Action: Johnnie To and the Hong Kong Action Film*, pp. 11–12.
6. Ibid., pp. 128–9.
7. For a discussion of the question of Bauer as hero, see Bokiniec, 'Who Can Find a Virtuous CTU Agent?', pp. 193–213.
8. The Unit was officially disbanded for Season 7, with much of the work being done from an FBI office, although elements of the former CTU (its servers) and some of its personnel reappeared. The Unit was reconstituted in New York for the final season.
9. As Jack complains bitterly to former Secretary of Defense James Heller, 'Earlier today, you said that I was cursed, that anyone I touched ended up dead or ruined. How dare you? How dare you? The only thing I did, the only thing I have ever done, is what you and people like you have asked of me' (Season 6, 5–6 am).
10. See Abbas, *Hong Kong: Culture and the Politics of Disappearance*.
11. Klein, *The History of Forgetting*, pp. 1–2.
12. For a recent collection of essays on series and serials, see Forrest (ed.), *The Legend Returns and Dies Harder Another Day*.
13. Tim Iacofano, one of the producers on the series, commented on its noir aspects: 'Noir, to me, is about dark, flawed characters in situations that could crush them. The story is generally about life and death matters and the film making mood reflects that by a texture that sometimes incorporates the physical decay of the surroundings. We had that in spades on "24." Noir, to me, is something with tension on multiple levels of the story. Again, "24" had tons of it.' (Iacofano, email to the author, 2010)
14. Three such analogues would be the protagonists of *Where the Sidewalk Ends* (Otto Preminger, 1950), *On Dangerous Ground* (Nicholas Ray, 1952) and *In a Lonely Place* (Nicholas Ray, 1950).

15. The playful, aleatory aspects of *Running Out of Time*, which also features as a central plot element a terminal illness, are absent here. No doubt is ever expressed that Bauer's illness is real. Instead, true to the melodramatic provenance of the series, a hint is dropped, and then reinforced, that a risky cure based on stem-cell tissue from a relative may be available. This becomes, in characteristic *24* fashion, a 'dangling cause' (Kristin Thompson's term [Thompson, *Storytelling in the New Hollywood*]), which brings into play all the complex emotional baggage surrounding Jack's relationship with his only surviving relative, his daughter Kim. No viewer should have been surprised to learn at the beginning of the next season that the cure was successful.
16. Penny Johnson Jerald, who played the unforgettable Sherry, notes that (as often happened with other characters, including Nina),

    > Sherry Palmer was not written as scheming and conniving until after episode 11 Season 1. I can't remember the line exactly. During a particular scene with David, Sherry was expressing that she was just as ambitious as David, and so the Lady Macbeth reference was birthed. The fans ate it up and wouldn't accept less . . . Another nickname [for Sherry, not used in the series itself] was Hillary McPalmer. (Jerald, email to the author, 2010)

    Both Sherry and Nina met their demise during Season 3.
17. The LA CTU offices, used in the series until Season 7, underwent a major redesign after Season 2. The set was specifically designed to allow for the spatially flexible cinematography so essential to the series: '. . . I build large spaces so we can shoot long lens, voyeuristic style' (Hodges, '24 Production Questions', p. 2). The series actors occasionally commented on the difficulty of working on the cloistered CTU set.
18. The manipulative and ruthless Philip Bauer (James Cromwell) fits quite well into the frame of '*père fatale*' discussed by William B. Covey in several examples of neo-noir films: Covey, '*Pères Fatales*', pp. 41–52.
19. Significantly, during the White House invasion, President Taylor and Jack Bauer are protected, or trapped, in a panic room, the ultimate in constricted interior space.
20. Skinner followed the actors very closely with his handheld camera, producing a sense of suspenseful intimacy in the two-shots. Writer and producer Evan Katz commented that in the series 'it's almost no Steadicam, it's all handheld, to look as shaky as possible' (Season 4, 3–4 pm). Greg Itzin, who played President Logan in numerous episodes, commented on Skinner's work in highly positive terms:

    > Guy, or 'Gee' (hard 'g') as Jeannie called him, was a constant amazement. The love affair between the '24' regulars and the crew was palpable, I think. And I am the one talkin' here. Guy, perhaps, especially. He became an actor in the scene. Perhaps a bit metaphoric but really true. When you work in front of a camera it is an exhilarating thing, when hitting on all eight. You work on a

> bunch of different planes: you the actor and your awareness of your place in the physical space (how big the frame, how long the shot, are you in the light, does it matter, what the lens sees), the character and his wants, his lies and truths (in other words; performance), the lines (are you being a good actor and delivering them as written), your relationship to others, what you say and whether you say it with words or a look or just think it so the camera sees it and the viewer interprets it. Exciting stuff. As good as it gets. On stage, it is different but just as exciting but in a different way. A different discipline but with overlapping rules of behaviour and preparation, but a different delivery system. I could go on.
>
> I don't remember specifically but I have very little doubt that the creeping reveal of the 'Logan revelation moment' is Guy's. (Itzin, email to the author, 2010, pp. 2–3)

21. The scores for *24*, which have won Emmy awards, are often highly propulsive, driving the visuals to create an ambience of extremely heightened tension. An excellent example can be found in Season 2, 7–8 pm, when Jack learns from Sayed Ali (the late Francesco Quinn) the location of the nuclear weapon set to detonate. The underlying score builds from background to a thunderously pulsing rhythm which fits perfectly with the anxious tension in Bauer's voice as he phones in the information. Sean Callery commented on his use of ostinato, of which the foregoing is an instance:

    > The ostinato articulations were born from my desire to give certain scenes a sense of ongoing tension and momentum without becoming a distraction. From the beginning the producers wanted a sense of the 'clock always running' energy – and that no matter where you were in the story or who you were watching, it is the concept of time that they were all tied to. The ostinato articulation helped address that request. The producers sometimes were distracted by my use of melody (I suppose any composer will always get in the way sometimes); at times they thought it interfered with dialog and story exposition. I had to curtail my approach a bit in this regard and the ostinato articulation became a valuable sonority in that it could be very present in the mix, enhance the energy of a moment without being intrusive. (Callery, email to the author, 2010, p. 1)

22. Additionally, a conscious effort was made from early in the series not to indulge in television glamorisation of the characters. Director Stephen Hopkins commented (Season 1, Special Features, 'The Genesis of *24*') that he preferred a cast of 'interesting-looking people who were good actors' rather than being typically telegenic. This laudable effort contributes much to the noir ambience of the series.

23. A similar though less complex employment of split-screen is found in To's *Breaking News*, which, like *24*, borrows from and comments on, or parodies, the structure of newscasts. Outlaws holding hostages and evading police inside a warren of

Running Out of Time, Hard-Boiled and *24-Hour Cityspace* 195

hallways and elevators in an apartment building are shown on several occasions in split-screen, when important events are imminently to occur – a bomb exploding, for example. Another Hong Kong film employing split-screen in a limited, though fluid and ingenious, way is *One Nite in Mongkok* (Derek Yee, 2004). *24* uses the same strategy, adding to it the complex placement of boxes, varying in shape and size and often moving around within one moment of screen time in order to display changing or unstable relationships between characters and situations. For discussion of the intricate nature of the box tactic in the series, see Allen, 'Divided Interests', pp. 35–47 and Jermyn, 'Reasons to Split up', pp. 49–57.

Figure 9.2 Cops and robbers in split-screen display (*Breaking News*, Johnnie To).

24. For more on *Hard-Boiled*, see Chapter 8 of Hall, *John Woo: The Films*.
25. Much of the final two seasons was actually shot in Los Angeles as well, with establishing shots and some other exterior work done on location in Washington and New York.
26. Stephen Hopkins, who directed several episodes and was instrumental in the creative initiation of the series, commented that 'LA . . . looks like a city of one-story warehouses' (Season 1, Special Features, 'The Genesis of *24*').
27. A good example is the shot from the director's office temporarily occupied by official Alberta Green (Tamara Tunie) in Season 1, 11–12 am (11:55). The dominating perspective of the shot underlines Green's attempt to impose her vision of order on the recalcitrant unit as a stepping-stone to career advancement. Ultimately she is frustrated in her efforts. A running motif of the series is the tension between CTU and

the supervisory officials at Division, who are generally perceived as bureaucratically leaden obstacles to progress at the CTU level.
28. Teo criticises the film for its heavy-handed 'symbolism': 'The symbolisms are clumsy, somehow suggesting that there is a link between global capitalism, communism and democratic socialism with Hong Kong's post-1997 economic decline' (Teo, *Director in Action*, p. 117). He refers chiefly to the use of the Internationale and other anthems to accompany key moments in the film.
29. Vosloo played Pik, henchman of Fouchon (Lance Henriksen) in *Hard Target*. See Hall, *John Woo: The Films*.
30. Joe Sullivan (Dennis O'Keefe) in *Raw Deal* escapes from prison and cannot restrain himself from carrying out a costly revenge on Rick Coyle (Raymond Burr). During the film, Joe shows not only the effects of injuries from gunfights and other physical confrontations but the residue of his boiling hatred, which finally costs him his life. Ralph Bigelow (Edmond O'Brien) in *D.O.A.* sickens gradually during the course of the narrative after being poisoned.
31. Although the Russian mob plays a role in the narrative of Season 8, and is placed directly within the New York urban ambience, in which cells of the mob are rooted, criminal organisations of this type are relatively unimportant in the general *24* narrative. The major exception to this is Season 3, which has several episodes dominated by the Salazar crime family. In this respect the series contrasts markedly with many Hong Kong films which place the triads at the centre of the plot: the *Infernal Affairs* films, the *Election* films, and so forth. The triads are also intimately connected with urban and even national politics in a way in which organised crime in *24* is not. The threats in *24* are externalised, although in some cases internal actors are at work as well (as in the case of Jonas Hodges). An interesting case is the terrorist threat engineered by a disaffected member of a mission led by Bauer. Stephen Saunders (Paul Blackthorne) is British, thus 'external' in citizenship, and is allied with, or purchasing bioweapons from, Ukrainian scientists; but importantly he had worked directly with Jack before being captured on the failed mission, thus combining an internal with an externalised threat. Sometimes as well, elements of the United States government are involved in conspiracies, most spectacularly in the excellent Season 5, when President Logan (Gregory Itzin) is at the centre of a complex plot. Unlike the Hong Kong films, though, threat in *24*, whether externally or internally driven, is not seen as societally integral in the way that triad influence is.
32. Itzin found this suggestion intriguing:

> I find the 'mirror Jack' image interesting. One of my . . . secrets? is that Logan was tremendously . . . I might say jealous, of Jack, but mostly I think he wanted to BE him, or get him, or be like him. He was a mystery to Logan, a man who not only said the things Logan said he believed in, but had the strength of his convictions and the skill set to pull them off and the singleness of purpose to never give up. Like Butch and Sundance looking back over their shoulders

and saying 'Who ARE these guys??', well, Logan wanted to understand Jack, perhaps befriend him, were the circumstances different. I think, perhaps, his greatest moments of self hate were when he was trying to stop Jack, kill him, ice him, stop him. (Itzin, email to the author, p. 2)

33. Ibid.
34. I would like to thank the following members of cast and crew of *24* for granting me interviews or answering questions by email: Xander Berkeley, Sean Callery, Duppy Demetrius, Bob Gunton, James Hodges, Tim Iacofano, Gregory Itzin, Penny Johnson Jerald, Hakeem Kae-Kazim, Michael Loceff, Anne Melville, James Morrison, Richard Rosser. Space did not permit citing all the useful material from their participation.

Chapter 10
Exiled in Macau: Hong Kong Neo-Noir and Paradoxical Lyricism

Jinhee Choi

A thematic continuity between *Exiled* (*Fangzhu*, Johnnie To, 2007) and *After This Our Exile* (*Fuzi*, Patrick Tam, 2006) is more easily prompted by the English titles than the original Chinese titles: '(*fang*) to let go, (*zhu*) to go after' and '(*fu*) father, (*zi*) son'. The English translations of these titles explicitly incorporate the notion of exile, which connotes both spatial displacement and social and cultural relegation. In each film, protagonists escape to a place of isolation (Macau) or reside in a place of lesser economic development (Malaysia). But what motivates – diegetically or extra-diegetically – these films to be set *outside* Hong Kong, and to what extent do they redirect one's attention to the experience of living *in* Hong Kong?

Hong Kong cinema has consistently been transnational at the level of text as well as industry, with characters in films travelling across national borders and targeted audiences for films spanning both domestic and overseas markets. Macau has emerged as one of the prominent locales for contemporary Hong Kong cinema, providing the space for such films as *The Longest Nite* (Patrick Yau Tat-chi, 1998), *Fu bo* (Lee Kung-lok and Wong Ching-po, 2003), *Isabella* (Pang Ho-cheung, 2006) and *Vengeance* (Johnnie To, 2009). Macau has also long served as a place of origin and sojourn for individual characters including Su Li-zhen in *Days of Being Wild* (Wong Kar-wai, 1990) or, as in the films that I will examine, a place for exile. Macau, like Hong Kong, attracted and bridged various political and cultural traffics within the region due to its geopolitical conditions. In *Song of the Exile* (Ann Hui, 1990), Macau provides a transitional place for Yueyin's family, whose members long to return or move to somewhere else for a different reason. In a flashback the childhood of Yueyin, who has grown up in Macau in the 1960s, unfolds. One detects a cultural tension between her grandparents, who still lead and insist on a

Chinese lifestyle with a hope to return to the People's Republic of China (PRC) in the near future, and her Japanese mother, who faces difficulty fitting into the Chinese customs and culture.

As a companion piece to Johnnie To's *The Mission* (1999), *Exiled* transports a group of gangsters from Hong Kong to Macau – a Portuguese colony – only a few days before its handover to China. *The Mission* features five bodyguards who are hired to protect triad boss Lung. The narrative takes an unexpected turn, as it is revealed that Shin, one of the younger bodyguards, has betrayed the boss' trust by having an affair with his young wife. Curtis, who is the leader among the group of five bodyguards, is ordered to kill Shin, but instead stages a gunfight standoff to spare Shin's life. Sharing the same cast with *The Mission*, except Jackie Lui, who played 'traitor' Shin in its earlier instalment, *Exiled* picks up what has been left open in the earlier film – the exile of a gangster. As Wo, who is comparable to Shin in *The Mission*, returns to Macau with his wife and an infant, hoping to settle in, they are paid visits by Wo's gangster comrades with two competing missions: to kill and to protect him.

The exile of a gangster protagonist in *Exiled*, though it may look trivial, still underscores the social disempowerment, as well as pointing to a changing perception of Macau. Vivian Lee notes that Hong Kong lost its privileged status over Macau during the economic downturn and the SARS epidemic of the late 1990s and early 2000s, and that Macau has been treated as 'something like its equal' in post-colonial Hong Kong cinema.[1] Parallel colonial histories between Hong Kong and Macau create a certain kinship; along with Hong Kong, Macau had become one of the two Special Administrative Regions of the PRC after its handover in 1999. In *The Longest Nite*, Hong Kong is substituted by Macau. In an interview, To, who took over the director role halfway through the film, claims, 'At the time, Macao was a hotbed of chaos. What motivated the chaos? Nothing but power – Some people wanted more power. We wrote the screenplay based on this idea.'[2] Macau, like Hong Kong, is governed by the power struggle of rival gangs, and doubling between the two protagonists – Tony (Lau Ching-wan) and Sam (Tony Leung Chiu-wai) – and their almost identical look at the end of the film further accentuates Macau's mirroring of Hong Kong.

Films set in Macau further add a 'foreign' atmosphere through its space. To claims that he chose Macau for the shooting of *Exiled* 'for its strong European flavour – the alleys, the streets and architecture retained their Portuguese and Spanish influence . . . If we had shot in Hong Kong, we couldn't have called it "Exiled".'[3] The disparity between the spatial proximity – Macau is only an hour away from Hong Kong via ferry ride and fifteen minutes by helicopter – and the character's forced immobility intensifies an exile in its psychological sense, as an interior experience.

South-east Asian countries, especially Thailand and increasingly Malaysia, also feature in contemporary Hong Kong and pan-Asian cinema. In the Pang brothers' *The Eye* (2002), rural Thailand is represented as a place that has forged an uneven relationship with Hong Kong, underscoring the economic disparity between East and South-east Asian countries.[4] Bangkok's Chinatown provides an atmospheric space for the investigation of a ghost-haunted murder mystery in *The Detective* (Oxide Pang, 2007). Malaysian-born Taiwanese director Tsai Ming-liang directs a feature set in Malaysia – *I Don't Want to Sleep Alone* (2007) – in which a migrant worker develops a quasi-romantic triangle relationship with both a male day labourer, who rescues and cares for him, and a waitress working in a nearby restaurant. Patrick Tam's *After This Our Exile*, which was released after Tam's seventeen years of hiatus since *My Heart Is That Eternal Rose* (1989), invites the viewer to a rural town in Malaysia – Ipoh – where working-class gambling addict Shing and his young son struggle to make a living after his wife has vanished.[5]

The increasing mobility and collaboration within the region, as well as the multinational backgrounds of filmmakers and talents, attract the already transnational Hong Kong industry to new spaces. In this chapter, however, I hope to examine how the idyllic imagery in *Exiled* and *After This Our Exile* evokes a sense of exile, and delineate how an experience of exile is constructed and negotiated within the generic conventions of gangster/crime films and family drama respectively. I will further discuss a shared aesthetic strategy between these two films, which I call a 'paradoxical lyricism', whereby the idyllic imagery produces paradoxical effects, counterbalanced by an undertone of, or an eruption of, violence. Such a paradoxical effect may perhaps be linked to the anxiety over the exile within one's own homeland or one's own home.

A Cinema of Exile

In both art and film, exile is often explored through the exilic status of artists and filmmakers and the ways their experiences of forced displacement find a cultural outlet, and are channelled through their artistic practices in the country of residence.[6] The exodus of Jewish and European artists, intellectuals and filmmakers during, between and after the two World Wars spurred artistic exchanges, altering the art scenes of host countries. Jacqueline Chénieux-Gendron poses the rhetorical question, 'Who, among the surrealists, was *not* in exile?', emphasising the voluntary exile as well as mobility that contributed to the initiation and formation of surrealism as an artistic movement.[7] Thomas Elsaesser examines the exodus of European filmmakers and talents, German filmmakers in particular, and their formative roles in shaping the Classical Hollywood cinema during the studio era.[8]

Although exilic cinema may be closely tied to a filmmaker in exile or derivative of the filmmaker's exilic status, a distinction needs to be made between a cinema of exile and a cinema in exile. According to Hamid Naficy, 'exilic cinema is dominated by its focus on there and then in the homeland',[9] contrasting it with 'diasporic' and 'ethnic' filmmaking, which foregrounds the relationship between the homeland and the country of residence and the experience of the country of residence respectively. Despite the text-based characterisation of this category, the exilic or emigrant status of filmmakers still matters or appears even necessary to be classified as such, with a heavier weight placed on filmmakers along with textual and stylistic manifestations. The national origin and diasporic experience of filmmakers such as Jonas Mekas, Atom Egoyan and Fernando Solanas, claims Naficy, become the passionate sources of their artistic endeavours.

Neither To nor Tam is an exilic or diasporic filmmaker in terms of his national origin; both were born in Hong Kong, unlike other Hong Kong directors such as Wong Kar-wai (PRC, Shanghai), Tsui Hark (Vietnam) and Peter Chan (Thailand), who boast multinational backgrounds. However, To and Tam share one of the principal characteristics of exilic cinema. Their filmmaking practices can be considered as 'interstitial', which is one of the major characteristics of 'accented cinema'. Naficy proposes what he calls 'accented cinema', defining it as a filmmaking practice or mode that encompasses all three types of filmmaking; it refers to the exilic, diasporic or ethnic filmmaking that arises under specific historical and political circumstances as an *alternative* to mainstream filmmaking, including the studio system.[10]

To is a prolific filmmaker, and many of his films are marked by their commercial sensibilities. However, what he calls 'exercises'[11] or 'personal films'[12] are geared more towards formal – both narrative and stylistic – experimentations, and often record relatively less successful box-office returns. To's edgier crime films marked relatively lower box-office returns, with *The Mission* earning 4.6 million, *PTU* 2.98 million and *Exiled* 5.47 million Hong Kong dollars. This is in sharp contrast to his other action and genre films, including the romantic comedy *Needing You* . . . (2000) (HK$35.21 million) and Chinese New Year comedy *Fat Choi Spirit* (2002) (HK$19.22 million), which enjoyed greater box-office success.¹³ By alternating the releases of formally experimental films with more commercially oriented films, To puts himself in a very intriguing position within the Hong Kong film industry as well as on the film festival circuits.

After This Our Exile is, in fact, a product of Tam's self-imposed exile in Malaysia, as its screenplay is a collaboration between himself and a former student of his whom he taught in Malaysia.¹⁴ Tam, a pioneering Hong Kong New Wave auteur, first worked in the television industry, and debuted as a film director along with Tsui Hark and Ann Hui in the late 1970s. But he had taken up a teaching post in Malaysia for the five years since 1995, and returned to Hong Kong. In one interview, he reveals that the increasingly commercialised Hong Kong film industry and a lack of creative freedom were the principal reasons why he stopped directing and moved to another country.¹⁵

Though the exilic status of a filmmaker may be conducive to the production of cinema of exile, the latter can neither be identified with, nor is reducible to, the former. In a film such as *Song of the Exile*, which is an autobiographical film by director Ann Hui, her personal and family history seeps into the film's narrative space and trajectory. Yet an attempt to tie a cinema of exile exclusively to a cinema in exile will have to exclude from the former category films that depict an exile experience that does not originate in the filmmaker's autobiographical experience. Instead of forging (or forcing) a tenuous relationship between the filmmakers' experiences (and filmmaking practices) and the two films in question, my approach here is to treat the cinema of exile as an independent category, which addresses the psychological dimension of exile. Exile in its usual definition refers to the forced spatial displacement imposed as a punishment by a society, or sometimes self-imposed, for political or religious reasons.¹⁶ However, as Chénieux-Gendron reminds us, 'emigration defines a voyage which impels one to leave one's place of origin or birth, for whatever reasons, political or economic; exile, however, is an interior experience.'¹⁷

Whose Exile Anyway?

Gangster-in-Exile

The gangster-in-exile, both external (that is, outside the country of origin) and internal (that is, within the country of origin), is a recurrent narrative trope in both Hollywood and Asian gangster cinema. A tug of war between rival gangs often impels the gangster's deportation and hideout. In *The Godfather* (Francis Ford Coppola, 1972), Michael Corleone flees to Sicily after his avenging of the near death of his father, and in *Sonatine* (Kitano Takeshi, 1993), yakuza Murakawa and his associates hide out in Okinawa, while waiting for things to be settled in the Tokyo headquarters. If, as Thomas Pavel characterises, exile is 'a subgenera of the more general notion of human mobility across geographical and political space',[18] both mobility and immobility are attributes embedded in the notion of exile. Exile is predicated upon the idea of forced displacement, and thus a desire to return, but without the means to do so.

The outcome of exile or hiatus in gangster cinema may vary – reluctantly continuing the family business in *The Godfather* and regressing to the liminal space where the usual gangster activities, though temporarily, come to a halt in *Sonatine*. Regardless of these diverging outcomes, what seems apparent is the idea of waiting. In her discussion of Francophone West African cinema, Lindiwe Dovey notes: 'alienation, as an outcome of both bodily and psychological exile, has to do, then with lack of movement: similarly, before one engages in bodily exile there is the alienation engendered by waiting – another immobilizing experience.'[19] Michael Corleone's exile is set against the bucolic scenery of Sicily. But scenes set in Sicily are alternated with the scenes taking place in New York, and as tension escalates in New York with Sonny increasingly losing his temper (and then dying), the pastoral beauty of Sicily, against which Michael's courtship of Appollonia unfolds, only accentuates its spatial remoteness and backwardness. *Sonatine* is filled with the juvenile leisure activities of Murakawa and his associates – dance, wrestling, Russian roulette and fireworks – the function of which is to reinforce their immobility and boredom, as they wait to be reconvened.

Such aesthetics – a juxtaposition of poignant, bucolic imagery and the eruption of sudden violence – yields what I call a 'paradoxical lyricism', a term I adopt from Chénieux-Gendron with a slight modification.[20] She characterises surrealist poetics as the paradox of a lyricism, noting a fissure between the poetic language/imagery and the opposing artistic intent manifest in surrealist writing: evident lyricism in the poems of surrealists-in-exile belies a tension underneath the artistic creation and writing, or the surrealist militant attitude and resistance to compromise.[21] What seems to be pertinent to my discussion of lyricism here is the disparity or incongruity between apparent euphoric lyricism and a counterbalancing tone or undertone that yields a paradoxical effect. Michael's exile in *The Godfather* embeds a violent undertone not only because of its juxtaposition with New York, but also because of its progression towards the death of Appollonia that culminates Michael's exile. Nino Rota's musical score in the Sicily sequence further evokes a sense of paradox, through its 'strong melodic vein tempered by irony, the indifference at the heart of the lyricism'.[22] Kitano's yakuza films also include examples of this aesthetic strategy, such as the final suicide scene by the beach in *Hana-bi* (1997). Violence may function as one of the devices that brings about paradoxical, and sometimes ironic, effects, but any stylistic choices that undercut the lyrical portrayal of space and landscape can engage the viewer in a similar manner. I would argue that To showcases a paradoxical lyricism in *Exiled*, especially in the way he captures the four gangsters' waiting and wandering.

One of the significant narrative twists in *Exiled* is that waiting and wandering befall Wo's gangster buddies, who are not the original subjects of exile. In the opening sequence, Wo's wife, Jin, is visited by the two sets of hitmen, first by Tai and Cat then by Blaze and Fat, and she denies the fact that it is Wo's residence. The four wait for Wo in the nearby square. In Leone-like slow-motion shots, the four greet one another with hand gestures and there is a soft smile on Blaze's face. After the establishing shot of the four, who 'pose' for the camera, Tai requests Blaze spares Wo's life. During their terse conversation, however, the camera repeatedly cuts to Jin, who looks warily out of a window. Her point-of-view shots add a female observer to this rather taciturn scene and colour it with her anxiety.

The arrival of Wo is first signalled by a sound cue – the engine sound of his truck. Through the lace-covered apartment window, the camera slightly zooms in to frame the blue truck driving down the hill, which is then shot at a slightly lower angle from the point of view of the four gangsters waiting in the square. The truck drives around the square, with the camera arcing to follow it as well as to show the other four who have been waiting for Wo. As the five walk towards the building to settle the fare, a car approaches from behind, in which sergeant Shan and his partner attentively observe the scene. All these glances exchanged make the scene polyvalent. To builds tension by adding to the scene each character's point of view one by one – first Jin, next Wo and then Sergeant Shan – signalling imminent violence.

It is neither the characters' literal immobility – in fact, the characters constantly move in and out of places – nor the absolute duration that conveys the exilic experience in *Exiled*. The scene analysed above lasts slightly less than five minutes. While the slow motion and the lethargic soundtrack by Guy Zerafa amplify the languor of the scene, the scene points to the impending shootout inside the house. What makes the scene paradoxical or even ironic is the tension between its dreamy qualities and its violent undertone. Compare this scene with one in *The Mission*, in which the five bodyguards are passing a paper ball to one another outside Lung's office. This may share the trope of waiting, but the five bodyguards' waiting is accompanied by bouncy electric music, which underscores their boredom as well as their unity, rather than conveying a tension of any magnitude.

After Wo's death, the four gangsters themselves become the wanderers in exile, as Boss Fay orders their execution. 'Where to?' is the question that is posed numerous times throughout the film, with a firm answer only given by Wo – 'Home'. From which roads to follow to which actions to take, the four subject their decision to sheer chance – flipping coins. The vehicles that carry them constantly break down, first Wo's blue truck and later the red car they have stolen after the shootout at the Yat Chat restaurant. A comparable malfunctioning vehicle motif is found in *Sonatine*; Murakawa does not know how to drive and when he does drive to town with a girl he 'rescued' from sexual assault, the car falls into a gutter.

While walking on a bridge in a forest (see Figure 10.1), which echoes the scenic beauty in films of Hou Hsiao-hsien such as *A City of Sadness* (1989) or *The Puppetmaster* (1993), Fat still lingers on the idea of stealing a ton of gold, a robbery that the four hitmen decided not to carry out. Fat wonders, however, how much a ton of dreams is, or how much a ton of pain, a ton of love, or a ton of leg hair, or a ton of dirt. The reciting of such questions makes Fat's utterances sound like a poem. His reflections are soon to be undercut when Tai and Blaze quickly turn them into a vulgar joke; Blaze asks how much a ton of bosom is. Fat's existential musings add a poetic rhythm to the already bucolic scene. But the juxtaposition of the poetic and the vulgar renders the scene paradoxical as well as humorous.

Figure 10.1 The four, led by Blaze, walk through the forest (*Exiled*, 2007).

What makes their wandering as well as waiting an exile resides in the fact that there is no way out. The doomed destiny of the four hitmen in *Exiled* is visually reinforced through *mise-en-scène* and the staging of action sequences. Their aimless journey unfolding in an open space is merely a sign of apparent mobility. As Lee notes, character movements are governed by two opposite forces, connoted by the Chinese characters of the original title *fang zhu* – 'to let go' and 'to go after'.[23] Their journey will end at Jeff's hotel, where an ambush awaits. These four hitmen, even with their temporary luck in securing the gold shortly after the forest scene, do not succeed in escaping Macau.

The visual entrapment is palpable throughout the film. For instance, there is the dome-shaped roof and the architectural design of the Yat Chat restaurant, where Wo gets shot; and the layout of Jeff's hotel, where the lobby is visible from all four sides upstairs (see Figure 10.2), invites a high-angle shot of the four, which suggests the slim prospect of their escape. Lee attributes To's sensitivity to compact indoor spaces to his training in *kungfu* and martial arts films during his earlier career.[24] Indeed, the hotel set, which was built on the rooftop of To's own production company Milkyway Image,[25] mirrors the architectural design of a common inn in martial arts films, with an open space in the middle surrounded by corridors upstairs. Such an interior space can become a space for both a triumphant rise, as in King Hu's *Come Drink With Me* (1966), and a tragic fall as in *Exiled*.

Figure 10.2 A high-angle shot of the hotel lobby (*Exiled*, 2007).

Many have identified To's hyper-stylisation and geometrical staging in his action sequences in such films as *The Mission* and *PTU*, while noticing the stylistic departure manifest in *Exiled*: '*The Mission* has clearer, cleaner, lines of violence. *Exiled* is messier';[26] 'The motion-in-stillness of [*The*] *Mission* gives way to "motion-at-random".'[27] Certainly *Exiled* carries some of the stylistic signatures of his earlier action crime films. To continues to rely on both lateral staging and staging-in-depth to set up the axes of action, which are prevalent stylistic choices in *The Mission* and *PTU*. During gunfight sequences, the axes of action remain perfectly intact, as characters are almost immobile when they fire their guns – consider the shopping mall sequence in *The Mission* or the final shootout in *PTU* that takes place in Canton Road.[28]

Exiled, in contrast, superbly transfers the psychological confusion and physical disorientation into the space. Consider the gunfights at the illegal clinic of an underground surgeon. When Wo's surgery for his chest wound is close to completion, Boss Fay barges into the clinic with his henchmen, as he is also in need of treatment for the gunshot wound on his genitals. Curtains and props instead of walls and doors demarcate the space, functioning similarly to the pillars in the shopping mall sequence in *The Mission*. These props create several pockets of space for hide-and-seek and the subsequent shootout. To clearly lays out two axes of action before the shootout begins: the horizontal axis is formed by Blaze, Tai and Fat who are hiding behind the curtains and a wooden partition (see Figure 10.3), with the vertical line being formed by Boss Fay, who is negotiating with the doctor, one of his guards in the near foreground and Wo in off-screen far background. As the doctor cleans the dripping blood from Fay's leg, the camera cuts to the opposite side to show Wo, who is framed in the centre of the far background, and now slowly waking up from anaesthesia (see Figure 10.4).

Figure 10.3 Both horizontal and vertical axes of action are established (*Exiled*, 2007).

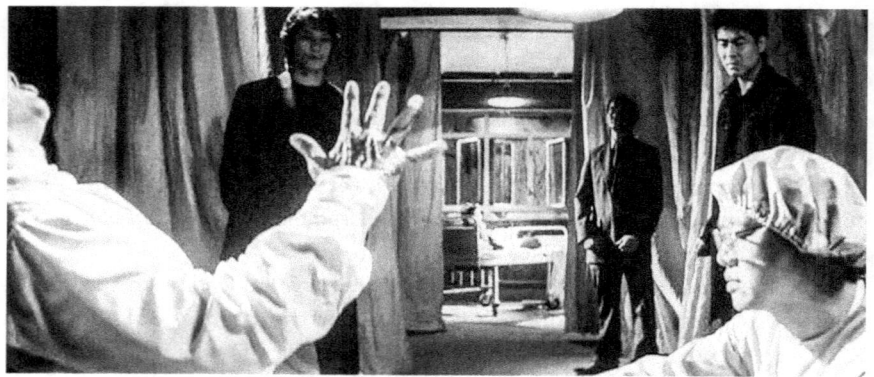

Figure 10.4 The camera cuts to the opposite end of the room, reinforcing the vertical axis of action, which is already established (*Exiled*, 2007).

As the shooting begins, gunpowder and falling curtains blur the vision of both the gangsters and the viewers with the once clearly marked axes of action disappearing to form more of a circle (see Figure 10.5). The visual chaos not only reflects the convergence and confrontation of the several groups of men in a confined space, but also the semi-conscious state of Wo, as he slowly wakes up from anaesthesia. Wo walks towards the window, being drawn to the sound of a wind chime, which recalls the sound of the bracelet he had put around his infant son's ankle, an important sound motif that accompanies the opening credit sequence.

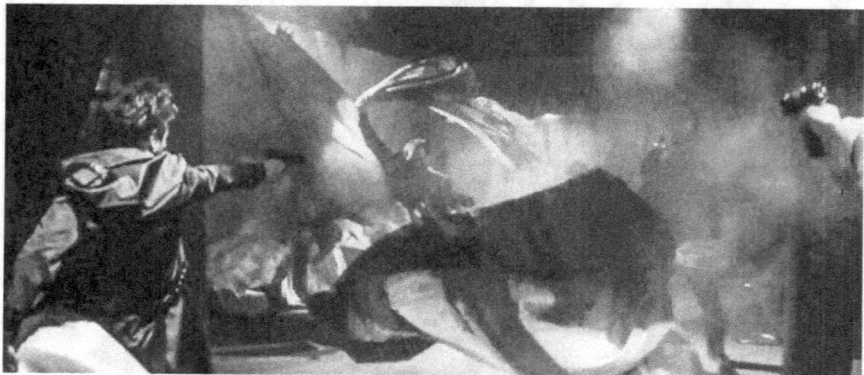

Figure 10.5 A darkly lit gunfight scene that blurs the audience vision (*Exiled*, 2007).

Stephen Teo characterises the crime zone in To's action cinema as an 'abstract' and 'mythic' space, comparable to the *jianghu* of wuxia films:[29] 'To's formalist-abstract approach to his action sequences transforms space from one of objectively-determinate space to one of subjectively-indeterminate space that changes the predilection of his characters toward fatalism.'[30] Teo's observation here is not specific to *Exiled*, but refers to To's crime films more broadly. Whether the action sequences in To's crime films *in general* are indeed vehicles to represent 'the inner world' is subject to debate, but the clinic scene is certainly transformed into a subjective, psychological space.

As characters' interiority is foregrounded, the exile increasingly becomes an internal one, both literally and metaphorically. The film is set in 1999 on the verge of Macau's handover to China, and passing the temporal threshold would in fact change their exile from an external to internal exile. Moreover, Macau as represented here is realistic as well as imaginary. Some of the scenes – the waiting scene in Lilau square for instance – are shot in Macau, while the hotel set is built on the rooftop of Milkyway Image in Hong Kong, and the forest scene in New Territory.[31] Expanded spaces associated with this imaginary 'Macau' can further be interpreted as an allusion to the unhomely condition of post-1997 Hong Kong, and the violence associated with it underlines the anxiety over exile within one's own homeland.[32]

It is interesting to note that *Vengeance*, directed by To, showcases more landmark places in Macau, including casinos and beautifully tiled squares with swirling patterns, compared to *The Longest Nite* and *Exiled*. But to the film's protagonist Costello, who is played by French singer-actor Johnny Hallyday, the two cities are not clearly demarcated. This is a consequence of both the fact that Costello is a foreign national – a French ex-hitman-turned-chef in Paris – and of his rapid memory loss. Travelling between Hong Kong and Macau, Costello needs to be informed where he is, and so too the viewers who are unfamiliar with the two cities. After a short boat ride, Chu, one of the hitmen hired by Costello to avenge the death of his daughter's family, says, 'We're in Hong Kong now.'

The wandering characters in contemporary Hong Kong crime films may be comparable to the 'drifters' in neo-noirs of the 1990s, who 'are cultural migrants fleeing a contemporary landscape defined by the 1990s negatives of post-1960s, postfeminist, postcolonial, postindustrial America'.[33] The increasing reliance on the extended or 'centrifugal' space, borrowing Edward Dimendberg's term,[34] in contemporary Hong Kong neo-noir films, points to the disappearing local identity and spatial boundaries that used to characterise Hong Kong cinema as well as the changing production circumstances in the Hong Kong film industry after 1997. The characters, who constitute and advocate the local identity of Hong

Kong, often musing over the beauty of the city of Hong Kong as in *A Better Tomorrow* (John Woo, 1986), are substituted or complemented by the characters who wander and drift in the 'foreign' space in Macau. The oscillation between the city's centripetal space – *PTU* (Johnnie To, 2003) and *Sparrow* (Johnnie To, 2008) – and its centrifugal spaces – *Infernal Affairs* (Andrew Lau and Alan Mak, 2002), *Election 1, 2* (Johnnie To, 2005, 2006) and *Exiled* – perhaps underscore the political and economic need and desire to forge a successful relationship with places outside Hong Kong, yet the psychological failure to do so. For Johnnie To, who is very self-conscious of the local history of Hong Kong as a city, the employment and incorporation of the 'foreign' space does not remain as a mere backdrop for the crime and violence to unfold, but rather becomes the site to point to and articulate the social and spatial relation between Hong Kong and the neighbouring spaces.

A Family-in-Sojourn

Shing's family is not in exile in the narrow sense of the term. Reasons for exile can vary but they are not usually economic.[35] The film is set in Ipoh in Malaysia, but the viewer remains uninformed with regard to the homeland or hometown of Shing and his wife Lin. A debate between Shing and Lin during their fight indicates that her marriage to him has resulted in her being estranged from her own family. But Shing's gambling habit leaves his family financially unstable and emotionally vulnerable. Boy is constantly and even humiliatingly reminded by the school bus driver that he has not paid the monthly fare; and Shing is chased by local mobsters for his gambling debts and later even attempts to flee to the UK, only to fail.

Ronald Skeldon characterises the patterns of Hong Kong and Chinese emigration as 'sojourn' rather than emigration or settlement. This is not a unique characteristic of Hong Kong emigration, but the idea of 'temporariness' and an eventual return 'home' is quite palpable both in terms of patterns of migration and discourses around Chinese emigration. Skeldon claims, 'the idea of sojourn has established a powerful image of exile, into which the current emigration of Hong Kong Chinese may be seen to fall'.[36] A heavy emphasis on Confucian family values allows a temporary absence from the native community with the assumption of a later return to the hometown.

In Tam's film, although the parents' national origin is left unidentified, their repeated attempts to leave home or even country, for various reasons, characterise their present life as a state of psychological exile. The juxtaposition between the confined, even claustrophobic, space of their temporary stay (both home and the hotel) and the idyllic imagery of the riverside betrays the gap between the hardship and conflict they face as a family and their yearning for a better life.

Hong Kong Neo-Noir and Paradoxical Lyricism   211

Figure 10.6   Lin is locked in the room after her futile attempt to run away (*After This Our Exile*, 2007).

The overarching narrative is framed through the perspective of Boy, beginning with his dream of a peaceful bike ride on the backseat with his father in front, and ending with his return to the riverside, where he has once admired its natural beauty. However, Tam repeatedly frames interior spaces and characters through horizontal grids, which either literally or metaphorically connote a sense of imprisonment. For instance, after a futile attempt to run away to be with the man she is having an affair with, Lin is locked up in a room (see Figure 10.6) while Boy is told by his father to keep an eye on her. If Lin is both visually and narratively foregrounded earlier in the film as the one who is desperately seeking opportunities to escape, the focus gradually shifts to Shing and then to Boy. Both Shing and Boy are trapped in unwanted situations – Shing's searching for his wife who ran way and being chased by mobsters for the debt, and Boy's stealing others' goods and money to maintain his father's gambling habit – and this is manifested through the persistent visual motif of grids, and aperture framing.

In addition to the rigorous visual motif and *mise-en-scène*, Tam also shows a penchant for paradoxical lyricism. The opening credit sequence is accompanied by a boy's singing of 'You Are My Sunshine'. It begins with a view of a river at dusk, followed by a shot of a blue-tinted night view of the river, with wooden poles and a boat in the foreground (see Figure 10.7). Such a view may remind the viewer of the bold use of colour characteristic of Tam's earlier films, such as *Love Massacre* (1981) and *Nomad* (1982). Throughout the film, this idyllic site

Figure 10.7 Opening sequence of *After This Our Exile*, a blue-tinted riverside view.

becomes a place which Shing and his son repeatedly visit and the site of their self-reflections; first the two together, then individually.

After several rounds of unfruitful stealing, Shing and Boy stand by the shore looking at the view. The scene is inserted between the two failed attempts that lead to the climax of the film. In the previous scene, Shing has just lied to the parents of an ill child that Boy is mentally ill, when Boy gets caught while hiding in the closet, waiting for the right time to steal. By the river, Shing is full of remorse, stroking Boy's hair. Oblivious of his father's heartache, Boy is struck by shining stars. This short interlude, however, is a bridge to Shing's last act of desperation and a prelude to his sinking to the lowest depths – abandoning his own son, when he is caught by the police.

Shing returns to the riverside after he has visited his son at a detention centre. He passes by the magnificent ruins of a deserted building. The viewer notices that his ear is severely wounded with blood seeping through the bandage, as he walks towards the camera. As Shing hunches over to sit on a white bench in front of the ruins, this atmospheric site is arrested by the sudden break into a flashback, in which we see his son biting off the tip of his ear. The eruption of unexpected violence unfolding against the scenic ruins intensifies the outburst of the boy's anger towards his father as well as the father's devastation. Shing sobs leaning against one of the columns of the façade of the ruins. The fluid and hovering camera connects the disparate spaces within the vast space, as well as foregrounding the psychological contiguity over the spatial and temporal discontiguity. There is a temporal ellipsis between the shot of Shing's walking away from the ruins, and the next shot of him slowly walking into the river, as if he is about to end his life. The initial camera movement in the latter, which is shortly afterwards replaced by Shing's figure movement, bridges the gap between Shing's separate figure movements.

A juxtaposition of violence against scenic beauty or rigorously controlled *mise-en-scène* is a persistent aesthetic strategy in Tam's oeuvre. In *Nomad*, an orgyesque amorphous shot of the bodies of the four main characters – Kathy, Pong, Louis and Tomato – sleeping outdoors in a mosquito net-covered bed, is quickly followed by the sudden massacre on the beach. As Pong waves at the ship on the ocean and swims towards it, he is suddenly attacked and slaughtered by a female Japanese Red soldier. In the finale of *Love Massacre*, Lin walks in and out of the rows of blue, white and red cloths hanging on the rooftop, before she finally encounters and kills Cheung.[37]

After This Our Exile ends with the boy's final visit to the riverside after some ten years. The theme of an exiled child is a recurrent one in seventeenth-century French heroic romance.[38] After undergoing a series of ordeals, the child returns home as a hero. Although Tam portrays the family in exile with the main emphasis on the downfall of both father and son, perhaps it is Boy who is the most exiled, as he is repeatedly abandoned by his parents – first by his mother, then his father – and imprisoned in the detention centre. But his visit to Long Hoke hotel, where he used to stay with his father after the latter had lost his job, and his returning of the watch he has stolen back to its owner is a sign of his moral redemption, if not a heroic return.

Boy's voiceover informs the viewer that his father is now settled and has started a new life. Boy spots, across the river, a couple strolling, who may be his father and his wife.[39] The camera probes the foliage of trees and weeds by the river as if wind caresses them. Triggered by the sight of a boy on a bicycle, a flashback to Boy's own childhood begins. The montage sequence brings back painful memories of his relationship with his father. Rapidly cut to the accelerating tempo of the pounding piano in Scriabin's Etude, the montage climactically ends with a close-up of Boy without any resolution. Classical music, which is consistently used throughout the film, including Tchaikovsky's Piano Trio in the scene of Shing and Lin's lovemaking in which Lin refuses at first but slowly gives in, not only connotes characters' aspirations towards a middle-class life, but also points to a chasm within (or amalgam in) Tam's own aesthetics between the Asian and the European sensibility.

As one reviewer of the film notes, there is something timeless and transcendental about the rural Malaysia represented.[40] An exilic journey of a father and son is specific yet quite universal. Tam informs us that the English title of *After This Our Exile* is taken from the phrases of Catholic prayer, *Hail, Holy Queen*.[41] Tam views life on earth as indeed a form of exile, in which one must go through a psychological journey of longing and loss. The pastoral and lyrical imagery, which provides a backdrop for such a trail, is constantly counterbalanced by the psychological intensity of characters, making their journey all the more lyrical as well as paradoxical.

In this chapter I have discussed two films of exile, and their paradoxical use of idyllic imagery. The juxtaposition of poetic imagery and violence – both literal and psychological – is not unique to these two films. Yet, such imagery accentuates not only the spatial and psychological isolation but also the disparity between where one resides and where one hopes to belong. If To's film subtly touches upon the fear of internal exile – exile within one's homeland – through an external one, Tam encompasses exile to make it a transcendental one – a life journey that one must expect and accept.[42]

Notes

1. Lee, *Hong Kong Cinema Since 1997*, p. 69.
2. Teo, *Director in Action*, p. 231.
3. Rothock, 'Macau Allure Attracts Biz', p. 16.
4. Knee, 'The Pan Asian Outlook of the Eye', p. 77.
5. Elley, 'Review: *After This Our Exile*', p. 34.
6. See the special issue on exile in *Poetics Today: Creativity and Exile: European/American Perspective 1* (Autumn, 1996), 17:3.
7. Chénieux-Gendron, 'Surrealists in Exile', p. 437.
8. Elsaesser, 'Ethnicity, Authenticity, and Exile', p. 98.
9. Naficy, *An Accented Cinema*, p. 15.
10. Ibid., p. 10.
11. Teo, *Director in Action*, p. 18.
12. Bordwell, *Planet Hong Kong*, 2nd edn, p. 251.
13. Davis and Yeh, *East Asian Screen Industries*, p. 45.
14. Lee, 'Director Patrick Tam is Anomaly in Prolific, Improvisational Hong Kong Industry', 16 December 2006.
15. Hui, '*After This Our Exile*: Interview with Patrick Tam Ka-ming': http://asiasociety.org/arts/film/after-his-exile-interview-patrick-tam-ka-ming (last accessed 6 January 2011); Symonds, '"Exile" Comes out at H.K. Film Nods': http://www.hollywoodreporter.com/news/exile-comes-at-hk-film-134075 (last accessed 14 January 2015).
16. Pavel, 'Exile as Romance and as Tragedy', p. 306.
17. Chénieux-Gendron, 'Surrealists in Exile', p. 439.
18. Pavel, 'Exile as Romance and as Tragedy', p. 306.
19. Dovey, 'Subjects of Exile', p. 63.

20. One must distinguish the term 'lyricism' employed here from the 'lyrical film', which Sitney characterises as one of the major movements in the American avant-garde in the 1960s. He defines the lyrical film as that which invites the viewer to postulate the filmmaker as the subject behind the camera and the camera as an extension of the filmmaker's perception and/or a vehicle to convey his or her reaction to the environment that is being filmed. See Stiney, *Visionary Film*, p. 160.
21. Chénieux-Gendron, 'Surrealists in Exile', pp. 444–9.
22. Dyer, *Nino Rota*, p. 38.
23. Lee, *Hong Kong Cinema Since 1997*, p. 97.
24. Ibid., p. 96.
25. Bordwell, 'A Many-Splendored Thing 4: Triangulating': http://www.davidbordwell.net/blog/2007/03/22/a-many-splendored-thing-4/ (last accessed 6 January 2011).
26. Teo, *Director in Action*, p. 191.
27. Lee, *Hong Kong Cinema Since 1997*, p. 98.
28. Teo, *Director in Action*, p. 132.
29. Ibid., p. 94.
30. Ibid., p. 22.
31. Bordwell, 'A Many-Splendored Thing 4: Triangulating.'
32. Esther Yau brought my attention to this point.
33. Stanfield, *Maxium Movies Pulp Fictions*, p. 178.
34. Dimendberg, *Film noir and the Spaces of Modernity*.
35. Pavel, 'Exile as Romance and as Tragedy', p. 306.
36. Skeldon, *Reluctant Exiles? Migration from Hong Kong and the New Overseas Chinese*, p. 6.
37. For a more detailed discussion of the use of colours in the film, see Cheuk, *Hong Kong New Wave Cinema (1978–2000)*, pp. 135–6.
38. Pavel, 'Exile as Romance and as Tragedy', p. 309.
39. It is rather ambiguous whether the man Boy sees is his real father, but I assume that he imagines or projects him to be his own father, due to the mismatch of the eye-lines. Boy looks off-screen left, while the man and a pregnant woman enter the next shot from screen right.
40. Elley, 'Review: *After This Our Exile*', p. 34.
41. Marchetti, Vivier and Podvin, 'Interview with Patrick Tam': http://www.hkcinemagic.com/en/page.asp?aid=270&page=1 (last accessed 19 January 2011).
42. Yau, 'Urban Nomads, Exilic Reflections', p. 91.

Chapter 11
The Tentacles of History: *Shinjuku Incident's* Return of the Repressed

Tony Williams

> What a hive of industry is a Chinese town. No industry is so minute, constant, and infinitesimally divided.[1]

Arriving in Hong Kong on 8 March 1859, the author of *Two Years before the Mast* cast an eye on the economic development of the recently acquired British colony. Richard Henry Dana Jr noted significant features such as Hong Kong's adverse summer climate, colonial business interests, the presence of coolies, and a hierarchical class structure strongly regulated on economic lines, as well as the presence of those lower-class girls from the 'flower boats'. He commented, 'If their lives are ever so polluted, they are decent and even completely modest in their dress and manners.'[2] Despite the well-regulated manner of that developing world of international trade, another darker realm of violence operated in uneasy co-existence. Dana observed the presence of a nearby river, 'a scene of piracy, robbery and violence for years'.[3] He also noted long narrow alleys not more than four feet wide that contained the presence of many local industries cramped together in limited spaces all contributing to an early Asian world of proto-capitalism. When Dana travels further into a China now the latest territory for western colonial incursion (a fact he, naturally, does not emphasise in his journal), he encounters a sign on the front door of a prosperous Chinese businessman: 'Many rich customers enter here!' He also recognises further contrasts between the prestigious decorum of mercantile prosperity and oppressive economic dominance of the less fortunate.[4] Dana visits an Execution Ground, the scene of capital punishment throughout the centuries. 'Tortures, the most frightful have been inflicted here, such as it can hardly enter into the mind to conceive, and the air has been rendered with shrieks and cries of the ultimate agonies of men.' This traveller mentions a gothic description of Oriental violence to genteel readers but not the fact that it is an indispensable part of a political and economic order that is also part of American Manifest Destiny in the Winning of the West. America is already engaged in reversing Horace Greeley's dictum into 'Go East, young man!'

By contrast, Japan is a much more regulated country with a strict currency exchange,[5] meticulously controlling tourism and trade in a land whose inhabitants are 'civil, yet remote'. It is a land that has experienced the incursion of Commodore Townsend Harris and that vainly attempts to combat the inevitable economic changes that have affected China, those which the Meiji Restoration will later accelerate. Had Dana the same types of access to Japan as with Hong Kong and China, would he have not discovered similar dark undercurrents of violence within an ordered Japanese society then reluctantly embracing western economic expansion? Despite references to the civility of those he meets, Dana says nothing about what might happen to any foreign intruder who may venture into a Shogunate forbidden zone with its racial bushido codes of regulation and institutional violence. He also remains silent about the gunboat diplomacy used by Harris to 'persuade' Japan to participate in the benefits of western influence, an element also repressed in John Huston's ludicrous *The Barbarian and the Geisha* (1958). *Shinjuku Incident* (Derek Yee Tung-sing, 2009) suffers from no such constraints but has its own historical reverberations.

These introductory paragraphs are not meant to suggest that those different worlds of nineteenth-century China and Japan bear any explicit parallels to Hong Kong neo-noir. They also have little connection to those twentieth-century urban worlds familiar to both classical film noir and its neo-noir successors from different national cinemas. Such introductory comments are meant to reveal the presence of significant historical seeds of economics and violence rooted in the past whose genesis foreshadows an even darker future. As indispensable units of capitalism, they will develop in different ways during the following century, taking on forms that will also change in a twenty-first-century world of global capitalism but also having certain distinctive historical antecedents.

Dana's premature insights reveal primitive formations that will eventually change into that future dark urban landscape familiar to us from the distinctive cinematography of film noir containing undeniable associations of capitalism and violence. Twenty-first-century capitalism is no new phenomenon emerging from a brave new world of an 'end of history' and a post-modernism that has supposedly erased its roots. It is really another development of its nineteenth- and twentieth-century predecessors. If Dana's descriptions foreshadow a future world, *Shinjuku Incident* echoes certain types of past historical economic and political antecedents as much as the stylistic world of contemporary Hong Kong neo-noir develops its visual predecessors.

Film noir is characteristically referred to as the 'dark side of cinema' usually associated with an American archetype. It is also a style present in other national cinemas, as is melodrama. Both genres have international and locally derived inflections of meaning. The urban experience characterises film noir in most representations so it is not surprising to find its neo-noir successor continuing this tradition. Neo-noir Hong Kong gangster films, present and past, represent one particular example, but so too do other generic inflections where Tony Miu Kin-fai's cinematography for Danny Lee Sau-yin's serial killer film *Dr Lamb* (Danny Lee Sau-yin and Billy Tang Hin-sing, 1992) amply captures bleak naturalistic environmentalist aspects of cramped living conditions and dysfunctional family behaviour, suggestively revealing repressed motivations influencing the violent behaviour of Simon Yam's psychotic character.[6] As well as well having a recognisable style, film noir also has historical and political resonances, as Thom Anderson pointed out in terms of its Hollywood model. It is not surprising to see such elements operating within the distinctive world of Hong Kong neo-noir, whether implicitly or explicitly, as other contributors to this anthology note. Law Kar documents how post-war Hong Kong cinema developed its own form of noir derived from both the American model and the brief world of post-war Shanghai cinema. Lisa Stokes sees *The Wild, Wild Rose* (Wong Tin-lam, 1960) as a film not only setting the tone for early Hong Kong noirs but also anticipating stylistic and thematic features seen in contemporary neo-noir in its context of globalisation. Bhaskar Sarkar notes how globalisation results in contemporary gangster films extending beyond national borders to chart the dark side of neo-liberal capitalist struggles for opportunity and economic dominance. Dana's early colonialist vision of a developing China and Japan will soon take on global dimensions. In terms of *Shinjuku Incident*'s themes, we must not forget Anthony Mann's *Border Incident* (1949), one of the few classical noirs to focus upon illegal immigration, as well as Jack Arnold's *Man in the Shadow* (1957) and *Touch of Evil* (Orson Welles, 1958), both starring Orson Welles, that also focus upon border crossings and the treatment of immigrant labour in a racist society.

Completed in 2008 but not released until after its premiere at the 2009 Hong Kong International Film Festival, *Shinjuku Incident* has received much attention due to Jackie Chan's decision to depart from his familiar star image to play a non-heroic dramatic role. Conceived a decade ago, filming was to begin in May 2006 but was postponed due to Chan's commitments to *Rush Hour 3* (Brett Ratner, 2007). Director Derek Yee Tung-sing and producer-investor Jackie Chan decided not to release the film in Mainland China to avoid censorship, supposedly due to its high level of violence. However, other factors may have contributed to this decision.

Shinjuku Incident also represents a radical change of image for its star, as if Sylvester Stallone had decided to return to the type of earlier more serious roles in *F.I.S.T.* (Norman Jewison) and *Paradise Alley* (Sylvester Stallone) (both 1978) rather than begin *Rambo 5*. Although Jackie made a lot of money with his *Rush Hour* series and *Mr Nice Guy* roles, this middle-aged actor has not decided to rest on his comedy *kungfu*, *Police Story* (Jackie Chan, 1985), *Project A* (Jackie Chan, 1983) laurels but play instead a deliberately low-key, non-action character role going far beyond anything he has done before. Precedents exist in *Island of Fire* (Chu Yen-ping, 1991), *Crime Story* (Kirk Wong, 1993) and *New Police Story* (Benny Chan, 2004) but this is the furthest he has gone in playing a morally compromised character in a film directed by someone specialising in studies of social losers who are never in control of the situations in which they find themselves. It is almost as if the star decided to change his image to reflect a different type of commodity in a global economic world, similar to Steelhead's decision to change his identity in *Shinjuku Incident*.

Even before *Rumble in the Bronx* (Stanley Tong Gwai-lai, 1995), the *Rush Hour* series (Brett Ratner, 1998, 2001, 2007), *Shanghai Noon* (Tom Dey, 2000), *Around the World in 80 Days* (Frank Coraci, 2004) and the recent version of *The Karate Kid* (Harald Zwart, 2010), Jackie Chan was already a transnational star. He has a following in Japan and also appeared in several films shot in Mainland China set in the safely distant historical past rather than the disturbing contemporary world of *Shinjuku Incident*. Like the character he plays in *Shinjuku Incident*, his star status has now become a transnational commodity subject to the variable demands of the international market at a time when his physical prowess has aged since his heyday in Hong Kong cinema of the 1970s and 1980s. Already popular in Japan and South-east Asia, he made several earlier attempts to break into the American market ranging from the ignominious *Cannonball Run* films (Hal Needham, 1981, 1984) to the flawed *The Protector* (James Glickenhaus, 1985), until *Rumble in the Bronx* appeared to give him that much-needed breakthrough.[7] Chan's later Hollywood films proved disappointing and, although still viable as a star commodity, his star status has fluctuated in the many vehicles he has since appeared in, such as *New Police Story* and *The Myth* (Stanley Tong Gwai-lai, 2005), *Rob-B-Hood* (Benny Chan, 2006), *The Forbidden Kingdom* (Rob Minkoff, 2008) and *Little Big Soldier* (Ding Sheng, 2010). Such films represent the unstable circulation of Jackie Chan as a still-viable star commodity in the early twenty-first century, one who is popular and appears to have relative control over his image. His current status achieves some success as a popular transnational marketable entertainment commodity. But it is dependent upon the changing expectations of a transnational audience looking for some degree of diversity rather than repetitive similarity that would make him anachronistic, like the later films of Charles Bronson and John Wayne. Continuing popularity often depends on some degree of change, appealing to some audiences always wanting something new in the market. Yet, at the same time, others find such variations difficult to accept. Jackie's role in *Shinjuku Incident* indirectly reflects his status as a star commodity in a global market that may find his 'use-value' as a star disposable at any moment.

Shinjuku Incident holds up a 'bleak mirror to [the] nature' (*Hamlet* III, ii) of a dark transnational world of illegal immigration and human commodification that differs significantly from Jackie Chan's other star vehicles, but also reveals a neo-noir image of him. He portrays a 'double' version of the character he usually plays in other films. Far from being in control of the situation via the use of comic technique and/or physical prowess, Chan's Steelhead becomes dominated not only by external forces he is powerless to change but also by flaws within his own psyche leading to his destruction. Jackie encounters a world paralleling one facing earlier illegal immigrants in *Border Incident* but one now reflecting a transnational global neo-noir 'brave new world'. He is now a noir hero caught up in situations of constant change, situations mirroring his vulnerable international popularity when increasing age will make him unlikely to perform previously expected physical stunts, rendering him as disposable as any worker within capitalism. Both in characterisation and narrative, *Shinjuku Incident* represents a dark noir mirror image of what could be if its star should suddenly disappear from sight in the same way Steelhead does in the climax of the film.

Shinjuku Incident also develops motifs previously seen in Derek Yee's *One Nite in Mongkok* (2004) and *Protégé* (2007), two recent neo-noirs both dealing with various aspects of the dark side of transnational capitalism, the first involving border-crossing assassination and prostitution, the other exploring the lucrative transnational Asian heroin industry. Both films (also starring Daniel Wu) depict the grim personal costs involvement has on its victims, an involvement having far more global associations than those contained within the limited urban environments of American classical film noir. *One Nite in Mongkok* ends with a particular history lesson. When Dandan (Cecilia Cheung) informs a Hong Kong customs official of her intention to return permanently to the Mainland, she also enquires as to why Hong Kong acquired its name of 'Fragrant Harbour', a question earlier asked by Lai (Daniel Wu) as he commented on its urban pollution. The official does not reply. Presumably, like Mainlander Lai, even he does not know the origins of the name of this now densely crowded colony. The final captions supply the answer. Hong Kong was once known as an incense (*Hong*) producing port (*Kong*). Seen within the context of Dana's description, the answer is ironic. Hong Kong was never a 'Fragrant Harbour', but polluted by capitalism and violence from its very beginning. Dana's Christian beliefs and those of the missionaries he encounters throughout his travels return with a vengeance in the final sequence of *One Nite in Mongkok* when Brother Wah appears wearing a Santa cap to violate hero and heroine. Individual missionaries may have been pacifists but their religion was associated with colonialist objectives: 'Onward Christian Soldiers!' Christmas time in this film has associations with a violent, non-fragrant type of capitalism.

Forces beginning in Dana's day now reach an advanced stage of violent development over a century later. In *Protégé*, ailing drug entrepreneur Quin (Andy Lau) takes putative successor Nick (Daniel Wu) on a trip to Thailand that is the geographical centre of a global industry he chooses to regard as just business, disavowing its deadly effects on human victims. After Nick's undercover cop has successfully dealt with his mentor's suspicion, Quin educates him into the contemporary global realities of the drug trade, revealing which countries are the most profitable throughout the world, the possibility that heroin may become an obsolescent commodity in the market due to challenges presented by new drugs such as Ecstasy, and the fact that even the Golden Triangle may become a tourist resort in ten years due to contemporary Asian political movements against the drug trade. *Protégé*'s neo-noir visual style operates as an appropriate visual counterpart for a world where humans are powerless to deal with global economic changes in their lives and resort instead to denial, whether it be Quin's attitude to just 'selling appliances', Nick's duplicitous role-playing or Fan's lies concerning the real cause of her dependence on drugs. The film ends on a bleak vision as Nick realises the betrayals his activities have caused and his final resort to drugs, one prevented by his now-adopted daughter Jane-Jane, a resolution that the bleak neo-noir lighting suggests as being far from effective. It places Nick in the category of those other characters in Yee's social dramas who find out that the worlds they inhabit no longer allow them the privilege of believing in any positive form of human agency that can change their personal dilemmas. These neo-noirs contain different types of history lessons. *Shinjuku Incident* delivers another one. Despite Daniel Wu's subordinate role, it also has claims to be regarded as Derek Yee's final chapter of a 'Daniel Wu Trilogy'.

The logo on the Hong Kong DVD version runs 'Jackie Goes in the Dark World of Film Noir', an apt description of the film. *Shinjuku Incident* develops its own themes, owing much to Johnnie To's exploration of contemporary social and political currents affecting the world of Triads in his *Election* films (2005–6) and Fukasaku Kinji's epic analysis of post-war Japanese yakuza politics in *The Yakuza Papers* (1973–4). Set in Japan during the 1990s, when

Figure 11.1 Chinese Invasion v. 2.

its booming economy attracted many illegal immigrants eager to escape the poverty of their own countries, the film evokes classical and modern parallels to 'rise and fall' narratives of the gangster hero. Derek Yee directs his version of a South-east Asian global economic film noir that has a revealing prologue and epilogue containing dark parallels to the now-changed economic world of Mainland China.

Jackie's different role in this film resembles the scandal of Henry Fonda playing a villain in *Once Upon A Time in the West* (Sergio Leone, 1968), a film dealing with an Old West facing the relentless surge of railroad capitalism. Although no actual villain, Jackie's north-eastern Mainlander character of Steelhead is never really in control of the circumstances in which he finds himself. Like Fonda's Frank, Steelhead will become neither a good husband nor a successful businessman, but face elimination in a new world that will make him obsolete. Like Quin in *Protégé*, he denies the fact that he is really responsible for the chaos that occurs in the latter part of the film. Chan's role resembles a different variant of those social loser characters seen in Derek Yee films such as *The Lunatics* (1986), *People's Hero* (1987) and *One Nite in Mongkok*. Like Daniel Wu's Mainland assassin in the last film, Steelhead is out of his depth in an alien and hostile urban environment. His futile heroic posturing in the latter part of the film resembles Ti Lung's Sunny Koo in *People's Hero*. Steelhead moves from being one type of commodity at the beginning of the film (a Mainland Chinese illegal immigrant) to being another more privileged version used as a pawn in yakuza power politics. His manipulation echoes

1930s Showa-era military treatment of its Chinese 'brothers'. Like many of Yee's central characters, Steelhead is never really in control of his place within this dark world of global capitalism.

As one of twenty-three wards in Tokyo, Shinjuku is a busy and commercial district by day (the obvious target for Wild 7 in *Battle Royale 2* [Fukasaku Kinji and Fukasaku Kenta, 2003]) and a red-light district at night, comprising the most mixed nationalities registered in Tokyo. By day, television monitors broadcast news about the arrest of illegal immigrants and rent-a-crowd demonstrators protest against anti-yakuza legislation resembling those vocal town hall opponents of American healthcare reforms. By night, the dark underworld of crime operates as freely as Count Dracula after twilight. This familiar film noir mirror imagery inflects Yee's chosen visual style, depicting characters who deny the worst features existing within their own personalities. Steelhead arrives in Japan as an illegal immigrant to find his girlfriend Xiuxiu (Xu Jinglei), who has taken the Japanese name of Yuko and is now married to yakuza Eguchi (Kato Masaya). During a later scene with her husband, a flashback reveals her earlier seduction by the material goods an affluent exile brought back home. Despite what she says, this reveals the real reason she left China. When Steelhead saves Eguchi from assassination by rival mobsters, the ambitious yakuza offers him legal status and help for his fellow illegal immigrants if two obstacles to his power are eliminated. But, far from being a friend to foreigners (despite mentioning the value of immigrant Chinese to the post-war reconstruction of Kabuki-cho to his racist second-in-command Nakajima (Sawada Kenya)), Eguchi really plans to exploit them as chess pawns in yakuza power politics. He allows them control of certain areas, confining them to ghettos of influence in the same way the Shogunate confined western traders in Japan during Richard Henry Dana Jr's visit. Despite the supposed benevolent nature of a global capitalism inviting an international workforce into formerly restricted national territories, identity politics still dominate. When a senior yakuza boss criticises Eguchi for his supposed inter-racial business activities – 'How can you allow foreigners to trample over your turf?' – Eguchi shows that he is not really a benevolent global entrepreneur and responds by unveiling a divide-and-rule strategy of using the Chinese to divert the unwelcome attentions of other Japanese gangs. During the time Steelhead is absent, Eguchi tempts his former friend, drug-addicted Jie (Daniel Wu), with the same type of 'offer you cannot refuse' earlier made to Steelhead. (This also ironically reflects contemporary star associations with Daniel Wu's rising status threatening Jackie Chan's veteran stardom.) Transnational global capitalism has no respect for previous commitments or people. It uses anyone for economic advantage.

Figure 11.2 Imperialist Echoes.

Mutilated by Taiwanese gangster Gao (Jack Kao), who runs the significantly named Club Formosa and works for the yakuza (motifs deliberately echoing the Japanese colonial occupation of Taiwan), Jie gradually turns into a leather-coated drug-taking punk vampire figure revealing a repressed 'Portrait of Dorian Gray' persona Steelhead denies within himself. Originally wanting to help fellow illegal immigrants, Steelhead initiates a situation that will eventually corrupt everyone, including himself. In the final scenes before the yakuza attack, Steelhead condemns the corruption of his Mainland compatriots who deny this indelible fact. Instead, like Quin they engage in denial, stating that they never sell drugs to fellow countrymen. When Steelhead says, 'What have you turned into?', the camera pans along the group before it stops at Jie. Steelhead compares his former friend to a ghost. 'Especially you, look at yourself!' Jie replies. 'If there was one, you let it out. You're the real ghost.' Jie is the 'Frank' character from John Woo's *Bullet in the Head* (1990) in this film. As a gentle person, unfit even for petty thieving, he only wishes to run a chestnut stand. But violence and psychological decline turn him into a violent thug whom Eguchi uses as his next chess pawn. In his garish wig and cosmetic make-up designed to hide the scars inflicted on him by racist Japanese, Jie functions as Steelhead's alter-ego, a mirror image representing the personal costs of his involvement in global capitalism. Depicted in the familiar type of dualistic mirror imagery of classical noir and neo-noir, Jie represents *Shinjuku Incident*'s Dorian Gray whose appearance displays Steelhead's corrupt inner persona that he denies within himself. Jie changes from gentle, non-criminal immigrant into a drug dealer and Steelhead's repressed *protégé*. Daniel Wu plays a different role from that in Yee's previous film but one having similarities to his earlier character. Yee's neo-noirs *Protégé* and *Shinjuku Incident* display significant variants on a common theme of mentor–younger man relationships, as well as being firmly rooted in historical awareness.

During their first meeting, Lilly tells Steelhead that 'When people are in a hurry, they stray from the faith.' The camera tracks into Steelhead as if recognising that his desire to gain legality and status in Japan will eventually involve his contamination from the money he initially refuses to take from other people. Steelhead later accepts protection money from collaborator Uncle Tak, who persuades him that it is legitimate business. Steelhead takes the money to help other illegal Chinese immigrants and prohibits drug dealing. But by taking this money he, unknowingly, triggers off other results. At this point of the film Jie becomes more alienated from Steelhead. When Tak (who has used yakuza connections to get Jie brutally beaten up earlier in the film) attempts to shake Jie's artificial hand, he sets in motion an outburst of violence. Having lost his hand from Gao's mutilation, Jie attempts to strangle Tak. He returns later as a leather-coated, white-wigged drug dealer who obviously enjoys the substance he sells. Steelhead's acquiescence to the underworld's 'business-as-usual' practices and denial of this involvement has dark consequences. Jie becomes Steelhead's neo-noir version of a 'return of the repressed' Frankenstein monster. Steelhead sells his soul to Eguchi to gain legal immigrant status by executing two rival yakuzas. During his second hit, Eguchi appears in the background like a Mephistopheles witnessing Steelhead's naive Faust fulfil his side of a bargain that will

Figure 11.3 Frankenstein Monster v. 1.

eventually lead to damnation. Steelhead commits consciously planned murder as opposed to an earlier accidental murder of a Mainland police officer as he fled across the border. He will later be reminded of this contrast.

During the film, a news commentator on one of the giant screens overlooking Shinjuku speaks about how when the oppressed rise up, their force turns into a power that 'changes people. That way tolerance and passivity become aggressive.' Images appear showing Steelhead on the street as the broadcaster mentions that '1.5 million foreigners now live in Japan'. These immigrants become trapped in a world of aggressive power and capitalist exploitation affecting both Steelhead and Jie. When Jie's Japanese girlfriend expresses shock at his changed appearance when they next meet, he responds, 'We're businessmen now.' Jie has now become corrupted by economic greed.

This scene ironically follows the final part of the flashback when Xiuxiu remembers how she once saw foreign goods brought to a neighbour's house in China. Then young Steelhead told her, 'You have to learn to be content.' The scene begins with Xiuxiu telling Eguchi, 'Since becoming a wife and mother, I know what I value in life.' These former Mainland lovers engage in their own forms of denial. Although Steelhead and Xiuxiu take different paths, they equally become corrupted by material values leading to their violent deaths. Although we see Steelhead floating to his death in the sewer at the end of the film, it is unlikely that the racist Nakajima will allow Eguchi's Chinese widow and his mixed-race child to survive after he has lured Steelhead to Okubo station.

Shot in appropriate neo-noir cinematography, *Shinjuku Incident*'s concluding sequence contains its own form of history lesson parallel to those in *One Nite in Mongkok* and *Protégé*. Despite its geographical location, the world of *Shinjuku Incident* uncannily resembles the divided China of the 1930s and 1940s. Nakajima's yakuza mobilise outside for an attack evoking memories of Imperial Army atrocities: 'Now is the time for us to use the Bushido way to get rid of the Chinese pigs.' Eguchi uses a perverse version of the Showa regime's East Asian Prosperity strategy to divide this Chinese community. He sets up Steelhead as his own version of Emperor Puyi, making Shinjuku resemble Manchukuo. But other gangsters plan their own type of Nanking Massacre. Like China in the pre-war era, Shinjuku is a divided territory, a battleground for different factions seeking control on racial as well as economic lines. Yakuza have allies such as Taiwanese gangster Gao and Uncle Tak, who is described as an 'old China hand', an appropriate term equating his involvement with Japanese gangsters to Chinese collaborators used by Japanese invaders in the 1930s and 1940s. Like many Chinese and Taiwanese during the Japanese occupation, Xiuxiu has married a Japanese husband and submerges her racial identity to resemble that of her spouse, as the Club Formosa scene shows. But this does not make her acceptable to other Japanese such as Nakajima. Although some criticise Daniel Wu's make-up and costume in the latter part of the film, his ghostly presence really embodies *Shinjuku Incident*'s particular history lesson. Jie is a ghostly presence from the past revealing that there is no 'end of history' for a contemporary China already re-experiencing the return of a capitalism that the 1949 Communist Party victory supposedly eliminated. He is also a new global version of Count Dracula, whom Franco Moretti[8] regards as a 'return of the repressed' embodiment of Victorian capitalism that has now returned from the grave. Although Jie dies from a wound inflicted by another, his death evokes a Japanese hara-kiri ritual suggesting guilt and shame stemming from his involvement in capitalist transactions. Like Steelhead, Chinese Communist Party authorities also engage in their own form of denial. *Shinjuku Incident*'s neo-noir style evokes its own allegorical return of the repressed, contradicting the official ideology of the 1949 liberation and revealing that capitalism has risen again like Count Dracula.

During an earlier scene an elderly Japanese politician presides over a meeting involving warring yakuza factions. It evokes memories of Chiang Kai-shek's supposed involvement with Shanghai Triads whom he used to massacre Communist Party members in 1926.[9] *Shinjuku Incident* contains repressed historical memories that reappear allegorically. Kitano spies on the meeting of 'black gold politicians', evoking the final sequence of Fukasaku's *Japan Organized Crime Boss* (1969), revealing the associations between politicians and gangsters. Kitano caustically comments, 'Gangsters, politicians, showbiz! You can't tell one from the other these days. It's called capitalism.' The scene echoes dark alliances between warlords, the KMT and Triads in Chinese history.

With the exception of Inspector Kitano (Takenaka Naoto), most characters have few redeeming features. Victimisers or victims, Japanese or foreigners, all inhabit a global capitalist neo-noir inferno, either consciously engaging in its benefits or denying involvement. In one scene, Xiuxiu remembers her former life in China and her first seduction by material affluence when a rich exile returns home with clothes, a refrigerator and a colour television for his family, stimulating capitalist desires on the part of envious villagers. Despite the line 'You have to learn to be content', few Chinese actually are in *Shinjuku Incident*. During the later part of the film Steelhead sublimates guilty feelings arising from his criminal activities by developing a tractor business. But his denial will not prevent the ensuing chaos. *Shinjuku Incident*'s first flashback casts doubt on his heroic agency. The tractor Steelhead drives in north-east China crashes into the ice, leading to teasing by his prospective brother-in-law who deliberately supplied him with misleading information concerning the supposedly solid nature of the ice he attempted to drive over. Like Sunny Koo, Steelhead is too trusting, easily betrayed and not in full control of the situation. Mainland Chinese corruption begins early in the film. Xiuxiu's aunt tries to leave China legally by deviously claiming that an inoculation scar on her arm was made by the Japanese during the occupation, thus making her Japanese not Chinese. Former dark and shameful memories of Japanese occupation become opportunistic excuses to escape from an impoverished homeland and participate in a former enemy's access to global capitalism. Despite his supposed humanitarian principles ('How can I take advantage of my own people?') and initial refusal to take money for humanitarian acts, Steelhead eventually succumbs to a contaminating lifestyle and becomes alienated from everybody as he plunges further into a dark global urban inferno. He refuses to entertain Lilly's suggestion that they leave Japan and immigrate to Brazil: 'What am I to do there?' Lilly replies, 'Something that lets you sleep at night.' Steelhead still entertains loyalty towards his fellow immigrants who now possess the same residential status but who have also changed drastically. He learns from a news report that they are involved in drug smuggling with Eguchi. Steelhead cannot accept the consequences of these new changes nor the fact that he is indirectly responsible for them: 'I can't leave them behind.' Although he affirms loyalty to his fellow Chinese, he is also prepared to betray Eguchi, thus echoing the devious strategy of his yakuza overlord who only regards him as a pawn in his own divide-and-rule political game. When Kitano appears, Steelhead tells him, 'As long as you don't arrest my people, I will give evidence against Eguchi.' Eguchi also suffers betrayal from his own people when his ambitions become too much for his organisation. A senior gang boss gives Eguchi's former Taiwanese colleague and betrayer Gao a contract to eliminate this chess player who is really just another disposable pawn in a dark world of global economic criminality.

Lilly condemns Steelhead's hypocrisy as he attempts a deal with Officer Kitano: 'Have you ever considered my feelings? Who do you live for? Your brothers? Xiuxiu? Me?' Although Steelhead will finally attempt to change things, his activities are too late. His actions actually contradict earlier words of encouragement to fellow Chinese in the film's last flashback that shows them all ironically reunited in a happier time when everyone has contributed generously towards a chestnut stall for Jie, recognising his inability to be a real criminal:'You can win if you put up a good fight.' Steelhead eventually dies in a Tokyo sewer with a punctured lung, the same place he rescued Kitano from earlier in the film. He flows away like a wasted commodity having no further use or value in the world he had embraced. Floating away like shit, Steelhead's body grimly resembles his real status as a capitalist waste product inside a sewer that the Japanese regarded as only fit for foreign immigrants to work within. As the old Japanese politician says earlier in the film, 'The dead have no more value but the riches of the world do.'

Steelhead attempts vainly to stop his friends becoming totally corrupted and being little better than Triads. When Lao Gwei (Lam Suet) attempts to intervene, 'Chinese don't fight Chinese', he receives a deadly slash on his throat by Hong Kong Boy who has earlier reacted against Steelhead's 'Without me, where would you be?' by reminding him of his earlier dependence: 'When you were in Japan who looked out for you?' Hong Kong Boy previously saved his boss Steelhead from retaliation in a restaurant they owned from young Katao-gumi members. Steelhead ironically berated these youths for their noisy behaviour in the same way that his Japanese landlord earlier complained about a Chinese New Year gathering. He prevented eviction by buying off the landlord with money, the first stage in his acquisition of Japanese business practices. When Steelhead learns that these young Japanese are Jie's multinational followers, he responds despairingly, 'Are we a Triad gang, now?' Hong Kong Boy responds, 'It's for survival. Don't interfere.' After Lao Gwei's death, all hell literally breaks loose with the once-close Chinese community turning in on itself. These and similar scenes probably made Chan and Yee hesitant about a Mainland release. The latter neo-noir scenes evoke too many grim historical memories.

Shinjuku Incident concludes with a sombre caption stating that since China's booming economy occurred, Mainland illegal immigration into Japan declined. Perhaps Party officials may have recognised certain relevant implications of this noir mirror imagery suggesting what China itself might face in the future? The bookend nature of the film's structure not only emphasises the grim naturalistic determinative mechanisms that have foredoomed Steelhead (as much as any character in Emile Zola's Rougon-Macquart series of novels) but also a future that may soon affect China itself. When the film began, it revealed Steelhead and his other Mainland illegal immigrants escaping from a boat on the beach. It ends with a long shot of the same beach as other illegals reach the shore. The caption mentions that illegal immigration from the Mainland peaked in the 1990s but dropped off after the millennium due to China's booming economy. This leaves viewers with the feeling that perhaps China will soon face its own type of problems similar to those facing Steelhead and his fellow illegal immigrants. One Mainland Chinese film suggests that such problems are already occurring.

Preceding *Shinjuku Incident*, Li Yang's *Blind Shaft* (2003) represents an ironic postscript to this later film despite the dates of their respective productions. Made in the Chinese Mainland ostensibly under the control of a Chinese Communist Party representing old nineteenth-century utopian hopes for the abolition of capitalism and a better life for everyone, Li's film reveals the return of a capitalist repressed with a vengeance. A century and a half ago, the ruthless world of Social Darwinism dominated western and eastern economies alongside progressive movements for its abolition. The beginning of this present century has seen not only the hegemony of capitalism in its global transnational manifestations but also the return of oppressive behavioural and social forces that characterised nineteenth-century naturalist observations by Zola and others. In several ways *Blind Shaft* represents the *Germinal* of its era. While Zola's original novel scrupulously documented the bleak personal and environmental facts oppressing the lives of those trapped within a mining community, it did end on a tentative note of hope. By contrast, *Blind Shaft* concludes pessimistically. Like Etienne Lantier, young Feng escapes at the climax and can return home. But he has witnessed the dark side of a Chinese economic miracle where unregulated mines and negligent managers allow Tang and Song to prey on their fellow workers like the ravenous dogs that prey on their weaker pack members in Jack London's *The Call of the Wild* (1903) and fulfil their appetites. In the case of Tang and Song, like Sergio Leone's bounty hunters in *For A Few Dollars More* (1965), they discover that 'Where Life has no Value; Death sometimes has its price.' Tang and Song inhabit the precarious world of the coal-mining industry of North-western China, staging a series of accidents by murdering fellow workers and profiting from their deaths by passing their victims off as relatives to gain hush money from a ruthless managerial bureaucracy intent upon suppressing knowledge of an economic miracle characterised by poor working conditions and the worthlessness of human life. It is a world where economic exploitation and prostitution supposedly eliminated by the 1949 revolution co-exist. Tang and Song immediately recognise that they can profit from a worthless human life until they encounter Feng, who will ironically become an economic beneficiary of the complex events that occur later in the film. *Blind Shaft* contains a mixture of styles comprising a cinematic neo-noir development of Italian neo-realism and classical film noir, both of which co-existed in earlier films such as Luchino Visconti's *Ossessione* (1943) and Jules Dassin's *The Naked City* (1948). Focusing upon the dark economic underworld lying beneath the glittering urban facades of contemporary Beijing and Shanghai contained in tourist depictions disseminated to the outside world, *Blind Shaft*'s particular stylistic world is another example of those dark social motifs motivating both neo-noir in general and *Shinjuku Incident* in particular. Mainland authorities banned *Blind Shaft*. *Shinjuku Incident* is a key example of Hong Kong neo-noir having both bleak social and economic discursive global meanings containing disturbing overtones for present and future.

Notes

1. Dana, 'Journal of a Voyage Round the World, 1859–1860', p. 649.
2. Ibid., p. 651.
3. Ibid., p. 652.
4. Ibid., p. 663.
5. Ibid., p. 719.
6. For an analysis of *Dr Lamb*, see Williams, 'Hong Kong Social Horror', pp. 209–12. Significantly, in his audio-commentary for the British neo-noir *Harry Brown* (2009), Michael Caine suggests that claustrophobic living conditions in lower-class estates may be one reason for the violent behaviour of working-class youngsters.
7. Fore, 'Jackie Chan and the Cultural Dynamics of Global Entertainment', pp. 239–62.
8. Moretti, 'Dialectic of Fear', pp. 92–108.
9. Peng, 'Introduction', p. 57.

Bibliography

Abbas, Ackbar, *Hong Kong: Culture and the Politics of Disappearance* (Minneapolis: University of Minnesota Press, 1997).

Abbas, Ackbar, 'Hyphenation: The Spatial Dimensions of Hong Kong Culture', in Michael P. Steinberg (ed.), *Walter Benjamin and the Demands of History* (Ithaca: Cornell University Press, 1996), pp. 214–31.

Abbas, Ackbar, 'The New Hong Kong Cinema and the *Déjà Disparu*', in Dimitris Eleftheriotis and Gary Needham (eds), *Asian Cinemas: A Reader & Guide* (Edinburgh: Edinburgh University Press, 2006), pp. 72–99.

Allen, Michael, 'Divided Interests: Split-Screen Aesthetics in *24*', in Stephen Peacock (ed.), *Reading 24: TV against the Clock* (London: I. B. Tauris, 2007), pp. 35–47.

Andersen, Thom, 'Red Hollywood', in Suzanne Ferguson and Barbara Groseclose (eds), *Literature and the Visual Arts in Contemporary Society* (Columbus, OH: Ohio State University Press, 1985), pp. 141–96.

'Article 23', *Hong Kong Human Rights Monitor*, n.d.: http://www.article23.org.hk/english/main.htm (last accessed 14 January 2015).

asianwack, 'Beyond Hypothermia', *Youtube*, 12 December 2010: http://www.youtube.com/watch?v=Mm0F3oOddlA (last accessed 18 February 2015).

Austen, David, 'CSB Interviews Johnnie To, Director of *Election* and *Election 2* (Triad Election)', *Cinema Strikes Back*, 23 April 2007: http://www.cinemastrikesback.com/?p=1470 (last accessed 15 January 2015).

Australian Cinematheque, Gallery of Modern Art Brisbane, 'Bond, JANE Bond: Hong Kong Action Women of the 1960s', *Australian Cinematheque, Gallery of Modern Art Brisbane*, n.d.: http://www.qagoma.qld.gov.au/cinematheque/past_programs/2010/bond,_jane_bond_hong_kong_action_women (last accessed 1 July 2014).

Baudrillard, Jean, *The Gulf War Did Not Take Place* (Indianapolis: University of Indiana Press, 1995).

Berry, Chris, and Mary Farquhar, *China on Screen: Cinema and Nation* (Hong Kong: Hong Kong University Press, 2006).

Bokiniec, Monika, 'Who Can Find a Virtuous CTU Agent? Jack Bauer as Modern Hero, Antihero and Tragic Villain', in Anna Fahraeus and Dikmen Yakali Çamoglu (eds),

Villains and Villainy: Embodiments of Evil in Literature, Popular Culture and Media (Amsterdam: Rodopi, 2011), pp. 193–213.

Bordwell, David, 'A Many-Splendored Thing 4: Triangulating', *Observations on film art*, 22 March 2007: http://www.davidbordwell.net/blog/2007/03/22/a-many-splendored-thing-4/ (last accessed 6 January 2011).

Bordwell, David, *Planet Hong Kong: Popular Cinema and the Art of Entertainment* (Cambridge, MA: Harvard University Press, 2000).

Bordwell, David, *Planet Hong Kong: Popular Cinema and the Art of Entertainment*, 2nd edn (Madison: Irvington Way Institute, 2011).

Chang, Cheh, *Chang Cheh: A Memoir*, Ain-ling Wong (ed.) (Hong Kong: Hong Kong Film Archive, 2004).

Charles, John, *Hong Kong Filmography 1977–1997* (Jefferson, NC: McFarland, 2000).

Cheng, Jihua, Shaobai Li and Zuwen Xing 程季華, 李少白, 邢祖文 (eds), *Zhongguo dianying fazhan shi* 中國電影發展史 [*The History of the Development of Chinese Cinema*] (Beijing: China Film Press, 1963).

Cheng, Yu, 'Anatomy of a Legend', in Cheuk-to Li (ed.), *A Study of Hong Kong Cinema in the Seventies*, rev. edn (Hong Kong: Leisure and Cultural Services Department; Hong Kong International Film Festival Society, 2002).

Chénieux-Gendron, Jacqueline, 'Surrealists in Exile: Another Kind of Resistance', *Poetics Today*, 17:3 (1996), pp. 437–51.

Cheuk, Pak-tong, *Hong Kong New Wave Cinema (1978–2000)* (Bristol: Intellect, 2008).

Cheung, Esther M. K, *Fruit Chan's* Made in Hong Kong (Hong Kong: Hong Kong University Press, 2009).

Cheung, Esther M. K., and Yiu-wai Chu (eds), *Between Home and World: A Reader in Hong Kong Cinema* (Hong Kong: Oxford University Press, 2004).

'Chinese Movies Fill the Void: But Don't Produce Cheaply in Bulk', *Qingqing dianying* 青青電影 [*Qing Qing Film*], 20 October 1948.

Chow, Rey, *Primitive Passions: Visuality, Sexuality, Ethnography, and Contemporary Chinese Cinema* (New York: Columbia University Press, 1995).

Chu, Yiu-wai, 'The Importance of Being Chinese: Orientalism Reconfigured in the Age of Global Modernity', *boundary 2*, 35:2 (2008), pp. 183–206.

Chung, Stephanie Po-yin, 'A Southeast Asian Tycoon and His Movie Dream: Loke Wan Tho and MP & GI', in Ain-ling Wong and Sam Ho (eds), *Cathay Story* (Hong Kong: Leisure and Cultural Services Department; Hong Kong Film Archive, 2002), pp. 36–51.

Ciecko, Anne T., 'Hong Kong: Cinematic Cycles of Grief and Glory', in Anne Tereska Ciecko (ed.), *Contemporary Asian Cinema: Popular Culture in a Global Frame* (New York and Oxford: Berg, 2006), pp. 169–81.

Clover, Carol, *Man, Women, and Chain Saws: Gender in the Modern Horror Film* (Princeton, NJ: Princeton University Press, 1992).

Collier, Joelle, 'The Noir East: Hong Kong Filmmakers' Transmutation of a Hollywood Genre?', in Gina Marchetti and See-Kam Tan (eds), *Hong Kong Film, Hollywood and*

the New Global Cinema: No Film Is an Island (London and New York: Routledge, 2007), pp. 137–58.
Conley, Tom, *Cartographic Cinema* (Minneapolis and London: University of Minnesota Press, 2007).
Conrad, Mark T. (ed.), *The Philosophy of Neo-Noir* (Lexington: University Press of Kentucky, 2007).
Copjec, Joan, 'Introduction', in Joan Copjec (ed.), *Shades of Noir* (London: Verso, 1993), pp. vii–xii.
Covey, William R., '*Pères Fatales*: Character and Style in Postmodern Neo-Noir', *Quarterly Review of Film and Video*, 28 (2011), pp. 41–52.
Dana, Richard Henry, 'Journal of a Voyage Round the World, 1859–1860', in Richard Henry Dana, Thomas L. Philbrick (ed.), *Two Years before the Mast and Other Voyages*, New York: Library of America; Penguin Putnam, [1840] (2005), pp. 541–870.
Deleuze, Gilles, and Félix Guattari, *Anti-Oedipus*, trans. Robert Hurley, Mark Seem and Helen R. Lane (London and New York: Continuum, 2004).
Desser, David, 'Global Noir: Genre Film in the Age of Transnationalism', in Barry Keith Grant (ed.), *Film Genre Reader III* (Austin: University of Texas Press, 2003), pp. 516–36.
Dimendberg, Edward, *Film Noir and the Spaces of Modernity* (Cambridge, MA: Harvard University Press, 2004).
Ding, Yaping 丁亞平, *Yingxiang Zhongguo: Zhongguo dianying yishu* 影像中國: 中國電影藝術, *1945–1949* [Imaging China: 1945–1949] (Beijing: Culture & Art Press, 1998).
Dorfman, Ariel, *Empire's Old Clothes: What the Lone Ranger, Babar, and Other Innocent Heroes Do to Our Minds* (New York: Penguin Books, 1996).
Dovey, Lindiwe, 'Subjects of Exile: Alienation in Francophone West African Cinema', *International Journal of Francophone Studies*, 12:1 (2009), pp. 55–75.
duriandave, 'The Black Killer (1967)', HKMDB, 12 April 2006: http://hkmdb.com/db/reviews/show_review.mhtml?id=11578 (last accessed 30 June 2014).
Dyer, Richard, *Nino Rota: Music, Film and Feeling* (London: BFI Publishing; Macmillan, 2010).
Elley, Derek, 'Review: *After This Our Exile*', *Variety*, 23–29 October 2006, p. 34.
Elsaesser, Thomas, 'Ethnicity, Authenticity, and Exile: A Counterfeit Trade? German Filmmakers and Hollywood', in Hamid Naficy (ed.), *Home, Exile, Homeland: Film, Media, and the Politics of Place* (New York: Routledge, 1999), pp. 97–123.
Fang, Karen Y., *John Woo's A Better Tomorrow* (Hong Kong: Hong Kong University Press, 2004).
Fay, Jennifer, and Justus Nieland, *Film Noir: Hard-Boiled Modernity and the Cultures of Globalization* (London and New York: Routledge, 2010).
Feng, Jing, '*Gang pian xiao zhang shi: dang jie pai qiang zhan 30 nian jia xi zhen zuo xia shi min* 港片囂張史: 當街拍槍戰30年 假戲真做嚇市民 [The Wild History of Hong Kong Films: Thirty Years of Using Streets to Shoot Gun Battles; So Realistic That

It Scares People]', *Sohu.com*, 30 October 2007: http://yule.sohu.com/20071030/n252952945.shtml (last accessed 6 March 2011).

Fore, Steve, 'Jackie Chan and the Cultural Dynamics of Global Entertainment', in Sheldon Hsiao-Peng Lu (ed.), *Transnational Chinese Cinemas: Identity, Nationhood, Gender* (Honolulu: University of Hawaii Press, 1997), pp. 239–62.

Forrest, Jennifer (ed.), *The Legend Returns and Dies Harder Another Day: Essays on Film Series* (Jefferson, NC: McFarland, 2008).

Foucault, Michel, *The Order of Things: An Archaeology of the Human Sciences* (New York: Vintage Books, 1973).

Fu, Po-shek, 'The 1960s: Modernity, Youth Culture, and Hong Kong Cantonese Cinema', in Po-shek Fu and David Desser (eds), *The Cinema of Hong Kong: History, Arts, Identity* (Cambridge: Cambridge University Press, 2000), pp. 71–89.

Fu, Winnie (ed.), *Hong Kong Filmography, Vol. 2 1942–1949* (Hong Kong: Leisure and Cultural Services Department; Hong Kong Film Archive, 1999).

Fu, Winnie (ed.), *Movement, Emotion and Real Sites @ Location* (Hong Kong: Leisure and Cultural Services Department; Hong Kong Film Archive, 2006).

Gellar, Theresa L., 'Transnational Noir: Style and Substance in Hayashi Kaizo's *The Most Terrible Time in My Life*', in Leon Hunt and Wai-Fai Leung (eds), *East Asian Cinemas: Exploring Transnational Connections on Film* (London and New York: I. B. Tauris, 2008), pp. 172–87.

Giddens, Anthony, *The Consequences of Modernity* (Cambridge: Polity, 1990).

Gledhill, Christine, 'Klute 1: A Contemporary Film Noir and Feminist Criticism', in E. Ann Kaplan (ed.), *Women in Film Noir* (London: BFI Publishing, 1980).

Glitre, Kathrina, 'Under the Neon Rainbow: Colour and Neo-Noir', in Mark Bould, Kathrina Glitre and Greg Tuck (eds), *Neo-Noir* (London: Wallflower Press, 2009), pp. 11–27.

Government Information Centre, 'Hong Kong Remains a Safe and Attractive Place for Filming', 22 March 2001, *Hong Kong SAR Government*: http://www.info.gov.hk/gia/general/200103/22/0322230.htm (last accessed 14 January 2015).

Government Information Centre, 'FSO Places HK on Map of Celluloid World', *Hong Kong SAR Government*, 29 March 2002: http://www.info.gov.hk/gia/general/200203/29/0328249.html (last accessed 14 January 2015).

Hall, Kenneth E., *John Woo's* The Killer (Hong Kong: Hong Kong University Press, 2009).

Hall, Kenneth E., *John Woo: The Films*, 2nd edn (Jefferson, NC: McFarland, 2012).

Hammond, Stefan, and Mike Wilkins, *Sex and Zen and a Bullet in the Head* (New York: Simon & Schuster, 1996).

Harootunian, Harry, *History's Disquiet: Modernity, Cultural Practice, and the Question of Everyday Life* (New York: Columbia University Press, 2000).

Harvey, David, *The Condition of Postmodernity* (Oxford: Blackwell, 1990).

Hayward, Susan, *Cinema Studies: The Key Concepts*, 2nd edn (London and New York: Routledge, 2000).

Ho, Erica, 'Can Hollywood Afford to Make Films China Doesn't Like?', *Time*, 25 May 2011: http://content.time.com/time/world/article/0,8599,2072194,00.html (last accessed 15 January 2015).

Ho, Sam, 'The Songstress, the Farmer's Daughter, the Mambo Girl, and the Songstress Again', in Law Kar (ed.), *Mandarin Films and Popular Songs: 40s–60s* (Hong Kong: Urban Council; Hong Kong International Film Festival Society, 1993), pp. 59–78.

Ho, Sam, 'Excerpts from an Interview with Ge Lan', in Law Kar (ed.), *Mandarin Films and Popular Songs: 40s–60s* (Hong Kong: Urban Council; Hong Kong International Film Festival Society, 1993), pp. 88–92.

Ho, Sam, 'Licensed to Kick Men: The Jane Bond Films', in Law Kar (ed.), *The Restless Breed: Cantonese Stars of the Sixties* (Hong Kong: Urban Council; Hong Kong International Film Festival Society, 1996), pp. 40–6.

Ho, Sam, and Wai-leng Ho (eds), *The Swordsman and His Jiang Hu: Tsui Hark and Hong Kong Film* (Hong Kong: Hong Kong Film Archive, 2002).

Holmlund, Chris, *Impossible Bodies: Femininity and Masculinity at the Movies* (London and New York: Routledge, 2003).

Hu, Jubin, *Projecting a Nation, Chinese Cinema before 1949* (Hong Kong: Hong Kong University Press, 2003).

Hui, La Frances, 'After This Our Exile: Interview with Patrick Tam Ka-ming', *Asia Society*, n.d.: http://asiasociety.org/arts/film/after-his-exile-interview-patrick-tam-ka-ming (last accessed 6 January 2011).

Hutcheon, Linda, *Narcissistic Narrative: The Metafictional Paradox* (London and New York: Routledge, 1980).

Ingham, Michael, *Johnnie To Kei-Fung's PTU* (Hong Kong: Hong Kong University Press, 2009).

Jaffe, Ira, *Hollywood Hybrids: Mixing Genres in Contemporary Films* (Lanham, MD: Rowman & Littlefield, 2008).

Jameson, Fredric, *The Political Unconscious: Narrative as a Socially Symbolic Act* (New York: Cornell University Press, 1981).

Jameson, Fredric, *Postmodernism: Or, the Cultural Logic of Late Capitalism* (Durham, NC: Duke University Press, 1991).

Jameson, Fredric, 'Postmodernism and the Consumer Society', in Hal Poster (ed.), *The Anti-Aesthetic: Essays on Postmodern Culture* (Port Townsend: Bay Press, 1983), pp. 111–25.

Jarvie, I. C., *Window on Hong Kong: A Sociological Study of the Hong Kong Film Industry and Its Audience* (Hong Kong: Centre of Asian Studies, University of Hong Kong, 1977).

Jermyn, Deborah, 'Reasons to Split up: Interactivity, Realism and the Multiple-Image Screen in 24', in Steven Peacock (ed.), *Reading 24: TV against the Clock* (London: I. B. Tauris, 2007), pp. 49–57.

Jost, Marie, 'The Rise of Johnnie To', *Hong Kong Cinemagic*, 28 February 2011: http://www.hkcinemagic.com/fr/pdf/The-Rise-of-Johnnie-To-Marie-Jost-HKCinemagic-PDF-version.pdf (last accessed 15 January 2015).

Kaminsky, Stuart M., 'Kung Fu Film as Ghetto Myth', *Journal of Popular Film*, 3 (1974), pp. 129–37.

Kaplan, E. Ann (ed.), *Women in Film Noir* (London: BFI Publishing, 1978).

Kaplan, E. Ann (ed.), *Women in Film Noir*, rev. edn (London: BFI Publishing, 1980).

Klein, Norman M., *The History of Forgetting: Los Angeles and the Erasure of Memory* (London: Verso, 2003).

Knee, Adam, 'The Pan Asian Outlook of the Eye', in Jinhee Choi and Mitsuyo Wada-Marciano (eds), *Horror to the Extreme: Changing Boundaries in Asian Cinema* (Hong Kong: Hong Kong University Press, 2009), pp. 69–84.

Krutnik, Frank, *In a Lonely Street: Film Noir, Genre, Masculinity* (London and New York: Routledge, 1991).

Lai, Linda, and Sam Ho, 'The Lucky One Becomes the Cop: Ringo Lam on *Full Alert*', in Law Kar (ed.), *Hong Kong Panorama 97–98* (Hong Kong: Provisional Urban Council; Hong Kong International Film Festival Society, 1998).

Lapsley, Rob, 'Mainly in Cities and at Night; Some Notes on Cities and Film', in David B. Clarke (ed.), *The Cinematic City* (London and New York: Routledge, 1997), pp. 186–208.

Lau, Andrew Wai-keung, '"City on Fire" Interview Part 2 of 3', *Youtube*, August 2007 (last accessed 30 April 2010).

Lau, Shirley, 'Painting over the Cracks', *scmp.com*, 26 April 2001.

Law Kar (ed.), *Fifty Years of Electric Shadows* (Hong Kong: Urban Council; Hong Kong International Film Festival Society, 1997).

Law Kar, and Frank Bren, *Hong Kong Cinema: A Cross-Cultural View* (Lanham, MD: Scarecrow Press, 2004).

Leary, Charles, 'What Goes around, Comes around: *Infernal Affairs II* and *III* and *Running on Karma*', *Senses of Cinema*, 30 (February 2004): http://www.sensesofcinema.com/2004/feature-articles/infernal_affairs_ii/ (last accessed 15 January 2015).

Lee, Hyangjin, 'The Shadow of Outlaws in Asian Noir: Hiroshima, Hong Kong and Seoul', in Mark Bould, Kathrina Glitre and Greg Tuck (eds), *Neo-Noir* (London: Wallflower Press, 2009), pp. 118–35.

Lee, Leo Ou-fan, 'The Popular and the Classical: Reminiscences on *The Wild, Wild Rose*', in Sam Ho (ed.), *The Cathay Story* (Hong Kong: Leisure and Cultural Services Department; Hong Kong Film Archive, 2002), pp. 176–89.

Lee, Min, 'Director Patrick Tam is Anomaly in Prolific, Improvisational Hong Kong Industry', *Associated Press*, 16 December 2006: http://english.sina.com/taiwan_hk/1/2006/1216/98198.html (last accessed 4 April 2015).

Lee, Nikki J. Y., and Julian Stringer, 'Film Noir in Asia: Historicizing South Korean Crime Thrillers', in Andrew Spicer and Helen Hanson (eds), *A Companion to Film Noir* (Oxford: Blackwell, 2013), pp. 479–95.

Lee, Pui-tak (ed.), *Colonial Hong Kong and Modern China: Interaction and Reintegration* (Hong Kong: Hong Kong University Press, 2005).

Lee, Vivian P. Y., *Hong Kong Cinema Since 1997: The Post-Nostalgic Imagination* (Basingstoke: Palgrave Macmillan, 2009).

Leyda, Jay, *Dianying/Electric Shadows: An Account of Films and the Film Audience in China* (Cambridge, MA: MIT Press, 1972).
Li, Cheuk-to, 'Postscript', in Cheuk-to Li (ed.), *A Study of Hong Kong Cinema in the Seventies*, rev. edn (Hong Kong: Leisure and Cultural Services Department; Hong Kong International Film Festival Society, 2002), pp. 127–31.
Liu, Jerry, 'Chang Cheh: Aesthetics = Ideology?', in Mo-ling Leong (ed.), *A Study of the Hong Kong Swordplay Film (1945–1980)*, rev. edn (Hong Kong: Urban Council; Hong Kong International Film Festival Society, 1996), pp. 159–64.
Longtin, 'The Buddha's Gaze', trans. Sandy Ng, in Cheuk-to, Li and Keith Chan (eds), *Wai Ka-Fai: Filmmaker in Focus* (Hong Kong: Leisure and Cultural Services Department; Hong Kong International Film Festival Society, 2011), pp. 88–9.
Loza, Susana, 'Orientalism and Film Noir: (Un)Mapping Textual Territories and (En)Countering the Narratives', *The Southern Quarterly*, 39:4 (2001), pp. 161–74.
Lu, Sheldon Hsiao-Peng (ed.), *Chinese Cinemas: Identity, Nationhood, Gender* (Honolulu: University of Hawaii Press, 1997).
Lui, Tai-lok, and Wai-hung Yiu, 'Intrigue is Hard to Defend: The Conditions of Transition and the Prototype of Hong Kong Culture', in Ain-ling Wong (ed.), *The Shaw Screen: A Preliminary Study* (Hong Kong: Leisure and Cultural Services Department; Hong Kong Film Archive, 2003).
Marchetti, Gina, *Andrew Lau and Alan Mak's Infernal Affairs – The Trilogy* (Hong Kong: Hong Kong University Press, 2007).
Marchetti, Gina, *From Tian'anmen to Times Square: Transnational China and the Chinese Diaspora on Global Screens, 1989–1997* (Philadelphia: Temple University Press, 2006).
Marchetti, Gina, and See-Kam Tan, 'Introduction: Hong Kong Cinema and Global Change', in Gina Marchetti and See-Kam Tan (eds), *Hong Kong Film, Hollywood and the New Global Cinema: No Film Is an Island* (London and New York: Routledge, 2007), pp. 1–9.
Marchetti, Gina, and See-Kam Tan (eds), *Hong Kong Film, Hollywood and the New Global Cinema: No Film Is an Island* (London and New York: Routledge, 2007).
Marchetti, Gina, David Vivier and Thomas Podvin, 'Interview with Patrick Tam: The Exiled Director', *Hong Kong Cinemagic*, 28 June 2007: http://www.hkcinemagic.com/en/page.asp?aid=270&page=1 (last accessed 19 January 2011).
Meehan, Paul, *Tech-Noir: The Fusion of Science Fiction and Film Noir* (Jefferson, NC: McFarland, 2008).
Mes, Tom, 'Zero Woman: Red Handcuff', *Midnight Eye: Visions of Japanese Cinema*, 14 May 2010: http://www.midnighteye.com/reviews/zero-woman-red-handcuffs/ (last accessed 29 April 2014).
Moine, Raphaëlle, *Cinema Genre*, trans. Alistair Fox and Hilary Radner (Malden, MA; Oxford: Blackwell, 2008).
Moretti, Franco, 'Dialectic of Fear', trans. David Forgacs, *Signs Taken for Wonders: Essays in the Sociology of Literary Forms*, 1st edn (London: Verso, 1983), pp. 83–108.
Morgan, Jack, 'Reconfiguring Gothic Mythology: The Film Noir-Horror Hybrid Films of the 1980s', *Post Script*, 21:3 (2002), pp. 74–86.

Morris, Meaghan, 'Transnational Imagination in Action Cinema: Hong Kong and the Making of a Global Popular Culture', *Inter-Asia Cultural Studies*, 5 (2004), pp. 181–99.
Muller, Eddie, *Dark City: The Lost World of Film Noir* (New York: St Martin's Griffin, 1998).
Naficy, Hamid, *An Accented Cinema: Exilic and Diasporic Filmmaking* (Princeton, NJ: Princeton University Press, 2001).
'Naked Killer', Wikipedia, the free encyclopedia, n.d.: http://en.wikipedia.org/wiki/Naked_Killer (last accessed 27 April 2014).
Naremore, James, 'Foreword', in Andre Spicer and Helen Hanson (eds), *A Companion to Film Noir* (Malden, MA: Wiley-Blackwell, 2013), pp. x–xx.
Naremore, James, *More than Night: Film Noir in its Contexts* (Berkeley, CA: University of California Press, 1998).
Neale, Steve, *Genre and Hollywood* (London and New York: Routledge, 2000).
Ng, Kenny Kwok-kwan 吳國坤, 'Lengzhan shiqi Xianggang dianying de zhenzhi shencha 冷戰時期香港電影的政治審查 [Political Film Censorship in Colonial Hong Kong]', in Ain-ling Wong and Pui-tak Lee 黃愛玲, 李培德 (eds), *Lengzhan yu Xianggang dianying 冷戰與香港電影 [Cold War and Hong Kong Cinema]* (Hong Kong: Leisure and Cultural Services Department; Hong Kong Film Archive, 2009), pp. 53–70.
Nix, '*Running on Karma* (2003) Movie Review', *Beyond Hollywood.com*, 5 October 2003: http://www.beyondhollywood.com/running-on-karma-2003-movie-review/ (last accessed 20 January 2015).
Pavel, Thomas, 'Exile as Romance and as Tragedy', *Poetics Today*, 17:3 (1996), pp. 301–15.
Peak, James, 'Hong Kong Producers Discuss Filming the City', *The Location Guide*, 28 October 2010: http://www.thelocationguide.com/blog/2010/10/interview-hong-kong-producers-discuss-filming-the-city/ (last accessed 20 January 2015).
Peng, Shu-Tse, 'Introduction', in Les Evans and Russell Block (eds), *Leon Trotsky on China* (New York: Monad Press, 1976), pp. 31–97.
Porter, Jonathan, '"The Past is Present": The Construction of Macau's Historical Legacy', *History and Memory*, 21:1 (2009), pp. 63–100.
Prakash, Gyan (ed.), *Noir Urbanisms: Dystopic Images of the Modern City* (Woodstock: Princeton University Press, 2010).
Preminger, Otto, *Otto Preminger: An Autobiography* (New York: Doubleday, 1977).
Prince, Stephen, 'Genre and Violence in the Work of Kurosawa and Peckinpah', in Yvonne Tasker (ed.), *Action and Adventure Cinema* (London and New York: Routledge, 2004), pp. 331–44.
Ramaeker, Paul, 'Realism, Revisionism and Visual Style: *The French Connection* and the New Hollywood *Policier*', *New Review of Film and Television Studies* 8:2 (2010), pp. 144–63.
Ray, Robert, *A Certain Tendency of the Hollywood Cinema, 1930–1980* (Princeton, NJ: Princeton University Press, 1985).
Read, Jacinda, *The New Avengers: Feminism, Femininity and the Rape-Revenge Cycle* (Manchester: Manchester University Press, 2000).
Rist, Peter, 'Neglected "Classical" Periods: Hong Kong and Korean Cinemas of the 1960s', *Asian Cinema*, 12:1 (2001), pp. 49–66.

Rist, Peter, 'Scenes of "in-Action" and Noir Characteristics in the Films of Johnnie To (Kei-Fung)', in Gina Marchetti and See-Kam Tan (eds), *Hong Kong Film, Hollywood and the New Global Cinema: No Film is an Island* (London and New York: Routledge, 2007), pp. 159–63.

Romao, Tico, 'Engines of Transformation: An Analytical History of the 1970s Car Chase Cycle', *New Review of Film and Television Studies*, 1:1 (2003), pp. 31–54.

Romao, Tico, 'Guns and Gas: Investigating the 1970s Car Chase Film', in Yvonne Tasker (ed.), *Action and Adventure Cinema* (London and New York: Routledge, 2004), pp. 130–52.

Rothock, Vicki, 'Macau Allure Attracts Biz', *Variety*, 9–15 October 2006, p. 16.

Said, Edward W., *Orientalism* (New York: Pantheon, 1978).

Saint-Cyr, Marc, 'REVIEW: Zero Woman: Red Handcuffs', *Toronto J-Film Pow-Wow*, 14 May 2010: http://jfilmpowwow.blogspot.hk/2010/05/review-zero-woman-red-handcuffs.html (last accessed 29 April 2014).

Schatz, Thomas, *Hollywood Genres: Formulas, Filmmaking, and the Studio System* (Boston, MA: McGraw Hill, 1981).

Sek, Kei, 'Cross-over Romanticism', in Ching-ling Kwok and Grace Ng (eds), *Director Chor Yuen*, Oral History Series (3) (Hong Kong: Leisure and Cultural Services Department; Hong Kong Film Archive, 2006), pp. 76–83.

'Sex, Fighting, Killing – Should Chinese Cinema Go This Way?', *Screen Voice*, 15 September 1948.

Shiel, Mark, 'A Regional Geography of Film Noir: Urban Dystopias On- and Off-Screen', in Gyan Prakash (ed.), *Noir Urbanisms: Dystopic Images of the Modern City* (Woodstock: Princeton University Press, 2010), pp. 75–103.

Shu Kei, 'Notes on MP & GI', in Ain-ling Wong and Sam Ho (eds), *The Cathay Story* (Hong Kong: Leisure and Cultural Services Department; Hong Kong Film Archive, 2002), pp. 86–107.

Silver, Alain, and James Ursini (eds), *Film Noir Reader* (Pompton Plains, NJ: Limelight Editions, 1996).

Skeldon, Ronald (ed.), *Reluctant Exiles? Migration from Hong Kong and the New Overseas Chinese* (Armonk: An East Gate Book, 1994).

Slethaug, Gordon E., 'The Exotic and Oriental as Decoy: Raymond Chandler's *The Big Sleep*', in Thomas Y. T. Luk and James P. Rice (eds), *Before and after Suzie: Hong Kong in Western Film and Literature*, New Asia Academic Bulletin No. 18 (Hong Kong: Chinese University of Hong Kong, 2002), pp. 161–84.

Song, Fagang 宋法剛, 'Lun Zhongguo kehuan dianying de queshi 論中國科幻電影的缺失 [On the Defects of Chinese Science Fiction Films]', *Dianying wenxue* 電影文學 [*Movie Literature*], 19 (2007), pp. 23–4.

Spicer, Andrew (ed.), *European Film Noir* (Manchester: Manchester University Press, 2007).

Spicer, Andre, 'Introduction: The Problem of Film Noir', in Andre Spicer and Helen Hanson (eds), *A Companion to Film Noir* (Malden, MA: Wiley-Blackwell, 2013), pp. 1–13.

Stanfield, Peter, *Maxium Movies Pulp Fictions: Film Culture and the World of Sam Fuller, Mickey Spillance, and Jim Thompson* (New Brunswick, NJ: Rutgers University Press, 2011).

Stiney, P. Adams, *Visionary Film: The American Avant-Garde 1943–2000* (Oxford: Oxford University Press, 2002).

Spicer, Andre and Helen Hanson (eds), *A Companion to Film Noir* (Malden, MA: Wiley-Blackwell, 2013).

Stokes, Lisa, 'Being There and Gone: Wong Kar-Wai's *In the Mood for Love* as Pure Mood Poem', *Tamkang Review*, 32:2 (Winter 2002), pp. 127–49.

Straw, Will, 'Urban Confidential', in David B. Clarke (ed.), *The Cinematic City* (London and New York: Routledge, 1997), pp. 110–28.

Stringer, Julian, 'The Gathering Place: *Lost* in Oahu', in Roberta Pearson (ed.), *Reading 'Lost': Perspectives on a Hit Television Show* (London: I. B. Tauris, 2009), pp. 73–93.

Swann, Paul, 'From Workshop to Backlot: The Greater Philadelphia Film Office', in Mark Shiel and Tony Fitzmaurice (eds), *Cinema and the City: Film and Urban Societies in a Global Context* (Oxford: Blackwell, 2001), pp. 88–98.

Symonds, Saul, '"Exile" Comes out at H.K. Film Nods', *The Hollywood Reporter*, 16 April 2007: http://www.hollywoodreporter.com/news/exile-comes-at-hk-film-134075 (last accessed 14 January 2015).

Teo, Stephen, 'The 1970s: Movement and Transition', in Po-shek Fu and David Desser (eds), *The Cinema of Hong Kong: History, Arts, Identity* (Cambridge: Cambridge University Press, 2000), pp. 90–110.

Teo, Stephen, 'Chinese Melodrama: The *Wenyi* Genre', in Linda Badley, R. Barton Palmer and Steven Jay Schneider (eds), *Traditions in World Cinema* (New Brunswick, NJ: Rutgers University Press, 2006), pp. 203–13.

Teo, Stephen, *Director in Action: Johnnie To and the Hong Kong Action Film* (Hong Kong: Hong Kong University Press, 2007).

Teo, Stephen, 'Hong Kong's New Wave in Retrospect', in Law Kar (ed.), *Hong Kong New Wave: Twenty Years After* (Hong Kong: Provisional Urban Council; Hong Kong International Film Festival Society, 1999), pp. 17–23.

Teo, Stephen, *Hong Kong Cinema: The Extra Dimensions* (London: BFI Publishing, 1997).

Teo, Stephen, 'Sinking into Creative Depths: Hong Kong Cinema in 1997', *Hong Kong Panorama 97–98* (Hong Kong: Provisional Urban Council; Hong Kong International Film Festival Society, 1998), pp. 11–13.

Thompson, Kristin, *Storytelling in the New Hollywood: Understanding Classical Narrative Technique* (Cambridge, MA: Harvard University Press, 1999).

Tong, Ching-siu, 'Notes on Wai Ka-Fai's Narratives of Redemption', trans. Sandy Ng, in Cheuk-to Li and Keith Chan (eds), *Wai Ka-Fai: Filmmaker in Focus* (Hong Kong: Leisure and Cultural Services Department; Hong Kong International Film Festival Society, 2011), pp. 94–6.

'The Top 100 Hitman/Assassin Films of All Time', *Flickchart*, n.d.: http://www.flickchart.com/Charts.aspx?genre=Hitman+/+Assassin+Film&perpage=100 (last accessed 28 April 2014).

Tsang, Steve, *A Modern History of Hong Kong* (London: I. B. Tauris, 2004).
Tsui, Clarence, 'Site Seeing', *South China Morning Post*, 21 December 2006: http://www.scmp.com/article/576113/site-seeing (last accessed 14 January 2015).
Ursini, James, 'Party Girl', in Alain Silver and Elizabeth Ward (eds), *Film Noir: An Encyclopedic Reference to the American Style* (Woodstock, NY: Overlook Press, 1992), pp. 222–3.
Van den Troost, Kristof, 'The Hong Kong Crime Film: Genre and Film Noir from the 1940s to the Present', PhD dissertation, The Chinese University of Hong Kong (2010).
Vernet, Marc, 'Film Noir on the Edge of Doom', in Joan Copjec (ed.), *Shades of Noir* (London: Verso, 1993), pp. 1–31.
Wang, Chaoguang 汪朝光, '*Minguo nianjian meiguo dianying zaihua shichang yanjiu* 民國年間美國電影在華市場研究 [Research on the Marketing of American Films in Republican China]', *Dianying yishu* 電影藝術 [*Film Art*] 1 (1998), pp. 57–65.
William, Darrell Davis, and Emilie Yueh-Yu Yeh, *East Asian Screen Industries* (London: BFI Publishing, 2008).
Williams, Tony, 'Hong Kong Social Horror: Tragedy and Farce in Category 3', in Steven Jay Schneider and Tony Williams (eds), *Horror International* (Detroit, MI: Wayne State University Press, 2005), pp. 203–19.
Wong, Ain-ling, and Angel Shing (eds), *Director Wong Tin-Lam* (Hong Kong: Leisure and Cultural Services Department; Hong Kong Film Archive, 2007).
Wong, Michael, 'Cameras Roll on Location as Office Chalks up Its 50th Successful Take', *Hong Kong Standard*, 10 May 1999: http://www.thestandard.com.hk/archive_news_detail.asp?pp_cat=&art_id=28454&sid=&con_type=1&archive_d_str=19990510 (last accessed 14 January 2015).
'Xianhua *Ye Dian* 閑話夜店 [Random Talk of *Night Lodging*]', *Qingqing dianying* 青青電影 [*Qing Qing Film*], 1948.
Xiang, Zi, 'Exploring the Hong Kong Film Scene', *Qingqing dianying* 青青電影 [*Qing Qing Film*], 15 September 1948.
Xu, Gary, *Sinascape: Contemporary Chinese Cinema* (Lanham, MD: Rowman & Littlefield, 2007).
Xu, Le 許樂, 'Xianggang kehuan dianying qianlun 香港科幻電影淺論 [On Hong Kong Sci-Fi Movies]', *Journal of Guizhou University (Art Edition)* 貴州大學學報 (藝術版), 20:2 (2006), pp. 51–6.
Yau, Esther C. M. (ed.), *At Full Speed: Hong Kong Cinema in a Borderless World* (Minneapolis: University of Minnesota Press, 2001).
Yau, Esther C. M., 'Ecology and Late Colonial Hong Kong Cinema: Imaginations in Time', in Law Kar (ed.), *Fifty Years of Electric Shadows: Hong Kong Cinema Retrospective* (Hong Kong: Urban Council; Hong Kong International Film Festival Society, 1997), pp. 107–13.
Yau, Esther C. M., 'Introduction: Hong Kong Cinema in a Borderless World', in Esther C. M. Yau (ed.), *At Full Speed: Hong Kong Cinema in a Borderless World* (Minneapolis: University of Minnesota Press, 2001), pp. 1–28.

Yau, Esther C. M., 'The Spirits of Capital and Haunting Sounds: Translocal Historicism in *Victim* (1999)', in See-Kam Tan, Peter X. Feng and Gina Marchetti (eds), *Chinese Connections: Critical Perspectives on Film, Identity and Diaspora* (Philadelphia: Temple University Press, 2009), pp. 249–62.

Yau, Esther C. M., 'Urban Nomads, Exilic Reflections', in Esther M. K. Cheung, Gina Marchetti and See-Kam Tan (eds), *Hong Kong Screenscapes: From the New Wave to the Digital Frontier* (Hong Kong: Hong Kong University Press, 2011), pp. 75–92.

Yau, Kinnia Shuk-ting, 'Interactions between Japanese and Hong Kong Action Cinemas', in Meaghan Morris, Siu-leung Li and Stephen Chan Ching-kiu (eds), *Hong Kong Connections: Transnational Imagination in Action Cinema* (Durham, NC: Duke University Press, 2005), pp. 35–48.

Zhou, Kelong, 'The Chinese Film Scene Today', *Qingqing dianying* 青青電影 [*Qing Qing Film*], 1 January 1949.

Žižek, Slavoj, '"The Thing That Thinks": The Kantian Background of the *Noir* Subject', in Joan Copjec (ed.), *Shades of Noir* (London: Verso, 1993), pp. 199–226.

Žižek, Slavoj, 'Da Capo Senza Fine', in Judith Butler, Ernesto Laclau and Slavoj Žižek (eds), *Contingency, Hegemony, Universality: Contemporary Dialogues on the Left* (London: Verso, 2000).

Filmography

Hong Kong

2046 (*2046*), Wong Kar-wai 王家衛, 2004
After This, Our Exile (*Fuzi* 父子), Patrick Tam Ka-ming 譚家明, 2006
Air Hostess (*Kongzhong xiaojie* 空中小姐), Evan Yang 易文, 1959
Ambush (*Maifu* 埋伏), Ho Meng-hua 何夢華, 1973
An All-Consuming Love (*Chang xiangsi* 長相思), Hoh Siu-cheung 何兆璋, 1947
The Angel Strikes Again (*Tieguanyin yongpo baozhadang* 鐵觀音勇破爆炸黨), Lo Wei 羅維, 1968
Angel with the Iron Fists (*Tieguanyin* 鐵觀音), Lo Wei 羅維, 1967
The Angry Guest (*Eke* 惡客), Chang Cheh 張徹, 1972
Anti-Corruption (*Lianzheng fengbao* 廉政風暴), Ng See-yuen 吳思遠, 1975
As Tears Go By (*Wangjiao kamen* 旺角卡門), Wong Kar-wai 王家衛, 1988
Asia-Pol (*Yazhou mimi jingcha* 亞洲秘密警察), Mak Chi-woh (aka Matsuo Akinori) 麥志和 (原名 松尾昭典), 1967
The Avenging Fist (*Quanshen* 拳神), Andrew Lau Wai-keung & Corey Yuen Kwan 劉偉強 & 元奎, 2001
The Awful Truth (*Shuohuang shijie* 說謊世界), Li Pingqian 李萍倩, 1950
Ballistic Kiss (*Shasharen、tiaotiaowu* 殺殺人、跳跳舞), Donnie Yen Ji-dan 甄子丹, 1999
Because of Her (*Jiaowo ruhe buxiang ta* 教我如何不想他), Evan Yang 易文, 1963
A Better Tomorrow (*Yingxiong bense* 英雄本色), John Woo Yu-sen 吳宇森, 1986
A Better Tomorrow II (*Yingxiong bense II* 英雄本色續集), John Woo Yu-sen 吳宇森, 1987
A Better Tomorrow III (*Yingxiong bense III xiyang zhi ge* 英雄本色III夕陽之歌), John Woo Yu-sen 吳宇森, 1987
Beyond Hypothermia (*Sheshi 32 du* 攝氏32度), Patrick Leung Pak-kin 梁柏堅, 1996
The Big Boss (*Tangshan daxiong* 唐山大兄), Lo Wei 羅維, 1971
Big Brother Cheng (*Dagecheng* 大哥成), Kuei Chih-hung 桂治洪, 1975
The Big Holdup (*Da jiean* 大劫案), Chor Yuen 楚原, 1975
Black Cat (*Heimao* 黑貓), Stephen Shin Gei-yin 冼杞然, 1991
Black Cat II (*Heimao II cisha yeliqin* 黑貓II 刺殺葉利欽), Stephen Shin Gei-yin 冼杞然, 1992

The Black Killer (aka *Dangerous Appointment*, *Hei shaxing* 黑殺星), Chiang Wai-kwong 蔣偉光, 1967
Black Mask (*Heixia* 黑俠), Daniel Lee Yan-gong 李仁港, 1996
Black Mask II: City of Masks (*Heixia II* 黑俠 II), Tsui Hark 徐克, 2002
The Black Rose (*Hei meigui* 黑玫瑰), Chor Yuen 楚原, 1965
The Black Swan: Female Detective (*Nütan heitiane* 女探黑天鵝), Ling Yun 凌雲, 1967
The Black Tavern (*Heidian* 黑店), Teddy Yip Wing-cho 葉榮祖, 1972
Blood Stained Azaleas (*Xueran dujuan hong* 血染杜鵑紅), Lee Sun-fung 李晨風, 1951
Blood Will Tell (aka *Blood Stained Begonia*, *Xueran haitang hong* 血染海棠紅), Yue Feng 岳楓, 1949
Boxer from Shantung (*Ma Yongzhen* 馬永貞), Chang Cheh 張徹, 1972
Breaking News (*Dashijian* 大事件), Johnnie To Kei-fung 杜琪峰, 2004
Broken Oath (*Pojie* 破戒), Jeng Cheong-woh 鄭昌和, 1977
Bullet in the Head (*Diexue jietou* 喋血街頭), John Woo Yu-sen 吳宇森, 1990
The Butterfly Murders (*Diebian* 蝶變), Tsui Hark 徐克, 1979
Cannonball Run I & II (*Paodan feiche I & II* 炮彈飛車 I & II), Hal Needham, 1981, 1984
Centre Stage (aka *Actress*, *Ruan Lingyu* 阮玲玉), Stanley Kwan Kam-pang 關錦鵬, 1992
Chungking Express (*Chongqing senlin* 重慶森林), Wong Kar-wai 王家衛, 1994
City on Fire (*Longhu fengyun* 龍虎風雲), Ringo Lam Ling-tung 林嶺東, 1987
City under Siege (*Quancheng jiebei* 全城戒備), Benny Chan Muk-sing 陳木勝, 2010
The Club (*Wuting* 舞廳), Kirk Wong Chi-keung 黃志強, 1981
Come Drink with Me (*Da zuixia* 大醉俠), King Hu Chin-chuan 胡金銓, 1966
Cops and Robbers (*Dianzhi bingbing* 點指兵兵), Alex Cheung Kwok-ming 章國明, 1979
Crime Story (*Zhong'anzu* 重案組), Kirk Wong Chi-keung 黃志強, 1993
The Criminals series (*Xianggang qi'an xilie* 香港奇案系列), Kuei Chih-hung, Ching Gong, Hua Shan, Sun Chung & Ho Meng-hua 桂治洪, 程剛, 華山, 孫仲 & 何夢華, 1976–7
Crouching Tiger, Hidden Dragon (*Wohu canglong* 臥虎藏龍), Ang Lee 李安, 2000
Dangerous Encounter – 1st Kind (*Diyi leixing weixian* 第一類型危險), Tsui Hark 徐克, 1980
The Dark Heroine Muk Lan-fa (aka *The Black Musketeer 'F'*, *The Dark Heroine Mu Lan-hua*, *Nüheixia Mulanhua* 女黑俠木蘭花), Law Chi 羅熾, 1966
Days of Being Wild (*Afei zhengzhuan* 阿飛正傳), Wong Kar-wai 王家衛, 1991
A Death Pass (*Siwan tongxingzheng* 死亡通行證), Chor Yuen 楚原, 1967
The Delinquent (*Fengnu qingnian* 憤怒青年), Chang Cheh & Kuei Chih-hung 張徹 & 桂治洪, 1973
Desire (*Yuwan* 慾望), Wang Yin 王引, 1946
Destroy (aka *Smash Up*, *Huimie* 毀滅), Bu Wancang 卜萬蒼, 1952
The Detective (*C+ zhengtan* C+偵探), Oxide Pang Shun 彭順, 2007
The Devil Woman in Black (*Hei yaofu* 黑妖婦), Hung Suk-wan 洪叔雲, 1949
Dr Lamb (*Gaoyang yisheng* 羔羊醫生), Danny Lee Sau-yin & Billy Tang Hin-sing 李修賢 & 鄧衍成, 1992
Dragon Heat (aka *Dragon Squad*, *Longhuo* 龍火), Daniel Lee Yan-gong 李仁港, 2005
The Drug Connection (aka *The Sexy Killer*, *Duhou mishi* 毒后秘史), Sun Chung 孫仲, 1976
Drug War (*Duzhan* 毒戰), Johnnie To Kei-fung 杜琪峰, 2012

The Duel (*Da juedou* 大決鬥), Chang Cheh 張徹, 1971
Duel of Fists (*Quanji* 拳擊), Chang Cheh 張徹, 1971
Eighteen Springs (*Banshengyuan* 半生緣), Ann Hui On-wah 許鞍華, 1997
Election (*Heishehui 1* 黑社會 1), Johnnie To Kei-fung 杜琪峰, 2005
Election II (*Heishehui yiheweigui* 黑社會以和為貴), Johnnie To Kei-fung 杜琪峰, 2006
Enter the Dragon (*Longzheng hudou* 龍爭虎鬥), Robert Clouse, 1973
Enter the Eagles (*Hunshun shidan* 渾身是膽), Corey Yuen Kwai 元奎, 1998
Everlasting Green (aka *Wild Fire and Spring Wind*, *Yehuo chunfeng* 野火春風), Ouyang Yuqian 歐陽予倩, 1948
Executioners (*Xiandai haoxia zhuan* 現代豪俠傳), Johnnie To Kei-fung & Tony Ching Siu-tung 杜琪峰 & 程小東, 1993
Exiled (*Fangzhu* 放·逐), Johnnie To Kei-fung 杜琪峰, 2006
Exodus (*Chu Aiji ji* 出埃及記), Edmond Pang Ho-cheung 彭浩翔, 2007
The Eye (*Jiangui* 見鬼), Danny Pang Fat & Oxide Pang Shun 彭發 & 彭順, 2002
Eye in the Sky (*Genzong* 跟蹤), Yau Nai-hoi 游乃海, 2007
Fallen Angels (*Duoluo tianshi* 墮落天使), Wong Kar-wai 王家衛, 1995
Fat Choi Spirit (*Liguligu xinniancai* 嚦咕嚦咕新年財), Johnnie To Kei-fung & Wai Ka-fai 杜琪峰 & 韋家輝, 2002
Female Spy 76 (*76hao nujiandie* 76號女間諜), Ren Pengnian 任彭年, 1947
The Fiery Phoenix (*Huo fenghuang* 火鳳凰), Wang Weiyi 王為一, 1951
A Fisherman's Honour (*Haishi* 海誓), Cheng Bugao 程步高, 1949
The Five Deadly Venoms (aka *The Five Venoms*, *Wudu* 五毒), Chang Cheh 張徹, 1978
Five Fingers of Death (aka *King Boxer*, *Tianxia diyiquan* 天下第一拳), Jeng Cheong-woh 鄭昌和, 1972
Flash Point (*Daohuoxian* 導火線), Wilson Yip Wai-shun 葉偉信, 2008
Floating Family (*Shuishang renjia* 水上人家), Gu Eryi 顧而已, 1949
The Flower Girl (aka *Flora*, *Hua guniang* 花姑娘), Zhu Shilin 朱石麟, 1950
The Flying Killer (aka *The Perilous Rescue*, *Chivalrous Girl in the Air*, *Kongzhong nushashou* 空中女殺手), Mok Hong-see 莫康時, 1967
Fong Sai Yuk (*Fang Shiyu* 方世玉), Corey Kwai Yuen 元奎, 1993
The Forbidden Kingdom (*Gongfu zhi wang* 功夫之王), Rob Minkoff, 2008
Forever Yours (*Qingshen sihai* 情深似海), Evan Yang 易文, 1960
A Forgotten Woman (aka *An Unfaithful Woman*, *Dangfu xin* 蕩婦心), Yue Feng 岳楓, 1949
Fu Bo (*Fubo* 福伯), Lee Kung-lok & Wong Ching-bo 李公樂 & 黃精甫, 2003
Full Alert (*Gaodu jiebei* 高度戒備), Ringo Lam Ling-tung 林嶺東, 1997
Future X-Cops (*Weilai jingcha* 未來警察), Wong Jing 王晶, 2010
Gang of Four (*Sierba* 四二八), Hua Shan 華山, 1978
Girl Detective 001 (*Diyihao nutanyuan* 第一號女探員), Lung To 龍圖, 1966
A Go-Go Teenager (aka *The Dreadnaught*, *Tiedan* 鐵膽), Chan Man 陳文, 1966
The Golden Cat (*Feizei jinsimao* 飛賊金絲貓), Chiang Wai-kwong 蔣偉光, 1967
The Golden Swallow (*Nuzei jinyanzi* 女賊金燕子), Chiang Wai-kwong 蔣偉光, 1967
Hard-Boiled (*Lashou shentan* 辣手神探), John Woo Yu-sen 吳宇森, 1992
He's a Woman, She's a Man (*Jinzhi yuye* 金枝玉葉), Peter Chan Ho-sun 陳可辛, 1994

Health Warning (aka *Flash Future Kung Fu*, *Da leitai* 打擂台), Kirk Wong Chi-keung 黃志強, 1983

Hearts Aflame (*Huozang* 火葬), Yuen Jun 袁俊, 1949

Her Name is Cat (*Baomei* 豹妹), Clarence Fok Yiu-leung 霍耀良, 1998

The Heroic Trio (*Dongfang sanxia* 東方三俠), Johnnie To Kei-fung 杜琪峰, 1993

Hit Team (*Chongzhuang jingcha* 重裝警察), Dante Lam Chiu-yin 林超賢, 2001

Home, Sweet Home (*Nanlai yan* 南來雁), Yue Feng 岳楓, 1950

Hot Blood (*Ruce* 入冊), Richard Yeung Kuen 楊權, 1977

The House of 72 Tenants (*Qishierjia fangke* 七十二家房客), Chor Yuen 楚原, 1973

I Want to Live (*Woyao huoxiaqu* 我要活下去), Lee Tit 李鐵, 1960

I Love Maria (*Tiejia wudi Maliya* 鐵甲無敵瑪利亞), David Chung Chi-Man 鍾志文, 1988

Infernal Affairs I (*Wujiandao I* 無間道 I), Andrew Lau Wai-keung & Alan Mak Siu-fai 劉偉強 & 麥兆輝, 2002

Infernal Affairs II (*Wujiandao II* 無間道 II), Andrew Lau Wai-keung & Alan Mak Siu-fai 劉偉強 & 麥兆輝, 2003

Infernal Affairs III (*Wujiandao III* 無間道 III), Andrew Lau Wai-keung & Alan Mak Siu-fai 劉偉強 & 麥兆輝, 2003

The Insulted and the Injured (*Haomen niezhai* 豪門孽債), Liu Qiong 劉瓊, 1950

Intimate Confessions of a Chinese Courtesan (*Ainu* 愛奴), Chor Yuen 楚原, 1972

Inter-Pol (*Tejing linglingjiu* 特警零零九), Yeung Shu-hei 楊樹希, 1967

The Invincible Fist (*Tieshou wuqing* 鐵手無情), Chang Cheh 張徹, 1969

Invisible Target (*Nan'er bense* 男兒本色), Benny Chan Muk-sing 陳木勝, 2007

Ironside 426 (*Sierliu* 四二六), Lam Gwok-cheung 林國翔, 1977

Isabella (*Yishabeila* 伊莎貝拉), Edmond Pang Ho-cheung 彭浩翔, 2006

Island of Fire (*Huoshao dao* 火燒島), Chu Yen-ping 朱延平, 1991

Island of Greed (*Heijing* 黑金), Michael Mak Tong-kit 麥當傑, 1997

Journey to the West: Conquering the Demons (*Xiyou xiangmopian* 西遊降魔篇), Stephen Chow Sing-chi & Derek Kwok Chi-kin 周星馳 & 郭子健, 2013

Jumping Ash (*Tiaohui* 跳灰), Josephine Siao Fong-fong & Leong Po-chih 蕭芳芳 & 梁普智, 1976

Kaleidoscope (*Renhai wanhuatong* 人海萬花筒), Chan Pei, Ng Wui, Cho Kei, Lee Fa, Lo Dun, Lee Ying-yuen, Chiu Shu-san, Lee Tit, Yue Leung & Wong Hok-sing 陳皮, 吳回, 左几, 李化, 盧敦, 李應源, 趙樹燊, 李鐵, 俞亮, 黃鶴聲, 1950

The Kid (*Xiluxiang* 細路祥), Fung Fung 馮峰, 1950

Kidnap (*Tianwang* 天網), Ching Gong 程剛, 1974

Kill Zone (aka *SPL*, *Shapolang* 殺破狼), Wilson Yip Wai-shun 葉偉信, 2005

The Killer (*Diexue shuangxiong* 喋血雙雄), John Woo Yu-sen 吳宇森, 1989

Killer Constable (*Wanrenzhan* 萬人斬), Kuei Chih-hung 桂治洪, 1980

Kiss of Death (*Du'nu* 毒女), Ho Meng-hua 何夢華, 1973

Kungfu Cyborg: Metallic Attraction (*Jiqixia* 機器俠), Jeff Lau Chun-wai 劉鎮偉, 2009

Lady Black Cat (*Nuzei heiyemao* 女賊黑野貓), Chiang Wai-kwong 蔣偉光, 1966

Lady Black Cat Strikes Again (aka *The Wild Black Cat, Part 2*, *Heiyemao bahai yangwei* 黑野貓霸海揚威), Chiang Wai-kwong 蔣偉光, 1967

Lady Bond (aka *Chivalrous Girl*, *Nushashou* 女殺手), Mok Hong-see 莫康時, 1966

Lady General Hua Mulan (*Huamulan* 花木蘭), Yue Feng 岳楓, 1964

Lady in Distress: The Invincible Fighter (aka *Dragnet of the Law*, *Wudi nushashou* 無敵女殺手), Mok Hong-see 莫康時, 1967

The Lady Killer (aka *Bat Girl*, *Yumian nushaxing* 玉面女殺星), Wong Fung 王風, 1967

The Lady Professional (*Nushashou* 女殺手), Kuei Chih-hung & Mak Chi-Woh (aka Matsuo Akinori) 桂治洪 & 麥志和 (原名 松尾昭典), 1971

Lady with a Cat's Eyes (aka *Cat-Eyed Beauty*, *Maoyan nulang* 貓眼女郎), Law Chi 羅熾, 1967

Laughters and Tears (*Jijia huanxiao jijia chou* 幾家歡笑幾家愁), Lau Fong 劉芳, 1950

Lee Rock (*Wuyi tanzhang Leiluo zhuan: lei lao hu* 五億探長雷洛傳: 雷老虎), Lawrence Ah Mon (aka Lawrence Lau Kwok-Cheong) 劉國昌, 1991

Lee Rock II (*Wuyi tanzhang Leiluo zhuan II zhi fuzi qingchou* 五億探長雷洛傳II之父子情仇), Lawrence Ah Mon (aka Lawrence Lau Kwok-Cheong) 劉國昌, 1991

The Lexicon of Love (*Fengliu baojian* 風流寶鑑), Wang Yin 王引, 1949

Life without Principle (*Duomingjin* 奪命金), Johnnie To Kei-fung 杜琪峰, 2011

Lightning Killer (*Shandian shaxing* 閃電煞星), Chiang Wai-kwong 蔣偉光, 1967

Little Big Soldier (*Dabing xiaojiang* 大兵小將), Ding Sheng 丁晟, 2010

Little Cheung (*Xiluxiang* 細路祥), Fruit Chan Gor 陳果, 2000

Little Godfather from Hong Kong (*Xianggang xiaojiaohu* 香港小教父), Ng See-yuen 吳思遠, 1974

Little Shrimp (aka *Kinship Marriage*, *Chunfeng qiuyu* 春風秋雨), Wu Zuguang 吳祖光, 1949

Long Arm of the Law series (*Shenggang qibing xilie* 省港旗兵系列), Johnny Mak Tong-hung and Michael Mak Tong-kit 麥當雄 and 麥當傑, 1984–90

The Longest Nite (*Anhua* 暗花), Patrick Yau Tat-chi 游達志, 1998

The Longest Summer (*Qunian yanhua tebie duo* 去年煙花特別多), Fruit Chan Gor 陳果, 1998

Love Massacre (*Aisha* 愛殺), Patrick Tam Ka-ming 譚家明, 1981

Love on a Diet (*Shoushen nannu* 瘦身男女), Johnnie To Kei-fung & Wai Ka-fai 杜琪峰 & 韋家輝, 2001

The Lunatics (*Dianlao zhengzhuan* 癲佬正傳), Derek Yee Tung-sing 爾冬陞, 1986

Mad Detective (*Shentan* 神探), Johnnie To Kei-fung & Wai Ka-fai 杜琪峰 & 韋家輝, 2007

Made in Hong Kong (*Xianggang zhizao* 香港製造), Fruit Chan Gor 陳果, 1997

Mambo Girl (*Manbo nulang* 曼波女郎), Evan Yang 易文, 1957

The Man from Hong Kong (*Zhidao huanglong* 直搗黃龍), Jimmy Wang Yu & Brian Trenchard-Smith 王羽 & Brian Trenchard-Smith, 1975

Man of Iron (*Chou lianhuan* 仇連環), Chang Cheh 張徹, 1972

Man on the Brink (*Bianyuan ren* 邊緣人), Alex Cheung Kwok-ming 章國明, 1981

The Mighty Peking Man (*Xingxingwang* 猩猩王), Ho Meng-hua 何夢華, 1977

Million Dollars Snatch (*Qibaiwanyuan da jiean* 七百萬元大劫案), Ng See-yuen 吳思遠, 1976

The Mission (*Qianghuo* 鎗火), Johnnie To Kei-fung 杜琪峰, 1999

My Darling Sister (*Zimeihua* 姊妹花), Evan Yang 易文, 1957
My Heart Is That Eternal Rose (*Shashou hudiemeng* 殺手蝴蝶夢), Patrick Tam Ka-ming 譚家明, 1989
Mysterious Murder (aka *Hong Ling's Blood*, *Hongling xue* 紅菱血), Tong Tik-sang 唐滌生, 1951
The Myth (*Shenhua* 神話), Stanley Tong Gwai-lai 唐季禮, 2005
Naked Killer (*Chiluo gaoyang* 赤裸羔羊), Clarence Fok Yiu-leung 霍耀良, 1992
Naked Killer 2: Raped by an Angel (*Xianggang qi'an zhi qiangjian* 香港奇案之強姦), Andrew Lau Wai-keung 劉偉強, 1993
Naked Weapon (*Chiluo tegong* 赤裸特工), Tony Ching Siu-tung 程小東, 2002
Needing You . . . (*Gunan guanu* 孤男寡女), Johnnie To Kei-fung & Wai Ka-fai 杜琪峰 & 韋家輝, 2000
New Police Story (*Xing jingcha gushi* 新警察故事), Benny Chan Muk-sing 陳木勝, 2004
No Retreat, No Surrender (*Meiyou tuilu, meiyou touxiang* 沒有退路，沒有投降), Corey Yuen Kwai 元奎, 1986
No Retreat, No Surrender 2 (*Zhanqinshu* 綻親陎), Corey Yuen Kwai 元奎, 1987
Nomad (*Liehuo qingchun* 烈火青春), Patrick Tam Ka-ming 譚家明, 1982
One-Armed Swordsman (*Dubidao* 獨臂刀), Chang Cheh 張徹, 1967
One Nite in Mongkok (*Wangjiao heiye* 旺角黑夜), Derek Yee Tung-sing 爾冬陞, 2004
Our Dream Car (*Xiangju meiren* 香車美人), Evan Yang 易文, 1959
Our Husband (*Chunlei* 春雷), Li Pingqian 李萍倩, 1949
Peasant Takes a Wife (*Xiao'erhei jiehun* 小二黑結婚), Gu Eryi 顧而已, 1950
A Peasant's Tragedy (*Shanhelei* 山河淚), Wu Zuguang 吳祖光, 1948
People's Hero (*Renmin yingxiong* 人民英雄), Derek Yee Tung-sing 爾冬陞, 1987
The Phantom Lover (*Yeban gesheng* 夜半歌聲), Ronny Yu Yan-tai 于仁泰, 1995
Police Force (*Jingcha* 警察), Chang Cheh & Tsai Yang-ming 張徹 & 蔡揚名, 1973
Police Story (*Jingcha gushi* 警察故事), Jackie Chan 成龍, 1985
The Professionals (*Jin'ou* 金鷗), Chan Man 陳文, 1967
Project A (*A jihua* A計劃), Jackie Chan 成龍, 1983
The Protector (*Weilong mengtan* 威龍猛探), James Glickenhaus, 1985
Protégé (*Mentu* 門徒), Derek Yee Tung-sing 爾冬陞, 2007
PTU (*PTU*), Johnnie To Kei-fung 杜琪峰, 2003
Public Toilet (*Renmin gongce* 人民公廁), Fruit Chan Gor 陳果, 2002
Purple Storm (*Ziyu fengbao* 紫雨風暴), Teddy Chen Tak-sum 陳德森, 1999
Quietly Flows the Jialing River (*Jingjing de Jialingjiang* 靜靜的嘉陵江), Zhang Min 章泯, 1949
The Rascal Billionaire (*Baifen shuangxiong* 白粉雙雄), Stanley Siu Wing 蕭榮, 1978
Return of Lady Bond (*Nushashou huxue jiu guer* 女殺手虎穴救孤兒), Mok Hong-see 莫康時, 1966
Return of the Lascivious Woman's Soul (*Dangfu hungui* 蕩婦魂歸), Chan Pei 陳皮, 1948
Rob-B-Hood (*Baobei jihua* 寶貝計劃), Benny Chan Muk-sing 陳木勝, 2006
Rouge (*Yanzhikou* 胭脂扣), Stanley Kwan Kam-pang 關錦鵬, 1988

Rumble in the Bronx (*Hongfanqu* 紅番區), Stanley Tong Gwai-lai 唐季禮, 1995
Running on Karma (*Dazhilao* 大隻佬), Johnnie To Kei-fung 杜琪峰, 2003
Running Out of Time (*Anzhan 1* 暗戰 1), Johnnie To Kei-fung 杜琪峰, 1999
Running Out of Time II (*Anzhan 2* 暗戰 2), Johnnie To Kei-fung 杜琪峰, 2001
Sasori (*Xiezi* 蠍子), Joe Ma Wai-ho 馬偉豪, 2008
The Secret (*Fengjie* 瘋劫), Ann Hui On-wah 許鞍華, 1979
Secret Agent No. 1 (*Shentan yihao* 神探一號), Walter Tso Tat-wah 曹達華, 1970
Seven Sisters (aka *Seven Maidens*, *Qijiemei* 七姊妹), Bu Wancang 卜萬蒼, 1953
Shaolin Soccer (*Shaolin zuqiu* 少林足球), Stephen Chow Sing-chi 周星馳, 2001
Shaolin Temple (*Shaolinsi* 少林寺), Cheung Yam-yim 張鑫炎, 1982
She's So Brave! (aka *The Heroine*, *Nutiedan* 女鐵膽), Ling Yun 凌雲, 1967
Shinjuku Incident (*Xinsu shijian* 新宿事件), Derek Yee Tung-sing 爾冬陞, 2009
So Close (*Xiyang tianshi* 夕陽天使), Corey Yuen Kwai 元奎, 2002
Somebody Up There Likes Me (*Langman fengbao* 浪漫風暴), Patrick Pak-kin Leung 梁柏堅, 1996
Song of the Exile (*Ketu qiuhen* 客途秋恨), Ann Hiu On-wah 許鞍華, 1990
The Soul of China (*Guohun* 國魂), Bu Wancang 卜萬蒼, 1948
Sparrow (*Wenque* 文雀), Johnnie To Kei-fung 杜琪峰, 2008
The Spring River Flows East (*Yijiang chunshui xiangdongliu* 一江春水向東流), Cai Chusheng & Zheng Junli 蔡楚生 & 鄭君里, 1947
Spring Song (*Qingchun ernu* 青春兒女), Evan Yang 易文, 1959
The Spy Lovers in the Dangerous City (*Weicheng dielu* 危城蝶侶), But Fu 畢虎, 1947
Spy with My Face (*Heimeigui yu heimeigui* 黑玫瑰與黑玫瑰), Chor Yuen 楚原, 1966
A Strange Woman (*Yidai yaoji* 一代妖姬), Li Pingqian 李萍倩, 1950
Story of a Discharged Prisoner (*Yingxiong bense* 英雄本色), Patrick Lung Kong 龍剛, 1967
The Story of Hua Mulan (*Huamulan* 花木蘭), Chan Pei & Gu Wenzong 陳皮 & 顧文宗, 1951
The Story of Wong Ang the Heroine (*Nufeixia Huang Ying qiaopo zuanshidang* 女飛俠黃鶯巧破鑽石黨), Yam Pang-nin 任彭年, 1960
Sun, Moon and Star (*Xingxing, yueliang, taiyang* 星星、月亮、太陽), Evan Yang 易文, 1961
The Super Inframan (*Zhongguo chaoren* 中國超人), Hua Shan 華山, 1975
Surprise (*Jinghunji* 驚魂記), Tao Qin 陶秦, 1956
Tactical Unit: No Way Out (*Jidong budui: juelu* 機動部隊——絕路), Lawrence Ah Mon (aka Lawrence Lau Kwok-Cheong) 劉國昌, 2008
Task Force (*Rexue zuiqiang* 熱血最強), Patrick Leung Pak-kin 梁柏堅, 1997
A Taste of Killing and Romance (*Shashou de tonghua* 殺手的童話), Veronica Chan Jing-yee 陳靜儀, 1994
The Teahouse (*Chengji chalou* 成記茶樓), Kuei Chih-hung 桂治洪, 1974
Tears of the Pearl River (aka *Tragedy on the Pearl River*, *Zhujiang lei* 珠江淚), Wang Weiyi 王為一, 1950
Teddy Girls (*Feinu zhengzhuan* 飛女正傳), Patrick Lung Kong 龍剛, 1969

Temptress of a Thousand Faces (*Qianmian monu* 千面魔女), Jeng Cheong-woh 鄭昌和, 1969

Three Females (aka *Three Women*, *San nuxing* 三女性), Yue Feng 岳楓, 1947

Torrents of Desire (*Shanhu yuchao* 珊瑚慾潮), Chiang Nan 姜南, 1958

Too Many Ways To Be Number 1 (*Yige zitou de danshen* 一個字頭的誕生), Wai Ka-fai 韋家輝, 1997

Tragedy in Canton (*Yangcheng henshi* 羊城恨史), Lo Dun 盧敦, 1951

Twinkle Twinkle Little Star (*Xingji duntai* 星際鈍胎), Alex Cheung Kwok-ming 章國明, 1983

Two Persons in Trouble Unsympathetic to Each Other (*Tongbing buxianglian* 同病不相憐), Zhu Shilin 朱石麟, 1946

Vengeance (*Fuchou* 復仇), Johnnie To Kei-fung 杜琪峰, 2009

Vengeance! (*Baochou* 報仇), Chang Cheh 張徹, 1970

Vice Squad 633 (*Liusansan* 六三三), Wa Yan (aka Chung Kwok-yan) 華仁 (本名 鐘國仁), 1979

The Victims (*Xuehaichou* 血海仇), Gu Eryi 顧而已, 1951

The Way of the Dragon (*Menglong guojiang* 猛龍過江), Bruce Lee Siu-lung 李小龍, 1972

A War Named Desire (*Aiyucheng* 愛與誠), Alan Mak Siu-fai 麥兆輝, 2000

The Warlord (*Dajunfa* 大軍閥), Li Han-hsiang 李翰祥, 1972

Way to Love (*Lianai zhi dao* 戀愛之道), Ouyang Yuqian 歐陽予倩, 1949

Where is My Darling? (*Yuren hechu* 玉人何處), Zhu Shilin 朱石麟, 1946

The Wicked City (*Yaoshou dushi* 妖獸都市), Peter Mak Tai-kit 麥大傑, 1992

The Wild, Wild Rose (aka *Love of the Wild Rose*, *Yemeigui zhi lian* 野玫瑰之戀), Wong Tin-lam aka Wang Tianlin 王天林, 1960

The Window (*Chuang* 窗), Patrick Lung Kong 龍剛, 1968

Wine, Women and Money (aka *Booze, Boobs, and Bucks*, *Jiuse caiqi* 酒色財氣), Ma-Xu Weibang 馬徐維邦, 1957

Wintry Journey (aka *Spring Comes and Winter Goes*, *Dongqu chunlai* 冬去春來), Zhang Min 章泯, 1950

Young and Dangerous series (*Guhuozai xilie* 古惑仔系列), Andrew Lau Wai-keung 劉偉強, 1996–2000

The People's Republic of China (1949–present)

Beijing Bastards (*Beijing zazhong* 北京雜種), Zhang Yuan 張元, 1993

Black Coal Thin Ice (*Bairi yanhuo* 白日焰火), Diao Yi'nan 刁亦男, 2014

Blind Shaft (*Mangjing* 盲井), Li Yang 李揚, 2004

The Blue Kite (*Lan fengzheng* 藍風箏), Tian Zhuangzhuang 田壯壯, 1993

Drifters (*Erdi* 二弟), Wang Xiaoshuai 王小帥, 2003

No Man's Land (*Wurenqu* 無人區), Ning Hao 寧浩, 2013

The Pickpocket (aka *Xiao Wu*, *Xiaowu* 小武), Jia Zhangke 賈樟柯, 1998

The Road Home (*Wode fuqin muqin* 我的父親母親), Zhang Yimou 張藝謀, 1999

A Touch of Sin (*Tianzhuding* 天注定), Jia Zhangke 賈樟柯, 2013

Republic of China (before 1949)

Angry Tide of the China Sea (aka *The Raging Tide*, *Zhongguohai de nuchao* 中國海的怒潮), Yue Feng 岳楓, 1933
Code No. 1 (*Tianzhi diyihao* 天字第一號), Tu Guangqi 屠光启, 1946
The Devils (aka *Ghosts*, *Qunmo* 群魔), Xu Changlin 徐昌霖, 1948
Doubt in the Boudoir (*Shengui yiyun* 深閨疑雲), Xu Changlin 徐昌霖, 1948
From Night to Dawn (aka *From Dark till Dawn*, *Heiye dao tianming* 黑夜到天明), Tu Guangqi 屠光启, 1946
The Incredible Rose (aka *Roses are Prickly*, *Meigui duoci* 玫瑰多刺), Yue Feng 岳楓, 1948
Murder in the Forest (aka *The Big Bloody Case in the Forest*, *Senlin daxue'an* 森林大血案), Yue Feng 岳楓, 1949
The Murderer (*Xiong shou* 兇手), Li Pingqian 李萍倩, 1948
Night Lodging (*Ye dian* 夜店), Huang Zuolin 黃佐臨, 1947
Night of the Killing (aka *The Night for the Killing*, *Sharenye* 殺人夜), Yue Feng 岳楓, 1949
Missing Document (*626 jian die wang* 626 間諜網), Chan Yik-ching & Yang Xiaozhong 陳翼青 & 楊小仲, 1948
Song at Midnight (*Yeban gesheng* 夜半歌聲), Ma-Xu Weibang 馬徐維邦, 1937

Republic of China – Taiwan (1949–present)

The Boys from Fengkuei (*Fenggui laideren* 風櫃來的人), Hou Hsiao-hsien 侯孝賢, 1983
A Brighter Summer Day (*Gulingjie shaonian sharen shijian* 牯嶺街少年殺人事件), Edward Yang 楊德昌, 1991
A City of Sadness (*Beiqing chengshi* 悲情城市), Hou Hsiao-hsien 侯孝賢, 1989
Eat Drink Man Woman (*Yinshi nannu* 飲食男女), Ang Lee 李安, 1994
I Don't Want to Sleep Alone (*Heiyanquan* 黑眼圈), Tsai Ming-liang 蔡明亮, 2007
Lust, Caution (*Sejie* 色, 戒), Ang Lee 李安, 2007
The Puppetmaster (*Ximeng rensheng* 戲夢人生), Hou Hsiao-hsien 侯孝賢, 1993
Rebels of the Neon God (*Qingshaonian Nezha* 青少年哪吒), Tsai Ming-liang 蔡明亮, 1992

Index

24, 178, 182–91; *see also* doppelgänger
1967 Riot, 48, 153
1997 Handover, 112, 162, 178
2046, 152–3; *see also* tech-noir

action cinema/film/movie, 132, 161, 187–8, 209
action-women film, 120, 123
adaptation, 2–3, 14, 21–2, 83, 132
aesthetics, 62, 83, 104, 115, 160–1, 163, 173, 200, 213
  and film noir, 99–100
  and location, 170–1
  and lyricism, 203–4
  realist, 147, 167
  scavenger, 144
After This, Our Exile, 198, 200, 202, 211–14; *see also* cinema of exile
agency, 124, 129, 162, 184, 221, 227
alienation, 3, 6–7, 90, 98, 113, 203
allegory, 8, 82, 101, 107, 148, 164, 172
allusion, 22, 84, 209
Alton, John, 61
ambiguity, 79, 119, 127
ambivalence, 119
  moral, 103, 107, 113
American television, 8, 123, 132, 178
anatomy, 8, 172
androgyny
  and female assassin, 119
android, 149
anti-hero, 103, 106, 113, 115, 178, 184
  hard-boiled, 98, 100
anxiety, 25, 30, 100, 143, 204
  and 1997 handover, 7, 178
  and cinema of exile, 200, 209
  and masculinity, 4, 152
  and neo-noir, 79, 87, 95
Article 23 (Hong Kong Basic Law Article 23), 99–101

Asaoka, Ruriko, 119
assassin
  female/woman, 7, 118–31, 135–7
  global, 23, 132–3
  see also La Femme Nikita; female/woman-killer film; *femme fatale*
assassination, 85, 137–8, 180, 185, 220, 223
assimilation, 2–3, 21, 95
attraction, 58, 136, 162
  same sex, 129
Australia, 57, 127
authenticity, 105, 167, 173
authorities, 55–6, 168
  and Chinese Communist Party, 227, 230
authority, 107, 147, 185, 191
  and creativity, 148
  patriarchal, 108, 152
axes of action, 207–8
Aylesworth, Reiko, 191

Bacharach, Burt, 136
Bai Guang, 6, 14, 39–42, 45
Bazin, André, 114
Beijing, 22, 42, 48, 102, 230; *see also* Peking
Bergman, Ingrid, 45
Bernard, Carlos, 184
Beyond Hypothermia, 136–8; *see also* female assassin
Black Mask, 149–52; *see also* tech-noir
Black Mask II: City of Masks, 149, 152; *see also* tech-noir
blockbuster (film), 31, 128–30, 134
  Chinese, 5
  Hollywood, 5, 128
bloodshed, 3, 101
  heroic, 25, 79, 85
body, 16, 112, 148, 150, 184, 187, 189, 228
  and female assassin, 138
  in *Running on Karma*, 104, 110–11, 114
bodyguard, 126, 132, 137

Index

border, 3, 24, 82–3, 100–1, 115, 226
   barred and controlled, 169
   crossing, 102–3, 134, 218, 220
   national, 198, 218
boundaries, 83, 87, 90, 94, 209
   and fluidity, 77, 148, 151
   and noir conventions, 101
box office, 6, 31, 36, 40, 56, 100, 145, 201–2
   Hong Kong, 14, 58, 132
Brazil, 82, 228
Brilliant Idea Group Ltd, 164
British colony, 3, 51, 112, 216
Bronson, Charles, 220
brotherhood, 150, 179
Bu, Wancang, 16, 37, 45, 49n13; *see also* Shanghai emigrés
Buddhism
   Buddhist, 97, 100–4, 108, 110–14, 132
   Buddhist asceticism, 112
   Tibetan, 102
bureaucracy, 151, 230

camerawork, 13, 46
Cameron, James, 143; *see also* tech-noir
Cantonese cinema/film/movie, 2, 24, 32, 36–7, 42, 44, 46, 55, 79–80, 120–3, 146
   Cantonese noir, 48
   Cantonese soundtrack, 152
capitalism, 4, 46, 54, 151, 183, 217, 220–2
   and China, 100, 227
   global, 183, 217, 223–4, 228
   proto-capitalism, 216
   transnational, 220
Carmen, 17–8, 20–2
Carmen Jones, 18, 20, 28n16; *see also* musical
Carné, Marcel, 82
cast, 20, 131, 133–4, 137, 152
   multi-ethnic, 132
castration, 93, 110
Cathay (Cathay Organisation), 43, 68
censorship, 2, 5, 31, 34–6, 42–3, 46
Chan, Connie Po-chu, 121–3
Chan, Fruit (Chan, Gor), 5–7, 80–1, 83, 85–7, 90–5
Chan, Jackie, 8, 218–23
Chan, Jordan, 152
Chan, Kuan-tai, 55
chanbara film, 62–3, 66, 131
Chang, Cheh, 52–3, 55, 58–63, 65–6, 67n8, 68n13, 72n46; *see also* crime cinema/film/movie
Chang, Eileen, 38, 137

characterisation, 32, 34, 44, 129, 164, 201
   and neo-noir, 79, 81, 104, 141, 220
   in *The Wild, Wild Rose*, 17, 21, 24
Charles, John, 164
Cheng, Ekin, 181
Cheng, Pei-pei, 132–3
Cheng, Sammi, 98
Chénieux-Gendron, Jacqueline, 200, 202–3
Cheung, Cecilia, 97–8, 103, 152, 220
Cheung, Jacky Hok-yau, 151
Cheung, Maggie, 152
Cheung, Nick, 180
Chiang, David Da-wei, 122
Chiang, Kai-shek, 227
Chiang, Wai-kwong, 122–3
chiaroscuro, 7, 60–2, 65–6, 97–8, 100
Chin, Fei, Tina, 119
Chinatown, 13–14, 100–1, 111
Chinese Communist Party (CCP), 227, 230
Chinese New Year film, 201, 229
Chinese sovereignty, 80, 88, 162
choreography, 24
   and fight action, 97, 122–3
Chow, Yun-fat, 25, 65, 137, 187
Chun, Robert, 16, 22
Chungking (city), 31, 37
CIA, 127, 133, 135
cinema
   accented, 201
   cinema of exile 200–2; *see also After this, our Exile; Exiled; The Godfather; Sonatine*
   crime, 5–6, 65
   crisis, 81
   Grey Cinema, 43
   Hollywood, 53, 60, 65, 77, 140, 201
   national, 1, 8, 80–1, 217–18
   Pan-Asian, 200
   post-modern, 98–9
   Shanghai, 1, 35
   world, 4, 83, 115, 119, 123, 133
   see also Cantonese cinema; Mandarin cinema
cinematography, 63
   and neo-noir, 184, 217–18, 226
   camera movement, 213
   colour, 2, 100
   location, 159–60
   city, 79–81, 141–2, 160–4
   in *Full Alert*, 164–74
   in *Made in Hong Kong*, 86–90
   in *The Longest Summer*, 92–4

city (Cont.)
    space, 24, 88, 161, 180–6; see also location filmmaking
    spectral, 87
    world city, 3–4, 23, 114
City on Fire, 3, 5, 57, 72–3n52, 79, 164, 179; see also noir urbanism
cityscape, 4, 7–8, 79–80, 87, 97, 168, 180, 188
Clark, Sarah, 183
class
    capitalist/upper/wealthy, 38, 121, 150
    lower, 87–8, 216
    middle, 15–17, 22–5, 125, 133, 213
    working, 32, 53–5, 63, 94, 200
cliff-hanger, 178, 184
climax, 45, 83, 109, 212, 220, 230
Closer Economic Partnership Arrangement (CEPA), 5
close-up, 17, 21–2, 24–5, 60, 90, 110, 213
Cold War, 99–100, 102
collaboration, 38, 97, 148, 165, 200, 202
collaborator, 16, 151, 173, 225
    Chinese, 226
coloniality, 80, 88
    colonial incursion, 216
    colonial period, 102, 112
Columbia Pictures Film Production Asia, 133–4
combat, 135, 217
comedy, 6, 38, 40, 45, 58, 101, 104, 129, 145, 149, 219
    Cantonese, 54
    Chinese New Year, 201
    dark, 97
    romantic, 16, 98, 201
commodification, 123, 219–22, 228
communist, 2, 23, 31–2, 43, 148, 227, 230
    Chinese, 227
Computer Generated Imagery (CGI), 133–4
conscience, 151, 190–1
constructivism, 128
context
    global, 4, 118, 218
    local, 127, 140, 142
    verisimilitudinous, 92
convention, 30, 34, 39, 81, 83, 200
    and women, 14, 24, 152
    narrative, 98, 100
    noir, 34, 97–9, 101, 105, 115
co-production
    China–Hong Kong, 5
    China–US, 6

China–US–Taiwan, 38
Hong Kong–Australia, 57
Hong Kong–Korean, 7, 137
Japan–Hong Kong, 119, 131
corruption, 4, 14, 32–3, 37, 40, 79, 82, 90, 100, 103, 124, 224, 228
    and police film, 57–8, 70n26–9
Counter Terrorist Unit (CTU), 183–6, 188, 191
crime cinema/film/movie, 30, 44, 51–4, 56–7, 63–6, 145, 190
    American, 3, 52, 163
    Hong Kong, 79, 141, 160–4, 200–1, 207, 209
    see also Chang Cheh
criminality, 79, 90, 228
cult film, 79, 124, 128, 131, 152
Curtiz, Michael, 13, 15, 28n16, 78; see also domestic melodrama
Cuthbert, Elisha, 185
cyberpunk, 14, 147
cycle
    gangster, 77–9
    generic, 110, 114
    Jane Bond, 121–3
    karmic, 59–60, 114
    production, 159–67, 172–3
cynicism, 13–14, 19, 58, 63–4, 99–100, 106, 113, 115, 121

Daai Chi Company, 122–3
Dalai Lama, 102
Dan, Duyu, 37
Dana, Richard Henry Jr, 216, 223
dance, 17, 19, 22, 24, 37, 93, 143, 145, 203
    flamenco, 20–1
Dassin, Jules, 15, 28n16, 78, 90, 230
death drive, 111
déjà disparu, 163
Deleuze, Gilles, 127
denial, 94, 221, 224–7
detection, 8, 161, 171
detective, 31, 34, 47, 78, 104, 114
    film, 39, 42, 62
    hard-boiled detective, 17, 52, 97
    stories, 7, 36–7, 45
deterritorialisation, 127, 132, 138
dialectic (dialectics), 95, 143
dialogue, 4, 80, 83, 90, 146, 171
Dimendberg, Edward, 79, 159–60, 163, 209
disorientation, 3, 207
displacement, 4, 198, 200, 202–3
D.O.A., 178, 189, 192n1, 196n30

doppelgänger, 105, 191; *see also Infernal Affairs*; *The Longest Nite*; *Running on Karma*; *Running Out of Time*; *Running Out of Time II*
double, 4, 17, 39, 84, 171, 190–1, 220
Dovey, Lindiwe, 203
dystopia, 147, 152, 178

Election, 3, 5, 196n31, 210, 221; *see also* Kowloon noir
Election II, 3, 5, 182, 196n31, 210, 221; *see also* Kowloon noir; handover
emigration, 202, 210
emigrés, 2, 13, 15, 35; *see also* Shanghai emigrés
emotion, 22, 40, 87, 92, 151–3, 167
 bleak emotions, 99
 in *24*, 184, 189–90
Empire, 1, 3
'end of history', 217, 227
engagement, 82, 95, 98, 152, 163, 167
entrapment, 184, 206
epilogue, 8, 94, 222
epiphany, 87, 105, 113
espionage film, 30, 36
exercise, 3, 39, 108, 166, 201
exile, 7–8, 37, 154, 198–206, 209–10, 213–14, 223, 227
 bodily exile, 203
 see also cinema of exile
existentialism, 7, 53, 78, 90, 92, 98, 103–4, 153, 184, 205
 angst, 7
 despair, 98
exodus, 200–1
exploitation, 46, 64–5, 124–6, 131–3, 136, 226, 230
expressionism, 89, 105, 146
 expressionist Rembrandt-like lighting, 121
 German expressionism, 15, 78, 100
 German expressionist cinema, 144
 see also chiaroscuro

façade, 24, 113, 212, 230
Fang, Ying, 119
Fantasia Film Festival, 131
fantasy, 32, 85, 98, 131, 145–6, 152
farce, 36, 145
fatalism, 6, 16, 59, 100, 102, 111, 209
 fatalistic hero, 59–60
FBI, 129, 190, 191

female
 -dominated audience, 18, 120
 warrior, 25, 118
femininity, 126, 150
feminism, 107, 130, 146, 152
 feminist consciousness, 146
femme(s) fatale(s), 4, 6, 25, 52, 64–5, 78, 84, 86, 93, 97, 100, 119, 124–5, 129, 138, 150, 184
 and Orientalism, 111–13
 in 1970s Hong Kong crime films, 60, 62
 in Hong Kong noir classics, 39–42, 45–6
 in *Running on Karma*, 107–8, 110
 in *The Wild, Wild Rose*, 15, 17–19, 22
 see also female/woman-assassin; female/woman-killer
femmes, 15, 42, 60, 62, 97, 125, 143, 184
Feng Huang Film Company/Feng Huang studios, 43, 45
figure, 118, 124
Film Censorship Standards (1953), 43
film festivals, 6, 18, 45, 48, 131, 218
Fincher, David, 77
flashback, 22, 34, 39, 135, 198
 in *After This, Our Exile*, 212–13
 in *Running on Karma*, 98, 102, 105, 108–9
 in *Shinjuku Incident*, 223, 226–8
Fock, Wing Foo, 165
Fonda, Henry, 222
Fong, Yim-fan, 14
formalism, 163, 201
 formalist-abstract approach, 209
Formosa, 42, 224, 227
Fox Studios, 22
fragmentation, 36, 86, 93, 153, 163
 fragmented spaces, 87
Fragrant Harbour, 220–1
frame, 77, 85, 90, 187, 189, 204, 207, 211
 conceptual frame, 3–5
 freeze frame, 63, 166
framework, 80, 92, 95, 97, 141, 183–4
France, 1, 118
Francophone West African cinema, 203
Franco-Prussian War (1870–1), 44
Frankenstein, 225
Freud, Sigmund, 111
Friedrich, Caspar David, 89
Full Alert, 8, 164–6, 168–73, 175n33, 176n35, 177n49, 181; *see also* handover; location

Gabin, Jean, 82
gangster, 15, 24, 52–5, 57, 78, 124, 126, 129, 182, 199–200, 208, 222
   cinema/film/movie, 5, 52–4, 56, 79, 147, 179, 188, 202–3, 218
   gangster-in-exile, 202–5
   in *Shinjuku Incident*, 224, 226–7
   mole, 4, 184, 191
Gardner, Ava, 42
gaze, 140–1, 152
   male, 17, 78
gender, 24, 108–9, 115, 125–6, 129, 137–8, 146, 152
   reassignment, 126
genre
   action genres, 3
   blending, 13
   crime genres, 5–6, 51, 54, 66
   sub-genre, 14, 62, 141, 144, 154
   see also detective films; family melodrama; killer-woman films; *kungfu* films; martial arts films; pinky violence films; science-fiction films
Gere, Richard, 102
ghetto, 53, 223
Giddens, Anthony, 127
Gilda, 18–19, 28n16; *see also* Hollywood noir, noir musical
Gledhill, Christine, 86
Global Positioning System (GPS), 134–5
globalisation, 1, 25, 68n15, 132, 218
   cultural, 2, 4
Godfather, The, 53–4, 69n21, 70n29, 71n45, 202–3; *see also* cinema of exile
Golden Harvest Studio/Golden Harvest, 3, 131
Golden Triangle, 221
Google Earth, 134–5
   eye-in-the-sky motif, 135
Grahame, Gloria, 42,
Great China Film Company/Studio, 35–6, 38
Great Depression, 100
Great Wall Pictures Corporation/Great Wall, 35, 39–40, 43, 45
Greeley, Horace, 217
Greenwich Village, 160
Greer, Jane, 42
Grey Film/Cinema, 43
Guattari, Félix, 127
guilt, 39, 107, 181, 227
gunboat diplomacy, 217

Habanera, 19, 20–1
hallucination, 14, 63
Hallyday, Johnny, 187, 209
Hammett, Dashiell, 60, 63
Hammond, Stefan, 99
Han, Ying-chieh, 132
handover, 32, 81, 98–9, 112, 162, 178–82
   and Macau, 179–80, 199, 209
   handover trilogy, 80, 91, 94
   in *Election II*, 182
   in *Made in Hong Kong*, 86, 88
   in *The Longest Summer*, 91–5
Hard-Boiled, 13, 25, 178–9, 181, 186–7; *see also* crime cinema/film/movie
Harvey, David, 87
Haysbert, Dennis, 184
Hayward, Susan, 95
Hayworth, Rita, 18, 19, 42
He, Feiguang, 37
He, Zhaozhang (aka Ho Siu-cheung), 37, 245
hegemony, 94, 140, 154, 230
heise dianying (dark film), 30
heist, 65, 168, 172
   film/thriller, 91, 161
heroic bloodshed, 25, 79, 85
High Sierra, 28n16, 78; *see also* noir western
Hitchcock, Alfred, 18, 34, 45
hitman (film), 118, 124, 180, 187, 209
hitwoman, 123–5, 129, 136–7; *see also* woman assassin
Ho, Li-li Lily, 62, 119–20
Ho, Luk-ying, 46
Ho, Meng-hua, 62, 64, 145
Hollywood
   blockbuster, 5, 128, 130
   cinema, 140–3, 201–2
   Hollywood of the East, 77
   musical, 13–14, 20, 23
   noir, 13–15, 18, 20, 32, 34, 46, 60–1, 65, 77, 90, 95, 159
   system, 2, 16
Holmlund, Chris, 104
Holocaust, 108
homeland, 200–1, 209–10, 214, 228
Hong Kong Basic Law, 99
Hong Kong Drama Troupe, 55
Hong Kong Film Archive, 161
Hong Kong Film Awards (HKFA), 164, 171
Hong Kong Film Services Office (FSO), 161
Hong Kong International Film Festival (HKIFF), 18, 29n23, 218

Hong Kong Jockey Club/Hong Kong Royal Jockey Club, 47–8, 165, 169–70
Hong Kong Military Service Corps, 91
Hong Kong New Wave, 57–8, 66, 79, 83, 142, 145–9, 202
Hong Kong Special Administrative Region (HKSAR), 4–5, 80, 98, 182, 199
Hope, Leslie, 185
horror film/genre, 30–1, 34, 78, 94, 97–8, 101, 104, 145
Huaying studios, 40
Hui, Siu-hung, 179
humanity, 37, 113, 130, 151
Hung, Kam-bo, Sammo, 132
Huston, John, 91
hybridity, 6, 14, 97, 111, 131 145–6, 149, 151, 154, 184
    hybrid cinema, 144
    hybrid noir, 19
    transnational, 113
hyper-stylisation, 206
hyphenation, 180

I Kuang, 121
iconography, 7, 81, 95, 145
identity, 4, 6, 45, 147, 150–2, 209
    and female assassin, 124–9, 138
    class, 53
    crisis, 82, 103
    Hong Kong, 51
    in *Made in Hong Kong*, 82–8
    national, 79, 91, 95
    politics, 223
ideology, 7, 141, 160, 227
immigrant, 17, 53, 55, 80, 100, 105
    illegal immigrants in *Shinjuku Incident*, 220, 222–9
    labour, 218
imagery, 8, 99, 203, 223–4, 229
    homoerotic, 147
    idyllic, 200, 210, 214
imaginary, 20, 80, 84, 92, 95, 209
immobility, 153, 200, 203–4
Imperial China, 52
Independent Commission Against Corruption (ICAC), 56–8
India, 3, 25, 112
indigenisation, 51, 54–5, 66
Infernal Affairs I, II, III, 57, 68n14, 95, 101, 105, 161, 173, 190, 196n31, 210; *see also* doppelgänger
inferno, 227–8

intertextuality, 79–81, 84, 88
intimacy, 103, 105
irony, 125, 149, 203
Italian neo-realism, 47, 230

James Bond, 7, 53, 118–22
    myth, 119
Jameson, Fredric, 7, 79, 84, 86, 98, 100, 104, 114
Jane Bond, 120–3
Japan, 1, 7–8, 30, 80–3, 86, 90, 111–12, 118, 126–7, 130–1, 134, 217–19
    in *Shinjuku Incident*, 221–9
Japanese Occupation, 23, 37–8, 102, 226, 228
jianghu, 83, 118, 209
Johnson, Penny Jerald, 184
justice/injustice, 37, 40, 46–7, 55–6, 58, 98, 102–3, 114

Kaminsky, 53
Kao, Jack, 224
karma, 97, 101–7, 112–15
    karmic connection, 103, 110
    karmic punishment, 108
killer, 124–5
    female/woman-killer film, 126, 128–30, 132, 136
    see also female assassin; *femme fatale*
Kinji, Fukasaku, 8, 221, 223
Klein, Norman M., 183
Koo, Louis, 152, 182
Kowloon, 42
    Kowloon noir, 3, 182
Kuala Lumpur, 187
Kun Lun Film Studio, 33
kungfu, 2, 51–4, 58, 62–4, 66, 103, 112, 131, 147–8, 153, 206, 219
Kuraki, Mai, 136
Kwan, Tak-hing, 122–3
Kwok, Phillip, 187
Kwong Ngai Film Company/Kong Ngee Company, 46, 123

La Femme Nikita, 7, 123–7, 132 *see also* female assassin
Lai, Fan Fanny, 119
Lam, Nyn Ngai, 164
Lam, Ringo (Lam, Ling-tung), 72n52, 79, 164, 173, 175n27, 175n33, 175n35–6, 176n42, 177n49; *see also* crime film/movie/cinema; location filmmaking; noir urbanism

Lam, Suet, 131, 181, 188, 229
landscape, 37, 82, 94, 181, 204, 209, 217
  modernist, 88
  post-modern, 88
Lapsley, Rob, 93
Lau, Andy, 97–8, 101, 106, 112, 128, 152, 180, 187, 191, 221
Lau, Ching-wan, 136–7, 151–2, 164, 180–1, 188, 199
Lau, Kar-leung, 122–3
Lau, Kar-wing, 123
Lau, Wing-kin, 164
Laura del Sol, 22
lawman, 57, 59, 66
Lee, Amanda, 165
Lee, Bruce (Lee, Siu-lung), 2, 53, 54, 133
Lee, Danny (Lee, Sau-yin), 58, 65, 218
Lee, Sam, 91, 131
Lee, Shannon, 133
Lee, Waise, 181
lens, 7, 63, 193–4
  fish-eye lens, 63
Leong, Po-chih, 57
Leung, Chiu-wai Tony, 149, 153, 191, 199
Leung, Gigi, 129
Leung, Siu-lung Bruce, 132
lesbian, 62, 128
lesbianism, 125–6, 133, 136; *see also Naked Killer*; *So Close*; *Zero Woman: Dangerous Game*
lighting, 46, 66, 146, 221
  chiaroscuro, 61–2, 98, 100
  dim and hazy, 147
  high-contrast, 60–1
  low-key, 7, 13, 16, 34, 60–1
  Rembrandt-like lighting, 121
Li, Lihua, 14, 40, 44
Li, Mei, 14
Li, Pingqian, 6, 37, 40, 49n13; *see also* Shanghai emigrés
Lin, Cui Jeanette, 14
Lin Dai, 14,
localisation, 52, 54
location, 3, 52, 55, 89, 93, 114, 132, 180, 185, 189–90, 226
  cinematography, 159–60
  controlled/uncontrolled, 168
  filmmaking/shooting, 8, 24, 63, 78, 161–2, 159–73
Longest Nite, The, 105, 198–9, 209 ; *see also* doppelgänger

Longest Summer, The, 80, 91–4 ; *see also* handover
Los Angeles/LA, 13–15, 101, 161, 182–5, 188–9
Lui, Kei, 123
lyricism, 200, 203–4, 211

Macao/Macau, 8, 179–80, 186, 198–9, 206, 209–10
Madama Butterfly, 20–2
Made in Hong Kong, 5–6, 80, 83, 86–94
Maggie Q, 132
Mainland China, 5–6, 15, 25, 32, 35–6, 42, 44–6, 55, 81, 97, 107, 111–13, 115, 126, 134, 141, 153, 164, 179, 182, 218–20, 222–30
Mak, Marco, 164
Malaysia, 8, 198, 200, 202, 210, 213
Manchu, 65
Manchukuo, 226
Manchuria, 30
Mandarin, 35, 42, 46, 122–3
  film, 2, 13, 36–7, 44, 51, 54, 68, 119–20
  Mandarin pop/Mando-pop, 14, 20, 21
  musical, 16; *see also* musical
  noir, 44
Mann, Michael, 164
Mao, Angela, Ying, 131
mapping, 95, 140, 170, 172
maps, 95, 169
martial arts cinema/film/movie, 2, 6, 51–2, 58–9, 61–3, 65–6, 97, 118, 121–3, 130, 132–3, 206
Masaya, Kato, 223
masculinity, 81, 126
  masculine anxiety, 152
  masculine fantasy, 152
Massie, Michael, 191
Maupassant, 44
Ma-Xu, Weibang, 16, 49n13, 137; *see also* Shanghai emigrés
Maxwell, Jacqui, 182
May, Corinne, 136
maze, 185
mechanisation, 143, 150
Meehan, Paul, 143
Meiji Restoration, 217
Mekas, Jonas, 201
melodrama, 17, 23, 30, 33, 35–7, 40, 42, 51–2, 101, 104, 137, 145, 179, 184, 188, 218
  blood, 39, 47
  Cantonese, 24

family/domestic, 2, 16, 38, 44–5, 77–8
musical noir, 14
noir, 46
romantic, 7, 16, 43
sensationalist, 59
Melville, Jean-Pierre, 1, 124
memory, 7, 18, 23, 77, 84, 94, 97, 109, 114, 127, 135, 183–4, 187, 209
Mephistopheles, 225
meta-fiction, 77–95
metaphor, 24, 90, 92, 150, 171, 178, 209, 211
metropolis, 90, 92, 189
Mérimée, Prosper, 20, 22
Mexico, 3, 101, 183, 185
milieu, 36, 64, 79, 84, 90–2, 141, 143, 147
Milkyway, 6, 25, 51, 97, 105, 136, 206
mirror, 37, 60, 91, 93, 199, 206, 223, 229
  character, 191; see also doppelgänger
  mirror image, 57, 77, 171, 190, 220, 224
mise-en-scène, 7, 16, 45, 61, 65, 78–9, 82, 88, 97, 103, 111, 145, 206, 211, 213
misogynist, 19, 21
misogyny, 24, 115
Mission, The, 173, 199, 201, 204, 206–7; see also Kowloon noir
Miu, Kin-fai, Tony, 218
Mizuno, Miki, 131
mobility, 121, 181, 200–1, 203–4, 206
modernisation, 7, 21, 23, 141, 150, 153
modernity, 4–5, 17, 41, 83, 95, 140–1, 148, 154
  capitalist, 2–3, 147
  urban, 2–3, 79, 87
Mok, Karen, 134, 136, 151
montage, 22, 65, 213
Montreal, 131
morality, 150–1
Moretti, Franco, 227
Morricone, Ennio, 63, 83
motif, 7, 20, 58, 60, 94, 102, 111, 120, 123–8, 135, 137–8, 143–4, 179–81, 185, 205, 208, 211, 220, 224, 230
motion, 8, 87, 90, 108, 178
  motion-at-random, 207
  motion-in-stillness, 207
  slow, 63, 85, 204
Motion Pictures and General Investments Co. Ltd (MP&GI), 13, 16, 18, 22–3, 25, 43, 47
Mui, Anita, 152

murder, 30–1, 33–6, 39, 45, 62, 65, 97, 105–6, 110, 112–13, 126, 131, 135, 143, 185, 189, 226
music, 19–20, 22, 37, 63, 90, 131, 136, 171, 204
  classical, 213
  electronic synthesizer, 147
  techno, 110
musical, 13–14, 16, 18, 20, 23, 30, 43, 45, 47, 145
  noir musical, 6, 13
  see also Carmen
mysticism, 103, 111, 113
  Buddhist, 103
  Eastern, 111

Naficy, Hamid, 201
Nagisa, Oshima, 82
Naked City, The, 90; see also Italian neo-realism
Naked Killer, 127, 133; see also female assassin; lesbianism
Nam Hung, 121
Nanking Massacre, 226
Nanyang, 36, 42
Naremore, James, 2, 99
narrative
  grand, 86, 95
  master, 92
  meta, 79, 86, 95
  micro, 86–7, 95
Nathan Road, 170
nationalist, 30–4, 43–4, 141–2, 153
  discourse, 141
  Nationalist government, 23, 30, 32, 34, 43
  resistance, 148
nationality, 80, 86, 95
Nazi, 1–2, 147–8
  Nazi-like dictatorship, 148
  neo-Nazi, 147–8
neo-noir, 1–8, 25, 48, 58, 60–1, 79, 81, 83, 86, 92, 95, 99–101, 104, 107, 111, 140, 160–1, 164, 167, 172–3, 184, 209, 217–18, 220–1, 224–30; see also noir
  and career women, 107–8
  notion of, 1–8, 25, 79, 81–3, 99–100, 218
  style, 227
  see also noir
New Ritz Club, 15
New York, 101, 127, 131, 159, 161, 163, 183–4, 188–90, 203
New York Asian Film Festival (NYAFF), 131
Ng, Carrie Ka-lai, 128

Ng, Chor-fan, 46
Ng, Francis/Ng, Francis Chun-yu, 164, 181
Ng, See-yuen, 54, 56
Ng, Sik-ho, 57
nightclub, 15, 19, 20, 23, 64, 97
Nikkatsu Studios, 119, 130
Nolan, Christopher, 77
noir
   American, 34, 47, 81
   Cantonese, 48
   Chinese, 37
   global, 3, 4, 140
   Hong Kong, 4, 6–7, 13, 25, 35, 42, 51, 58–9, 61, 63, 66, 98–9, 104, 218
   Japanese, 90
   Kowloon, 3, 182; see also Election; Election II; The Mission; PTU
   noir hero, 93, 104, 220
   noir musical, 6, 13; see also musical
   noir Orientalism, 111
   noir road movie, 78
   noir sensibility, 4, 7, 145–6
   noir style, 13–14, 45, 58, 78, 142, 145, 227
   noir urbanism, 79; see also City on Fire
   noir western, 17
   noir women, 107–8; see also femme fatale
   procedural, 92
   Shanghai, 30–4, 38, 42, 46
   tech-noir, 7, 14, 141–5, 147–9, 151
North Point, 15, 17
nostalgia, 7, 14, 46, 84, 86, 100, 108, 114, 153
nushashou, 120, 122; see also woman assassin

obsession, 101–2, 138, 143
Old West, 222
One Nite in Mongkok, 5, 195n23, 220–2, 226
opera, 60, 137
   Peking, 16, 40
   Western, 20
Oregon for Palmer, 183
Orientalism, 111–13, 115
origin, 14, 198, 201–2, 210
Ouyang, Shafei, 42
Ouyang, Yuqian, 44

Pacific War, 102
Pak Yin, 14, 46
paradigm, 79–80, 88, 141
paradox, 147, 203
paranoia, 4, 115
Paris, 169, 209
parody, 145, 152, 178

pastiche, 88, 101, 115, 130
patriarchy, 81, 108, 146, 152
   patriarchal-capitalist gender economy, 146
patriotism, 33, 190
Patton, Will, 191
Pavel, Thomas 203
Peckinpah, Sam, 180
Peking, 30–31, 40; see also Beijing
   Peking Opera, 16, 40
People's Republic of China (PRC), 5, 99–102, 107, 115, 129, 180, 199, 201
persona, 102, 224
Philips, 189
pinky violence, 124, 130
Po Sang Bank, 56
poetics, 8, 173, 203
point of view, 58, 87, 204
police
   film, 57–8
   mole, 4, 184
   police procedural, 5
policiers, 4
politics, 8, 24, 84, 109, 152, 172–3, 183, 221–3
Porter, Jonathan, 180
'Portrait of Dorian Gray' persona, 224
Portugal, 199
   Portuguese colony, 199
post-1997 Hong Kong, 5, 8, 105, 179, 209
postcolonial, 5, 80, 92, 94–5, 141, 199, 209; see also colonialism
post-coloniality, 87–8, 92–5; see also coloniality
postfeminist, 107, 209; see also feminism
post-Handover Hong Kong, 98
post-modernism, 79–80, 83–4, 87–8, 92, 95, 98–100, 104, 113–14, 135, 217
postscript, 58, 229
predestination, 98, 143
Preminger, Otto, 18, 20, 28n16, 78, 178
production
   convenience, 146
   cross-border, 134
   Production Code, 2
   production cycle(s), 159–60, 167, 172–3
Progressive Cinema (1947–57), 30, 33
prologue, 8, 90, 222
prostitution, 220, 230
protest, 45, 102, 191, 223
   Tibetan, 102
psyche, 91, 102, 220
psychoanalysis, 45

psycho-geography, 172
PTU, 3, 5, 182, 201, 206–7, 210; see also Kowloon noir
Puccini, 20, 40
punishment, 53, 55, 62, 108, 110, 202, 216

Qing dynasty, 65
Qiu, Gangjian, 64

rape-revenge films, 64–5, 72n50
realism, 1, 14, 47, 55, 78, 82, 94, 167, 201, 230
   French poetic realism, 1, 78, 82
   gritty, 14
   magical, 94
rebirth, 105, 110, 113, 131
reconciliation, 15, 102
Red Harvest, 60, 63
redemption, 7, 107, 110, 113, 125, 185, 213
reflection, 14, 24–5, 183
region, 2, 4–5, 23, 80, 98, 112, 126, 130, 133, 182, 198–200
reinvention, 2–3
Reis, Michelle, 151
remembrance, 86, 94, 184
Ren, Pengnian, 36, 37
return of the repressed, 94, 225, 227
Rigoletto, 20–1
road movie, 78; see also noir road movie
romance, 6, 16, 44, 46, 97, 98, 101, 128–9
   heroic, 213
Rougon-Macquart, 229
Royal Hong Kong Police Force, 48
Running on Karma, 7, 97–9, 101, 103–5, 109, 111, 113–15; see also doppelgänger
Running Out of Time, 105, 178–80, 186–7, 190–1, 193; see also doppelgänger; handover
Ryo, Ishibashi, 131

sadomasochism (S&M), 125
   sadomasochistic scenes, 147
Samsung, 189
samurai film, 3, 130–1
San Francisco, 101
Sang, Woo-han, 137
Santa Clarita, 189
Severe Acute Respiratory Syndrome (SARS), 25
   epidemic, 99–101, 199
Sarkar, Bhaskar, 218
satire, 44–6, 98, 145

Sawada, Kenya, 223
schizophrenia, 104, 138
science fiction/sci-fi (film), 7, 140–50
   Chinese sci-fi, 142, 153
   comedy, 145, 149
   see also noir sci-fi
scientism, 143
Scorsese, Martin, 83, 91, 102, 145
seduction, 3, 4, 17, 24–5, 39, 42, 119, 128, 223, 227
Sek, Kin, 122–3
Seoul, 137, 161
September 11th, 178, 182, 189
serial killer, 113, 218
Seven Princesses of the Cantonese Cinema, 122
sexploitation, 64
sexuality, 19, 22, 111, 119, 133
shadow, 13, 48, 218
Sham, John, 149
Shanghai, 1, 6, 14–16, 22–3, 30–40, 42, 46, 48, 53, 55, 100, 111, 120, 201, 230
   Chinese/Shanghai emigrés, 15, 35
   Communist-occupied, 2
   Japanese occupation of, 38
   noir(s), 30–6, 38, 42, 46
   post-war Shanghai, 1, 32, 34, 40, 218
   triads, 227
Shaw Brothers Studio, 43, 47, 52, 56, 58, 61, 119–20, 123, 145
Shek Kong, 170
Shenzhen, 101, 103
shidaiqu, 21; see also Mandarin pop
Shinjuku, 130, 223, 226
Shinjuku Incident, 5, 8, 217–21, 224–7, 229–30; see also illegal immigration
Shiri, 7, 129–30, 132; see also female assassin; femme fatale
Shishido Jo, 119,
shootout, 135, 204–5, 207
Shu Qi, 134
Shum, Tin-ha Lydia, 123, 134
Siao, Fong-fong Josephine, 57, 122–3
Sichuan Earthquake, 102
Sicily, 202–3
Singapore, 32, 43, 136
Sino-Japanese War, 32
Sit, Ka-yin Nancy, 123
Siu, Yin-fei, 46
Skeldon, Ronald, 210
slapstick, 145–7
Slethaug, Gordon, 111

social problem film/picture, 66, 78
Soderbergh, Steven, 77
sojourn, 198, 210
Solanas, Fernando, 201
Sonatine, 190, 203, 205; see also cinema of exile
Song Seung-heon, 134
songstress, 14, 17, 21, 24, 39, 41
sound
   sound pollution, 161, 171
   sound stage, 15, 19, 24–5, 159
soundscape, 171
soundtrack, 63, 152, 171, 204
South East Asian Film Festival (SEAFF), 45
South-east Asia 8, 45, 123, 200, 219, 222
   Chinese communities of, 31, 36
   market, 43, 54
sovereignty, 80, 88, 99, 114, 162, 165, 172
space
   amorphous, 92–3
   centrifugal, 91, 159, 209
   centripetal, 159, 210
   claustrophobic, 210
   illusory, 92, 95
   in *24*, 185–6, 188
   in *Full Alert*, 161–3, 166–72, 176n39
   in *Hard-Boiled*, 187–8
   in *Made in Hong Kong*, 80–90
   in *Running Out of Time*, 187–8, 191
   in *The Wild, Wild Rose*, 20, 24–5
   liminal, 203
   objectively-determinate, 209
   political, 203
   subjectively-indeterminate, 209
   urban, 24–5, 80, 93, 95, 159, 163, 182, 184–5, 187
Special Administrative Region(s) (SAR), 4–5, 182, 199
spectacle, 3, 5
split-screen, 183, 186, 194–5n23
staging, 5, 66, 167, 230
   geometrical staging, 206
   in-depth, 207
Stallone, Sylvester, 84, 219
Stanwyck, Barbara, 42
Stone, Sharon, 102
studio
   era, 62, 77, 201
   production, 23, 80
   system, 2, 16, 81, 201
stunt, 165, 167, 173
subgenre, 7, 14, 62, 79, 141, 144, 154

subjectivity, 86, 91, 93, 95, 127
   social, 93, 95
subplot, 178, 183–4
subtext, 14, 25, 91, 178
Suet Nei, 122–3
Sugimoto, Miki, 124
sukeban, 124
superhero, 103–4, 152
superhuman, 143, 152
surrealism, 201
Surrealists-in-exile, 203
surveillance, 135–6, 170, 191
suspense, 45, 143, 178, 180, 189, 191
Sutherland, Kiefer, 183, 189
Suzuki, 22, 81
swordplay, 3, 36, 52, 62, 65
swordsman, 119, 152

Taiwan, 38, 42–3, 80–1, 102, 134, 224
taiyozoku, 82
Takenaka, Naoto, 227
Takeshi, Kitano, 190, 203
Takumi, Furukawa, 81–2
Tang, Ching, 119
Tarantino, Quentin, 77, 79, 130, 132
Tatsuya, Nakadai, 151
Tchaikovsky, 213
Television and Entertainment Licensing Authority, 161
temporality, 7, 84, 86
   anachronistic, 114
tension, 14, 24, 39, 44, 78–80, 87, 100–1, 140, 187, 198, 203–5
Tentacles, 216
Teo, Stephen, 3, 79, 104, 164, 182, 209
Terminator, The, 143; see also tech-noir
text, 8, 48, 98, 198, 201
textual, 7, 92, 95, 132, 172, 201
   contextual, 79, 90, 172
   extra-textual, 171
   intertextual, 78–81, 84, 87–8, 114
   intra-textual, 114
   sub-textual, 91
Thieves Highway, 78; see also noir road movie
thriller, 4, 18, 31, 34, 36, 39–40, 44–5, 47, 51, 79, 91, 97, 172
   cop/police, 57–8, 70n29
   crime, 7, 51, 164
   cyberpunk, 147
   erotic, 62
Ti, Lung, 60, 222
Tiananmen Square massacre, 99

Index

Tierney, Gene, 42
To, Chapman, 152
To, Johnnie (To, Kei-fung), 101, 114–15, 155n19, 186, 201–2, 210, 221
Toei Video Company, 126
Toei-produced films, 124, 130
Tokyo, 124, 126, 130, 161, 203, 223, 228
Tolstoy, Leo, 39
Tong, Gai, 122–3
Tosca, 40
traitor, 31–2, 36, 38, 125, 199
transformation, 66, 88, 110, 124–5, 127–8, 135, 143, 149, 153
transgender, 126, 190
transgression, 8, 149, 161, 168, 171
transition, 21, 162, 172
  political, 151, 163, 166
transnationalism, 79, 140
trauma, 36, 64, 65, 98, 102, 107, 112, 114, 138
triad, 8, 54–7, 83, 126, 129, 136, 138, 179, 191
  boss/leader, 55, 91, 182, 199
  culture, 161
  gangster, 54–5
  rituals, 57
  triad-style justice, 56
Triads, 8, 221, 227, 229
trickster, 181, 188
Tsang, Kong Kenneth, 122–3
Tse, Yin, Patrick, 121–3
Tso, Tat-wah, Walter, 123
Tsui, Hark, 114, 145–6, 148–9, 164
Tu, Chuan Margaret, 119
Tu, Guangqi, 31, 42, 46, 49n13; *see also* Shanghai emigrés
Tung, Chee-hwa, 161

undercover, 38, 40, 56, 107, 110, 122, 190
  cops, 57, 221
underworld, 3, 17, 124, 142, 223, 225, 230
Union Film Enterprise Ltd, 47
United Kingdom (UK), 3, 127–8, 210
United States (US), 3, 6, 16, 25, 35, 38, 42, 77, 79–82, 87, 127–8, 130–3, 138, 140, 152, 159, 163, 167–8, 182–3, 185, 191
'Untouchables', 126; *see also* triad

Van Damme, Jean-Claude, 164
Verdi, 20
victim, 34, 78, 109, 147, 164
video, 109, 113, 124–6
monitors, 135
surveillance, 136
Vietnam, 111, 201
  War, 100
vigilante, 53, 56, 121
villain, 19, 53, 104, 106, 119, 121, 146, 150, 172, 222
violence
  Oriental, 216
  pinky, 124, 130
  realistic, 52
  stylised, 6
Visconti, Luchino, 230
voiceover, 21, 84, 152–3, 213

Wang, Yu, Jimmy, 119
Wayne, John, 220
Wersching, Annie, 190
warlord, 40, 145
Warner Bros, 78–9
Washington, DC, 183–4
Watergate, 100
Welles, Orson, 100–1, 218
western (film), 13, 17–18, 130
  Italian spaghetti western, 83
  revisionist western, 63
White House, 183, 186
The Wild, Wild Rose, aka *Love of the Wild Rose*, 6, 13–25, 26n2–3, 47, 218; *see also* noir musical
Wilkins, Mike, 99
woman
  action-women film/movie, 120, 123
  assassin, 7, 118, 126, 133, 136; *see also* female assassin
  in neo-noir, 7
  in *The Wild, Wild Rose*, 20–1
  killer-women, 120, 130, 132, 138
  killer-women film/genre, 126, 130, 138
  policewoman, 97, 102, 108, 112
  strong woman, 14, 17–18, 24–5, 40
  woman's picture, 18, 25
  see also femme fatale
Wong, Almen/Wong, Pui-ha, 129, 132
Wong, Anthony, 179, 181
Wong, Kar-wai, 81, 83, 87, 99, 153, 198
Wong, Tin-lam (aka Wang, Tianlin), 6, 13–15, 20, 23, 28n14, 28n18, 47, 218
Wong Jing's Workshop Ltd, 127
Woo, John (Woo, Yu-sen), 25, 48, 51–2, 56, 59, 66, 79, 129, 135–6, 187
world cinema, 4, 83, 115, 119, 123, 133

world city, 3, 4, 23, 114
Wu, Chien-lien, 136–7
Wu, Daniel, 132–3, 220–4
wushu, 135
wuxia, 52, 62, 65, 209
   wuxia chivalry, 104
   wuxia pian, 97

Xander Berkeley, 183
Xu, Gary, 111, 113
Xu, Jinglei, 223

yakuza, 8, 83, 126, 203–4, 222–8
   politics, 221
   The Yakuza Papers, 221
Yam, Tat-wah Simon, 128, 131, 179, 182
Yan, Jun, 39–40
Yang, Gongliang, 37
yanggang, 52, 119; *see also* Chang Cheh
Yao, Ke, 40
Yasuaki, Kurata, 134
Yau, Chingmy Suk-ching, 128
Yeh, Feng, Julie, 14
Yeh, Sin-man, Sally, 65, 149
Yen, Donnie, 25, 179
Yeoh, Michelle, 152
Yokosuka, 130
You Min, 14
Yuan, Meiyun, 37
Yue, Feng, 6, 26n2, 37–9, 44–5, 49n13, 121; *see also* Shanghai emigrés
Yumiko, Nogawa, 22
Yuen, Anita, 128
Yuen, Corey (Yuen, Kwai), 7, 132–4
Yuen, Woo-ping, 123
Yung Hwa Motion Picture Industries Ltd/ Yung Hwa Studio, 35, 40

Zerefa, Guy, 204
Zero Woman: Dangerous Game, 126; *see also* lesbianism
Zhang, Shichuan, 37
Zhao, Wei, 134
Zhu, Shilin, 6, 37–8, 49n13; *see also* Shanghai emigrés
Žižek, Slavoj, 100
Zola, Emile, 230

EU representative:
Easy Access System Europe
Mustamäe tee 50, 10621 Tallinn, Estonia
Gpsr.requests@easproject.com

www.ingramcontent.com/pod-product-compliance
Lightning Source LLC
Chambersburg PA
CBHW061708300426
44115CB00014B/2603